Ante-Bellum Southern Literary Critics

EDD WINFIELD PARKS

Ante-Bellum Southern Literary Critics

GREENWOOD PRESS, PUBLISHERS
WESTPORT CONNECTICUT

Library of Congress Cataloging in Publication Data

Parks, Edd Winfield, 1906-1968.
  Ante-bellum Southern literary critics.

  Reprint of the ed. published by University of Georgia
Press, Athens..
  Bibliography: p.
  Includes index.
  1. Criticism--Southern States. I. Title.
[PN99.U52P3 1978]   810'.9   77-17953
ISBN 0-313-20103-X

TO

GERALD AND HELEN HUFF

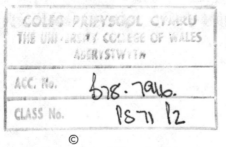

Copyright 1962 University of Georgia Press

Reprinted with the permission of University of Georgia

Reprinted in 1978 by Greenwood Press, Inc.
51 Riverside Avenue, Westport, CT 06880

Printed in the United States of America

CONTENTS

v

INTRODUCTION

ALTHOUGH every book must in the long run stand on its merits, perhaps a few preliminary remarks about the plan and organization of this one may not be out of order. I have attempted to present, fairly and without bias, the intellectual literary history of the South from 1785 to 1861; in particular, to indicate the concepts that led to a change from Classicism and Neo-Classicism to a full-bodied, yet at times a tempered, Romanticism. The men whom I have selected are meant to be representative. At the same time, I have tried to select the best critics rather than merely the representational ones. This may give too favorable a picture of the region, intellectually. It may also explain certain omissions. Since Paul Hamilton Hayne seemed to be doing much better approximately what John R. Thompson was also doing, I have glanced at Thompson but have concentrated on Hayne. The terminal date has also caused trouble. With those critics who lived and wrote during and after the Civil War (for example, Simms, Timrod, Hayne, and John Esten Cooke), I have attempted to complete the critical picture, but not in such detail, usually, as I have given to their pre-war works. Fortunately, each man's thinking had mainly been fixed in the earlier period: their thought developed in post-war years, but did not basically change.

There is one notable omission: Edgar Allan Poe. I do not consider him, especially as a critic, out of place or out of time. However, his work seems important enough to treat it separately in a monograph, instead of trying to compress his critical thought into a chapter.

Originally, I had planned to open this book with a chapter on

William Byrd, as representative of colonial criticism. Byrd wrote well and wittily; he had a library of nearly four thousand books; he was a friend of William Congreve and William Wycherley. In the surviving portions of his shorthand diary, he noted that nearly every morning he read Hebrew, Greek, or Latin; later in the day he usually read English, French, or Italian authors. A few of his translations are extant, most notably a free and racy version of "The Ephesian Matron," from the *Satyricon of Petronius Arbiter*. Rarely does he comment on a work, or even identify an author. Sometimes he will list the number of verses (usually two hundred to three hundred) that he had read in Homer, or specify that he had read two chapters in the Old Testament, or, more generally, a "great deal in Anacreon." Milton's Latin poems interested him enough that he followed them with "some English in Milton"— not even specifying whether it was poetry or prose. He encouraged a young lady to keep on writing by admonishing her that "there was a time when Dryden was a lame poet"; he enjoyed reading *The Beggar's Opera* aloud to an audience, but thought its success "not owing altogether to the Wit or Humour that Sparkled in it, but to some Political Reflections, that seem'd to hit the Ministry." His ironical observations on literature are interesting, but they are few in number and slight in content. I have embodied them in an article that appeared in the *Georgia Review,* Summer, 1960.

There is also a sprinkling of good if incidental criticism in some of the Colonial newspapers, especially in the *Virginia Gazette* and the *South Carolina Gazette,* as Elizabeth Cook and Hennig Cohen (among others) have shown. But it was difficult to find a respectable body of critical work that could be identified even with a pseudonymous author. Regretfully, I have omitted Colonial critics from this book.

There are many later critics who might have been included, but whose omission seemed to me less regrettable. Shortly after 1800, Isaac Harby in Charleston was writing discerningly of actors and acting and the production of plays, but the comments on literature of this belated tragi-comedian seem less important and certainly less discerning. In Charleston, also, William Crafts was stating that all he wanted of English literature was that written "Anteriour to the Revolution," and voicing his hearty dislike of the Romantic poets. On the other hand, some twenty-five years later, A. B. Meek in Alabama was advocating a Romanticism even more thorough-going, if far less persuasive, than that of Hayne. Crafts and Meek were extremists, and the body of their work was small. I have tried to incorporate a few items that would indicate their position, but I do not feel that they deserve to be treated at length. In the same way, I have drawn on other minor critics for pertinent illustrative material.

This book had its beginning in 1935, when at the suggestion of Harry Hayden Clarke I included a section on poetic theory in my *Southern Poets*. Since then, I have treated this and other aspects of Southern critical thought in *Segments of Southern Thought*, in the Introduction to *The Essays of Henry Timrod*, in *William Gilmore Simms as Literary Critic*, and in various articles that have appeared in the *Georgia Review, Mississippi Quarterly, South Atlantic Quarterly, Southwest Review, Tennessee Studies in Literature*, and *Georgia Historical Quarterly*. I have levied on this earlier material freely, but in almost every instance I have made extensive additions and revisions. The book was unduly delayed because certain essential material has only recently become available; I hope it has profited by this slowness in its making.

I am indebted to many scholars and to many libraries for valuable help. Foremost among these are my colleagues at the University of Georgia. Dean John Olin Eidson has constantly given personal and tangible encouragement; he has also read the manuscript and made discerning suggestions. Deans George Hugh Boyd, Gerald B. Huff, and Robert A. McRorie have provided research time and aid, and warm friendliness toward the task. The Library staff, as always, has been unfailingly cooperative even when faced with unreasonable demands; among those who have helped most are Porter Kellam, Evelyn Fritz, John Marshall, John Bonner, Sue Fan Tate, and Christine Burroughs. I appreciate also receiving the M. G. Michael Award, since it made part of this research possible. From the University Press, especially from Ralph Stephens, Callie McWhirter, and Anna Pryor Cobb, I have received intelligent editorial and proof-reading aid.

In the English Department, various friends read all or part of the manuscript, and made perceptive criticisms: Rayburn S. Moore, Edwin M. Everett, John E. Talmadge, and Robert H. West. Friends at other universities have also assisted me untiringly. Chief of these are Jay B. Hubbell of Duke, Donald Davidson of Vanderbilt, C. Hugh Holman of North Carolina, Scott Osborn of Mississippi State, and Richard Beale Davis of Tennessee. I am also indebted for gracious assistance to Mary C. Simms Oliphant, and for her permission to use Simms material in her own possession and in the Charles Carroll Simms Collection in the South Caroliniana Library.

After this work was in page proof the Harvard University Press published a reprint of the first volume of Simms's *Views and Reviews,* excellently edited by Hugh Holman. I had no chance to incorporate references to this volume in the notes. However, I have used to advantage Holman's articles and his dissertation on Simms.

I could not have written this book without permission from several libraries to use unpublished material. The officials of the Charleston Library Society have given me free access to their resources, especially the Timrod material. The South Caroliniana Library, through E. L. Inabinett, has permitted use of the Simms, Grayson, and Timrod manuscripts, and other documents. The Duke University Library, through Ben Powell, has allowed me to publish freely from the Chivers and Hayne Collections, and to make use of other items; Jay B. Hubbell, Jr., guided me through the sometimes bewildering maze, especially the manuscripts of Chivers.

My greatest debt is to my wife, Aileen Wells Parks. She has constantly and intelligently helped with the research, and discerningly suggested revisions in the writing. She has also given that most unselfish of all scholarly assistance, the compiling of the index.

E. W. P.

University of Georgia
Athens, Georgia

1

THOMAS JEFFERSON
Humanitarian

WHEN George Washington was questioned about the relative advantages of knowing Greek and French, he answered that he could not pretend to judge of Greek but that French was useful to a traveler.[1] This practical response was probably typical of Virginian thought of his day, or of thought anywhere, at any time. Usually, philosophical and literary values are casually disregarded. A wide-ranging curiosity, an instinctive desire to judge facts and values, an almost tireless mental and physical energy, a quick interest in any matter that might extend the boundaries of man's knowledge—these are traits rarely possessed. Thomas Jefferson had them in abundance, and this quality gives importance to his work in fields where he remained a gifted amateur. He could get excited over measuring the fall of rain, over a new type of seed or plow, over the rights of man and the principles of government, and over the correct scansion of a poem. Although his statements and ideas have, naturally, a varying value on the subjects he touched upon, his first-hand observation and reasoned, independent thought give to most of his reflections a personal validity and a wide interest.

If he took many fields of knowledge as proper for his own inquiries, he was never satisfied with merely idle speculation. It was not enough that a thing be good; it should serve a tangible and preferably an immediate end. He did not ask that profit or credit accrue to him: if he could add to the knowledge of French scientists by sending them strange bones, increase the yield of rice on Carolina farms, or inculcate the ideas of democratic freedom by encouraging the study of Anglo-Saxon, he had helped somewhat in the slow, continuous battle against ignorance, against poverty, against injustice. By such work, a gentleman justified his existence, and his right to live. In addition to giving time and energy, he spent money with a free-handedness that finally impoverished him: "The glow of one warm thought is to me worth more than money," he wrote to Charles McPherson when he was trying to secure the works of Ossian in the original Gaelic.[2] As the quotation indicates, his concept of tangible good went beyond the needs and comforts of the body. A man's mind and soul were to be reckoned with as living entities which must be nourished in their own right. He desired to systematize and order the knowledge available to man, but he desired with equal fervor to expand the realm of man's knowledge.

Early in life he gained a reputation as a skillful writer. When he entered the Continental Congress in 1775, John Adams noted that Jefferson "brought with him a reputation for literature, science, and a happy talent for composition. Writings of his were handed about remarkable for the peculiar felicity of expression."[3] That he took some pride in authorship, he confesses in a sketch of Franklin: when the Declaration of Independence was being considered by Congress, he chafed under the criticisms of words and phrases, until Franklin "perceived that I was not insensible to these mutilations" and as consolation told him the story of a hatter whose carefully worded sign was gradually pared down to a name and a picture.[4] He was proud of his style, but it was not pride in writing which caused him to reckon among his finest achievements the authorship of the Declaration of Independence and of the Statute of Virginia for religious freedom: they were symbols rather than personal achievements; they illustrated certain principles; and they helped to extend the freedom of mankind. His writing had a definite object; it was strictly occasional, and was meant to serve an immediate purpose. He was master of a clear, dry, classic style, which could occasionally take on emotion and color; he sought hard for the precise word, and generally he found it; he could adjust and sharpen and heighten his style until it said admirably what he wanted to say and what the occasion demanded. But interest in good prose writing was a personal, almost an aristocratic, interest. His felicity of expression appears in public documents, state papers, and private letters.

Only once, and then inadvertently, did he publish a book. In 1781, the French government sent him "a number of queries relative to the State of Virginia." Jefferson's answer was lengthy, partly because he embodied the substance of many loose memoranda which he desired to get into a more usable form. Friends pestered him for copies, and he desired to gratify them. But he set a limited value on the work: in America, the price "exceeded the importance of the project"; in Paris, he had two hundred copies printed. None was for sale; he would not permit himself, he wrote, to be arraigned at the bar of public opinion. But a copy got into the hands of a bookseller, "who engaged its translation, and when ready for the press, communicated his intentions and manuscript to me, suggesting that I should correct it, without asking any other permission for the publication. I had never seen so wretched an attempt at translation. Interverted, abridged, mutilated, and often reversing the sense of the original, I found it a blotch of errors, from beginning to end. I corrected some of the worst material, and, in that form, it was printed in French. A London bookseller, on seeing the translation, requested me to permit him to print the English original. I thought it best to do so, to let the world see that it was not really so bad as the French translation had made it appear."[5]

In a preface to the English edition, Jefferson notes that imperfections may be ascribed to the circumstances of composition, and "to the want of information and want of talents in the writer." His greatest concern was that his book might do harm if it appeared in America. He had spoken harshly of slavery, and his words might produce an irritation that would "retard that reformation which I wish, instead of promoting it." For that reason, he had "taken measures to prevent its publication" in America.

This attempt to prevent re-publication is indicative of Jefferson's attitude toward his own writing. *Notes on Virginia* was not a book; it was meant to be a long memorandum. The factual information was, as far as he could make it, accurate; the opinions were personal and honest. But a misguided honesty could do great harm. It was not important that he advance his own views on slavery, if his words would give offense; it was important that slavery be checked, and eventually abolished. It is worth noting that Jefferson never hesitated to express his own mind or personality. If possible, however, these opinions must be so phrased as to hasten, and not to retard, a cause.

II

Jefferson's taste in literature was formed early in life. His father, Colonel Peter Jefferson, was a land-owner and surveyor; he helped "to make the first map of Virginia which had ever been made." Thomas notes that his father's education "had been quite neglected; but being of a strong mind, sound judgment, and eager after information, he read much and improved himself." Randall mentions his "well-worn and fine old edition" of Shakespeare, his copy of the *Spectator,* some of Swift's and Pope's works. But Peter Jefferson was determined that his son's reading should not be limited to English literature; when Thomas was nine, he was sent to a Latin school, and later to study for two years under "a correct classical scholar." His gratitude to his father for this classical training is expressed without Jefferson's customary reserve: "I enjoy Homer in his own language infinitely beyond Pope's translation of him, and both beyond the dull narrative of the same event by Dares Phrygius; and it is an innocent enjoyment. I thank on my knees him who directed my early education, for having put into my possession this rich source of delight; and I would not exchange it for anything which I could then have acquired, and have not acquired."[6]

To him, Homer was always "the first of poets." The work of Homer was a criterion of poetic judgment and a guide to conduct. In Gilbert Chinard's phrase, he "evidently saw in Homer a repository of the wisdoms of an ancient civilization." There is evidence in Jefferson's literary commonplace book that he was interested in a poet's philosophy, and in those descriptions which were as applicable to Virginia as to ancient Greece and Italy. There seems evidence, also, that Jefferson was not then master of Greek to the point that he could disregard a translation: there are eighteen passages from Pope's version of Homer, and thirteen taken directly from the original. But his knowledge of the *Iliad* and the *Odyssey* was thorough enough that, in a commentary on slavery, he remembered Homer's statement that slavery takes away half of a man's worth; when he read the account of a new wheel, he could turn instantly to a similar description. After his wife's death he chose for her epitaph two lines from the *Iliad.*[7]

If his quotations are an index, Jefferson got from Homer primarily a sense of man's weakness, his faith, his moral strength, and his capacity for stoic endurance. No poet could lessen the chances of adversity or the certainty of death, but poetry wisely read could strengthen the mind to endure them. As he grew older, Jefferson's taste constricted. It became more austere, until he was satisfied only with the highest and deepest of poetry. The small doses of sense, imagination, and rhythm were no longer enough, and he wrote, in "Thoughts on English Prosody": "I suspect we are left at last only with Homer and Virgil, perhaps with Homer alone."[8]

Constantly he went back to the classics for models and for comparisons. Remembering as an old man Patrick Henry's speech against the Stamp Act in 1765, he recalled vividly hearing "the splendid display of Mr. Henry's talents as a popular orator. They were great indeed; such as I have never heard from any other man. He appeared to me to speak as Homer wrote."[9] Possibly the term "popular orator" delimits the praise, for Jefferson distrusted any oratory that appealed primarily to the passions: "In a country and government like ours, eloquence is a powerful instrument, well worthy of the special pursuit of our youth. Models, indeed, of chaste and classical oratory are truly too rare among us, nor do I recollect any remarkable in England. Among the ancients the most perfect examples are perhaps to be found in Livy, Sallust and Tacitus. Their pith and brevity constitute perfection itself for an audience of sages, on whom froth and fancy would be lost in air. But in ordinary cases, and with us particularly, more development is necessary. For senatorial eloquence, Demosthenes is the finest model; for the bar, Cicero. The former had more logic, the latter more imagination."[10]

In his youthful *Commonplace Book*, Jefferson copied out many quotations from Cicero. But in maturity he distrusted the Roman author. In 1810, after recommending his favorite trio as models, he made a drastic exclusion: "most assuredly not Cicero. I doubt if there is a man in the world who can now read one of his orations through but as a piece of task-work."[11]

As a young man, Jefferson evidently preferred Euripides to the other classical dramatists. Apparently eighteen pages of manuscript containing excerpts from his plays are missing from his *Commonplace Book;* even so, he had copied out nearly seventy passages, with the greatest number from *Hecuba.* Clearly Jefferson found in Euripides "a treasure of experience and of disenchanted and yet courageous wisdom."[12]

He enjoyed such diverse writers as Herodotus and Anacreon,

but he was completely blind to the merits of Plato. Jefferson was rarely interested in metaphysical speculation. To his old friend John Adams he wrote:

I amused myself with reading seriously Plato's Republic. I am wrong, however, in calling it amusement, for it was the heaviest task-work I ever went through. I had occasionally before taken up some of his other works, but scarcely ever had patience to go through a whole dialogue. While reading through the whimsies, the puerilities and un-intelligible jargon of this work, I laid it down often to ask myself how it could have been, that the world should have consented to give reputation to such nonsense as this? How the *soi-disant* Christian world, indeed, should have done it is a piece of historical curiosity. But how could the Roman good sense do it? And particularly, how could Cicero bestow such eulogies on Plato? Although Cicero did not wield the dense logic of Demosthenes yet he was able, learned, labo-rious, practised in the business of the world and honest. He could not be the dupe of mere style, of which he was himself the first master in the world.[13]

Virgil, Horace, and Seneca were more to his taste. He copied excerpts from their work in his *Commonplace Book;* after he re-tired from the Presidency, he wrote that "I read one or two newspapers a week, but with reluctance give even that time from Tacitus and Horace, and so much other more agreeable read-ing."[14] In Virgil's work there was prophecy as well as sublimity, and Seneca is indeed "a fine moralist, disfiguring his work at times with some Stoicisms, and affecting too much of antithesis and point, yet giving us on the whole a great deal of sound and practical morality."[15]

With this interest in literature and in philosophy went also an interest in pronunciation and in prosody. He believed that by a study of modern Greek practice one should be able to gain a juster concept of ancient standards: "Thus we may live to see the Greeks re-established as a people and the language of Homer again as a living language. Little will be wanting to amend the modern into ancient Greek."[16] In Paris he proposed to study "the rythm of Homer" and the work of "your divine countryman" with an expatriate lady; for this purpose he prepared a manu-script, "A Short Greek Prosody," in which he summarized "the few rules of Greek prosody which must be indispensably known."[17]

III

Early in life Jefferson developed a tenable if limited aesthetic, which mainly guided his appreciation of creative writing. When in 1771 he drew up for a friend a long list of books that might advantageously be purchased for a gentleman's library, he included the novels of Richardson, Fielding, and Smollett, as well as individual works like *Gil Blas, Don Quixote,* and *The Vicar of Wakefield.* Some of his recommendations "would I suppose extort a smile from the face of gravity." This was a short-sided view. Using the term *fiction* in the generalized sense of the word, he defended such reading vigorously:

A little attention however to the nature of the human mind evinces that the entertainments of fiction are useful as well as pleasant. That they are pleasant when well written, every person feels who reads. But wherein is its utility, asks the reverend sage, big with the notion that nothing can be useful but the learned lumber of Greek and Roman reading with which his head is stored? I answer, everything is useful which contributes to fix us in the principles and practice of virtue. When any signal act of charity or of gratitude, for instance, is presented either to our sight or imagination, we are deeply impressed with its beauty and feel a strong desire in ourselves of doing charitable and grateful acts also. On the contrary when we see or read of any atrocious deed, we are disgusted with its deformity and conceive an abhorrence of vice. Now every emotion of this kind is an exercise of our virtuous dispositions; and dispositions of the mind, like limbs of the body, acquire strength by exercise. But exercise produces habit; and in the instance of which we speak, the exercise being of the moral feelings, produces a habit of thinking and acting virtuously. We never reflect whether the story we read be truth or fiction. If the painting be lively, and a tolerable picture of nature, we are thrown into a reverie, from which if we awaken it is the fault of the writer. I appeal to every reader of feeling and sentiment whether the fictitious murther of Duncan by Macbeth in Shakespeare does not excite in him as great horror of villainy, as the real one of Henry IV by Ravaillac as related by Davila? And whether the fidelity of Nelson, and generosity of Blandford in Marmontel do not dilate his breast, and elevate his sentiments as much as any similar incident which real history can furnish? Does he not in fact feel himself a better man while reading them, and privately covenant to copy the fair example? We neither know nor care whether Lawrence Sterne really went to France, whether he was there accosted by the poor Franciscan, at first rebuked him unkindly, and then gave him a peace offering;

or whether the whole be not a fiction. In either case we are equally sorrowful at the rebuke, and secretly resolve *we* will never do so: we are pleased with the subsequent atonement, and view with emulation a soul candidly acknowledging its fault, and making a just reparation. Considering history as a moral exercise, her lessons would be too unfrequent if confined to real life. Of those recorded by historians few incidents have been attended with such circumstances as to excite in any high degree this sympathetic emotion of virtue. We are therefore wisely framed to be as warmly interested for a fictitious as for a real personage. The spacious field of imagination is thus laid open to our use, and lessons may be formed to illustrate and carry home to the mind every moral rule of life. Thus a lively and lasting sense of filial duty is more effectually impressed on the mind of a son or daughter by reading King Lear, than by all the dry volumes of ethics and divinity that ever were written. This is my idea of well-written Romance, of Tragedy, Comedy, and Epic Poetry.[18]

His admiration for Sterne continued. Shortly before her death in 1782, Martha and Thomas Jefferson arranged a prose passage from *Tristram Shandy* in the form of a poem; five years later, he advised his nephew to "read good books because they will encourage as well as direct your feelings. The writings of Sterne particularly form the best course of morality that ever was written." For a different reason (because in the United States women had greater freedom and his own daughter's chances of marrying "a blockhead I calculate at about fourteen to one"), he wished his daughter to be familiar not only with "the best poets and prose writers," but with some of "the graver sciences"; he also left with her, however, "a *Gil Blas* and *Don Quixote* which are among the best books of their class as far as I am acquainted with them."[19]

Yet novels must be read with discretion. Too often they did not illuminate life, as far as the reader was concerned, and he noted with concern, when asked to draw up a "plan of female education" that a "great obstacle to good education is the inordinate passion prevalent for novels, and the time lost in that reading which should be instructively employed. When this poison infects the mind, it destroys its tone, and revolts it against wholesome reading. Reason and fact, plain and unadorned, are rejected. Nothing can engage attention unless dressed in all the figments of fancy, and nothing so bedecked comes amiss. The result is a bloated imagination, sickly judgment, and disgust toward all the real business of life. This mass of trash, however, is not without some distinction; some few modelling their narratives, although fictitious, on the incidents of real life, have been able to make them interesting and useful vehicles of a sound morality. Such, I think, are Marmontel's new moral tales, but not his old ones, which are really immoral. Such are the writings of Miss Edgeworth, and some of those of Madame Genlis. For a like reason too, much poetry should not be indulged. Some is useful for forming style and taste. Pope, Dryden, Thomson, Shakespeare, and of the French, Moliere, Racine, the Corneille's, may be read with pleasure and improvement."[20]

The specific purpose treated in this letter may explain some of the omissions. Apparently for a young woman Jefferson thought that French was the one really important foreign language, whereas for young men he almost invariably recommended a knowledge of Greek, Latin, French, and Spanish.[21] Milton and the classic dramatists and poets appear on nearly all of the extensive lists that he prepared for young men. Jefferson may have thought such reading would be too difficult for girls. But he never doubted that, when properly used, fiction aided the mind and enriched life.

He enjoyed making out lists of reading for younger friends. Perhaps the best of these, and the one most indicative of Jefferson's own tastes, is the one that he prepared for his nephew, Peter Carr:

For the present I advise you to begin a course of ancient history, reading everything in the original and not in translations. First read Goldsmith's history of Greece. This will give you a digested view of that field. Then take up ancient history in the detail, reading the following books in the following order: Herodotus, Thucydides, Xenophontis hellenica, Xenophontis Anabasis. Quintus Curtius. Justin. This shall form the first stage of your historical reading, and is all I need mention to you now. The next will be of Roman history. From that we will come down to Modern history. In Greek and Latin poetry, you have read or will read at school Virgil, Terence, Horace, Anacreon, Theocritus, Homer. Read also Milton's Paradise Lost, Ossian, Pope's works, Swift's works in order to form your style in your own language. In morality read Epictetus, Xenophontis memorabilia, Plato's Socratic dialogues, Cicero's philosophies.[22]

Books were to be read for a purpose. But Jefferson's aesthetic seems at once to broaden and deepen when we realize that among the useful values to be gained were generosity, charitableness, humaneness, warmth of thought and sentiment—that they were to help make a man true, just, firm, orderly, courageous, and steadfast. Here is no narrow didacticism, no doctrine of immediate utility, but a firm belief that books existed to illuminate life. He did not ask for a complete illumination. It was sufficient if the land of make-believe adumbrated the world of reality, but the cross-reference must be implicit in the work. He wanted to yoke together the practical and the imaginative. Reading is at once an "innocent and elegant luxury," a source of taste, and a source of information—all good things.

IV

His taste was formed by eighteenth century standards. The romantic poets who came into prominence after 1800 did not interest him. There is reason to believe that he was not speaking the full truth when in 1801 he wrote to John D. Burke about his close friend Joel Barlow's poem, *The Columbiad*: "To my own mortification. . . I am the last who should undertake to decide as to the merits of poetry. In earlier life I was fond of it and easily pleased. But as age and cares advanced, the powers of fancy have declined. Every year seems to have plucked a feather from her wings, till she can no longer waft one to those sublime heights to which it is necessary to accompany the poet."[23]

Not all the feathers had been plucked, or ever were. All his life Jefferson enjoyed, in addition to Homer and Virgil, the work of Shakespeare, Milton, Dryden, and Pope; and he remembered well the works of Otway, Congreve, Young, Collins, Gray, Shenstone, Akenside, and Ossian. But he did not seek out new worlds in literature. Although he kept any occasional verse that was sent to him, and pasted up in a commonplace book a collection of contemporary poems that praised liberty and freedom, he clearly valued the ideas they expressed more than he did their literary merit. Such work might do some good, and whatever of it came to his hand he kept, but for his own purposes he turned back to the older men.[24]

Jefferson's approach to English and American literature was that of a classicist. It is all the more remarkable, therefore, that he wrote one of the first technical essays on English prosody ever produced in this country.

The manner of its writing was typical of his attitude toward literature. At Monticello and in France he had discussed versification with a French friend, F. J. de Chastellaux. Jefferson started with the assumption that English prosody depended, like Greek and Roman verse, "on long and short syllables arranged into regular feet. You were of a different opinion." He set out to convert a foreigner. In leisure hours while serving under great pressure as Ambassador to France, he relaxed by walking and at the same time "turning this subject in my mind."[25]

He knew little about prosody, and contented himself with noting that of those who "have mounted the English poetry on Greek and Latin feet," the commentaries of Samuel Johnson are the best. But he did not turn back to the scholars and critics for guidance; he went directly to the poets. Reading and reflection convinced him that he had been wrong, and somewhat ruefully he confesses to de Chastellaux that it was a Frenchman who "recalled me from an error in my native tongue, and that, too, in a point the most difficult of all others to a foreigner, the law of its poetical numbers."[26]

His method was simple. He tested lines and verses by pronouncing the words aloud, drawing upon the works of minor as well as of major poets. This simple and practical test soon convinced him that English prosody had an accentual, not a quantitative, basis. Essentially an amateur, he was alert, independent—and little concerned with precedent. His reason indicated that even Dr. Samuel Johnson was in error on this point; it was useful for Thomas Jefferson and M. de Chastellaux to be aware of the truth. But it was not important that the world know, for this was a private and not a public interest. Although he ended by writing a long essay, he apparently thought of it only as another long memorandum, much less important than his *Notes on Virginia,* and this time he was not forced into publication. In fact, the essay was not published until 1903.

No poet himself, Jefferson arrived at conclusions that are almost startling in their rigidity. The fundamental law of English verse, he decided, was that "the accent shall never be displaced from the syllable whereon usage hath established it." He tried to reduce the kind of feet to three (the equivalent of trochaic, iambic, and anapaestic), but in those to allow for a certain amount of elision: "There are but three arrangements into which these accents can be thrown in the English language which entitle the composition to be distinguished by the name of verse. That is: 1. Where the accent falls on all the odd syllables; 2. Where it falls on all the even syllables; 3. Where it falls on every third syllable. If the reason of this be asked, no other can be assigned but that it results from the nature of the sounds which compose the English language and from the construction of the human ear."[27]

On this basis he tests many lines of poetry, working out for himself a method of indicating the relative strength of accents.[28] But technical rules for reading are not enough. The gradations of sound and tone and accent are intimately connected with usage, and with the sense of the poem. If a man has "a well-organized ear," he will be conscious of the verse: to prove this, Jefferson prints as prose a passage from the Greek of Homer and proclaims that the man who can read it without pausing at every sixth foot "is an unfavored son of nature." For such persons little could be done, but for those who had a natural ear some knowledge of the technical rules would improve their art.[29]

In one respect he was before and after his period, in preferring blank verse to rhyme. In every form of literature he demanded the condensed, the well-digested, and the reasonable. Rhyme had a jingly quality but, even worse, it forced the poet into padding his lines with "feeble nothings necessary to introtrude the rhyming word. With no other trammel than that of measure he is able to condense his thoughts and images and to leave nothing but what is truly poetical."[30]

The time spent on a technical study of prosody, if only as a relaxation from political work and worries, seems to contradict Jefferson's demand that literature be useful. He saw no contradiction. His definition of use was so wide-ranging that it provided for spiritual as well as material good. He advocated the study of a simplified form of Anglo-Saxon because it would enable us better to use and understand modern English, but also because it would enable people to "read Shakespeare and Milton with a superior degree of intelligence and delight." There was a second, perhaps more potent, reason: from the Anglo-Saxons we had inherited our love of freedom, and students would "imbibe with the language their free principles of government."

V

Jefferson's introduction to Anglo-Saxon was casual enough: while studying law, he read a preface which mentioned "the advantages to be derived to the English student generally, and particularly the student of law, from an acquaintance with the Anglo-Saxon." He immediately secured the necessary books and "devoted some time to the study." His letters intimate that his study of the language was almost as casual as his introduction to it, and that he had found the subject chaotic rather than difficult. With his instinct for ordering and simplifying, he had noted down some ideas "for facilitating the study by simplifying its grammar, by reducing the infinite diversities of its unfixed orthography to single and settled forms . . . there I have left them, and must leave them, unpursued, although I still think them sound and useful."[31]

These ideas are rooted, fundamentally, in one idea: that Anglo-Saxon is an older form of English, "some ages earlier than that of Piers Plowman" and that the language has been made unduly complicated by men who attempted to give it "the complicated structure of the Greek and Latin languages."[32] It was the basis of our present tongue and a full-formed language, but its structure, its declensions, and its syntax were fundamentally different from "those of the South." Later additions to the language, from Latin, Greek, French, or Italian, were but engraftments on its idiomatic stem; its original structure and syntax remain the same, and can be but "imperfectly understood by the mere Latin scholar."[33] With this in mind, Jefferson proposed simplifications and modernizations in the alphabet, the orthography, the pronunciation, and the grammar.

His first suggestion was that all Anglo-Saxon characters be printed in Roman forms: the mixture of the two, and the fact that students were accustomed to the Roman, made the Anglo-Saxon part seem "uncouth, and appalling" to the eye. He argues ingeniously that the change of a character did not represent a change in the sound or in the language; hence there is nothing to be lost and much of practical value to be gained, by printing all Anglo-Saxon works in Roman type. With regard to orthography, Jefferson maintained that few men in Anglo-Saxon days knew how to read and write; those who knew had no examples to refer to, and thought the arrangement of letters "indeed not important"; in short, no one knew how to spell. The vowels, especially, were used indiscriminately: Jefferson quotes several times the word *many,* and gives the twenty different ways in which it was spelled. Since the Anglo-Saxons had never imposed order upon the language, Jefferson believed that "we are surely at liberty equally to adopt any mode which, establishing uniformity, may be more consonant with the power of the letters, and with the orthography of the present dialect, as established by usage." As for pronunciation, he would simply take that "now in general use as the legitimate standard," although he proposed this reluctantly, as "irregular and equivocal." But it was hopeless, he believed, to try to recover a lost pronunciation: with Anglo-Saxon, as with Greek and Latin, the best expedient was to accept as fact that "their pronunciation has been handed down, by tradition, more nearly than it can be known to other countries."[34]

His reforms in grammar were more drastic. He would "dismiss the learning of genders [for nouns and adjectives] from one language, whether in its ancient or modern form," and he gives a common-sense reason: "although the thing designated may have sex, the word designating it, like other inanimate things, has no sex, no gender." Those cases which are distinguished by change of termination could be reduced to three. He would remove also the "cumbrous scaffolding, erected by too much learning" from around numbers, moods, and especially gerunds; he quotes at length to show that Anglo-Saxon does not have supines. Grammar should be made clear and understandable; if a subtle philological damage was done to the language, that mattered little. "Is it worth while," he asked, "to embarrass grammar with an extra distinction for two or three, or half a dozen words?" Clearly, to his mind, it was not. A man must set a proper value on his time and energy.[35]

There was much to be gained from a study of Anglo-Saxon. The English Constitution had as "its rightful root, the Anglo-Saxon," and, though never written down, "they have left fragments of their history and laws, from which it may be inferred." Jefferson believed that "the difference between the Whig and the Tory of England is, that the Whig deduces his rights from the Anglo-Saxon source, and the Tory from the Norman." Jefferson, a hater of Tories, saw then as one advantage that students "will imbibe with the language their free principles of government."[36] Its acquisition, also, "will richly repay us by the intimate insight it will give us into the genuine structure, powers and meaning of the language we now read and speak. We shall then read Shakespeare and Milton with a superior degree of intelligence and delight, heightened by the new and delicate shades of meaning developed to us by a knowledge of the original sense of the same words." These were positive values. But the work of certain Anglo-Saxon scholars had resulted in "such an infinitude of minute rules and observances, as are beyond the power of any human memory to retain. If this be the true genius of the Anglo-Saxon language, then its difficulties go beyond its worth . . . and, in that case, I would recommend its abandonment in our University, as an unattainable and unprofitable pursuit."[37]

Jefferson was interested also in the language of the Indians, although for a different reason: "We generally learn languages for the benefit of reading the books written in them. But here our reward must be the addition made to the philosophy of language." This was not unimportant, for he had "long considered the filiation of languages as the best proof of the filiation of nations."[38] These were philosophical reasons. There were personal reasons, also. Jefferson had been brought up on the frontier, and this has too often been minimized in the treatments of Jefferson's thought. Ontassaté, on his way to and from Williamsburg, had frequently stopped at Peter Jefferson's house; Thomas had spent much time with the Indians, and liked them; he cited among the greatest of speeches Logan's response to Lord Dunmore; he noted to the editor of *The American Speaker* that his own copy of Chief Cornplanter's speech "has much in it, which yours has not. But observing that the omissions relate to special subjects only, I presume that they are made purposely and indeed properly."[39]

Jefferson regretted the extreme mistreatment of the Indians. Mainly, this was for humanitarian reasons, but in the extinction of so many Indian tribes we had lost, also, "they general rudiments" of their languages. "Were vocabularies formed of all the languages spoken in North and South America, preserving their appellations of the most common objects in nature, of those which must be present to every nation barbarous or civilized, with the inflections of their nouns and verbs, their principles of regimen and concord, and these deposited in all the public libraries, it would furnish opportunities to those skilled in the languages of the old world to compare them with these, now, or at any future time, and hence to construct the best evidence of the derivation of this part of the human race."[40]

What he could do to prevent the complete disappearance of these languages, Jefferson did. The work was a hobby only, but an engrossing one. "I endeavor," he wrote to James Madison in thanking him for a pamphlet on the Mohican language, "to collect all the vocabularies I can, of the American Indians, as of those of Asia." In this work, he called on friends who might have access to records, and he commanded the aid of subordinates. In March, 1800, he wrote to the Indian Agent Benjamin Hawkins that he was "about to print" his collection of Indian vocabularies, but he lacked "the great Southern languages, Cherokees, Creeks,

Choctaw, Chickasaw." Jefferson wanted only a vocabulary of particular words; he enclosed a list, with precise details, and requested that Hawkins send him the Creek words immediately (Hawkins had promised, rather vaguely, information on the Creek language), and the others as soon as possible. From William Dunbar he received "little vocabularies of Bedais, Tankawis, and Teghas," and noted that, with these, he had "thirty tolerably full." He notes also that in publishing them he will "keep them in the orthography in which they were taken down, only noting whether that were English, French, German, or what."[41] Evidently any friend or acquaintance of Jefferson's, regardless of his nationality or business, was likely to be drafted into service. The collection of Indian vocabularies was made a duty of the Lewis and Clark expedition, Captain Lewis being "instructed to take those of every tribe" beyond the Mississippi. Jefferson adds that he "was very attentive to these instructions, never missing an opportunity of taking a vocabulary"; and that he never met "with a single Indian of a new tribe, without making his vocabulary the first object."[42]

But this hobby came to nothing, and that at the moment when he had the leisure to prepare his study for publication. He had hoped to publish them before, as he modestly puts it, "the last of my stay in Washington," but had lacked the leisure to put Lewis's collection in order, and "put it off till I should return home. The whole, as well digest as originals, were packed in a trunk of stationery, and sent round by water . . . while ascending James River, this package on account of its weight and presumed precious contents, was singled out and stolen. The thief being disappointed on opening it, threw into the river all its contents, of which he thought he could make no use. Among them were the whole of the vocabularies. Some leaves floated ashore and were found in the mud; but these were very few, and so defaced by the mud and water that no general use can be made of them."[43] Thus he felt, after 1809, that his own share in the work was reduced from the possibility of scientific proof to the relatively fruitless field of speculation. This was pleasant enough, in one way, but it was distressing, at the end of a long life, to be able to add little to his earlier surmises. In the *Notes on Virginia,* he had stated that "there will be found probably twenty in America for one in Asia, of those radical languages, so called because if they were ever the same they have lost all resemblance to one another. A separation into dialects may be the work of a few ages only, but for two dialects to recede from one another till they have lost all vestiges of their common origin, must require an immense course of time; perhaps not less than many people give to the age of the earth. A greater number of those radical changes of language having taken place among the red men of America, proves them of greater antiquity than those of Asia."[44]

Although he grew doubtful of this apparent proof, he remained impressed with how languages "so radically different have been preserved by such small tribes in coterminous settlements of moderate extent": in his own collection, a third of his carefully chosen words, "if not more, were perfectly insulated from each other."[45]

At least, the Indian languages could be used to dispose of error: for example, that all words were originally monosyllables. Man might come from one stock, but languages as we know them did not: "I should conjecture that the Cherokees . . . have formed their language not by single words, but by the whole phrases. . . . Thus the Cherokee has no name for father in the abstract, but only as combined with some of his relations. A complex idea being a fasciculus of simple ideas bundled together, it is rare that different languages make up their bundles alike, and hence the difficulty of translating from one language to another. European nations have for so long had intercourse with one another, as to have approximated their complex expressions much toward one another. But I believe we shall find it impossible to translate our language into any of the Indians, or any of theirs into ours."[46]

His own research had proved nothing. Perhaps it had disproved Adair's belief that the Indians were descended from the Jews; it certainly had disproved Adair's generalization that "the hundred languages of America . . . have all one common prototype." Each man who started with a set theory "had his kink," and therefore tended to retail "such absurdities as zeal for a theory could alone swallow." Since ignorance was preferable to false knowledge, Jefferson felt that his work had not been completely wasted. But on the problem which he set out to solve, he could confess to John Adams that "the question of Indian origin, like many others, pushed to a certain height must receive the same answer, "Ignoro."[47]

VI

The problem with history, and especially with contemporary history, was not so much ignorance as deliberate distortion. He set a high value on a knowledge of the past, and he desired that all students in this country have their minds stored with the most useful facts from Greek, Roman, European, and American history:

History, by apprizing them of the past, will enable them to judge of the future; it will avail them of the experience of other times and other nations; it will qualify them as judges of the actions and designs of men; it will enable them to know ambition under every disguise it may assume; and knowing it, to defeat its views.[48]

These words represented his honest belief. By nature, Jefferson was optimistic; he believed that people needed only to know the truth in order for them to act by it. The major difficulty was in finding out the truth. Too many historians were prejudiced, and deliberately colored the facts; many of them were careless or downright ignorant. The errors of ignorance one could find amusing, if distressing; when a French historian wrote that John Dickinson, alone, had stood for independence, Jefferson sent to the editor of a Paris newspaper a mighty and in places a mock-serious protest: "When young I was passionately fond of reading books of history and travels. Since the commencement of the late Revolution, our country, too, have been thought worthy to employ the pens of historians and travellers. I cannot paint to you, Sir, the agonies which these have cost me, in obliging me to renounce these favorite branches of reading, and in discovering to me at length, that my whole life has been employed in nourishing my mind with fables and falsehoods. If contemporary histories are thus false, what will future compilations be? And what are all those of preceding times?"[49]

Carelessness was harder to forgive. In 1814, he attempted to help William Wirt give a true record of Patrick Henry's legislative career. Two earlier historians had presented false copies of the record, although printed copies were in existence, and Jefferson could only question: "When writers are so indifferent as to the correctness of facts, the verification of which lies at their elbow, by what measure shall we estimate their relation of things distant, or of those given to us through the obliquities of their own vision?" It was only too easy, when exact records were missing, for history to become "fable instead of fact. The great outlines may be true, but the incidents and coloring are according to the faith or fancy of the writer."[50] Jefferson was afraid of what he considered fables; he feared the power of the historian.

A great part of Toryism in England could be traced to the works of David Hume: "Every one knows that judicious matter and charms of style have rendered Hume's history the manual of every student. I remember well the enthusiasm with which I devoured it when young, and the length of time, the research and reflection which were necessary to eradicate the poison it had instilled into my mind. . . . It is this book which has undermined the free principles of the English government . . . and has spread universal toryism over the land." Jefferson praises an adaptation of Hume's work, which "corrected in the text his misrepresentations, supplied the truths which he suppressed . . . . And it is wonderful how little interpolation has been necessary to make it a sound history, and to justify what should have been its title, to wit, 'Hume's history of England abridged and rendered faithful to fact and principle.' I cannot say that his amendments are either in matter or manner in the fine style of Hume."[51]

The item quoted above is significant. Jefferson undoubtedly wanted a true recording of history; but he wanted it, also, to be faithful to his own democratic principles. When judgments or outright calumnies were directed at him personally, he ignored them; and with all that seemed simply malicious, he preserved an amazingly detached attitude. His personal relations with Hamilton were amicable, and only Aaron Burr, it seems, stirred in him a deep personal resentment. Even Burr's case is doubtful: he was far more concerned with Burr's and Marshall's attacks on his concept of government than by attacks on himself as an individual. As to his personal reputation, he had an implicit faith in the long-range verdict of the people, and an aristocratic contempt for his detractors. He wrote to Thomas Jefferson Randolph in 1808 that "My character . . . is in the hands of my fellow citizens at large, and will be consigned to honor or infamy by the verdict of the republican mass of our country. . . . Never, therefore, consider these puppies in politics as requiring any notice from you." Variance of opinion was nothing new in the world. There had always been Whigs and Tories in the world; there always would be, no matter what party labels they might use. When a man was honestly convinced, nothing could be gained by argument, and Jefferson had no intention of becoming "a Don Quixote, to bring all men by force of argument to one opinion."[52]

Jefferson looked upon Marshall's biography of Washington as

a partisan document; it was a "five-volume libel" and a "party diatribe." He planned to correct by notes of his own the entire fifth volume of the biography, and he started the task, but apparently never got beyond page 33. In these notes, Jefferson attacks the "artful complexion" which Marshall gave to the Federal and Republican parties; but he does not present any documented rejoinder.[53]

The whole truth, if honest history of his time could ever be written, would plainly show that republicanism had been right in principles and in acts. But an error of fact, once made, could hardly be corrected. Of the Committees of Correspondence, he noted despairingly: "Botta, copying Marshall, has repeated his error, and so it will be handed on from copyist to copyist, *ad infinitum.*" (I, 184). He objected even more strongly to "the factitious speeches which Botta has composed" for various historical characters: these were patent falsifications of history, and Jefferson greatly preferred the "modern practice" of presenting the reasons in the author's own words. (XVIII, 306-07). Yet these were but surface blemishes; in general, Jefferson approved highly of Botta's *History of the American Revolution,* and according to La Fayette it was translated into English under Jefferson's "auspices." (XVIII, 326-27).[54]

To Destutt de Tracy's commentary on Montesquieu, Jefferson gave even more help. He arranged for the translating and printing of the work, but he found "the style of the translation was so bungling" that he revised the entire work—a "horrible job." Tracy's name was kept secret, as a protection to him; in answer to an inquiry about the book, Jefferson wrote: "I may only say at present that it was written by a Frenchman, that the original MS. in French is now in my possession . . . it is a most valuable work, one which I think will form an epoch in the science of government, and which I wish to see in the hands of every American student." For Montesquieu, Jefferson had less respect; he wrote to Monsieur Tracy that "I had, with the world, deemed Montesquieu's work of much merit; but saw in it, with every thinking man, so much of paradox, of false principle and misapplied fact, as to render its value equivocal on the whole." Tracy had written a commentary and review, in which he confirmed or confuted the older author, and when necessary had substituted "true for false principle, and the true principle is ever that of republicanism."[55]

Men were frequently calling on him, especially in his later life, for help; if they would come in person, he would turn over to them letters and documents "so tattered and tender as not to admit removal further than from their shelves to a library table." He helped Wirt with his biography of Patrick Henry, and wrote several sketches of characters and events; he read proof on the book, and wrote the author that "Your characters are inimitably and justly drawn." But he added, later, that Wirt must expect criticism ("By the Quarterly Reviewers you will be hacked and hewed, with tomahawk and scalping-knife") from prejudiced Anti-Americans, from adherents of the familiar manner of Plutarch, or the scanty manner of Nepos; these classicists, however, "can only prove that your style is different . . . not that it is not good." Wirt's manuscript had much to commend it, but in one respect the author had departed from truth: "You have certainly practised rigorously the precept of *de mortuis nil nisi bonum*. This presents a very difficult question,—whether one only or both sides of the medal shall be presented. It constitutes, perhaps, the distinction between panegyric and history."[56]

Jefferson admitted that "opinions are much divided" on this point; for himself, he preferred history. Generally he could look at himself in an amazingly detached and impersonal manner; he wrote to one historian of Virginia, L. H. Girardin, an explicit statement: "As to what is to be said of myself, I of course am not the judge. But my sincere wish is that the faithful historian, like the able surgeon, would consider me in his hands, while living, as a dead subject, that the same judgment may now be expressed which will be rendered hereafter, . . . too little is safer than too much; and I sincerely assure you that you will please me most by a rigorous suppression of all friendly partialities."[57]

This attitude was characteristic. All his mature life he had a curiously impersonal and detached point of view concerning his own achievements. He was enormously concerned about the causes and the principles for which he fought, but quite indifferent about his own part. All that he asked of history was that the facts and the ideas be presented honestly. If this was done, the people would find out and judge the truth for themselves. That was all that mattered, and he asked only that history provide the materials on which unbiased judgments could be formed.

VII

Knowledge was meant to dispel error, to widen and deepen mental horizons, to strengthen the moral sense. These were essential tests. It did not matter whether the book purported to be fact or fiction. Homer and Shakespeare and Sterne, Herodotus and Euclid and Newton, all were to be judged finally by the same tests. The immediate canons of criticism were changed, but the ultimate canon remained always the same. A good book or a sound piece of knowledge enlarged the domain of man's mind. This was the most important field of human endeavor—more important to him than wealth or success or personal well-being. In many ways a practical man, Jefferson spent most of his life in the hurly-burly of politics, and he climaxed a distinguished career with eight years in the presidency. Yet he was always willing to steal time from the immediately practical to give it to the long-range intellectual concept. What one did was no more important to him than how one thought.

Always his knowledge was at the service of others. But he never forced it upon them, or desired personal credit. It was important that a job be well done, but not important that he do it. That was his feeling about architecture as well as about writing. He preferred to share with friends rather than to expose his work for judgment before the world. When the occasion demanded, he did not hesitate; but he preferred when possible to limit his remarks to private letters.

This was his attitude toward literature. He never looked upon himself as a writer, but always as a discriminating reader who was sometimes forced into writing for the public. Yet out of his books and his literary speculations he evolved a clean, distinguished style—a distinction of thought that found expression in words. His taste was sound, if a bit austere, and his standards high, for himself as well as for the books he read. In this field, as in many others, he remained in his own mind an amateur. But the independent-minded amateur can contribute something that the professional might overlook. Jefferson does this. Whether he felt himself qualified to write on the subject or not, his scattered remarks on literature have a two-fold value: what he says about literature reveals much about Jefferson, but his critical insights help also to reveal much about literature, and even a bit about ourselves. Jefferson would have liked this double-barreled usefulness.

2

HUGH SWINTON LEGARÉ
Humanist

FOR A FOUR-YEAR period (1828-32), Legaré was an exceedingly active literary critic, as the principal and most prolific contributor to *The Southern Review,* and for approximately the last two years its editor. This was strictly an avocation; he was by profession a lawyer, recognized as an authority on civil law. From October 1830 until after the magazine ended with the February 1832 issue, Legaré also served as Attorney-General of South Carolina.[1] He was in wide demand as a speaker, for he was one of the most famous orators of his time. Yet his qualifications as critic, his background of literary knowledge, are impressive. He had read extensively in English literature, especially poetry and drama; he enjoyed reading plays informally with friends, often making discerning comments on them. Yet he was better grounded in Greek literature than in English. In addition, he knew Latin, French, Italian, and Spanish, and had read in the original all the standard and many of the obscure works in those languages. Although he did not learn German until after he became Chargé d'Affaires in Belgium in 1832, his reviews indicate that he was familiar with many works in translation. After graduating with highest honors from South Carolina College, he had travelled in Europe and studied for a year at the University of Edinburgh.[2]

Emphasis should be placed on his knowledge of and his enthusiasm for Greek literature. He was a critic in a time of transition. Many Southerners had enthusiastically accepted the Romantic writings of Scott, Wordsworth, Coleridge, Byron, and their fellows; others had summarily and even contemptuously rejected them.[3] Charleston in particular retained a strong classical bent. For this, Legaré and his friends were to some degree responsible. The two Stephen Elliotts, James L. Petigru, Henry Junius Nott, and Robert Henry were essentially classicists with a rather limited taste for contemporary works; Legaré, with somewhat wider and more catholic tastes, nonetheless approached contemporary English, American, and French literature from a background which had convinced him of the supremacy of the Greeks.[4]

The editors adhered strictly to the title. They were not editing a magazine, but a review. Every article started with one or more books and pamphlets as a springboard. Sometimes the connection of article with book was exceedingly tenuous, so that what was practically an independent treatise resulted; in one instance, the reviewer apologetically noted on the eighteenth page that he would begin his criticism of the novel listed at the beginning of the article.[5] Since many of the books discussed were not readily available to readers, it was deliberate editorial policy to give lengthy excerpts even from novels, and to quote generously from books of poetry.[6] The *Review* intended to familiarize its readers with the work under discussion at least as much as to present the analyses and judgments of its contributors. Although a reviewer might range widely over a given field, he was to some extent limited by the books that happened to be published, and to be available in Charleston. This explains some of the surprising choices that Legaré made, and some of the omissions from his critical canon.

Legaré adhered to the policy which he had helped to set. His discussions of Cooper are based on two of the weaker novels; his treatment of Scott likewise starts with an inferior work; his major literary reviews—the two on Byron—were written because of the timely appearance of Tom Moore's *Letters and Journals of Lord Byron*. Especially near the end, when he was writing half an issue himself, Legaré undoubtedly padded it because of the necessity of filling the number. After three pages on Bryant's poetry, he quotes (usually with a one-line introductory) fourteen pages of poetry before giving a brief summation. The attentive reader certainly had an excellent chance to become familiar with Bryant's work.

At the same time, Legaré consistently judged creative work by certain defined standards. A great work of literary art must have, to be considered "a composition of genius," three qualities "essential to all excellence . . . perfect unity of purpose, simplicity of style, and ease of execution—and it is in these things that the literature and art of Greece exhibit their matchless perfection. Other nations have produced works indicating as rare and fertile invention, as much depth of thought, as much vigor of conception, as much intensity of feeling—but no body of literature or art can be compared to the *antique* for the severe *reason*, the close, unsparing *logic* of its criticism. Unity of design, especially, which is more immediately connected with the subject in hand, they rigorously exacted. They considered a work of art always as a *whole*—a sort of organized body—to the very structure of which certain parts and proportions, and none others, were essential, and in which the least violation of this fitness and harmony was a deformity, more or less uncouth and monstrous. The details were sacrificed without mercy to the general effect."[7]

These ideal standards which Legaré attributed to Greek literature were the ones by which he judged. Rightly or wrongly, he made them his own. Paraphrasing Sidney, he wrote that "True poetry—like true eloquence—is the voice of nature appealing to the heart with its utmost sublimity and power";[8] after asking "what is poetry," he presented a definition that has misled some literary historians into calling him a romantic critic: Poetry "is but an abridged name for the sublime and beautiful, and for highly wrought pathos. . . . It is spread over the whole face of nature—it is in the glories of the heavens and in the wonders of the great deep, in the voice of the cataract and of the coming storm, in Alpine precipices and solitudes, in the balmy gales and sweet bloom and freshness of spring. It is in every heroic achievement, in every lofty sentiment, in every deep passion, in every bright vision of fancy, in every vehement affection of gladness or of grief, of pleasure or of pain. It is, in short, the feeling—the deep, the strictly *moral* feeling, which when it is affected by chance or change in human life, as at a tragedy, we call sympathy—but as it appears in the still more mysterious connections between the heart of man and the forms and beauties of inanimate nature, as if they were instinct with a soul and a sensibility like our own, has no appropriate appellation in our language, but it is not the less real or the less familiar to our experience on that account. It is these feelings, whether utterance be given to them, or they be only nursed in the smitten bosom—whether they be couched in metre, or poured out with wild disorder and irrepressible rapture, that constitute the true spirit and essence of poetry."[9]

The key to this definition is in the last seven words. The subject-matter of poetry is unlimited: in all these things, animate or inanimate, spoken or mute, there is the spirit of poetry; but where realized and not potential poetry is under discussion, Legaré demands of the poet (as he does of novelist or dramatist) that he give form, design, wholeness to the finished product.

With these critical standards as touchstones, Legaré surveyed a goodly if miscellaneous body of world literature, with enlightening although incidental commentary on a host of other writers. The death of the *Southern Review* almost coincided with his appointment as Chargé d'Affaires to Belgium; near the end of his four years there, when various South Carolinians urged him again to edit the *Review,* he politely but flatly refused.[10] Instead he returned to take up law and politics, serving as Congressman and then at his death holding the combined jobs of Attorney-General and Interim Secretary of State. In this period he wrote for the *New York Review* three of his finest articles, although they are not concerned with literature. But he always looked back with pride on his work as a literary critic, and on his close connection with the *Southern Review.*[11]

II

It was appropriate that the first essay was by Legaré, since he was to become its principal contributor; it was equally appropriate, considering his interests, that it was entitled "Classical Learning."[12] Although he lists three pamphlets at the head of his article, he was fundamentally concerned with refuting Thomas S. Grimké's contention that classical studies were no longer useful, and with presenting his own positive arguments as to their usefulness. After briefly describing the pamphlets and complimenting their authors, Legaré notes that there are two distinct questions involved in the controversy: "first, what are the merits of Greek and Roman classics, considered merely as works of art, and as models for imitation; and, secondly, how far is it worth while, under existing circumstances, to study them."[13] Grimké had appealed to the authority of men like William Wirt and Timothy Dwight. Legaré brushes this aside as worthless. Except when national pride has led British critics to place Milton above Homer, or Italian critics Tasso, or Portuguese critics Camoëns, "there is but one voice throughout the whole of civilized Europe" respecting the matchless excellence of Greek literature and art.[14] There can be no real question as to their merits.

Even worse, Grimké had unduly and meretriciously narrowed the meaning of usefulness. Grimké assumes that "Our youth are to be trained up as if they were all destined to be druggists and apothecaries, or navigators and mechanists." If this is true, Legaré notes, he must fairly give up the controversy, for he "cannot, with a clear conscience, undertake to promise, that Greek and Latin will make better artisans and manufacturers," and admits that an itinerant preacher might find "more profitable doctrine, in honest John Bunyan, than in all the speculation of the Lyceums and the Academies; and we do conscientiously believe, that not a single case, more or less, of yellow fever would be cured by the faculty in this city, for all that Hippocrates and Celsus have said." But there is another usefulness, broader and deeper, for it "ought to be the capital object of education, to form the *moral* character, not by teaching what to think but persuading to act well; not by loading the memory with cold and barren concepts, but forming the sensibility by the habitual, fervid and rapturous contemplation of high and heroical models of excellence; not by definitions of virtue and speculations about the principle of obligation, but by making us *love* the one and *feel* the sacredness of the other."[15]

Grimké had presented a plausible argument for our material well-being. In Legaré's eyes, this was not enough. Truly patriotic Americans desired also that we become "a cultivated and a literary nation. Upon this assumption, what we contend for, is that the study of the classics is and ought to be an essential part of a *liberal* education—that education of which the object is to make accomplished, elegant and learned men—to chasten and to discipline genius, to refine the taste, to quicken the perceptions of decorum and propriety, to purify and exalt the moral sentiments, to fill the soul with a deep love of the beautiful both in moral and material nature, to lift up the aspirations of man to objects that are worthy of his noble faculties and his immortal destiny."[16]

If this definition is accepted, as Legaré thinks it should be, then utility is not enough. But there is the parallel argument often presented that even in this respect the Moderns have more to offer, that "the literature, but more especially the poetry. . . is more various, profound and passionate than that of Greece and Rome." The German critics in particular have emphasized the objectivity of the classical writers, and the subjectivity (and therefore superiority) of the moderns, whom they call Romantics, because they are "more conversant with the depths of the heart and its passions, with abstract ideas and the operations of the world of spirits." Legaré demurs. He admits that the Greek and Roman poets drew "their figures of speech from external or material objects." But so did the Old Testament poets, and Romantic critics had extolled this as a "distinguished excellence."[17]

This concept, Legaré argues, must be limited strictly to modern writers. The critics cannot find support in the works of the English poets: "Even Milton, who has drawn together his materials from a greater variety of sources than any other writer, and whose mighty genius is for nothing more remarkable than the apparent ease with which it appropriates and applies, and melts and moulds into new and original combinations, the most multifarious learning that ever fell to a poet's lot, is still distinguished by an antique and severe simplicity, even in his boldest and vastest conceptions. We do not remember, in any of his works, rich even to gorgeousness and redundancy, in all sorts of imagery, any tropes or figures, that in their external form and character merely, give the least countenance to this notion of a romantic, or spiritual or mystical poetry, essentially distinct from the classical (not in its subjects or spirit, for that is certainly true, but) in its rules and proportions, its lineaments and contours. The same thing may be said of Shakespeare, and of all our great English classics. The poets of our day, indeed, have in quest of —novelty—a pursuit which ever led to the corruption of taste, deviated from this primitive simplicity. Byron, especially, is remarkable for far-fetched allusions and quaint conceits, that are more worthy of Cowley than of himself, and this straining after effect, is precisely the besetting sin of his muse."[18]

With some reluctance, Legaré admitted that there was a fundamental difference between the classical and the modern Romantic writers. He quoted at length from A. W. Schlegel, who had argued that the "principle, by which it is attempted to account for this mighty revolution in art and criticism, is *religion*."[19] Legaré was "disposed to assent, in general," to the justness of Schlegel's observations that "modern literature does differ from that of the Greeks in its *complexion* and *spirit*—that it is more pensive, sombre and melancholy, perhaps we may add, more abstract and metaphysical—and it has, no doubt, been 'sicklied o'er' with this sad hue, by the influence of a religious faith which connects morality with worship." The modern writers were certainly "more given to *spiritualizing* than the Greeks were—sensible objects suggest more reflections more readily—the external world is treated as if it were the symbol of the invisible, and the superiority of mind to matter, of the soul to the body, is almost as much admitted by the figures of rhetoric and poetry, as in the dogmas of philosophy." The spirit had changed, perhaps for the better, but in Legaré's estimation the forms and proportions of beauty had not changed.[20]

Parts of this beauty Legaré found in the superiority of the Greek language. This was not apparent even in the best translations: "The wonderful, the magical powers of certain expressions, cannot by any art of composition be transfused from one language into another."[21] This was particularly true of Greek, for "All the other tongues that civilized men have spoken, are poor and feeble, and barbarous, in comparison of it. Its compass and flexibility, its richness and its powers, are altogether unlimited."[22]

But this "wonderful idiom happens to have been spoken . . . by a race as wonderful. The very first monument of this genius —the most ancient relic of letters in the Western world—stands to this day altogether unrivalled in the exalted class to which it belongs." Legaré qualifies this statement in a note: "Milton is, perhaps, more sublime than Homer, and, indeed, than all other poets, with the exception, as we incline to think, of Dante . . . . the Paradise Lost, like the Divina Commedia, is more remarkable for Lyrical, (and sometimes for Dramatic) than for Epic beauties—for splendid details, than an interesting whole." Homer was not only the first, he was also the greatest of the strictly epic poets.[23]

The Greek dramatists were equally superior. He agreed with A. W. Schlegel in preferring Sophocles to Euripides,[24] but he used Aeschylus as a touchstone when examining Byron's *Manfred*. These plays had indeed served him well, for in 1832 "I was crossing the ocean in horribly low spirits, and I do not know what I might not have been driven to by my despair, had I not taken the precaution to buy in Philadelphia a collection of all the Greek dramatists. I read a tragedy every day, so that, in the course of a voyage of three weeks, I got through Aeschylus, Sophocles, and many of the plays of Euripides."[25]

Greek subjects had been attempted by many later dramatists, from Roman times on, but always with a relative lack of success:

"No poets of any nation can expect to handle those subjects with the same effect as Aeschylus and Sophocles. Turn from the Oedipus Tyrannus to the Oedipe of Voltaire, which has always been considered by the French critics as one of that author's happiest efforts, and by some of them, we believe, as decidedly superior to the original. The difference between the Greek name and the French mutilation of it (bad as that is) is not, by any means, so great as between the things themselves. Even Racine, with all his admirable talents for this department of poetry, has fallen far short of the Greeks, whenever he has attempted the same subjects, as we think is clearly made out by Schlegel, in his comparison of Phedre with the Hippolytus of Euripides." The story of Oedipus in a French or Italian re-working was likely to be revolting and disgusting, but in the glorious trilogy of Sophocles the reader felt "the touching interest and awful grandeur of the theme."[26]

Legaré remarked in conversation that in his opinion "justice has not yet been done to the depth and power of Aristophanes, the great political satirist of Athens. Mention my idea of the *'Clouds'*—that its purpose is to show that, if men affect to reason about everything, they infallibly end in *libertinism.*"[27] Yet, considered simply as a dramatist, Aristophanes was not to be considered in the same category with Menander or Plautus or Terence: "a good comic poem, and a good comedy, are two very distinct things. We may illustrate the difference by the plays of Aristophanes. We think those critics in the right who consider these dramas as *sui generis*—as poems in the nature of comedy (to borrow a phrase from the bar) rather than as comedies. Aristophanes was not eminently remarkable as a painter of individual character or an observer of private society. He was a man of extraordinary genius, the first of poets in his own way . . . a severe satirist of public abuses—a vehement and relentless enemy of great state criminals, whom he thinks it quite fair to hold up to derision, even by the exaggerations of buffoonery and caricature, and to overwhelm with the most bitter and unmerciful mockery."[28]

For the Roman writers of comedy Legaré had considerable admiration, especially for Plautus. Terence's style was faultless, although sometimes "insipid and spiritless. . . . It is quite evident that his genius is not above mediocrity, and we do not suppose that without the aid of the Greek originals, his name would ever have been known to posterity. In short, nature intended him for a good translator, and he is so." Plautus was less dependent on the Greek versions, and he lacked the stylistic merits that had caused writers "from Julius Caesar downwards" to extol Terence's work. Where Terence excelled in "the portraiture of character," Plautus excelled in *vis comica*: he seems "a blunt, downright, hearty lover of fun, and to have written for those who are for the most part equally so—the lowest of the populace. He is always in a good humour, and never misses an occasion for raising a laugh, even by a coarse joke or by low buffoonery. His *dramatis personae*, like some of those in Shakespeare's comedies, are shrewd cavillers and wordcatchers, always on the watch for a *double-entendre*, and unmercifully given to forced and farfetched conceits, and to all the abominations of professed punning and wit with malice aforethought. . . . It is impossible to read Plautus without feeling that he was born to write comedy. His coarse jests, his broad humour, his buffoonery, and extravagance—these are no doubt vices, but they are the rank growth of a fertile and generous soil."[29]

Legaré freely admitted that he was less interested in Roman literature than in Roman law. Where Greek literature was "perfectly original," the Roman was "altogether exotic and imitative."[30] In summarizing the early literary history, Legaré especially laments the loss of the works of Ennius, the only one who had "produced anything like a *national* work," the *Thyestes* of Varius, and the *Medea* of Ovid; he does not consider the tragedies of Seneca.[31] Of the pre-Augustan poets, he concentrates on Lucretius and Catullus, calling them "in point of original genius, the two first poets of ancient Rome." Catullus undoubtedly owed much to the Greek lyricists, but "of all imitators he has the most originality. . . . There is no constraint whatever in his movements—no parade or pedantry in his style. On the contrary, there never was a poet—we do not even except Shakespeare—who seemed to write more as the mood happened to prompt, and whose verses are stamped with such a decided character of facility and of spontaneity."[32]

Legaré confessed that he was suspicious of didactic poetry. Yet Lucretius had taken utterly unmalleable material, which did not seem to have "an *atom* of poetry" in it; he had stuck rigorously and logically to the development of his (or Epicurus's) philosophy and science; but since he was "withal a true poet," he had written "a most interesting and beautiful poem." Only one work in this *genre* had surpassed it, and that was less strongly and uniformly so: "Of all Didactic poems, except the Georgics of Virgil, his is incomparably the first. There is a very great difference, however, between the characters of these immortal poems. To say of the Georgics that it was the most elaborate and finished composition of its author, in the maturity of faculties, is to pronounce it a masterpiece of its kind. It is, accordingly, a model of that high-wrought and studied elegance of which it is scarcely too much to say that no writer was ever so great a master as Virgil; and is full of the most beautiful and lofty poetry . . . the perfection of the Georgics is unapproachable in Didactic poetry, and were it not that we have that work and Lucretius' De Rerum Naturâ before our eyes, we should even doubt whether the very phrase 'Didactic poetry' were not somewhat of a contradiction in terms."[33]

Legaré had high praise for such Roman prose writers as Varro, Cato, and Cicero. But even the best had never equalled in style or content the work of such Greek philosophers as Plato and Aristotle, such historians as Herodotus and Thucydides, such an orator as Demosthenes.[34] The failure of the Romans was especially notable in philosophy and—allowing full merit to Catullus, Lucretius, Horace,[35] and Virgil—in poetry. A fundamental defect was in the language. Latin was eminently fitted for law and jurisprudence; it was ideally suited "for a race of conquerors and of politicians." But it was unsuitable for philosophy and for the highest creative achievements: "there is an awkward and, as it were, foreign air about the Latin language when applied to such subjects, which not even Cicero's unrivalled skill in composition could altogether change or conceal. This defect would, of course, be more felt by the poet than by prose writers."[36]

III

Dante was the "Father of modern poetry."[37] Legaré suspected that Dante did not realize the full originality of his own work. He mistakenly thought himself a follower of Virgil. True, he had back of him the early literature of Southern Europe and the magnificient Spanish ballads about Charlemagne, and this early work was distinguished by a striking air of originality: "The lay of the Troubadour, full of gallantry and sentimental love, was indebted for none of its charms to the lyrical poetry of antiquity. These simple effusions, the first language, perhaps the first lessons of chivalry, breathed a spirit which had never animated the numbers of Anacreon and Tibullus. It was evident, even from them, that a new order of ages was beginning from a new era.

The Divina Comedia, the Decamerone, and the Canzoni of Petrarch, although the productions of men who had read more, and who rank among the most renowned votaries and restorers of classical learning, are certainly not formed upon the ancient models. They exhibit all the freedom, the freshness and originality of a primitive literature. Dante, indeed, avows himself a follower, an humble follower of Virgil, but no two things can be more unlike than the original and the supposed copy. The antique grandeur and simplicity of the Aeneid, and the perfect regularity of its proportions are not more strikingly contrasted with the wildness and eccentricities of his fable, than its whole spirit and character with the dark, dismal, and dreadful imaginings of the Inferno, or those dazzling visions of glory and beatitude, which are revealed by Beatrice in the Paradiso. The same thing may be said of Ariosto, and, with all his classic elegance and accuracy, of Tasso too."[38]

There were four great Italian poets to whom Legaré returned again and again. In discussing and denying Sir Walter Raleigh's claim that Sidney was entitled to be called "the English Petrarch," Legaré makes a specific comparison of them. He could not understand how anyone who had read Petrarch properly could "fail to award him all the praise which the best critics among his own countrymen have bestowed upon his sweet and elegant muse. Certainly he is not a poet of the very highest order—he is not equal to Tasso and Ariosto—and there is a gulph 'thrice from the center to the utmost pole,' between him and his mighty master and precursor, Dante." Even as a writer of sonnets about love, Dante was superior, but "it is not disparaging any poet to say that he is not equal to Dante—one of the most extraordinary of men, whose 'soul was as a star and dwelt apart' from the whole species—far above the highest, brighter than the most shining." Even so, Petrarch in spite of forced conceits and puling sentimentalism had enough poetic virtues to "have given immortality to any poet in any age."[39]

Works which had their origin in Christian belief, tradition, doctrine, and conflict seemed to Legaré to speak more directly to the modern reader than works rooted in a classical mythology. This was true of Dante, Ariosto, and Tasso. The old English, Spanish, and French ballads had the additional virtue of revealing national history, manners, and culture. It would no longer be necessary for an Addison or a Percy to defend these "artless lays" that are "the very language of nature—at once heroic and simple." In spite of his affection for *Don Quixote* and for "my favorite Gil Blas," his estimate of Spanish literature was fairly low: "it will be long before Calderon or Herrera or Garcilaso de la Vega, shall rival Dante, and Ariosto, and Tasso, in the estimation of the world." This inferiority did not extend to the older ballads of Spain: "Her old national poetry is second to none—if it is not superior to any in Europe."[40] The conflict between Christian and Saracen had given them a deep, poignant, passionate character. Engrafted upon them, also, were the concepts and fables of Chivalry—notably "the exploits of Arthur's Round Table, and those of Charlemagne and his Twelve Peers." The Spaniards took over Charlemagne, and they created "the great model of this school . . . the famous Amadis de Gaul, well known to the readers of Don Quixote, for the honorable exception made in its favour by the Curate and Master Nicholas, in the auto-da-fe of the knight's library."[41] There is something more: "the splendor of oriental imagination," and the "dreams of that 'delightful londe of faerie,' where the fancy of Spenser lingered so fondly."[42]

His admiration for the French writers of classical tragedy was tempered by his conviction that the Greek dramatists had done a far better job.[43] When, however, Racine turned to Biblical subjects, he proved himself a great dramatist in his own right. Legaré thought *Athalie* "a work, with which, in our opinion, nothing that modern genius has produced in the same kind can compare." This did not mean that religious subjects were easy. Instead, they could be treated successfully only by men of "transcendent genius. Our ideas of every thing connected with religion, have been raised to too high a pitch by those sublime and ravishing strains of Hebrew poetry, which are become the common property of Christendom," for these subjects to be easily handled.[44] After Dante, who "but a Milton or a Racine is worthy to strike the harp of the Prophets and the Psalmist? Paradise Lost, and the Choral odes of Esther and Athalie, preserve that sublime and somewhat stern simplicity, that awful grandeur, that comes up to our conception of the divine power and majesty."[45]

He had but scant regard for Voltaire, as dramatist or as critic. He declared without qualification that if "we were called upon to exemplify the difference between sound criticism and the petulant and presumptuous dogmatism of prejudice and ignorance, we should refer to W. Schlegel's course of dramatic literature for the one, and Voltaire's strictures upon the Greek tragedies, in his various prefaces, commentaries, etc., upon the other."[46] Although various quotations from and allusions to *Candide* indicate a thorough familiarity with that novel and presumably an enjoyment of it, although he declared that "Voltaire's prose style is more Attic than that of any writer, we remember, within the last century—except, perhaps, Goldsmith,"[47] he felt that Voltaire and Rousseau were mainly responsible for the present low state of French literature. Moderns should contrast writers like Homer, Horace, Dante, and Milton with "such a soulless, superficial, presumptuous scoffer as Voltaire, half eagle, half ape." It was Voltaire who had pointed the way to a "want of *faith* . . . *faith* in religion; *faith* in morals; *faith* in political doctrines; *faith* in men and women."[48]

Rousseau was even worse. He could admire and praise Rousseau's "matchless style" and recommend to other writers the remarks in the *Confessions* on "his extreme slowness and labor in composition," but never, "perhaps, has a writer exercised a more terrible influence."[49] Grudgingly he admitted that Rousseau had "an admirable genius," but he remained always the *parvenu,* the obsessed victim of a "morbid and jealous vanity." As a result, Rousseau had attempted to overthrow the steady, conservative progress of the Civil Law with a wildly impractical ideal of government; he had attempted to overthrow reason and morality by exalting an "extatical and frenzied delight in love, by exalting a false sentimentalism and an erotic emotionalism."[50]

French literature in his own time Legaré considered inferior, but by no means worthless. The works of Lamartine and Chateaubriand he found attractive. In Germany he read "Balzac's *livre Mystique,* which, although it shews the author to be undoubtedly a man of talent, does not please. It is a wild story, intended to illustrate Swedenborg's nonsense." Yet the very next afternoon he started *Père Goriot* and "found it so interesting that I laid it down with regret, and hasten to resume it."[51] This was characteristic. Legaré's critical principles were fairly rigid, but they did not prevent him from recognizing excellent work in fields essentially alien. His ideas on morality were likewise rigid, but an incidental comment helps to illustrate that in judging literature they were not invariably narrow: the simplicity of a group of German mountaineers "contrasts strangely with the manners painted by Balzac and Paul de Kock, whose *ni Jamais, ni Toujours,* I have read *ces jours ci,* I found, par parenthèse less immoral in their tendency, than those of his less decried contemporaries, who pervert the head, which is worse than exciting the senses."[52]

Since he learned German late and distrusted translation, his remarks on that literature are scant and fragmentary. A. W. Schlegel he regarded as the most important and germinal of modern critics; when he planned a tour of Germany he especially included Bonn so as "to make the acquaintance of August William Schlegel"—an acquaintance that Legaré describes at some length, and quite evidently enjoyed mightily, although he was amused by Schlegel's vanity.[53] On this tour, Magdeburg reminded him of certain features in Schiller's *Wallenstein,* and the Brocken of Faust's witches."[54] But his most suggestive and illuminating comment on a German author was made earlier: "Whoever has considered the scheme and drift of Goethe's famous drama of Faustus, understands the history of Lord Byron."[55]

IV

Byron was, Legaré thought, easily the best of contemporary English poets. When he pondered the matter carefully, he decided that except for Shakespeare and Milton and "Pope and Dryden who are writers of quite another stamp—we do not know who is to be placed, all things considered, above Byron. We doubt between him and Spenser—but no other name is prominent enough to present itself to us in such a competition."[56]

This was high praise, and the more forcible because Legaré thought poorly of Byron's character. True, he admitted that "there was, amidst all its irregularities, something strangely interesting, something occasionally, even grand and imposing in Lord Byron's character and mode of life. His whole being was, indeed, to a remarkable degree, extraordinary, fanciful and fascinating."[57] It was also true that although his conduct in his mature years seemed "wholly indefensible," it was necessary, in order to be just, to "be merciful to men of genius." Yet the fact remained, Legaré thought, that when all possible qualifications had been made, Byron was still "an unprincipled man." The good features in his character could appear only "by fits and starts," for he "seems to have been altogether the creature of *impulse.*" The result of this was that his "whole nature was in process of time perverted and poisoned. The irregularities of his temper and disposition, instead of being corrected by experience, were confirmed by excessive indulgence. . . . He never learned the first, last, great lesson of man's existence—submission. He became more and more impatient of contradiction, rebellious against authority, wilful and obstinate in his course of conduct, peculiar and fantastical in his manner of living . . . and to expect that the laws of nature should yield to his wanton caprices."[58] This self-pride and self-indulgence resulted inevitably in his greatest rival being himself. Magnificient as his accomplishment was, Legaré felt that readers "throw down his book dissatisfied. Every page reveals powers which might have done so much more for art—for glory—and for virtue!"[59]

Yet the positive accomplishments ought not to be minimized, but rather to be examined and analyzed. The first item to be noted was the intensely personal, autobiographical nature of his poems. They were, in a sense, his own journals and commonplace books. The scenery was the same scenery that he had looked at, changed, and illumined only by his own feelings and associations; more important, Byron was himself "uniformly the *dark* sublime he drew." His heroes were himself, and toward the end he "scarcely took the trouble" to hold up a poetic mask to disguise his own countenance. Yet the revelation of the "fiercest and fellest passions," aided as it was by "the wizard tones of genius," entitled his work to a very high place "among the achievements of creative mind."[60]

Byron's prose was almost equally felicitous. In one respect, indeed, it was better, for the "besetting sin of his poetry . . . was exaggeration and effort; but nothing can be more off-hand, dashing and lively than his prose. He expressed himself with all the literary freedom of table-talk."[61] Byron's letters could not equal in grace or elegance those of Gray, or in uniqueness those of Madame de Sévigné, but "like the epistles of Cicero, they not infrequently rise from the most familiar colloquial ease and freedom into far loftier regions of thought and eloquence. . . . We scarcely read one of them without being surprised into a smile—occasionally into a broad laugh—by some felicitous waggery, some sudden descent from the sublime to the ridiculous, while there is many a passage in which the least critical reader will not fail to recognize the hand that drew Childe Harold."[62]

Byron's literary opinions were frequently admirable; many passages revealed that "he had formed his taste, or nature had formed it for him, upon the models of *Attic,* not of *Asiatic* eloquence—of classical, not of romantic poetry."[63] But Byron's

poetry belonged to the new school. To help explain the difference, Legaré turned to A. W. Schlegel and quoted a long paragraph that ascribed the concreteness of the Ancients and the
mysticism of the Moderns to the differences between Paganism and
Christianity. Somewhat guardedly, Legaré assented that in general
"modern literature does differ from that of the Greeks in its
complexion and spirit."[64] To illustrate this, Legaré embarked
upon a lengthy comparison. For this purpose he chose what
seemed to him Byron's best work, although he cautioned that
when "we speak of Manfred as the master-piece of Lord Byron,
we speak of it as a *whole*. There are to be found in most of his
other compositions, especially in Childe Harold, many passages
of unsurpassed beauty and power." But these passages were short
and isolated; they were not, therefore, comparable to works in
which the beauty of design and composition is added to all other
beauties. A lyrical rhapsody is a much easier thing to write than
a "sage and solemn drama, exhibiting a rare portraiture of character, combining many incidents, introducing the difficult and
even perilous machinery of magic, incantations, and the spirits
of the air or the deep, and withal unfolding an impressive moral
truth. There is a great deal more of *invention* and of art, more
creative genius, in short, required."[65]

The style of *Manfred* was "more sober and subdued" than
that of *Childe Harold*. In place of ornateness and lavishness,
Byron has given to *Manfred* "a degree of austere and rugged
force, which reminds us as strongly of Dante, as the spirit and
character of the poem itself does of the Inferno."[66] But the character of Manfred reminded Legaré most closely of Orestes, in
the *Eumenides* of Aeschylus—and later he regretted that he had
not developed the idea at more length. Each is "a picture of remorse, but there can be no better illustration of the difference,
which we admit to exist between ancient and modern literature, than is afforded by the manner in which this affection is
exhibited, respectively, in the Greek tragedy and the English
Drama. In the former it is made a sensible object—it is personified—its office is performed by the Furies." The moral lesson is
the secondary rather than the principal object; the allegory is
deliberately veiled; the picture of remorse is presented by Aeschylus through "types and sensible images, but it is remarkable for
scenic effect and profound philosophical analysis."[67]

In contrast, Manfred stands alone. Byron "derives no help
from such external symbols—nor does he darkly shadow his pur-

pose in Allegory." The story is so intensely personal and subjective that, except for the monotony, it might have been told as a
monologue. But Manfred's aspiring genius cannot be presented
through ordinary situations or contacts with ordinary men; he
must be given "such a knowledge of the visible world, as shall enable him to control the invisible. . . . The machinery of the
poem then answers two great purposes—it relieves its monotony,
without violating its plan, and it exalts the dignity of the hero
without disturbing the characteristic solitude—the essential loneliness of his being." Legaré thought that Byron was right in never
stating the cause of Manfred's guilt, but only darkly hinting of
unnatural love and a wilful or perhaps even an involuntary
destruction of his beloved. It was not the explicitness of fact that
Legaré demanded, but the objectifying of subjective feelings. He
was convinced that *Manfred* was the finest achievement of modern Romanticism; he was equally certain that it was inferior to
the *Eumenides*.[68]

Apparently Legaré had scant interest in the other English poets
of his own time. Wordsworth seemed the best, and Legaré occasionally quoted from his poetry, but "even his simplicity is
often affected, and always visibly elaborate—as different, as it
is possible to imagine any thing, from the naked, unsophisticated nature of the best Greek writers."[69] He labelled Coleridge
"an ingenious admirer of the philosophy of Kant" and agreed
heartily with his dictum that frequently it is we who are ignorant
of the understanding of writers (especially the Greek) rather
than understanding their ignorance, but he was not interested in
Coleridge's poetry.[70] Scott's early poetry had been magnificently stirring, but Legaré bluntly declared that everybody knew
"there was an immense falling off in the later poetry of Sir Walter Scott; and, in truth, that to call things by their right names,
he had begun to indite insufferable doggerel," when his "good
genius interposed" and turned him to the prose romance.[71]

Legaré was more interested in religious poetry. Something of a
mystic, a man proud of his Huguenot and Scottish ancestry yet
fascinated by the beauty and music of the Roman Catholic mass,
he brought to the problems of religion a complex yet reasonably
consistent point of view. Byron under other circumstances might
have become "enthusiastically religious," for he had a deep-rooted
sympathy with nature's "mighty and mysterious powers."[72] Lesser poets might be enkindled to write to the full extent of their
natural powers, but they might also be tempted so far that the

poet wound up with a miscellany of mawkish sweetness. Legaré thought the latter true of Robert Montgomery's *The Omniscience of the Deity*:[73] the poems were "very pretty and very pious," but he ironically notes that the poet begins with "the creation of the world, and ends with its final conflagration and the Day of Judgment. Within these *narrow* limits, our poet wanders about at random, moralizing in a very edifying strain of sentimentalism, and turning into rhyme whatever happens to hit his fancy." Yet Montgomery had not completely failed, for a tone of benevolence and piety prevaded his work, and he had at times been able "to clothe in the charms of elegant diction and poetical fancy, those subjects about which the thoughts and sensibilities of civilized and Christian men ought to be most constantly engaged."[74]

Legaré uses Robert Pollok's *The Course of Time*[75] as an excuse to discuss religious poetry. The poem ostensibly treated has some positive merits, as well as faults: Pollok was a "man of true poetical talent, writing verses with almost as much freedom and facility as he could prose, not very curious about their cadence, and occasionally indeed even violating prosody by gross negligence or unauthorized metrical liberties; but, pouring out numbers equally remarkable for strength and simplicity, always with the zeal of an evangelist, and sometimes with a 'prophet's fire.' Indeed, considered merely as a Didactic Poem, we do not know any thing in the language that is better than 'The Course of Time.' " But when reviewers compared it with *Paradise Lost,* Legaré objected stoutly. Pollok had painted some "touching and beautiful pictures," but he had written a sermon in verse rather than an epic, and it would be quite ridiculous to compare his style and diction with Milton's. Pollok was fervid, enthusiastic, declamatory; he was frequently verbose and diffuse, so that only his sincerity, simplicity, and seriousness redeemed him.[76]

In fact, of all the poets writing in English on religious subjects, only three had earned a widespread, permanent reputation: Milton, Young, and Cowper. Of these three, Young and Cowper had rarely ventured "beyond the region of an elevated, it is true, but rather didactic and unimaginative morality."[77] Only Milton had achieved a religious poetry comparable with that of Dante. In one respect he surpassed all other poets: "It is true he is the greatest master of the sublime that any language has to boast of—greater than Shakespeare—greater than Dante—greater than

Homer."[78] Yet he never had been, and never would be, a really popular poet. This was traceable to his merits more than to his demerits: Milton put an exorbitant demand on his readers. His mighty genius is "every where visible. . . . His style is of a piece with the characters and the fable. He speaks as no other man ever spoke. His diction is fraught—overcharged with richness and power, yet every where perspicuous, precise and *classical*. But a reader must be somewhat of a scholar to have a just idea of its immeasurable treasures. Master of every branch of knowledge, but especially of ancient literature, he turns all he knew into poetry, and this unequalled and astonishing union of a daring creative genius, operating upon materials drawn from every quarter of the universe, and from every repository of learning, is what constitutes at once his peculiar excellence, and with a view to popularity, one of his capital defects. . . . His whole poem is a creation. Design is evident in every part of it—design projecting, composing, combining, harmonizing all."[79]

Following Dugald Stewart in defining *imagination* as designating exclusively the creative power, Legaré concluded that imagination "may be considered as the first faculty of Milton's, and he as first among the possessors of that faculty."[80] By contrast, Edward Young was strictly a poet of fancy. There was some question in Legaré's mind whether *Night Thoughts* should be classed as poetry, for there was no blossom or fragrance or genial warmth in it; all was bleak, desolate, sepulchral. His range was limited: "His flight was certainly not the eagle's, nor did he at any one time fly for long; but he was always on the wing. Every thing he sees, hears, or thinks of—the commonest objects in nature, the most trivial incidents in life, suggest to him impressive and original associations . . . the almost Shakesperian fertility of his fancy, and the terrible truth of his reflections upon life, death and immortality, must always secure Dr. Young, in spite of his inharmonious versification and prosaic tone, the great popularity he enjoys among those whose character or situation incline them to serious meditation."[81]

Byron had gone too far when he declared that Cowper was no poet. But those critics who thought Cowper one of the great English poets were even more in error, for in his work there was little of invention, originality, deep pathos, or sublime thought. He lacked genius, but "he had much talent, a ready command of language, and of an easy, flowing versification." His purity of heart and love of mankind, his tenderness and simplicity, all combine to "make his verses the delight of sentimental and philanthropic, and especially of pious readers."[82]

Legaré complained that in general English Romantic poetry had not been "sufficiently elaborated." The besetting defects were feeble and prosaic lines, carelessness of diction, and inequality of style. Even Byron was frequently guilty. Legaré suggested that readers compare what Byron had done in "the Spenserian Stanza, with Spenser himself, or with the first part of Thomson's 'Castle of Indolence.' Whatever may be thought of their relative merits in other respects, we fancy everybody, who has either ear or taste, must agree that, as far as mere language goes, there is a richness, harmony and uniform finish in the works of those masters, which are sadly wanting in Byron. So in satire, he has produced nothing to be talked of in comparison to Dryden's vigorous and bold pen, or the condensed and sententious elegance of Pope."[83] Byron had somewhat redeemed himself, at least in critical judgment, by defending Pope against the ignorant "modern Grub-street" critics; he should have written a new Dunciad and "gibbeted a few of that great man's detractors. . . . Having tried his own hand at satire, with some degree of success, Byron was the better able to appreciate the matchless excellence of Pope."

Of the early English poets, Legaré has relatively little to say. Coeval with the ballads and legends, the romances and troubadours, came a few men of creative genius: at "the daybreak, as it were, while twilight, with its spectral imagery and shadowy wonders, still lingered in the vale and in the wood. It is such an age that produced Dante and Chaucer."[84] Gower also had written admirably, but neither he nor Chaucer had had any worthy successors: at the best, "meritorious, but still inferior poets" like Surrey, Wyatt, and Sackville.[85]

Legaré tried to find this successor in Sir Philip Sidney.[86] He admired the man greatly, and he admired "The Defense of Poesy," as well as Sidney's minor prose writings. With complete approval he paraphrased Sidney's statement that true poetry "is the voice of nature appealing to the heart with its utmost sublimity and power. . . . Instead of teaching merely, it persuades, elevates, inspires."[87] Sidney's theory was excellent, but his practice in "Astrophel and Stella" convinced Legaré that Sidney was only a minor poet—an interesting and respectable follower of Petrarch, but by no means the equal of the Italian poet. Regretfully, Legaré concluded that "Sir Philip's prose was more poetical than his verse."[88] Not until Spenser was English poetry to have a worthy successor to Chaucer. Spenser had allegorical power, richly complex wording, and smooth versification; although he had wandered long in fairyland, he had at the same time a remarkable power in a "homely strength of expression and painful minuteness of delineation in painting objects that can properly be described in no other way."[89]

The irregularities in the Elizabethan dramas troubled Legaré. He preferred the order and regularity of Aeschylus, Sophocles, and even Racine. His doubts did not extend to Shakespeare: genius had triumphed over the difficulties inherent in a loose form. He quoted constantly from the plays; he noted casually in a letter that "those blackguards of Shakespeare are so taking, one never loses sight of them"; he closed an oration on Washington by paraphrasing Milton on Shakespeare: Washington, like the great dramatist, needed no tomb. Shakespeare was a writer of "incomparable genius," but in "the drama, *we* have no tragedies but Shakespeare's."[90]

Legaré revealed little interest in American poetry. Reluctantly, and out of a sense of duty to a fellow Charlestonian, he reviewed the writings of the late William Crafts. The two men had been lawyers together, closely acquainted though apparently not friends. As lawyer, orator, and poet, Crafts had been essentially a dilettante, priding himself on quickness of performance rather than on finish of execution. Sir Philip Sidney had been, as author, essentially an amateur, but when he devoted time to writing he gave himself completely to the subject at hand.[91] Crafts did not. Although not a man of genius, he had great talent; but he was content to write for the "poetical corner" of a newspaper or magazine. His best poems were "far from being bad." Legaré thought that, of Crafts' best work, the "poem entitled 'Raciad' is lively and spirited, and may be read with interest. 'Sullivan's Island' is equally commendable—but their merit is not high enough to challenge honor from gods, or men."[92]

With a one-time Charlestonian he showed even less patience. James Gates Percival's *Clio* seemed to him page after page "of mere musings—of such incoherent, undefined and shapeless fantasies, as may be supposed to float at random in the brain of a poetical opium-eater." It had become quite fashionable to dignify this type of "mystical and rambling—we had almost said raving—style under the plausible title of the Romantic, and to prefer it greatly to the studied regularity of the classical models."[93] Legaré believed these critics and readers to be absolutely in the wrong; if they were right, his own judgment of Percival's work was indeed in error, for "if what principally distinguishes the modern or romantic poetry from the classical is, that the former is more concerned about *spiritualities* than *temporalities*—about soul than body—about the shadowy abstractions of the mind than the objects of the senses, Mr. Percival is entitled to a very high rank in the school." Percival ought to write better poetry, for as a good scholar he knew that "Design and *unity* of design are essential to a work of art." But his facility too often tempted him to write before he was ready, with pathos and with "a certain tender and poetical pensiveness," but without genius or profound sensibility: "In this respect Mr. Percival resembles in some measure, another of our men of talent, we mean Washington Irving, who (whether it be heresy or not, we will say it) appears to us to have much more sentimentalism than sensibility." Percival had, in Legaré's estimation, hared off after the wrong models. If he desired to leave something that posterity would remember, he should undertake "a work like the Castle of Indolence."[94] Then he might avoid his prevailing poetical defects: "want of perspicuity and distinctness, of condensation and simplicity."[95]

After he got to Brussels, Legaré was pleased when an intelligent English woman talked with him "of Bryant's poetry—another wild-bird of my country,—whose touching natural notes had awakened her pure sensibilities, and won her precious imagination."[96] Yet the year before (1832) when he had reviewed Bryant's *Poems,* he noted that he had heard the author "advantageously spoken of," especially as editor of "one of the most respectable daily journals in the country." But Legaré's ignorance of any earlier work did not lead to quibbling or hesitation: this was "the most faultless, and we think, upon the whole, the best collection of American poetry which we have ever seen."[97]

Admitting that it was not safe to judge from fugitive pieces, Legaré none the less decided that Bryant had more talent for the beautiful than the sublime, for pensive tenderness than harrowing pathos, for effusions of fancy than creations of imagination. Bryant seemed to him an excellent rather than a great poet. Some of his merits might be negative, but they were "not the less solid and important on that account. To say of a writer that his language is simple, natural, precise, idiomatic—and to add of what he writes that it is poetical, is to pronounce him one whom the gods have made a poet and who can make himself what he pleases."[98] After lengthy quotations, and a short aside on the Italian sonnet,[99] Legaré concluded with one of his few statements on literary nationalism. It is mild enough. After recommending "this excellent little volume" simply for its poetic merits, he concluded: "Decided poetical merit is a great desideratum, in the social character of our country. A most exalted merit it is—precious in itself, still more precious as an index of what is thought and felt by a people, and as tending to foster and to warm into enthusiasm, all the sentiments that do most honour to human nature. In this point of view, Mr. Bryant deserves well of his country."[100]

V

Legaré's reading of novels seems to have been rather casual. Although he admired Sir Walter Scott greatly as man and novelist, he confessed when reviewing *The Fair Maid of Perth* that he had never got around to reading the first volume in the new series, "Chronicles of the Canongate." He had often seen Scott "diligently hobbling up to his daily task" in the Parliament House in Edinburgh "and going about his task with business-like formality"; mentally Legaré had compared him with Byron, the only man not overshadowed by his genius. Never did two "competitors in the highest walks of creative imagination . . . present such a strange antithesis of moral character, and domestic habits and pursuits, as Walter Scott at home, and Lord Byron abroad. It was the difference between prose and poetry." Scott had never yielded to self-indulgence, or attempted to deny or transcend the realities of existence.[101]

Their lameness also invited comparison. Byron had bitterly and openly cursed his affliction; Scott had repressed his emotions, but that he had felt intense mortification was apparent in *The Black Dwarf*: "That novel appears a piece of fantastic nonsense to superficial readers—it is, on the contrary, a profound and masterful conception, which nothing but such a genius, instructed by personal experience, could have formed." Here Legaré spoke with personal authority, for he was conscious always of his own stunted legs. Shakespeare had admirably depicted one of the effects of deformity in the character of Richard III, but Scott "had dived much deeper than Shakespeare into this dreadful mystery of the heart." Richard's wickedness is "downright *devilry,* to use a home phrase. There is nothing of the 'archangel ruined' there. . . . He is never surprised into 'tears such as angels weep.' " There is little or nothing to arouse sympathy in us for Richard. But in Scott's "terrible picture . . . there is every thing to move us to compassion—much to plead even for forgiveness."[102]

The Fair Maid of Perth was second-rate Scott. The first hundred pages were excessively heavy and slow-moving, although the author had "selected one of the most admirable subjects that can be imagined for the historical romance." After the novel gets under way, there is increasing interest "amidst such scenes as no hand could conjure up but Sir Walter Scott's," and the novel bears "the stamp of his extraordinary genius."[103]

Legaré had evidently followed the career of James Fenimore Cooper with considerable interest. Although in the first sentence of his review he flatly pronounced that *The Wept of Wish-ton-Wish* "is a failure,"[104] he used it as an excuse to survey Cooper's achievement as novelist. There was much to commend. Cooper was at his best in novels of the sea: when Legaré "perceived that the scene was laid on shore, we anticipated no rivalry of the novelist's achievements on his own element." On land, Cooper seems at home only in the wilderness; with a limited subject, a certain monotony has crept in, so that the present novel "is but an echo of the Pioneers, the Last of the Mohicans, and the Prairie." Legaré hoped that Cooper's maturer genius would "make wider explorations, explore deeper recesses, and unfold new and lavish resources" of American life; so far, Cooper had not lived up to his promise.[105]

Even so, his achievement is considerable. Even passages in this weak novel are "highly wrought, well-sustained, and distinguished by many of those masterly touches which characterize our author in scenes of hurried excitement."[106] But the book has been padded: a "moderate episode" expanded into a novel. Worse, Cooper has used the same material that Catharine Maria Sedgwick had handled more richly and artistically in *Hope Leslie*. Legaré makes no direct accusation of plagiarism; he is willing to accept Cooper's claim that the material had been furnished to him directly; but he adds wryly that "in fairness" Miss Sedgwick should have been "honoured by the dedication." Cooper has also "laid violent hands on a historical incident" that the "mighty master," Sir Walter Scott, had used with sublimity in *Peveril of the Peak*; Cooper has "tamed down" the episode.[107]

The Indians are the best characters in *The Wept*; in fact, "No one can paint them as Cooper does." But here, as in earlier novels, there are indications of hasty composition, of loose threads left dangling; Cooper has never yet produced a finished performance. "There are interspersed through all his novels, graphic pictures, which the imagination retains with delight. The panther hunt and the burning mountain in the Pioneers—the escape of the prisoner in the Spy; the chase on the Lake in the Mohicans—the crossing of the river, and the burning plains in the Prairie—the irruption on the farm in the work before us—all, once read, are never forgotten; and the unique splendour, we had almost said powerful poetry of his ocean scenes, would redeem a thousand failures."[108]

Except for Leatherstocking, common sailors, and Indians, Cooper has largely failed in the delineation of character. His heroes are "half-bred dull young gentlemen; his females as fictional characters" disagreeable; his people nearly all "prosers when they speak." Leatherstocking is different: "We always meet him with affection, and take leave of him with regret. . . . His sagacity, his simplicity, his heroic presence of mind, his fortitude, his innate gentlemanly delicacy . . . ," these and other elements "harmoniously mingle to fix the impress of genius on this noble original. He is a creation which proves that Shakespeare has not exhausted the new world if he has the old." Cooper lacked humor and wit; he had power, but lacked instinctive taste; he had as novelist many defects, "yet all other sea pictures are tame to Cooper's!"[109]

In a lengthy review of *The Disowned,* Legaré identifies Bulwer only as the author of *Pelham.*[110] Both novels belong to the "Beau-Brummel School," for they profess to hold the mirror up to "the very reverse of nature, viz. English fashionable life." D'Israeli in *Vivian Grey* likewise had treated "fops and fashions . . . with a gravity and profoundness, befitting its singular importance, and highly edifying to connoisseurs in this department of liberal knowledge." Legaré soon abandons irony to state flatly that he has no patience with such characters, or with the structure of English society. *Pelham* seemed to him the best novel of this kind that he had read, "but the *kind* is miserable." It owed much to *Vivian Grey,* which is "a very clever book, but its popularity and reputation were out of all proportion beyond its deserts"—in part at least, because it portrayed "living characters of some celebrity." *Pelham* was a better novel: it "dived much deeper below the mere surface of life, and mixed up, with the portraiture of its follies and frivolities, more of profound pathos and more of permanent and universal interest." But the idea of morality presented in both novels seemed to Legaré "out of the question."[111]

Considered simply as a novel, *The Disowned* was inferior in execution and interest. But it had more pathos and more power; it had also "a deeper and more novel delineation of character"; it "abounds in striking situation and pathetic incident."[112] This novel, like *Pelham,* is in part derived from an earlier work: Charles Robert Maturin's *Melmoth the Wanderer.* Legaré suggests influence but not plagiarism. Although "it is probable that the first conception of the character and situation was suggested by Mr. Maturin's book, there is quite enough in the turn which is given to them here—in the manner in which they are wrought up and appropriated, to support his claim to a good deal of originality in them."[113] Unfortunately, the fashionable tittle-tattle is "rather stupid," and several of the characters are "great bores." But one objection frequently made against Bulwer seemed to Legaré fallacious: Bulwer's moral sense, like his style, was objectionable, but it is no proper "objection to the instructive and salutary moral tendency of the novel, that it does not distribute what is called 'poetical justice' among its chief personages. We have always thought that nothing was, at once more fallacious in a philosophical point of view, and more at variance with the analogy of nature and of human life, than such a principle."[115]

In the same article, but treated separately, Legaré reviewed George Croly's *Tales of the Great St. Bernard.* The plan was suggested by Boccaccio's *Decameron,* but the stories would increase the reputation of the author of *Salathiel*: "In point of *style,* for example, they are very superior to the more elaborate work which we have just been reviewing—there is far more spirit, simplicity and force in Mr. Croly's composition—in short, it is a nearer approach to the perfect propriety and chastened elegance of our classical authors." The best of the stories, Legaré noted, "bears a strong resemblance to the Vicar of Wakefield, and is not altogether unworthy to be mentioned in connection with that charming novel, not only for the general drift and structure of the fable, but for the simplicity of its style, the candor and *bonhomie* with which the hero tells the story, and a certain sly and quiet humor that pervades it throughout."[116]

Legaré appears to have been rather more interested in the historical romance than in the domestic novel. He had no doubt that, in fiction, Sir Walter Scott was the undoubted master. He gave Scott credit for accuracy and verisimilitude in characterization. But he gave him credit for something, also, that is outside the field of aesthetic judgment and that may help to explain Legaré's limited interest in the novel. Dealing specifically with *The Fair Maid of Perth,* he noted: "There is so much historical truth in his narrative, that we are willing to believe all, and this seems to us to be the very perfection—so far as the fable and costume are concerned—of the Historical Romance."[117]

VI

Legaré was a conservative but not a reactionary critic. Although only in the review of Sidney did he treat directly a work of literary criticism, he had read most of the standard classical and neo-classical works. In discussing *Paradise Lost,* he cited Aristotle's dictum that the perfect man is not a fit subject for tragedy; he praised Horace, but of all Roman critics he thought Quintilian "the most enlightening and unerring, as the most dispassionate and impartial";[118] for background material on Roman literature, he relied heavily on the judgment of Aulus Gellius. He noted in passing that Julius Caesar Scaliger, "who finds fault with every thing," started by denouncing Catullus as vulgar and ribald, but concluded by praising him as lavishly as Martial ever had.[119]

In his own time, he leaned most heavily on A. W. Schlegel for definition and precepts of Romanticism. Yet he drew frequently on Madame de Staël and on Coleridge to buttress his own (often derogatory) remarks.[120] He had great admiration for the thoroughness and the fairness of German scholarship and German literary criticism: not only had they effectively defended the "immortal master-pieces" of Greek literature against "the flippant ignorance of the Parisian wits"; they were also "the first among strangers" to offer homage to the "genius of Shakespeare and of Calderon."[121]

Scholarship was not, however, a satisfactory substitute for taste. This must be founded on wide and discriminating reading, on a well-grounded knowledge of classical literature, and on personal sensitivity. Legaré had no patience with bowdlerization or with censorship: it was "fit and desirable" that truth be told, for there are passages "in the book of life which all would and some *should* read."[122] He never doubted the value of literature for this purpose, but agreed firmly with Milton that "our sage and

serious poet, Spenser," is a better teacher of moral philosophy
and conduct "than Scotus and Aquinas."[123] At the same time,
relatively few people could recognize excellence. Personal standards could be formed only after a thorough familiarity with the
finest models. He liked the comparative method in criticism.
Epic poems should be judged in comparison with Homer's; religious poems, in comparison with Milton's and Dante's. A man
who did not know *Paradise Lost* was in no position to judge Edward Young's *Night Thoughts* or Robert Pollok's *Course of
Time*.

The best works deserved several readings. The mawkish and
sentimental becomes as quickly cloying in the literary as in the
culinary art; illogical and bombastic work soon palls. Genuine
work does not: "the true test of excellence is, that you like it
more and more at every repeated examination of it. Who was
ever tired of Shakespeare or Homer, or to come down to mere
mortals, of Burns or Goldsmith, or any other poet remarkable
for simplicity as well as talent?" He preferred works that showed
"almost superhuman inspiration," as the early novels of Scott
had done, but he was ready to praise excellent work wherever
he found it.[124]

When he wrote on literary matters, Legaré had constantly in
mind a closely reasoned and consistently applied body of critical
standards. They were based on his own study of ancient and
modern literatures. Few readers had his wide-ranging knowledge; few readers, probably, were interested in his glancing allusions, his elaborate comparisons, or his analytical criticisms.
Most of them were undoubtedly willing to accept or to reject the
new poetry without bothering to formulate reasons for acceptance or rejection. Legaré was not. A critic in a time of transition,
he was faced with a literature demonstrably different from the
kind that he valued most. He did not like abstract reflection,
moral musing, pensive woe, or mystical soul-searching; he did not
like subjective writing. Yet when confronted with a *Manfred* he
recognized its essential vitality, its true greatness. He praised it
highly, but he also attempted to make an impartial examination
of its good and its bad qualities. As a result, he was willing to
broaden the base for poetry by widening the scope of its subject-
matter, without loosening his demand for unity and form and
wholeness. In a romantic age, he continued to proclaim that
every truly great work of literature must have unity of purpose,
simplicity of style, and ease of execution.

3

RICHARD HENRY WILDE
Expatriate

AT THE BEGINNING of 1835, Richard Henry Wilde was discontented with himself and with his life. He was a prosperous lawyer in Augusta, Georgia, but after serving intermittently in Congress he had just been defeated, and he had no desire to return immediately to the scene of his humiliation. He had long been interested in writing poetry, but some of his experiences in that field had not been happy. When his lyric, frequently entitled "The Lament of the Captive," was published apparently without his knowledge in 1815, Wilde was soon charged with plagiarism. Although the charge was absurd and easily disproved, it left Wilde embittered at the unpleasant notoriety.

By 1835 he had decided, also, that he lacked the requisite invention for writing original poetry and that the United States lacked the rich complexity needed for great poetry. In addition, his health was poor and he suffered from melancholia. He felt the need for new scenery and new interests; above all, for a complexly-ordered society with its roots in antiquity. Travel in Europe was the immediate answer; an extended residence in Italy might open a literary career more favorable to his own talents and desires.[1]

He had long been interested in the Romance languages. As early as November 2, 1821 he published in the Augusta *Chronicle* a translation of a Portuguese sonnet; in December 1834 he re-published it in the *Southern Literary Messenger*. He began to read Italian assiduously, and in February 1835 he published in the same magazine his translation of an Italian poem by Francisco da Lemene.

In June of 1835 he sailed for Europe; in February of 1836 he settled in Florence, and began his new career of scholar and translator. Before he left Europe in January of 1841, he had completed the only book published in his lifetime, *Conjectures and Researches concerning the Love, Madness, and Imprisonment of Torquato Tasso* (1842); and he had completed most of the work that he ever got done on his unfinished and unpublished *Dante and Italian Lyric Poets.*[2]

Although he modestly claimed in the preface to his *Dante* that he had written the *Tasso* "as an exercise in translation and composition,"[3] this two-volume work reveals a care in marshaling evidence, a scrupulous use of documents, and a felicity in translating Tasso's poems that belie Wilde's modest disclaimer. Before he completed the work, Wilde had become the advocate rather than the judge. There can be little doubt that he believed Tasso in love with Leonora d'Este, that his love was returned, that he was imprisoned for loving above his station, and that he feigned madness to avoid torture or death. But Wilde does not assert this; instead, he plays variations on the theme that the reader must decide for himself. The value of Wilde's own conjectures "will depend on their probability, and that, again, on the number of incidents collected and compared, and the candor and sagacity employed in their collation. To draw, as far as possible, from his [Tasso's] own writings, whatever light they may afford concerning the most doubtful events of his life, is the object of this essay."[4]

At the conclusion of his work, with its many long quotations, Wilde characteristically and modestly disclaims having done more than present the evidence: "Either the thing proves itself, or we should fail to prove it." He was convinced that his case was proved for him, partly by the quoted documents but mainly by the works of Tasso himself. As a final sentence he claims that he has "but followed the advice of Michelangelo: 'The statue is in the marble; seek it there and you will find it.' "[5]

This direct seeking in Tasso's poems Wilde believed to be fully justified. When in the Preface to *Hesperia* he had lamented his "want of invention," he seemed to be acknowledging a personal deficiency. Apparently, however, he sincerely thought this lack of invention or imagination not merely personal, but a quality or defect shared by many poets. The poet may disguise or dis-

tort the truth, but he can never completely conceal it; there is a
kernel of truth in his supposed fictions: "It is a vulgar error," he
writes in the first chapter of *Tasso*, "to suppose that they who
paint passion with the pen deal chiefly in fiction. On the contrary they exalt, combine, and embellish much more than they
invent. . . . Poets are, in fact, like the rest of our species. What is
most deeply felt by them is apt to be most clearly and forcibly
expressed. By the flight of the shaft, we may guess the strain of
the bow."[6]

Wilde returns to this theme in the Introduction to Petrarch's
works (*Italian Lyric Poetry*), when he considers whether or not
Laura was a real or an imaginary person. The final authority is
Petrarch himself: "Giving credit to Petrarch then, for only as
much sincerity as is necessary to explain his poetic success, it may
be possible from his own verses, to trace, at least in outline, the
story of his love." Because this love was real, it "wrung from
his lyre a new species of amatory poetry," marked by romantic
and melancholy tendencies. Wilde thought poorly of Laura as a
person, but he gives her full credit for awakening the poet in her
lover. He notes sharply yet perceptively that "Love is not kindled
by rhyme, but self-love is fed by it, nor should we without reflection condemn Laura for not valuing more highly nor making
a more grateful return for the offering. *We* behold in Petrarch
the restorer of learning, the creator of a new poetry, the beauti-
fier of a language which is all melody. She saw in him only a
persevering sonneteer, who annoyed her with complaints or
soothed her with flattery."

This in Wilde's view did not bring Petrarch's sincerity in question, since the poet's feelings were not dependent on those of the
lady. "Verse never fully described, much less exaggerated, real
passion," he declared roundly, and added: "This very power indeed of transmitting our own sensations vividly to others is the
great attribute of genius. The die is in our own memory, and its
fidelity and sharpness decide the value of the medal."[7]

Although he does not overlook the problem, Wilde showed
much less interest in the question of morality involved in these
liaisons, or in the literature about them. Characteristically he remarks that "the philosophy and logic and morality of Tasso, as
manifested in these papers, are not intended to be approved without reserve. Much of them, indeed, is open to censure; but they
were the logic and philosophy, and morality, of his age and country and education." When he dealt with a famous and notorious

book, Boccaccio's *Decameron,* he presented much the same defense. The morality might not suit Wilde's own time; indeed, he undoubtedly gave his own sincere judgment when he wrote that its "literary merits can hardly be too much praised, while its occasional licentiousness is open to severe censure." Nonetheless, neither the thought nor the language shocked the taste of the author's age, and unprejudiced minds in more fastidious times "may excuse the author though they cannot absolve the work."[8]

<h1 style="text-align:center">II</h1>

When he dedicated his book-length poem *Hesperia* to a patronymically disguised but not entirely fictional lady, Richard Henry Wilde wrote that she had "advised me to attempt a poem of some length, in hopes that an occupation suitable to my inclinations might divert my inexplicable weariness of life and spirit." Wilde does not explain the cause of his weariness and there may have been some Byronic attitudinizing in it, but he was keenly aware of "the difficulties of such an undertaking. Few write well, except from personal experience, from what they have seen and felt,—and modern life, in America especially, is utterly commonplace. It wants the objects and events which are essential to poetry."[9]

His feeling that America "excludes all romance" was shared in varying degrees by such diverse but fundamentally romantic writers as Washington Irving, Nathaniel Hawthorne, and Paul Hamilton Hayne. A new country, primarily interested in establishing itself politically and economically, could not have the long background of human history, thought and emotion that alone could give meaning to nature. To Wilde, nature by itself, no matter how beautiful, was insufficient; he was not interested in communing in solitude with liveoaks or rivers or primroses. In the first canto he notes his affection for his native town, Augusta, and his desire to "die at home"; he notes also that the United States could and did furnish "matter that the eye and mind, Heart, fancy, memory, could brood upon." He had traveled widely in his own country and remembered with intense pleasure the Spanish town of St. Augustine and a totally dissimilar New England town; he had marveled at Niagara Falls, watched frightening forest conflagrations, and explored strange caves in Virginia. These he had seen and known, with eyes and mind; potentially they offered as much as his beloved Italy could offer.

This would be fit material, after it had been enriched by historical associations, for future poets; for himself, "Stream, grove, cliff, fountain, cataract, and lake,/Transient and slight emotions only wake."[10]

In a letter to William Gilmore Simms, Wilde qualified some of these statements: "How rich and varied the traditions truly American, nay if you will, exclusively Southern, that might be wrought up by the magic of your pencil, if Time, and encouragement only were allowed!" But some allowance must be made for the fact that Wilde was writing to a friend who had dealt with these subjects many times, yet in Wilde's view with only partial success: "though what you have effected under the most unpromising auspices moves my wonder and despair, you must allow me to say, I hold them as comparatively little to that which you are capable of accomplishing."[11]

But for Wilde himself, neither America nor nature was enough. Like Byron and quite unlike Wordsworth, he demanded something more: the "classic recollections" that only history and story could provide. Disregarding the Indians and whatever romance there might be in colonial settlements or the Revolutionary War, he declared roundly

> But the heart seeks, and has forever sought,
> Something that man has suffered or enjoyed,
> And without human action, passion, thought,
> Nature, however beautiful, is void:
> 'Tis from deep feeling poetry is wrought. . . .[12]

In Wilde's view, the poet gets that intense feeling not directly, but from "Memory's exhaustless store" which invests scenery with "history, or legendary lore." Shakespeare, not the trees, had given importance to the forest of Arden; Surrey in his love poetry had been like a morning-star before the "bright mass" of Shakespeare. These ideas expressed in poetry are made even more explicit in a prose note: "Civilized men, the inhabitants of countries made classic by a thousand memories, tired of the eternal presence of their kind, and satiated with all common emotions, may long for the wilderness, and suppose savage Nature the true and only source of the sublime. But let them try to embody their feelings and ideas so as to impart pleasure to others; let them attempt to extract poetry from inanimate or irrational objects apart from man, and see how soon monotony produces weariness."[13]

Just as Surrey had preceded Shakespeare, we in our turn must have good poets before we could have great ones. Wilde could detect no one who might usher in "our dawn"; he stated flatly, sadly, and honestly that he was not the one. All the fictional trappings of *Hesperia* (the use of the pseudonym Fitzhugh de Lancy, the prefatory address to La Signora Marchesa Manfredina, the familiar tone imparted by addressing many stanzas directly to this disguised lady) indicate that he had no intention of publishing a work "written for you alone." If he had ever decided on publication, there seems little doubt that he would have preserved the obscuring devices and perhaps added to them; in fact, the manuscript was edited by his son and published in 1867 —twenty years after Wilde's death.

That he was not seeking romantically to impress a lady is made evident in sources meant to remain private. In letters to the sculptor Hiram Powers, he expressed his desire to return to Italy "for about three years, that, I might finish what I have already devoted so many years to"; for the arts, and literature especially, "can't live in the atmosphere of Law and Commerce. It is like putting some innocent warm-blooded animal into carbonic gas."[14] If Wilde's statement is meant to apply primarily to his own situation, it also reflects his attitude about the intellectual atmosphere of the United States, for in 1842 he had written to Simms (after refusing to allow publication of excerpts from his *Dante* but praising *The Magnolia*) that "We are yet a long way behind other countries—and unfortunately we do not know how much. But considering the absorbing nature and universal diffusion of American cares and occupations it is truly wonderful that any good comes of reading and writing."[15]

This unfavorable intellectual climate caused ordinary men to suspect any writer, and to avoid doing business with him. When Rufus W. Griswold asked for one or more prose pieces for his anthology, Wilde obligingly listed eight articles in addition to his speeches in Congress, but he added wistfully: "As literature does no good to an advocate's reputation, I should be pleased if you will give my place among the *Prosaic* to somebody else."[16] Many other writers complained bitterly about this prevailing attitude; Wilde lists it as one of several reasons why he had made so little progress on his unfinished *Life and Times of Dante* and his *Specimens of the Italian Lyric Poets*.

Supplementing this was his doubt of the literary taste of most Americans. Since the public did not demand works of high quality, they were given mediocre productions: "In our day of fear while the public taste relishes little but fictitious narrative, and craves novelty with the greediness of a pampered and depraved appetite, the standard of what *sells profitably,* has fallen with the rapidity of production, and the flimsiness of the *material,* of books. The greater part of the novels and romances now published, scarcely hold together while we read them, and have passed apparently from the author's desk to the printer's devil, the pen running a race with the press."[17]

He was a slow writer, addicted to constant revision. He complained also in the Preface to *Hesperia* of "my own want of invention," and wrote to Simms that "I envy you your Invention, and your facility, the one of which seems to give you such a boundless command of incident for fiction, and the other such a ready power of weaving it into song or story." These were precisely the abilities that in his own estimation he himself lacked.[18]

III

Although an amateur keenly aware of his lack of training, Wilde was a zealous and scrupulous scholar. In personal letters, in the *Tasso,*[19] and in the Introduction to the *Dante* he had described his difficulties in gaining entrance to Italian libraries and access to essential documents. As excuse for dilatoriness in answering a letter, he wrote Charles Sumner that "Probably the scent of some old worm-eaten parchment or chronicle, with certain indecipherable names or dates that smelt of the 'Secolo decimaterzo' was just then warm, & the hunt being up and my blood fired, I could think of nothing else until I had effectually wearied myself."[20] Sometimes this zeal seemed to him a mere antiquarianism, but many of his letters reveal a thorough knowledge of documents and of archives.

This interest in the Italian renaissance was not all-absorbing. He was interested in his own time and in other arts. Antiquarianism played its part in the work he did in helping to discover a portrait of Dante (attributed in Wilde's time to Giotto), but his constant praise of the sculptors Hiram Powers and Horatio Greenough indicates his interest in the contemporary. Allied with this was a desire to help develop a favorable intellectual climate in his own country: "As Americans whatever an American does in the arts should be dear to us. . . . For that reason I would rather have a statue of Powers or Greenough than of

Canova or Thorvaldsen."[21] For the same reason he fought for a copyright law[22] and attempted to get Congress to buy a distinguished foreign library.[23] When these efforts failed, he was disappointed but not surprised.

Apparently that was also his feeling about his own failure as a writer. He was not satisfied with his own work, although in several letters he admitted that he hoped for literary immortality through his *Dante,* and noted the many revisions he had made of each page and, indeed, each sentence. He asked one correspondent to "tell me honestly, all my offenses against Tasso and Leonora . . . one fault, justly found, is better to an author or an artist than a thousand flatteries. Who knows but that the 'Life and Times of Dante' may profit. . . ."[24] He was scrupulous about acknowledging indebtednesses to other writers, whether it was a general one to Lord Byron and Tom Moore, or a specific one to some poem (usually Italian) that had stimulated his own poetic fancy. The lengthy notes to *Hesperia* indicate his awareness of this, for he points out his own imitations of poems by Dante, Tasso, Filicaja, Alfieri, and many others; he also notes the borrowing of a line from Lord Byron.[25] He tried to be equally scrupulous about including the original version of a poem when he allowed any of his translations to be published, but some editors published only the translations.

He was interested in the making and enjoying of literature, not in criticizing it; in relating the poem to the poet rather than in analyzing the work. After reading *Donna Florida,* he wrote Simms that Ponce de Leon seemed "a frail and feeble thread of cotton on which you have strung your beads of gold and pearl. The very tone of levity and caricature adopted would be fatal to its continuation as a grave poem." Byron had succeeded with abrupt transitions from "graceful levity to deep-heart-stricken-grief," but for other poets the imitation of *Don Juan* was "a thing almost always fatal." Yet Wilde characteristically tempers this criticism by noting that "I have found beauties everywhere."[26]

As he noted, he preferred to read not analytically but enthusiastically. He preferred books which aroused "a warm glow of feeling" in him. A few Southern writers—especially his personal friends, the novelists Simms, Kennedy, and Caruthers—could awaken a mild and intermittent enthusiasm; he called on Longfellow, embodied the equivalent of an article on Tasso manuscripts in a letter to J. K. Paulding, and praised the work of Hal-

leck and Bryant.[27] More significant is his praise of Irving and
Cooper, for they seemed to be finding in New York those historical and legendary qualities that Wilde considered necessary
in literature:

> Around us are the haunts that Cooper loved.
> The glens were Irving's Muse her revel kept:
> Here are the woods where Leatherstocking roved,
> Yonder the dell where Rip Van Winkle slept:
> Hence came the legends that so often moved
> Our admiration as we laughed or wept;
> For here it was our Country's Genius found
> Fresh and untouched her own first fairy ground![28]

Wilde could admire without envy the work of his American
friends, but the English poets of the seventeenth and nineteenth
centuries interested and influenced him more profoundly. He
wrote poems that have at least a remote kinship with the Cavalier lyrics, and among his poetic tributes are sonnets addressed
to Lord Byron and Elizabeth Barrett Browning. But his deepest
enthusiasm was for the Italian lyric poets of the Renaissance.
These poets and their poems he wished to present in such a way
that his fellow-countrymen might share the enthusiasm for them
that Wilde himself felt.

4

THE INTENT OF THE HUMORISTS

THERE IS abundant justification for describing the work of the Southern humorists as "spontaneous, hilarious pencillings."[1] No doubt most of these widely scattered, highly varied writers simply sat down and described a realistic incident or concocted a tall tale, with no particular concern about why they were writing as they did. But a few men felt the need for a rough-and-ready aesthetic that would justify a new way of writing.

Some men never doubted either its originality or its validity. By 1845 William T. Porter was convinced that his weekly *Spirit of the Times* had become "the nucleus of a new order of literary talent . . . who have subsequently distinguished themselves in this novel and original walk of literature."[2] His associate editor, George Wilkes, later noted accurately that Porter had "brought out a new class of writers, and created a style which may be denominated as American literature—not the august, stale, didactic, pompous, bloodless method of the magazine pages of that day; but a fresh, crisp, vigorous, elastic, graphic literature, full of force, readiness, actuality and point."[3]

Although the humorous sketch and the tall tale found a congenial home in the *Spirit*, Porter rightly puts the greatest emphasis on realistic stories, sketches, and essays. In fact, the tall tales began as an exaggeration of reality, as James K. Paulding indicated when he described his purpose in the rip-roaring *Lion of the West* (1830) as "to embody certain peculiar characteristics of the west in one single person, who should thus represent, not an individual, but the species."[4] Some falsification naturally ensued, but the best of them have a semi-epic quality and flavor: Constance Rourke sees in Mike Fink "a Mississippi river-god, one of those minor deities whom men create in their own image and magnify to magnify themselves," and in the legendary Davy Crockett a figure closely allied to mythology.[5] The contemporary novelist John Neal was most impressed by their zestfulness: "*live* stories I should call them," and always "brimful of energy and vivacity."[6]

Crockett himself enjoyed at times stretching the long bow to its fullest extent, but in the Preface to his autobiographical narrative he (and possibly also his collaborator) roundly declared that "I have endeavored to give the reader a plain, honest, homespun account of my state in life," and he protests valiantly against the "bundle of ridiculous stuff" incorporated into the *Sketches and Eccentricities of Col. David Crockett* (1833). Although acknowledging help in his own book's preparation, he concludes with the advice: "just read for yourself, and my ears for a heel tap, if before you get through you don't say, with many a good-natured smile and hearty laugh, 'This is truly the very thing itself—the exact image of its Author'."[7]

They may be equally honest, but there is certainly nothing plain or homespun about such full-dress biographies as Wirt's life of Patrick Henry, or John P. Kennedy's life of William Wirt. Crockett was presenting in embryo a case for realism in biography; if he did not go very far, he at least made a beginning.

More important are the ideas of the creative writers. The best of them emphasized realism, but they recognized that a literal truthfulness was not enough. Realism must be heightened and enhanced by imagination and by art.

Augustus Baldwin Longstreet recognized the necessity for fusing these into a unified whole. His friend and fellow-humorist William Tappan Thompson quotes him as desiring that through *Georgia Scenes* "we may be seen and heard by our posterity two hundred years hence just as we were."[8] Fidelity came first, but obviously any book that was to last for two centuries must "enliven the family fireside" of a contemporary, and the author "used some little art to recommend them to the reader of my own times" because "the chance of their surviving the author would be increased in proportion to their popularity upon their first appearance." Artistry could help but it must not be allowed to distort authenticity: the sketches "consist of nothing more than fanciful *combinations* of *real* incidents and characters," he writes, but he quickly qualifies even this statement by adding that he had used "some personal incident or adventure of my own, real or imaginary, as it would best suit my purpose."

He objected vigorously when the design of the book was "misapprehended" as mere "entertainment." His characters, episodes, descriptions, and dialect were drawn directly from the immediate life around him, and the "aim of the author was to supply a chasm in history which has always been overlooked—the manners, customs, amusements, wit, dialect, as they appear in all grades of society to an eye and ear witness of them. . . . I have not confined myself to strictly veracious historic detail; but there is scarcely one word from the beginning to the end of the book which is not strictly *Georgian.*"[9] With some justice Longstreet was praised by his contemporaries both for the skill of his artistry and for his exact fidelity.

At times Longstreet's desire for a documentary accuracy effectively though perhaps inadvertently buttressed his artistry. After using "d--n," the author apologizes: "I should certainly omit such expressions as this could I do so with historic fidelity; but the peculiarities of the times of which I am writing cannot be faithfully represented without them. In recording these things, *as they are, truth* requires me. . . ."[10] Truth and candor constrained him to record various crimes and follies that reflected no honor on his countrymen, but these too were a necessary part of the total picture.

Longstreet was a limited artist. He digressed, sermonized, and moralized all too freely, no doubt with the feeling that his essay-intrusions helped to justify the writing of fiction. But the Addisonian echoes in his work are precisely the qualities in them that we value least. Fortunately it was also the part his contemporaries valued least. He was at his best when he portrayed live and living persons he had known, talking as he had heard them talk, and moving about in a region whose geography and customs he knew at firsthand. Then he fully earned Poe's judgment that he was "imbued with a spirit of the truest humor, and endowed moreover with an exquisitely discriminating and penetrative understanding of character in general, and of Southern character in particular."[11]

Although suspecting that the Americans, like the English, were not a humorous people, William Gilmore Simms thought that an indigenous humor had developed on the Southern frontier. He was less inclined to emphasize the strictly realistic elements than Longstreet, and he thought the published specimens rather pale and weak in comparison to the oral versions which he had heard, but "in the buoyant life and animation of its speech,—in its copious fund of expression,—in the audacity of its illustration,— its very hyperbole,—the singular force of its analogies,—the pregnant, though ludicrous vitality of its pictures,—its queer allusions, sudden repartee, and lively adaptation of the foreign and unexpected to the familiar,—we recognize the presence of a genius as likely to embody the humorous as the eloquent." This was a "rare, racy, articulate, native humor," which Simms himself sometimes effectively employed in episodes and in stories although it was incidental to his main purpose; of the published books of humor he thought *Georgia Scenes* "unquestionably, far beyond any comparison . . . the best specimens in this field that the American genius has produced."[12]

William Tappan Thompson, like Longstreet, put the emphasis on particular characters in a particular place. True, when he wrote under the fictional guise of Major Jones, his prefatory comments employ the trappings of the professional humorist: if the letters in the *Courtship,* he tells the reader, "will serve to draw a few nails out of your coffin, by makin you laugh, they will serve a equally benevolent purpose by puttin a few dollars in the pocket" of Joseph Jones. The determinedly humorous approach, though with a different intent, is continued by the imaginary Major when he writes that his *Sketches of Travel* "was rit with no higher aim than to amuse the idle hours of my friends, and if it fails to do that, its a spilt job." But when Thompson wrote under his own name and voiced his own intentions and convictions, he states explicitly that his attempt is to "depict some of the peculiar features of the Georgia backwoodsman . . . to present to the public a few more interesting specimens of the genus Cracker."[13]

Unlike such tall tale writers as George Washington Harris and even more unlike the somewhat later professional humorists, Thompson never used dialect merely for humorous effect. His purpose, rather, was the realistic one of making the language and pronunciation of his characters consistent with that of the Middle Georgia farmer: "For this purpose the local dialect or *patois* peculiar to the rural district of Georgia was employed, with the orthography necessary to convey the peculiar pronunciation of the word. Consistency, and not an effort at cheap wit, compelled the resort not only to incorrect grammar, but also to a mode of spelling many words, more simple than is found in our standard lexicons."[14] He firmly believed that the "mangling and murdering of etymology is no part of humor," and he confined himself in that respect to such malapropisms as transgression for digression.[15]

Thompson protests with quite evident sincerity that he liked, respected, and even admired these people, but he enjoyed their oddities and peculiarities. He could see that both their happiness and their usefulness might well be improved by the standardizing influences of education, but the result also would be, regrettably, that individualities would be absorbed into a mass uniformity: such education would "by polishing away those peculiarities which now mark his manners and language, reduce him to the common level of commonplace people, and make him less a curious 'specimen' for the study of the naturalist. As he now is, however, I have endeavoured, in a small way, to catch his 'manners living as they rise.' "[16]

Here Thompson significantly extends the aesthetic that Longstreet at least hinted at. He recognizes that it is the original, not the typical, that forms the proper basis for art, just as in his review of Longstreet's *Georgia Scenes* he recognized that Ned Brace and Ransey Sniffles were sublimations and not mere descriptions, were in fact imaginative creations based on reality. Along with this recognition there is also a definite limitation: Thompson, like Longstreet, believed that if the author could find strikingly typical incidents and, in the old sense of the word, original people, he would be well advised to stick closely to actuality. It seems never to have occurred to them that, although real life might provide an adequate foundation for sketch or story, too much reliance on observation and too little employment of the imagination might ultimately prove a handicap.

Whether or not it turned out to be a handicap or a benefit, the Southern humorists tied their work closely to the life around them. Joseph G. Baldwin, more a social historian than a creative writer, announced his purpose clearly: The *Flush Times,* he wrote, was intended "to illustrate the periods, the characters, and the phases of society" of frontier life in Alabama and Mississippi.[17] By contrast, Johnson J. Hooper's *Simon Suggs* is fiction closely tied to fact. To increase the semblance of verisimilitude, Hooper adopts the mellow device of the mock or satirical biography and assures the reader that he has no doubt of the "perfect genuineness" of the story; although, perhaps as a warning to the reader not to carry a belief in the author's truthfulness too far, he quickly adds that it is to be a campaign biography.[18]

Richard Malcolm Johnston has summed up the intent of the humorists in a specific remark on his own work and in a brief general commentary. He was so dependent on a specific locale that he confessed, "As long as my people have no fixed surroundings, they are nowhere to me; I cannot get along with them at all."[19] Even more significant is his belief that "an artist can create interesting concretes only if he can re-enact scenes from human life." Successful story-telling, oral or written, required artistry, but it should be so concealed that the listener or reader would be conscious only of the "naturalness" of the story. A writer could achieve this only by re-creating life as he had personally known it, directly and intimately, as a child and as a man. Of one collection he notes that "While these sketches, like their predecessors, are imaginary, except as to the scenes and certain characteristics which have been selected here and there, they are in harmony with the rural society which the author remembers as a lad, and later as a young lawyer."[20] So Johnston defined his purpose as "to illustrate some phases of old-time rural life in middle Georgia," and some "characters and scenes among the simple rural folk of my native region," and he acknowledged freely that he took as his artistic models the story-tellers he had known in his youth.[21]

There were, of course, literary influences on practically all of the humorists. Simon Suggs, as Thackeray recognized,[22] fits naturally in the tradition of literary rogues. It is not by accident that *Georgia Scenes* "forcibly" reminded Poe of the *Spectator,* or that some of Johnston's work reminds us of Dickens. But they were not slavish imitators. When the humorist and editor George W. Bagby had read too many ultra-literary but derivative poems submitted to him, he adjured American poets to "kick Tennyson and all other models into the middle of next week . . . and come right down to the soil that gave them birth." No such advice was needed by the Humorists. They stayed close to the soil. If their home-grown literature was often crude, it reflected directly the life they had known.

5

THE INTENT OF THE NOVELISTS
Kennedy, Caruthers, J. E. Cooke

OF THE ANTE-BELLUM Southern novelists, only William Gilmore Simms attempted to develop a considered and rounded aesthetic of the novel. In a huge number of prefaces, articles, and reviews he argued that a distinction must be made between the romance and the novel, presented his own concept of the proper uses of history in fiction, and argued forcibly for such important but diverse ideas as nationalism and realism.[1] Simms was an exception. He was a professional writer, absorbingly interested in his craft and its possibilities; among his Southern contemporaries, only Poe and possibly John Esten Cooke deserve to be considered as professionals. Men like John Pendleton Kennedy and Nathaniel Beverley Tucker thought of themselves first of all as lawyers. William Alexander Caruthers gave first allegiance to medicine. They were novelists only by avocation.

Most Southerners, when they essayed to write a novel, simply patterned their work on accepted English and American models. In the main, they were primarily interested in telling a story. They might have other interests. As early as 1824, in *The Valley of Shenandoah*, George Tucker set out to depict faithfully rural life (including slavery) in Virginia, but he hitched his keen, first-hand observations to an improbable plot strongly reminiscent of Richardson's *Clarissa Harlowe*. He also used the time-worn device, beloved by Defoe and Scott, of pretending to edit a manuscript turned over to him by a dying man who had given him permission "to make such alterations, either as to matter or style, as he should think proper." The ostensible editor was puzzled as to whether this carelessly-written manuscript was "a history of real life, or one of those fictitious representations" which "mingle instruction with pure and rational amusement." From personal knowledge, he suspected the work to be based on fact, with some disguise of characters. He presented it to the world, partly because of his promise to do so, partly because he will be "presenting to the public not only a faithful picture of the manners and habits which lately prevailed in one of the most distinguished states of our confederacy, but also an instructive moral to the youth of both sexes."[2]

N. B. Tucker, in *The Partisan Leader* (1836), used the novel as a form for sugar-coating a political tract: at once a campaign document against Van Buren and "a textbook of rebellion in disguise." The structure was so unimportant that he breaks the story off abruptly. Many characters are merely sketched in. He considered a villainous Van Buren Cabinet member adequately described when he referred the reader to Scott's Olivier le Diable. But Tucker's extreme anti-Northern bias comes through clearly, and the political message was complete.[3]

This is the extreme case. In the work of three significant ante-bellum novelists, there are occasional illuminating comments. Kennedy, Caruthers, and Cooke did not attempt to develop an aesthetic of fiction; they too were content with the accepted models and practices of their time. Yet their ideas and theories, however rudimentary and however incompletely conceived, may have value in understanding Southern fiction and Southern thought.

II

John Pendleton Kennedy was a bookish youth, though not a bookworm. In addition to his regular academy and college classes, he did additional study in Greek, read French and Spanish, began German, and read widely in the English poets and essayists. In forming his early literary tastes and his style, and influencing his early writing, the last-named is the most important. When Kennedy and Peter Hoffman Cruse in 1818 started *The Red Book*, they modelled it on Addison and Steele's *Spectator* and (only slightly nearer in place and in time, intrinsically) on the *Salmagundi Papers*, by James K. Paulding and the Irving Brothers. The prose essays in this occasional Baltimore periodical were by Kennedy, and their Addisonian flavor was unmistakable; the poetic satires by Cruse had the significant title, "Horace in Balti-more."[4]

When in 1828 Kennedy began writing *Swallow Barn,* he did not attempt a new form. Probably the most immediate influence was Washington Irving's *Bracebridge Hall*; closer to home, and the work of a personal friend, was William Wirt's *Letters of a British Spy.*[5] Not far in the background were Oliver Goldsmith's reports on England by an imaginary Chinese traveller, in *The Citizen of the World*; Addison's loosely-unified Sir Roger de Coverley papers; and probably Voltaire's *Persian Letters.*[6] Kennedy dedicated his first book to Wirt, his second to Irving. But if he borrowed something of structure from them, his descriptions, characterizations, and commentaries were solidly based on first-hand observation. His fictional disguise was slight. He adopted the pen-name of Mark Littleton, with a residence in New York rather than in Maryland; and he makes Littleton more of a stranger to Virginia than Kennedy was. He set the plantation on the James River, but transplanted to it many of the characteristics of the Shenandoah region, which he knew better. If he presented his impressions in a somewhat detached and ironically humorous manner, he did not stray far from his purpose: "to portray the impressions which the scenery and the people made upon him [Mark], in detached pictures brought together with no other connection than time and place."[7]

Fundamentally, he seems to have been interested primarily in fiction as it could be employed to represent actuality. He cared little for the domestic novel. In the first sentence in the original Preface to *Swallow Barn* (1832), Kennedy writes: "I have had great difficulty to prevent myself from writing a novel." He admits that there is "a rivulet of story wandering through a broad meadow of episode. Or, I might truly say, it is a book of episodes, with an occasional digression into the plot."[8] This is certainly true. One thread of plot is resolved half-way through the story: the owner of Swallow Barn contrives by dubious legal means to settle a long-continued lawsuit by giving some worthless acres to his neighbor. The second, the courtship by Ned Hazard of Bel Tracy, must be as often-interrupted and as desultory as any love affair in fiction; the author was so little interested in it that news of Hazard's success reaches Mark by letter, after he has left Virginia. Kennedy's real design was not to advance the story "according to the regular rules"; instead, "my design in this work has been simply to paint in true colors the scenes of domestic life as I have found them in Virginia."[9]

Partly because of the style (based, to some extent, on the oral style of a skilled raconteur),[10] partly because of the shrewdness and the geniality of the observations, *Swallow Barn* remains a highly readable book. Wisely or unwisely, Kennedy abandoned the contemporary scene and the casually constructed novel for the historical romance. One cause, no doubt, was his admiration for the works of Sir Walter Scott and of his own friend, James Fenimore Cooper. Perhaps he was conscious also of the great popularity of this relatively new form. These may have been subsidiary. True, he employed the conventional romance form in *Horse-Shoe Robinson,* and if such a form had not been readily available he probably would not have troubled himself to invent one. But Kennedy's liking for history was great. Yet formal history frequently left him unsatisfied. True history, whether fictionalized or not, should give life to the past. This concept he presented persuasively in his own semi-fictional "A Legend of Maryland":

That which makes history the richest of philosophies and the most genial pursuit of humanity is the spirit that is breathed into it by the thoughts and feelings of former generations, interpreted in actions and incidents that disclose the passions, motives, and ambitions of men, and open to us a view of the actual life of our forefathers. When we contemplate the people of a past age employed in their own occupations, observe their habits and manners, comprehend their policy and their methods of pursuing it, our imagination is quick to clothe them with the flesh and blood of human brotherhood, and to bring them into full sympathy with our individual nature. History then becomes a world of living figures,—a theatre that presents to us a majestic drama, varied by alternate scenes of the grandest achievements and the most touching episodes of human existence.[11]

This was Kennedy's purpose in writing *Horse-Shoe Robinson.* The work had been suggested to him, he claims in an elaborate Introduction to the 1852 edition, by a personal though accidental meeting with the titular hero, who later vouched for the accuracy of everything in the story, "excepting about them women —which I disremember." More pertinent, however, are his remarks in the Preface to the 1835 edition: the events narrated came to his knowledge in connection with "researches into the personal history of some of the characters." He had embodied

characters and events "in a regular narrative for two reasons:
First, because they intrinsically possess an interest that may
amuse the lovers of adventure, and Second, because they serve to
illustrate the temper and the character of the War of our Revolution." The formal writers, Kennedy complains, have given
"only the political and documentary history of that war."[12] They
have neglected the romantic, the picturesque, the traditional,
and the social. These have been left to the novelist. In answer to
those who thought the war too recent and too well-known for fiction, Kennedy responded that the fiftieth anniversary had converted "tradition into truth." But his claim for romantic license
was a very mild one, since he immediately added: "I have been
scrupulous to observe the utmost historical accuracy in my narrative."[13]

Kennedy's interest in the love story was slight. He gets rid of
the romantic hero for many chapters at a time by having him un-
heroically captured and re-captured by the British. Pathos also
was felt to be needed, and Kennedy provided this in a subsidiary
love affair, although he is rather more careful than most romancers by revealing in action, well ahead of time, the impetuosity of character which led to the young man's death. Undoubtedly
the titular hero has some kinship with Cooper's Leatherstocking, but the relationship is generic rather than direct: Horse-
Shoe is clearly-drawn and individualized; he may well have been
created out of Kennedy's personal observations. In the same way,
there is a generic relationship between various minor characters and those of Shakespeare and Scott.[14] However, these seem
no more than the unconscious natural parallels that would be reflected in the writing of an exceedingly well-read man. Whenever Kennedy needed or wanted an apposite quotation or chapter
head-note, he could draw with equal ease on the Bible, Shakespeare, Scott, Ben Jonson, James Shirley, Lovelace, an old ballad, or an obscure song. He was an appreciative reader, and
he never hesitated to make use of his reading in his own writing.

This appears to greatest advantage in *Rob of the Bowl.* The
conflict between Catholics and Protestants in Maryland in the
1680's was, Kennedy notes, "involved in great obscurity." Remote-
ness of time and lack of knowledge gave him greater freedom; a
better-educated group of characters allowed more room for literary allusions, as well as play of wit. Yet Kennedy's purpose was
the same as in *Horse-Shoe Robinson.* He was excited by the discovery of long-lost documents, and to them he was "indebted for

no small portion of the materials" that he embodied in the story. Kennedy walked over the ancient ruined site of St. Mary's, and found it "sunk to the level of Tyre and Sidon"; the blank field seemed to him "a book whose characters I could scarcely decipher." But within the limits of his knowledge he intended to be accurate: "In his endeavor to illustrate these passages in the annals of the state, it is proper for him to say that he has aimed to perform his task with historical fidelity." Kennedy might err, as he himself realized, but he had no intention of twisting history to fit the needs of his story. Fiction was added onto fact, to gain the attention of readers; but where fact was known, it should neither be distorted nor disregarded.[15]

III

William Alexander Caruthers also was a novelist by avocation. As a physician he did yeoman service in one plague, and a few times he turned his medical knowledge to use in his novels. Perhaps unfortunately, he rarely confused his vocation with his avocation. As he saw it, a writer had little chance of making a living: "no man in this country can afford to write, unless he pursues some lucrative employment at the same time." There was of course the lack of a copyright law, with unscrupulous publishers taking full advantage of it. With less justice, Caruthers also blamed English writers for taking unfair advantage of Americans, and asked, indignantly, "Is this just, is it fair, is it honorable?" The English and French insisted on the superiority of their respective cultures; their authors had a status even in this country which we denied to our own. In spite of this, our literary progress had been remarkable, for we had "built our literature confessedly on an English basis," yet a few American authors (notably Charles Brockden Brown, Washington Irving, James Fenimore Cooper, and Catharine Maria Sedgwick) had done notable work. But they and later writers were handicapped because "we do not live for the arts; we make the arts merely subservient to us."[16] He was referring directly to himself when he complained that, in literature and history especially, "few in this country have the fortune of the elegant leisure necessary to pursue these matters uninterruptedly; such is the fate of the author of the following imperfect and crudely-digested effort, and he must offer it in extenuation of his many shortcomings."[17]

Caruthers was a comparatively mild literary nationalist. He

was less mild in his belief in American expansionism. In his novels, Nathaniel Bacon and Governor Spotswood are confident that the English must steadily advance westward until they have conquered the entire country, advancing "in a semicircular wave like a kindred billow of the watery ocean, sweeping all obstruction before it." Caruthers predicted confidently (though with some advantage of hindsight) that Spotswood in crossing the mountains had started a movement that "would be renewed from generation to generation, until in the course of little more than a single century it would transcend the Rio del Norte, and which, perhaps, in half that time may traverse the utmost boundaries of Mexico." Spotswood, Caruthers thought, deserved to rank with Columbus.[18]

In his one contemporary novel, Caruthers was heavily concerned with intersectional amity and understanding. Before the nation could attain its destiny, it must be emotionally and spiritually, as well as politically, unified. Caruthers was aware of difficulties. As an author, making his "first embarrassed, and perhaps awkward, bow before the public," he was aware that his work would meet with prejudice: "there is evidently a current in American Literature, the fountain-head of which lies north of the Potomac, and in which a southern is compelled to navigate up the stream if he jumps in too far South."[19] But Northerners were not alone in holding unfair prejudices. With a background of Virginia up-bringing, Pennsylvania medical training, and extensive practice in New York City, Caruthers was prepared to combat unfounded prejudices wherever he met them. So he declared roundly that "Every southern should visit New York. It would allay provincial prejudices, and calm his excitement against his northern countrymen. The people here are warm-hearted, generous, and enthusiastic, in a degree scarcely inferior to our own southerns."[20]

For this tale of sentiment and of social observation, Caruthers in *The Kentuckian in New York* adopted the conventional epistolary form, although it was already going out of fashion. Caruthers mixes his characters plentifully. Two young South Carolinians who had been educated in Virginia meet on their way to New York a Kentucky frontiersman (who owes something to the legendary Davy Crockett and to the literary concept of the frontiersman embodied in such a work as James K. Paulding's *Lion of the West*). In turn a Virginia friend visits in South Carolina. Caruthers does not stint the romance, for all four men fall in love—one with a New York girl, and the Kentuckian with a girl he had met at a circus there. At the end of the story there are four weddings, which is about par for a Caruthers novel. But if the romantic and sentimental elements obscure the social commentary, they do not vitiate it, for Caruthers intended to give pictures of slavery in Virginia and South Carolina, the plague in New York, the Northern mobs, and the Virginia Reel. There are descriptions of typical and sometimes of beautiful places in the North and in the South, for Caruthers wished to give his readers a fair and tolerant picture of many sections in the United States. But he felt it necessary to interest and amuse his readers, if he was to hold their attention.[21]

Although his second novel may be interpreted as continuing his plea for national unity and understanding and expansion, it is so only indirectly. Probably influenced by the popularity of Scott and Cooper, in *The Cavaliers of Virginia* he turned back to a dramatic episode in Virginia's history: Bacon's Rebellion. To Caruthers this was the first great conflict of democracy against aristocracy, of frontier against seaboard, of expansionism against timid conservatism. Bacon represented the cavalier at his best, while the villain Governor Berkley is allowed only the virtue of bravery. The story is told in black and white, with practically no shading. Yet Caruthers had a dual purpose: he intended "to sketch the lives and manners of these early cavaliers of Virginia," before it was too late to depict men "around whose jovial memories there lives such a rich store of traditionary lore, and so many manuscript relics of antiquity fast crumbling into oblivion." But something more was needed than a factual record: not only should the storyteller weave these historic and tradition- ary accounts into "such a shape as would at once preserve the general features of historic truth," but he should go well beyond this and "throw around these venerable relics the richer and more attractive hues of romance."

Caruthers provides an occasional footnote or internal comment to reassure the reader that he is faithful to "the grave words of History," and he apologizes for one digression with the explana- tion that "we could not pass it over with any kind of regard to historical accuracy," but he does not hesitate to rearrange facts for the advantage of his story. He transplants a Puritan regicide to Virginia; he alters or omits known facts about Bacon's life; and of course he throws in a generous if unhistorical num- ber of love affairs.

Three unfavorable reviews apparently forced Caruthers into a consideration of what the historical romance should be. He denied the charge that he had mistakenly made Bacon a callow, Byronic hero; instead, he claimed to be "the first writer that ever described Bacon as a hero and a patriot." In his bitter rejoinder, Caruthers labels his hostile reviewers as "sparrow hunters" and denies practically all their charges of historical and geographical inaccuracies. But Caruthers justly claimed that in the novel he had "distinctly avowed that the author had intentionally transposed the historical order of events." The reviewers had not only misunderstood the author's purpose, but had failed to understand that there was a difference between fiction and history. Caruthers indignantly asks: "Was there ever a historical novel which did not violate historical accuracy?" How, also, could one have a romance without a romantic hero: "Did any body ever hear of such criticism as this? Was there ever a hero of Romance, from Waverly down to ——*, who was not employed upon petty schemes of matrimonial alliance? How the mischief would he construct a novel without it? A writer who could suggest such an idea, is not only incapable of giving a judicious opinion upon a work of fiction, but he is ignorant of the very first principles upon which a plot is constructed, so as to sustain the interest of the reader."[24]

Caruthers never doubted the value of the romantic idea, in literature or in life. He identified it with the true spiritual ideal, inhabited by persons who had spent too many "sad and solitary hours" to be content with the real. It is these choicest spirits who remain apart from "the busy and the gay world, and are called romantic."[25] All great writing comes from the imagination, and for that matter all important thinking, for "there is no such thing as reasoning without imagining." It is man's greatest gift from God, "a glorious power: and almost independent of all gross and earthly thralldom. Taste, reason, and judgment are all subject to be check-mated by the senses and are dependent on them for existence, but the imagination is a soul of itself—almost emancipated from earth, and living in a world of its own. It bears in its essence both the power and the truth of immortality."[26]

To a large degree, certain men live beyond or outside the real: "It is this which forms the nucleus of that passion for the

——* Caruthers' note: "We leave the reader to fill up the blank."

Ideal, which is commonly called a romantic disposition. The more vivid the picture which memory presents, the more completely will they be blended with all imaginary persons presented to the mind." When he narrowed this to a specific group, Caruthers believed that "a great writer of Romance is communicating in spirit with a whole world of ideal personages, and rousing up, like an enchanter, the dead heroes of a thousand Romances in real life."

Viewed in this light, what a master magician was Scott. He "waved his potent wand over seas and continents." Scott, "the great wizard of Abbottsford," was preeminent in creating characters like Guy Mannering and Edward Waverley that the reader transforms into living beings: G. P. R. James had done it with Henry Masterson. Scott could conjure up ghosts and transform this "every day world of ours into a land of spirits." To do so, however, even he must have the imaginative assistance of readers: "Every work of imagination depends for its success upon this assimilative power in the mind of the reader. Some one character is at once singled out and personified, and the book is not read one page after the marriage or death of that individual."[27]

Although he frequently used Gothic elements in his own stories, he kept them subordinate and rationally explainable. For the *genre* in and of itself, Caruthers had only contempt: "there is a bastard romantic vein in some minds which idealizes after its own morbid visions all the stern realities of life, but these are not the genuine children of song and romance. A weak understanding is almost a sure concomitant of this false ideal. There is a want of taste and judgment in them to humanize the images. They delight in gloomy castles — imprisoned damsels — hair breadth escapes — and at least a thousand murders to the duodecimo. Cervantes has, fortunately for common sense, gibbeted the whole class to the everlasting gaze and derision of posterity."[28]

When he re-wrote his last novel, *The Knights of the Horse-Shoe*,[29] Caruthers no doubt felt that he had lived up to all his own requirements, however imperfectly. Older readers could identify themselves with Governor Spotswood; young men with Frank Lee; young women with Kate Spotswood or Ellen Evylin. Despite the seduction of an Indian girl, the story is undeniably pure in tone. There are stirring and pathetic events, disguises, and above all an important and hazardous expedition. Caruthers heightens the dangers and difficulties; with even greater freedom, he bestows a wife and four grown or nearly grown children on the bachelor governor. He took other liberties with history, although at the end of the book he appends a letter to prove that golden horseshoes once existed, and the order had been established; on the title page he thanks five Virginians for their aid, and in the Introduction describes his own research. But once again he warns the reader that he is not writing history: this is a "Traditionary story." The author felt that he was entitled to the justifiable liberties of fiction.[30]

It is possible, however, that Caruthers did not desire to separate legend and history. There was a definite value in re-creating the past. After he had surveyed the ruins of Jamestown and had pondered their meaning, Caruthers concluded that "The tendency of such reminiscences is humanizing in the highest degree. It leads us gently away from the strifes of personal and political warfare—from the turbulence of passion engendered amidst the clashing of interests and turmoil of busy life, to ponder over the venerable relicks and monuments of a former generation." It might help if we could "see them as we ourselves," but too close an inspection might reveal deformities. So in his romances Caruthers attempted to get rid of the deformities before he gave his readers a chance to see their ancestors "as we ourselves."[31]

IV

John Esten Cooke expressed his ante-bellum literary ambitions rather modestly yet with fair exactness when he wrote: "My aim has been to paint the Virginia phase of American society, to do for the Old Dominion what Cooper has done for the Indians, Simms for the Revolutionary drama in South Carolina, Irving for the Dutch Knickerbockers and Hawthorne for the weird Puritan life of New England."[32] He was, at least in diluted part, a social historian; he was also a Virginian who believed that "everything connected with the history and family romance (that is *truth*) of Virginia" would be listened to with ardor throughout the country. With Simms and Kennedy, he believed that the formal historians had failed to give a complete picture: "Alas for the historians! They tell us many things, but so little! They relate with much dignity, how the battle was fought and the treaty made—they tell us the number of the combatants, and spread every protocol upon the page. But the student of the past asks for more. Of the historian we ask a picture of the elder day—portraits of the Virginian and his household. We would know the peculiarities of character and manners which marked a great race."[33]

Perhaps the last-quoted words indicate Cooke's limitations. In the 1850's he drifted into professional writing, after an abortive attempt to practice law. He wrote poems, essays, stories, novels; he also wrote a fair amount of miscellaneous literary criticism. It is not impressive. One reason may have been John Esten Cooke's astounding facility: if engaged on a novel, apparently he thought it a poor day if he failed to write one hundred pages of 5 x 8 manuscript. Even more to the point, however, is Cooke's idea that it is "a just maxim that true criticism is appreciation."[34] This indicates why Cooke's criticism, considered purely as criticism, lacks the incisiveness and the character of his brother Philip's. Yet some of his parodies and his sharply-phrased commentaries indicate that he was by no means completely soft-minded. But these are intermittent flashes: his comments on Carlyle and his objections to certain Northern writers were rather signs of temporary intransigence than of a settled philosophy. Unless he had a special reason, Cooke was too kind by nature to hate anybody for very long.[35]

Cooke had also in the preface to his first novel in book form indicated his own serious limitations, when he wrote that "If the book be found entertaining, and (above all else) the spirit of it pure, the writer will be more than satisfied." The reader is not satisfied, for the simple reason that Cooke has failed to live up to his fictional obligations. The author never recognized this. He had set out to present, through the character of a well-known hunter, John Myers, "some of the personages, and modes of life and thought in Virginia, at the commencement of the present century." The chief character was drawn from life, and many of the incidents taken from his own or his father's experience. But Cooke had set the time fifty years earlier, at the beginning of the century, with the result that *Leatherstocking and Silk* is a historical novel with contemporary overtones.[36]

In his next work, *The Virginia Comedians,* he became frankly the romancer as well as the social historian. He turned back to the troubled pre-Revolutionary Virginia of 1765. But though "many pages are dedicated to historic events and men" (especially to a highly mysterious, unidentified Patrick Henry), he notes that "the aim of this book is scarcely to follow the course of public events, or reflect the political spirit of the period." The real personages of his narrative were fictitious, and "the simple design he proposed to himself was a rapid delineation of some social pecularities in their passionate and humorous development. . . . Everywhere the writer has endeavored to preserve the traits of the period, and above all to make his characters flesh and blood." But the story, he insisted, was not paramount. He wished "simply to depict some Virginia scenes and personages ten years before the Revolution. He trusts his picture is at least truthful, as far as it extends."[37]

Sometimes "the fidelity of history" forced him to draw unpleasant or unworthy characters. Cooke semi-apologizes for his harsh portrait of an Episcopalian clergyman by claiming that far too many men of this caliber had been sent to Virginia, and that "Here, as on all important occasions, imagination has yielded to history; fancy, to recorded fact." But even more important was its moral tone: "Every book should be judged, first for its purity and healthfulness: afterwards for what it contains of novel character, incident, or idea. The writer trusts that in the first particular these pages are irreproachable: he is too well aware of his deficiencies on the remaining point."[38]

Cooke threw around his novel all the mysterious trappings that Scott and Irving loved so well. He purports to be editing a manuscript written by one C. Effingham, a descendant of a main character; in the prologue and from time to time in the story Effingham speaks in his own right, in a style even more ornate than Cooke's; the presumed editor claims that with one exception he has followed the manuscript faithfully: "The sequence of events has been somewhat altered, to give more artistic point to certain pages—since art is all in all after honesty—and many moral digressions of the worthy gentleman have been omitted, as unnecessary and superfluous."[39]

In the sequel, *Henry St. John,* he retains the same cumbrous machinery. There is an elaborate prologue and epilogue by C. Effingham, who proposes "composing a book of the revolutionary period, based on family archives." Through Effingham, Cooke again states his quarrel with the formal historians, who have "bloody minds and delight in carnage; or legal minds, and wander in the flowery fields of legislative enactments." As a result, from history "we have nothing but the skeleton, when we want the warm blood, the flushed brows, and the flashing eyes." It is difficult, he confesses, to "revive a whole period, or many periods, with all their peculiarities of life and thought and manners," but

Cooke as a boy had dreamed of doing just that for Virginia, and he felt it could best be done through the historical romance. So his book had two themes, as he stops the action to inform the reader: "the story of a man and a woman; the history, also, of a period in the annals of a nation." [40]

The reality of fiction troubled him far less. He did not hesitate to use the same melodramatic devices over and over. *The Virginia Comedians* is resolved by having the heroine kidnapped, and then rescued; in the sequel, *Henry St. John,* another heroine is kidnapped, and again is rescued. A fictional character is given equal credit with Henry, Jefferson, and Washington for Virginia's part in starting the revolution. Champ Effingham twice tears at his breast until his fingers are "stained with blood." The same descriptive epithets ("Curling lip" to denote contempt, for example) are used over and over. And Cooke is lavish with his love affairs: typically, at the end of *The Virginia Comedians,* four weddings have been arranged for.[41]

In spite of his protestations, Cooke on occasion took liberties with history. In *Fairfax* he presents a mysterious young man who turns out to be the son of Lord Fairfax, although the Governor had no son; and an equally mysterious young Mr. George proves to be George Washington. He took even greater liberties in *The Youth of Jefferson,* which in spite of its title is fiction and deals with an almost imaginary love affair. Cooke himself was amused when the book was considered authentic: in the Preface he wrote modestly, "If its grotesque incidents beguile an otherwise weary hour with innocent laughter, the writer's ambition will be satisfied."[42]

Yet in all his romances there are many effective touches. One of the most convincing is a transposition of a personal experience. In 1853 Cooke was on close terms with Kate and Ellen Bateman and their father, the manager of a theatrical troupe. Kate was an excellent actress; but she was old enough to recognize and to be ashamed of "unworthy double-entendres" in her speeches: "Poor child! She is getting old enough to feel as an incipient woman the unworthy part she plays. Thank heaven for it and may they both soon leave the stage and become children again." Cooke effectively transfers this dislike of acting to a slightly more mature Beatrice Hallam in *The Virginia Comedians,* and through it gives richness and complexity to his best-achieved feminine character.[43]

These pre-war romances are Cooke's best work. Technically he was not an innovator. He was content to accept the historical romance as he found it, to follow in the footsteps of Scott and Dumas and G. P. R. James, of Cooper and Kennedy and Simms. Undoubtedly the most influential single book, however, was Thackeray's *Henry Esmond,* which appeared in 1852—just before Cooke started writing his own romances. He simply adopted a model that he liked and adapted it to the needs of a chronicler of Virginia life and manners.[44]

Cooke served in the Confederate Army throughout the Civil War. This brought to an abrupt end one phase of his writing. After the war, in desperate need of money, he quickly wrote inadequate biographies of Lee and Jackson, and embodied some of his own experiences as a staff officer in three romances: *Surry of Eagle's Nest, Mohun,* and *Hilt to Hilt.* But the history and the romance run tandem; they are never fused. When Cooke was accused by a Boston critic of providing fare too highly seasoned, with "duels and murderous settlements of deadly feuds" to add to the excitement of war and battles, and when his style was described as "excessively florid" and "exaggerated," Cooke was indignant. He has his narrator Colonel Surry respond that he had supposed the earlier book "composed in a most compact, terse, and altogether faultless style." He hoped that the style of *Hilt to Hilt* was "not florid; I know the events, strange as they appear, are not exaggerated . . . whatever seems strangest in this book is substantially, when not literally, true."[45]

One novel had a didactic purpose. Cooke had become a farmer, and in *The Heir of Gaymount* advocated that Southerners should turn to truck farming in order to become prosperous. The remedy for the South's troubles was to be found in intelligent work. In many ways Lieut. Carteret is Cooke himself: his war experiences parallel Cook's; he too is a writer; he too is a truck farmer. But the message is somewhat obscured by a love affair and a family feud, and effectively ruined when the heir deciphers a cryptogram and discovers buried treasure. This solves Carteret's problem, but it was hardly a workable solution for most Southern farmers.

Cooke felt that he was obliged to write for money, and mainly he continued to pour out romances. Sometimes he was disgusted with them. Of *Out of the Foam,* set on the rocky coast of Wales, he admitted that the "sort is not literature and Reade invented it to make money. I am in want thereof." He had written it to sell, "as I would raise wheat or corn. . . . I follow 'the fashion'—when I should set in! . . . I have attempted a style and treatment not natural to me, and I do not propose, D. V., ever again to return to it. . . . 'Out of the Foam' is mere melodrama."[47] Although he wrote other novels with foreign settings, he was happier when he kept his characters in Virginia and set the action in the time of the Revolution. There was one exception. With the encouragement of Thomas Dunn English, Cooke wrote *My Lady Pokahontas*. It is mainly set in England, and purports to be written by Anas Todkill, a contemporary "Puritan and Pilgrim," and edited with notes by John Esten Cooke. This has at least the virtue of justifying an archaic style and choice of words. It is a slight but graceful romance, with Shakespeare as a character and the Mermaid Tavern as a setting for his conversation with Captain John Smith. Appropriately, it was Cooke's last successful work, though not his last book.[48]

But Cooke knew full well that such books were out of favor. Shortly before his death, he surveyed himself in relation to the contemporary literary world, and concluded: "I still write stories for such periodicals as are inclined to accept romances, but whether any more of my work in that field will appear in book-form is doubtful. Mr. Howells and the other realists have crowded me out of popular regard as a novelist, and have brought the kind of fiction I write into general disfavor. I do not complain of that, for they are right. They see, as I do, that fiction should faithfully reflect life, and they obey the law, while I cannot. I was born too soon, and am now too old to learn my trade anew. But in literature, as in everything else, advance should be the law, and he who stands still has no right to complain if he is left behind."[49]

V

One way to glorify the South and to defend it against outside attack was to present persuasively some of the finer aspects and episodes from its past. There was a need for understanding, and the novel or romance seemed a persuasive and easily comprehended, if indirect, means of bringing this about. Simms was fully aware of the value of fiction for this purpose. Kennedy was not immediately concerned, but when he wrote in 1852 "A word in Advance, from the Author to the Reader" as a preface to the second edition of *Swallow Barn*, he thought the twenty-year-old story of some historical importance. The older states were "losing their original distinctive habits and modes of life, and in the same degree, I fear, are losing their exclusive American character." This seemed to him a pity. The older, nobler, more individual- istic way of life should not be forgotten under the pressures toward standardization. He had tried to write with tolerance and understanding of a way of life, to deal fairly with the problem of slavery, and to depict characters who for all their foibles were intrinsically good; he was not willing to allow these sketches, "a faithful picture," entirely "to pass away." The sketches might in turn encourage tolerance and comprehension.[50]

Caruthers also believed that understanding might result in tolerance. In his first novel, social commentary was subordinate to his love stories, but it was not incidental to his plan. He did not approve of slavery, although in Virginia it seemed to him not too bad; in South Carolina, with Negro drivers and absentee land- lords, it had little excuse for being. Yet if he had no desire to excuse the evil aspects of slavery, he had no easy remedy to offer. Citizens of a nation should know what an entire nation had to offer. If at times *The Kentuckian* sounds like a guide-book, this is not accidental. But Caruthers, like Kennedy, turned away from the contemporary field. He too had a love of history. Moreover, Scott had made the historical romance respectable, in a way that the novel was not.

Cooke began as a romancer, and mainly he stayed within that genre. Even when he wrote about his own time, he continued to use melodramatic plots and mysterious characters. Like Kennedy and Caruthers, he was intensely concerned with the reality of history, but he had even less concern than they did with the reality of plot and of characterization. This neglect of technique and structure, this failure to develop an aesthetic of fiction, weakens even their best work. In general, they are better as social his- torians than as novelists.

6

WILLIAM GILMORE SIMMS
Realistic Romanticist

IT IS NATURAL that Simms's best and most influential criticism deals with fiction. Although he sometimes expressed distrust of that medium and fancied his true forte was as poet or dramatist, he was most at home writing or writing about prose fiction. He had so many other interests that for almost a decade (1842-51) he neglected fiction to concentrate heavily on writing history, geography, and especially biography; he devoted an inordinate amount of time and thought to politics, military strategy, and the defense of slavery; he yielded easily to requests for occasional poems and orations; he edited too many impecunious magazines and filled far too many of their pages with hasty hack work.

There were good and possibly quite valid reasons for all this activity. He was a professional man of letters living in Charleston or on his father-in-law's plantation "Woodlands": that is, at a far remove from the center of profitable literary and publishing activities, yet largely dependent on that activity for a livelihood. It is to this necessity rather than to other interests that C. Hugh Holman attributes "Simms's virtual abandoning" of fiction between 1842 and 1850: the writing of novels was no longer profitable because of "the devastating effect on American fiction of the [continuing] Panic of 1837, the pirating of English popular novels and the development of the 'mammoth weeklies' and the 'cheap book' publishers."[1] Simms frequently and bitterly noted how the sales of his novels had declined. Thus in 1841 he wrote that "Irving now writes almost wholly for magazines and

Cooper and myself are almost the only persons whose novels are printed—certainly, we are almost the only persons who hope to get anything from them. From England we get nothing. In this country an Edition now instead of 4 or 5,000 copies, is scarce 2,000. My Damsel of Darien [1839] was 3,000. My Kinsmen [1841] not more than 2,000; and it is seldom now that the demand for novels carries them to a 2d Edition. . . . Nothing, in short, but the great popularity of an author will secure the publication of a novel now."[2]

These conditions led his friend and publisher Mathew Carey to advise Simms to stop writing novels. Partly influenced by economic conditions but even more by a general distrust of the value of fiction, his friends James H. Hammond and Benjamin F. Perry counselled him to write only histories and biographies. Simms yielded to what he must have regarded as necessity, but by 1850 he was convinced that he had been wrong to do so. Except for the biography of Francis Marion, the sales of these books had been disappointing, and his history of South Carolina "did not yield me as much money as I have earned in three nights, penning legends for the Annuals."[3] Perhaps equally important was his considered belief that "the works that make fame are works which admit of the exercises of originality, and chiefly belong to the imaginative faculty."

This included all forms of creative writing, but as one pertinent illustration he noted that "Boccaccio undervalued his stories and built upon his treatises. The last are forgotten and he lives by the former."[4] Even more relevant is the fact that when he mentions Homer and Aeschylus, he is not talking of practitioners of an alien craft, but as in a sense his own direct literary ancestors. Like many of his contemporaries, Simms attempted to draw a sharp line of demarcation between the novel and the romance. Most of his own works, he wrote emphatically to E. A. Duyckinck, "are *romances,* not novels," and therefore "involve sundry of the elements of heroic poetry."[5]

He developed this theme at some length in the 1853 Preface to the revised *Yemassee.* He demanded that critics recognize the distinction and judge the book by the "standards which have governed me in its composition."[6] These standards were reasonably clear in his own mind: "The Modern Romance is the substitute which the people of the present day offer for the epic. The form is changed; the matter is very much the same; at all events, it differs much more seriously from the English novel than it does from the epic and the drama." The reader who employs Fielding and Richardson as his touchstones can never satisfactorily read *Ivanhoe*, for the domestic novel deals with ordinary characters in ordinary conditions of society; the romance, differing in material even more than in mode, "is of loftier origin than the Novel. It approximates the poem. It may be described as an amalgam of the two. It is only with those who are apt to insist upon poetry as verse, and to confound rhyme with poetry, that the resemblance is unapparent."

The standards of the romance are similar to those of the epic, and to these the writer is "required religiously to confine himself." Simms's definition may seem inadequate both for the epic and the romance, but he explained frankly what he was trying to do: The romance as he wrote it "invests individuals with an absorbing interest—it hurries them rapidly through crowding and exacting events, in a narrow space of time—it requires the same unities of plan, of purpose, and harmony of parts, and it seeks for its adventures among the wild and wonderful."

This distinction was clear-cut, but its application was not always easy. Sometimes he described his stories of the Revolution as novels, sometimes as romances; at least one of them, *Eutaw*, was "at once a novel of society and a romance."[7] For him this was a remarkable concession. Ordinarily he thought poorly of domestic novels, "a very inferior school of writings," because the "imagination can have little play. The exercise of the creative faculty is almost entirely denied."[8] As a result, the author must depend on "analysis of minute shades of character," and description of tame social events. Simms preferred works that were "imaginative, passionate, metaphysical"; he preferred, as a general rule, "to give a story of events, rather than of persons."[9]

Although he felt that readers preferred action to analysis and tended to agree with them, he recognized that "success in drawing character" was "one of the most important requisities in modern romance and novel writing."[10] He semi-apologizes for stopping the action in *Beauchampe* (p. 46) to give "proper characterization," but defends himself on the ground that the "novel only answers half its uses when we confine it to the simple delineation of events, however ingenious and interesting." In *Confession*, the story depended almost wholly on an analysis of the passions, of "the heart in some of its obliquities and perversities"; Simms admitted in the Preface to the second edition that he had revised the work "with many misgivings." It lacked variety, color, incident; it appealed to the brain rather than to the blood. He did not expect it to be popular, for success of this kind "is rarely possible in any work of fiction where events, which naturally speak for themselves, are mostly rejected from use."[11]

In general, he preferred simply that his characters be portrayed truthfully, as the author had known similar persons in life, with their inconsistencies as well as their basic governing attributes.[12] This emphasis on actuality extended to conversation: R. M. Bird in *The Infidel* was wrong aesthetically and realistically in letting his "Cavaliers all speak the same language."[13] With certain historical personages the author was closely bound, and Simms notes, for example, that General Marion in *Mellichampe* is "correct to the very letter of the written history."[14] The story of Captain Barsfield's conversion to Toryism "is not less so," although it is based on tradition rather than records; Simms notes its "close resemblance to the recorded history" of another and more famous Southern loyalist. The romancer also had the right to transpose incidents from the life of a known character to that of a fictional one, as Simms did when he borrowed freely from the career of Col. Isaac Hayne to round out his portrait of Col. Walton.[15] One could likewise transpose incidents, as he did when he described the "destruction of the mansion-house at 'Piney Grove' by Major Singleton . . . the means employed to effect this object [fire-bearing arrows supplied by the owner's daughter], will be recognized by the readers of Carolina history, and the lover of female patriotism, as of true occurrence in every point of view; the names of persons alone being altered, and a slight variation made in the locality."[16]

Sometimes he transposed unlikely incidents from his own personal knowledge, especially from his experiences on the frontier; thus, after describing how an outlaw escaped by floating down an Alabama river on a bag of cotton, Simms added a footnote: "This is a fact; such a mode of escape would not readily suggest itself to a romancer's invention, but it did to that of a very great rogue."[17]

Incidents from history, legend, or personal knowledge could be used effectively provided they were used in such a way as to add verisimilitude to the story. But an accumulation of facts, even though each might in itself be true, was not enough to prove a case. This was one fundamental error that Harriet Beecher Stowe had made in *Uncle Tom's Cabin*. Many of her isolated facts were true, yet the novel was "a wholesale lie. . . . Admit all her statements to be true, and they prove nothing. Her facts may be susceptible of proof, while her inferences are wholly false."[18] The romancer could use uncharacteristic or isolated facts to advantage because they are rare but possible; the writer of social protest could not. Mrs. Stowe had ignorantly confused the *genres,* so that *Uncle Tom's Cabin* was as deficient artistically as it was sociologically: "The structure of the romance, to which class of writings Mrs. Stowe's story belongs, is one that demands extraordinary events. In this respect it transcends the privileges of the ordinary novel of society. The interest is maintained by startling incidents, and these require constantly to rise in their excitements in order to produce the proper effects. The standards, measurably, are those of the drama. Scene follows scene; act, act; event crowds upon the heels of events; one incident prepares the way for another still more imposing, till the gradually swelling spectacle finds its *denouement* in an event of such magnitude and importance to the parties, as leaves it beyond the power of the dramatist to go further."[19] To Simms's mind, although she wrote with passion and power, Mrs. Stowe's novel was deficient as "art and argument."

Yet his concern with strict artistry was limited. In most novels he is the omniscient author who does not hesitate to tell what is or is not true, what must or must not be supposed; to announce bluntly in the middle of a chapter that "we must now return" to another group of characters; or naively to assure the reader that he can listen in on secret conferences, in which he will remain unseen to the participants.[20] Occasionally he used the device of the fictional narrator and let the supposed speaker present the story, usually although not completely according to his own developing knowledge, as in *Confession;* but in *Richard Hurdis* he endows his narrator with practically total recall as to the exact words of long conversations. Simms attempted to justify the method in a Preface written eighteen years after its first publication: "It will be seen that there is a peculiarity in the arrangement of the story. The hero tells, not only what he himself performed, but supplies the events, even as they occur, which he yet derives from the report of others. Though quite unusual, the plan is yet strictly within the proprieties of art. The reader can readily be made to comprehend that the hero writes after a lapse of time, in which he had supplied himself with the necessary details, filling up the gaps in his own experience. I have persuaded myself that something is gained by such a progress, in the more energetic, direct and dramatic character of the story; and the rapidity of the action is a necessary result, from the exclusion of all circuitous narrative. The hero and author, under the plan, become identical."[21] To the modern reader, however, Simms appears to have sacrificed whatever advantages there may be in the first person narrator, without any compensations. There is rather less awkwardness in his transitions when he is himself the omniscient author.

When he provided direct historical information in an Introduction or even as part of the first chapter, the material seems relevant and properly placed. But he did not hesitate to interrupt the action in order to interpolate historical matter, without any attempt to weave it into the story, or hesitate to include a lengthy and argumentative footnote in order to set a somewhat irrelevant record straight.[22]

Yet the writer of historical romances was not a historian. He should be factually accurate and he should have as much personal knowledge as possible; thus Simms wrote that he could not complete *The Yemassee* "until I have in *pro. per.* gone over the ground of the story, and become acquainted with its localities."[23] But the subject must have a "certain degree of obscurity," and the events "must be such as will admit of the full exercise of the great characteristic of genius—imagination. He must be free to conceive and to invent—to create and to endow;—without any dread of crossing the confines of ordinary truth, and of such history as may be found in undisputed records. His material must be of such a kind as to leave him without danger of rebuke for impropriety; and the only laws and criteria against which he must provide, must be those of good taste and probability, with such other standards as he himself sets up in his progress, as gauges by which to work, himself, and by which others are to judge of his performances. When we are told that a history is too fresh for fiction, it is because of this danger that it is so. When it is objected that America is too young for the production of a national literature, it is chiefly because of this difficulty, which fetters and defies domestic invention. Genius dare not take liberties with a history so well known, and approaches her task with a cautious apprehensiveness which is inconsistent with her noblest executions."[24]

Both the regular historian and the romancer needed first of all to be an artist, so that readers would feel that the historical "drybones were once covered with flesh." To a large degree, history is informed conjecture; it is raw material to be handled honestly and scrupulously, but "the chief value of history consists in its proper employment for the purposes of art. . . . It is by such artists, indeed, that nations live."[25] For a major defect with history is that as written it is "the history rather of princes than of people,"[26] and it pays little or no attention to social customs and manners, ordinary human beings, and minor events: the historical romance "supplies those details which the latter, unwisely as we think, but too commonly, holds beneath her regard."[27]

Without disparaging history, he valued most "the free use which the imaginative mind may make of that which is unknown, fragmentary and in ruins—the *debris* of history, and not the perfect fragment."[28] The imagination was all-powerful and all-important, and it derived at least in part from the intuition. It came before invention and design; it could be shaped but not wholly controlled by conscious discipline. Simms apparently believed, contrary to his own practice, that the main work of the imagination should be complete before a particular work was begun; he advised his younger friend and fellow-novelist John Esten Cooke to "Give yourself time enough to contemplate your ground and materials fully, so as to *design* with a better grasp of the *absolute* in your subject. It is thus that it always shows itself arbitrarily fixed in its object. It must go in one direction—speak in one character—pursue one outline, and has no choice. The imagination, if not a will itself, seems to work under a will which is imperative as fate, and allows it no caprices. It is the fancy which wanders and has a frequent choice."[29]

Here and elsewhere (notably in a review of Bulwer's work) Simms equates the imagination with the creative faculty; whereas fancy equates with the decorative ornamental faculty: "Imagination may be described as the architect who designs the noble temple . . . fancy, that subordinate artist who lays out the grounds below."[30]

Although more limited, the function of invention was equally important. No man could be a first-rate novelist who did not have in a high degree the "constructive faculty"; it was James Fenimore Cooper's major weakness that he "seems to exercise none of his genius in the invention of his fable. There is none of that careful grouping of means to ends, and all, to the one end of the denouement, which so remarkably distinguished the genius of Scott."[31] Instead, Cooper relied on the "spirit and success of certain scenes," disregarding the fact that in the romance "all the standards are dramatic," and that "the per-fecting of the wondrous whole—the admirable adaptation of means to ends—the fitness of parts—the propriety of the action—the employment of the right materials,—and the fine architectural proportions of the fabric,—these are the essentials which deter-mine the claim of the writer to be the BUILDER."

Through invention, then, the author provided a continuous, harmonious action. Simms objected to writing short stories be-cause in them "no room is allowed you for the development of character, you have to rely chiefly on incident and this tasks in-vention to the uttermost."[32] He believed, rather, that incidents should grow out of the development of character.

As some of the preceding quotations suggest, design has to do with the over-all pattern of the story, rather than with artistry. In the Preface to *Mellichampe,* Simms admitted that critics of *The Partisan* had been justified in calling it crude and unfin-ished; it was rapidly prepared, and "the finish of art can only be claimed by a people with whom art is a leading object." But when objection was made "simply to the story, *as a story,*" Simms at once defended the novel, although he confessed that the "design may have been unhappy, and in that my error may have lain."[33] Perhaps Simms is half-way admitting here that in the Revolutionary stories he had thrown in too much undigested history and given too much attention to military strategy and tactics. When Simms was revising his work for the collected edition, J. H. Hammond advised him to "use the knife freely and cut out every thing that impedes the action. I used even as a boy to curse Scott for his long twaddling scenes and you must not blame me if I say that you have caught that failing from him . . . the writer who has fine things to say must weave them so closely into his very framework that they will appear to belong necessarily to the tale."[34]

In theory Simms agreed fully with Hammond. He noted that Cooper often rode his intellectual hobbies too hard, to the disquiet of his readers,[35] and that Ainsworth, lacking design, de-pended on the accumulation of details to hold interest.[36] Fiction required both more invention and a more elaborate treatment than non-fiction; it must be shaped "with proper care, with a becoming purpose, and under a severer, sublimer design."[37] To a young writer he indicated clearly the defects caused by faulty design: "You have too many persons to manage. You cannot group them into consistent and condensed action. You bring forward too prominently persons who do not help on the action, and several of the early scenes which delay the reader have no obvious connection with the catastrophes."[38]

He admitted freely his own similar errors, but he attributed them in part to the indifference of American readers to careful artistry, and in part to his own impetuosity of temperament and consequent over-hasty writing. Of *Beauchampe* he wrote to his friend B. F. Perry that "The work was written *stans pede in uno,* goon like, literally, as fast as pen could fly over paper,—pretty much as I write to you now. A mode not very favorable to a work of permanent merit, but particularly suited to a temperament like mine."[39]

Possibly as a rationalization of his own defects, Simms tended to set a low value on artistry. The essential qualities, the best proofs of originality, were "passion or power";[40] if a writer had these, he could safely disregard the time-consuming niceties: "fame does not so much follow polish and refinement as Genius—not so much grace and correct delineation as a bold adventurous thought."[41] Yet the mercurial Simms—though always ready to lash out at publishers, editors, and critics, and to advise that a literary work might better be tried on the cook—had many moments of uneasiness. When he was not defending himself, he was capable, typically, of confessing to N. B. Tucker that "I do not know that I should desire you to read the things which I have sent you. I feel all their feeblenesses and crudenesses. They were written most of them at an extremely early age, and under the pressure of necessities which left me too careless of any but present and momentary considerations. You will find them wanting in symmetry and finish, and grossly disfigured by errors of taste and judgment." But in them, he hoped, Tucker would find "proofs of original force, native character, and some imagination."[42]

If Simms was inconsistent about the need for artistry and about his accomplishment, he was steadily consistent about morality in literature. Any work of the imagination must be ultimately useful in the "most elevated meaning" of that word, for it must "answer to our want as human beings, of mixed earth and spirit: having a human necessity before us which however lowly, is the absolute essential to any higher or more hopeful condition."[43] So Bulwer makes a common but unwholesome error when he places the ideal in opposition to the real; Simms, with rather more grasp of good sense than of philosophy, argued that this placed the ideal beyond the reach of men, whereas the moral purpose of art should be attainable, for "the ideal is nothing more than the possible real. . . . To show the real as it is, is the subordinate but preliminary task of genius. It is the holding the mirror up to the common nature. To contrast with this the image of the real, such as it may become, is the holding the mirror up to the universal nature." In this, Simms roundly declared, "consists the morals of art; writers like Shelley and Bulwer might think otherwise, but Homer, Dante, Shakspeare, and Milton never made this error."[44]

One function of genius is to lead "people out of the bondage of the present." For this exalted and frequently agonizing task, prose fiction was not a satisfactory medium: "The mere business of novel-writing, as it is ordinarily conducted, is about the humblest way in which genius can employ itself."[45] Even so, the novel could be useful, for it is of value in the highest sense when it "ministers to morals, to mankind, and to society."[46]

This did not require sermonizing, or pointing a moral. The writer must always keep in mind that we do not take up a poem or novel "in the same frame of mind with which we approach a volume of sermons." The preacher attempts to inculcate moral and religious truth, but the business of the novelist is simply to be truthful. Since human nature is seldom wholly good or bad, "a character either wholly good or bad never yet entered into the imagination of the dramatist or novelist." It is the "mixt" character that the novelist deals with, and if he presents a true picture, "the author has succeeded—and the reader or critic may cavil, if he please, about the 'cakes and ale'."[47]

Simms returned to this theme time and again, perhaps nowhere more clearly than in a review, "Modern Prose Fiction": "As truthfulness is never without its moral, and as the great end of the artist is the approximation of all his fiction to a seeming truth, so unavoidably he inculcates a moral whenever he tells a story." It does not follow that all authors are moral, for many of them did not aim at truthfulness at all; but any author who deserved to be called an artist would be moral in proportion as he succeeded in being truthful.[48]

When his own work was attacked as low, vulgar, and immoral, Simms presented as a personal defense the same arguments he had presented generally. Reviewers who had objected to the "preponderance of low and vulgar personages" in *The Partisan* had not properly understood the function of the romancer. He was not presenting the equivalent of a rosy-hued fairy tale, or an account of "inane perfectibility." He claimed for himself a realistic purpose: "My object usually has been to adhere, as closely as possible, to the features and the attributes of real life, as it is to be found in the precise scene, and under the governing circumstances—some of them extraordinary and romantic, because new—in which my narrative has followed it." Certain portraits in his novels might not be pleasing to some readers, but Simms was persuaded that in them he had "done mankind no injustice."[49]

When the publication of "[Caloya; or] The Loves of the Driver" in the *Magnolia* brought forth horrified but unfounded objections, Simms responded vigorously to the attack, protesting that in his story there was nothing "that can, in the slightest degree, prove hurtful to the delicacy of the purest mind." He had not made vice beautiful or attractive, or virtue ugly. True, it was "a tale of low life—very low life," but there was nothing salacious or prurient in it. So many people were afflicted with "mock modesty" that authors were reluctant "to call things by their proper names. We dare not speak of legs, or thighs, in the presence of many very nice ladies."[50] He adds that if Shakespeare were writing *The Merry Wives* for nineteenth century readers, certain words would be objected to, but the real evil would be in the mind of that person who objected to the correct use of an exact word; even Shakespeare would have "to soften one of the words used into 'female dog,' 'feminine dog,' or something equally inoffensive and equally stupid; but while it would be perfectly moral to say 'bitch' where the sense called for it, it would be a proof of an immodest thought, in the mind of the speaker, who should say 'female dog'!"[51]

This plea for the use of "appropriate language" was a minor part of his defense. He felt that he had re-created characters as he had known them in real life; that moral justice had been allowed to triumph by "natural and ordinary" means; and that the Indian woman in his story embodied a high order of morality. He had presented strong passions, but he had not falsified them; so in earlier days had many of the Biblical writers, and after them Homer, Shakespeare, Massinger, Scott, and Byron: In fact, the "whole tribe of great names, employ the deadly sins of man, as so many foils to his living virtues and whether he falls or triumphs, the end of the moralist is attained, if he takes care to speak the truth, the whole truth and nothing but the truth! In this, in fact, lies the whole secret of his art. A *writer is moral only in proportion to his truthfulness*."[52]

This did not mean that the author, especially the romancer, was bound by the literal fact. As Alexander Cowie has indicated, Simms had read Aristotle's *Poetics* to good purpose, and conformed to the Aristotelian dictum that a "likely impossibility is preferable to an unconvincing possibility."[53] Although he praised its "fearlessness and ingenuity," he condemned Mrs. Shelley's *Frankenstein* for its "extreme violation of natural laws,"[54] and he was careful that his own Gothic effects were rationally explainable; but he never wavered from his belief that imaginative or intuitive understanding was fundamentally more truthful than historical fact or rational comprehension. Only through the skill and imagination of the artist could history be made to yield its ultimate meanings.

II

The best writer of prose fiction, in Simms's estimation, was clearly Sir Walter Scott; with the possible exception of Milton and Dryden, he was the best English writer since Shakespeare. He lacked intuitive insight, but his success in depicting characters was "the grand secret" of his pre-eminence. His one defect was in the feebleness and passivity of his heroes, in comparison with relatively minor characters, but Scott's willingness to give himself completely to his subject and to his characters redeemed what otherwise would have been fatal to a dramatic composition. Also, Scott had boldly broken away from the inferior domestic novel, so that the works of Fielding and Richardson did not provide adequate, correct, or even relevant standards by which to judge Scott's romances.[55]

He was equally outstanding in his power to impose on his material a design that carried the reader step by step, naturally and easily, with no sense of artistic impropriety or violence, until the complete story was a "harmonious achievement."[56] In his letters, articles, and books Simms made casual allusions to Scott's phrases and characters in such a way as to reveal a thorough familiarity; more important, in his criticism he constantly used Scott as a touchstone by which to judge other novelists. He was especially inclined to use *Ivanhoe* in this way, for it seemed to him "one of the most perfect specimens of the romance that we possess. . . . Impaired, however, by the single piece of mummery toward the

close, which embodies the burial rites of Athelstane and his resur-
rection. But for this every way unbecoming episode, the romance
would be nearly perfect."[57] Moreover, with it Scott had done what
the romancer should always strive to do: he had changed the pre-
viously-accepted historical concept of the period.

Simms's admiration for the earlier English novelists was limited.
He remembered that as a boy he "used to glow and shiver in
turn" over *Pilgrim's Progress*,[58] and in *Eutaw* he presents
through several chapters the way in which that book literally
saved the life of an outlaw, and effected a partial if temporary
regeneration of a previously ruthless desperado.[59] Parts of the
Vicar of Wakefield threw him "into paroxysms of laughter";
Sterne, although a humorist of a superior order, erred in making a single character responsible for the "whole interest of his
story"; Defoe and Swift, masters in handling detail, helped
bring about the "natural merging" of the drama with prose fiction.[60] But he seems to have thought more highly of Fielding
and Smollett, "English masters of comic fiction," as humorists than
as novelists: they were working directly in the tradition of Chaucer, with the grafting on of some "foreign attributes." This
means that their humor "grew naturally out of the situation . . .
the spontaneous effusion of a faculty in themselves, and in the
character and the event upon which they were engaged." They
did not rely on quaintness of phraseology, odd nomenclature, or
cunning contrivances, but allowed their humor simply to grow out
of life as they knew it.[61]

Scott shared this ability, but in him humor was tributary,
"always subservient to the tragedy—a foil rather than a constitu-
ent." Dickens also had a genuine sense of humor, but one too
frequently distorted; if Chaucer had written modern prose narratives "like those of Mr. Dickens," they would have been constructed "with better plots, less extravagance, and something
less of the pathetic." But Dickens, like Chaucer, had as a
prominent part of his genius "that pliancy of mood, for example,
which we call mental flexibility, and which enables him to go out
of himself, to forget himself, to forget his favorite thoughts and
fancies, and to throw all the strength of his intellect into the
dramatis personae that grow under his hands." Homer, Shakespeare, and Scott possessed this ability; Byron and Bulwer did not,
and Milton was "a kingman . . . who impressed all persons with
his own nature, and made all speak after the fashion of his own

soul . . . he made the world after his own models." Although admitting the superlative genius of Milton, Simms in general preferred what he called "many-sidedness" in an author.

Yet one of the most powerful immediate influences on Simms as novelist was by an intense, single-track writer. As he frankly admits in the Introduction, *Confession* belongs to "the class of works which the genius of William Godwin has made to triumph in 'Caleb Williams,' even over a perverse system." *Martin Faber* also clearly reveals the influence of Godwin. Although he was doubtful that such works could be made popular, Simms was interested both in reading and writing psychological novels about crime.

The "many-sided" author could compensate for looseness of structure in a way that the intense novelist could not. That was clearly an advantage which Charles Dickens enjoyed over William Godwin. The weaknesses of Dickens were to be found, typically, in *Bleak House,* with its "exaggeration in the portraiture" and its failure in the overall design—a failure that Simms in several notices of Dickens' works blamed on serial publication of parts of a book, to the neglect of the unified whole.[62] Occasionally he was outdone by Dickens' carelessness: he declared roundly that if *The Haunted Man* had "been issued by an unknown writer, it would have been generally pronounced a wretched piece of drivel."[63] He praised *Hard Times* as "very characteristic. . . . Its portraiture is mournfully true and terribly human throughout. The story is painfully pleasing; the softening features in *Hard Times* admirably contrasting with the iron of the age." But his verdict on Dickens at his best is well summed up in his comment on *David Copperfield:* "The delineation of character is inimitable in particular cases, and unexceptionable in most. The 'Child Wife' portrait is very happy, and Micawber, in his miseries, extremely so."[64]

His admiration for Thackeray was at once more limited and more complex. As editor of the *Southern Quarterly Review* he accepted and published an article describing Thackeray as the finest delineator of human nature since Fielding;[65] in the next issue, in reviewing *Pendennis,* Simms dissents sharply: Thackeray's "art is not of the highest character, and we are very far from concurring with one of our contributors, who . . . gave us a very spirited and well-written, but highly exaggerated, estimate of the genius of Thackeray."[66] Thackeray had "a wonderful faculty in minute painting—in social detail"; he had also a "keen insight into human frailties and vanities . . . stripping bare the fraud, and cant, and hypocrisy of pretentious people."[67] But this faculty was too often, as in *The Virginians,* greatly overworked: "the bad and the base—the mean and the malignant—are allotted as usual, too large a proportion of its pages."[68] This had led many readers to misunderstand Thackeray, as man and as writer. His talent was "eminently essayical," and his "art is genial. His art, in fact, is truer than his sentiments. . . . His genius is more just than his sympathies." Simms as novelist and critic liked "mixt" characters, but the cynicism of Thackeray offended one who believed that "Man is a much better animal, in his worst rags, than we are inclined to think him";[69] when Thackeray changed the "stern, simple, sublime character of Washington" to an undignified, raging, roaring, ordinary man, Simms was thoroughly infuriated.[70]

Yet his distaste for Thackeray's philosophy of life did not blind him to Thackeray's mastery in fiction of construction and design. Technically, Thackeray was a master of his craft, and Simms set a high value on any novelist who could impose an artistic design on his material. He enjoyed also Thackeray's "felicitous and peculiar vein of drollery and humor," especially in his shorter works, but he indulged himself too much in "a harsh and savage portrait of humanity." Rather oddly, but almost entirely because of what he considered faulty characterization of real people, Simms in reviewing *Henry Esmond* expressed a preference for Thackeray as a "domestic and social humourist" rather than as a writer of romances. *Henry Esmond* had many attractions for the reader, and Simms admitted that some characters were well drawn and forcible, but the exaggerated and unbalanced portrait of Sir Richard Steele and the tone of the book alike roused him to protest. He could admire Thackeray's skill, but he apparently did not in his heart either like or admire Thackeray.[71]

One of Simms's major critical essays is "Bulwer's Genius and Writings."[72] In it he gave his own definition, previously noted, of imagination and fancy, and one of his best statements on the use of the real and the ideal. The article is more critical than the title indicates: at the beginning he admits Bulwer's genius, but here as elsewhere he uses the term to include spirit, intention, characteristics, and performance, by those men who were struggling "constantly to leave the common track." Bulwer had large and various natural endowments; he thought with boldness, conceived with courage, and painted with ardor. But the genius of Bulwer had within itself two startling flaws. The first was the more serious: "a certain obliquity of the moral sense, which seems to make it impossible for him, under certain lights, to distinguish between right and wrong";[73] and with this, a boyish and vain desire to startle by vehement novelties simply for the pleasure of gratifying his own egotism. As a result, "Bulwer is rather a writer of fancy than imagination"; although credited with boldness, he is really not bold enough in his imaginative grasp of concepts—possibly because of his weak creative powers, his deficiency of artistic imagination. Bulwer fascinated Simms, and he was highly pleased when a reviewer wrote that he had read *The Yemassee* "with a deeper interest and more unalloyed gratification than any preceding work of imagination since the *Last Days of Pompeii*";[74] he had in many short notices and reviews a sincere praise for Bulwer's accomplishments. But he was forced, somewhat reluctantly, to declare that he could not rank Bulwer "among the fathers of his time."[75]

A writer with some of Bulwer's characteristics, Benjamin D'Israeli, presented an easier critical case. He had been unjustly neglected by some English critics, notably R. H. Horne; he had not, like Scott, Carlyle, Wordsworth, Coleridge, and Bulwer, profoundly affected his age, but novels like *Coningsby* and *Venetia* had individuality and power. The neglect was primarily D'Israeli's own fault; his "endowments . . . are various and showy. He has never made the best, or even a proper, use of them."[76] Yet in spite of many faults, arising mainly out of vanity and ambition, D'Israeli knew well the society that he described with a lively fancy, and he had "a power in conversational dialogue, which is not often surpassed among novel writers." To offset these virtues, "His invention is small. His mind is too versatile for that degree of concentrativeness which is required for weaving together, in harmonious connection and dependency, the intricate details of a story, and his tales are accordingly deficient in cohesion and compactness."[77]

Possibly because of pro-Irish and anti-British sentiments, possibly because of unprejudiced critical standards, Simms had a higher regard for contemporary Irish romancers than for their British fellows. He praises William Carleton mildly for his warmth and color, and his good sketches of Irish life, but objects to his lack of taste. He is more enthusiastic about Samuel Lover, "a rare good fellow," who strains too much after merriment at times but succeeds in depicting Irishmen who are true to life, and about Charles Lever, badly underrated by the English but nevertheless the author of novels that were well-constructed and alive with action.[78]

By contrast, the English G. P. R. James had turned himself into a highly popular romancer "by merely imitative industry . . . through the paths opened by Walter Scott."[79] In fact, Simms enjoyed James's works and freely proclaimed that they had certain virtues, especially a "sustained and lively interest,"[80] although it is exceedingly doubtful that he approved of J. H. Hammond's comment that James knew how to "throw in the words that bring the tear. . . It is about the *whole* of his secret of success, such as it is. He beats Scott, Bulwer, Cooper and all of you here."[81] Simms was not quite prepared to admit this, but he evidently counted James not only as a worthy rival but also (at some time after 1852, when James was appointed British Consul at Norfolk) as a personal friend: a notice in 1858 in the Charleston *Mercury* was not "designed as a criticism," but only that "I keep you in grateful recollection."[82] Simms as critic knew full well that James was at a far remove from Scott; Simms as reader and as friend liked James and his works.

For W. H. Ainsworth, and the other lesser English writers of romance, he had only mild and qualified praise. They drew for their material upon Eugene Sue, but they did not "possess a tithe of his genius, his power, the skill with which he combines, or the courage with which he conceives." The English writers are nearer to Dumas, and possibly have patterned their works after his, but the French romancer is infinitely the superior in invention, in good taste, in variety of costume and character, and in "the light and shade which are essential to the picture."[83]

Sue and Dumas were unjustly neglected; so, for that matter, were most novelists who wrote in any tongue other than English. He thought that "Goethe was emphatically the great artist of the age," and that his *Wilhelm Meister's Apprenticeship* was second only to his *Faust;* it was in fiction "the masterwork of the great author of Germany." Simms objected heartily to the tendency to call Goethe's *Wilhelm Meister* merely a domestic story; it was a fiction designed for amusement, but it was at the same time "social, political, and philosophical." In it, Goethe demonstrated that through a "domestic story" an author could design a book for profound thought and meditation.[84] To Simms, this was undoubtedly the highest praise to be given to a domestic novel, but when some reviewer thought an Italian novel "the best specimen extant of Italian prose fiction," he did not hesitate to pronounce it inferior to Manzoni's *I Promessi Sposi*.[85] Simms, preferred in English or Italian a book that showed or at least indicated originality. Few writers did that. Manzoni did.

So did the Brontës. Simms was at first convinced that the authors were men. In various notices he praised their hard masculinity and rough native powers, and was quite surprised in 1850 to read that the author of *Jane Eyre* (his favorite among the Brontë novels) was a woman. *Wuthering Heights* seemed "clumsy," but in Jane the heroine and the woman were fused, and the novel, in spite of some coldness, monotony, and lapses of taste, exhibited "design, as well in the persons as the story."[86] He found George Borrow harder to place, and doubted that he was a novelist at all, but anyone who would read *Lavengro* "with regard to the writer himself, as his own subject," would find it "eminently provocative and commonly interesting."[87]

His enthusiasm for Anthony Trollope was genuine but somewhat limited. Books like *Dr. Thorne* and *The Bertrams* were "charming works of fiction"; the author was "generally amiable and clever"; his works were not dull or tedious, but the highest praise that Simms could give them was that they "might be held truthful" and show an "extreme fidelity to nature."[88]

In the "Literary Docket," George Eliot was "charged with a volume of domestic fiction called Adam Bede." The critical jury pronounced it "a good moral story; Adam was declared to be an admirable fellow, and to have worked out his mission in society with credit to himself and family; and George Eliot, to whom we owe the creation of this Adam, was bade go and make as many more of the same sort of persons as he pleased." Unfortunately, in her next attempt, George Eliot did not fully succeed: *The Mill on the Floss* was not up to the earlier novel, although the "author of Adam Bede is incapable of a positively bad book—incapable of a book which shall not interest, and in which there shall not be picturesque development and fine characterization . . . the catastrophe seems in conflict with all our ideas, not only of poetical and human justice, but of completeness and propriety." George Eliot had been guilty of resorting to the device of the inferior playwrights, "according to Latin satire," in requiring a *deus ex machina* (the flood) to resolve the novel.

When he reviewed *Felix Holt*, Simms had to make even sharper reservations and distinctions. The reviewers "all conspired to praise her, even in the face of her evident deterioration as a *novelist,* as a teller of interesting and absorbing stories. We make this distinction carefully, for as a woman of genius, a master of strong, graphic, good English, a keen appreciation and delineation of scenery and character, she still holds the high position which she reached almost at a bound. . . . But who can as a story compare 'Felix Holt' with its long side issues of local political discussion, its impossible plots and improbable personages, with 'Adam Bede,' 'The Mill on the Floss,' and the 'Scenes from Clerical Life.' "[89]

Although he was prejudiced against the English, he was not prejudiced against English novelists. Apparently he started a book with the idea, or at least the hope, that he would like it. He read many books unemotionally, for the sake of the information they contained, but his first and his ultimate test of a novel was that it should move him emotionally and interest him intellectually. Scott could almost always do it; Dickens, most of the time; Thackeray, rarely. He told his readers bluntly his own reactions to a particular book. Whether or not these reactions were right or wise, they were entirely his own.

III

Quite possibly the best of Simms's critical essays is on James Fenimore Cooper. Bryant praised it highly; so did Trent. Certainly it deserves praise. Simms expresses many times his personal disgust at being called a follower or imitator of Cooper, but Cooper was the best of American novelists; Cooper as writer had many defects, but his positive virtues had never been fully acknowledged; Simms attempted to point out the bad and the preponderantly good in Cooper's work. It is a magnanimous essay, yet even today it seems just.

Cooper's most notable achievement in *The Spy* and later romances was to open "the eyes of our people to their own resources." It was Cooper who "first awakened" Americans and Englishmen to a new and indigenous literature. Washington Irving with his "sweet and delicate essays" had not done this, for he "was not accounted in England an American writer, and he . . . took no pains to assert his paternity." Cooper let it be clearly understood that he was an American writer, and in his conflicts between hunters and Indians, in pursuits, flights, traps, pitfalls, captures and rescues, in cunning opposed to cunning, "Mr. Cooper

has no superior as he has had no master." His conception of
the frontiersman was "less true than picturesque," and even the
redoubtable Hawkeye was a "sailor in a hunting shirt," but the intensity that marked Cooper's best work made these portrayals "as
perfect, of their kind, as the artist of fiction has ever given
us."[90]

Cooper depended too much on highly dramatic scenes, and
too little on a carefully-wrought design. The defect in *The Spy,*
Simms thought, "was rather in its action than in its characters.
This is the usual and grand defect in all Mr. Cooper's stories."
But the author more than compensated for these defects by
"felicitous display of scenery," by "fine moral and dramatic pictures," by "intensifying every subject which affects his mind,"
and above all by superb native characters acting out their dramas
in a native scene.[91] Simms had no patience with local critics
who carpingly denigrated Cooper's achievement by emphasizing
his defects and minimizing his positive accomplishments, and he
protested vigorously against such treatment of the first writer "to
begin fairly the career of American letters."[92]

From his earliest days as a magazine editor, Simms had ar-
dently encouraged the development of a national and a regional
literature. When in 1828 he and James Wright Simmons started
the *Southern Literary Gazette,* they announced in the Prospectus
that their primary object was "to encourage the efforts and do
justice to the claims of native genius. . . . The Editors invite the
contributions of the literary gentlemen in general, and especially
of the South. Favors from their own immediate townsmen will
not, they trust, be withheld." These sentences might have fittingly served as an introductory to most of the magazines that
Simms later edited. Consistent also with his later point of view
was the insistence that our literature must be emancipated "from
its present state of feudal bondage and allegiance to those 'Master Spirits' of Great Britain."[93]

Simms (perhaps with the collaboration of his fellow-editors)
re-stated his belief in native genius in "Le Debut," the prefatory
article in *The Cosmopolitan* (1833). There was abundant talent
in country, state, and city, but too often it found an outlet only in
turbulent partisan controversy.[94] Although they did not invite
outside contributions, the authors hoped that as pioneers they
would encourage their fellow-citizens to write.

For those men who wrote even reasonably good American
books, there should be just recognition, and their Americanism

should be noted as a virtue. When he asked permission to dedicate *The Damsel of Darien* to James Kirke Paulding, he put it on the ground that Paulding was "among the most successful of our native authors,—as indeed, one of the fathers of our forest literature,—a leading Pioneer,"[95] and in the Preface itself as an author who had "never made any concessions to . . . foreign sway."[96] He did not care greatly for Paulding as a humorist, thinking him successful only in "his least ambitious efforts,"[97] but "admired him more as a downright sensible writer, hearty, frank and unaffected"; his work was not highly spiced, but it was not likely to pall upon the appetite.

Although he was on friendly terms with Robert Montgomery Bird and John Pendleton Kennedy, exchanged new books with them, and dedicated a book to each one, he was never unrestrainedly enthusiastic about their work. Bird's *Adventures of Robin Day* and, surprisingly, Kennedy's *Rob of the Bowl* he described as "very small performances."[98] Bird's work was "rich in merit," but except in *Nick of the Woods* he tended to dissipate his fictional energies on too many characters and to give too much information that, though "highly useful," is "out of place in such a rapid work as the romance";[99] Kennedy, "one of our most accomplished authors and orators,"[100] was better: in *Swallow Barn* he had given "genial and natural pictures of Virginia Life" and had effectively answered the abolitionists.[101] *Horse-Shoe Robinson* was even better, but here Kennedy had trespassed on Simms's own territory, and Simms in a letter warned him that "I join issue with you upon certain points of your Historical Summary, and suggest some shortcomings in the details of the story. . . . But all my fault-finding is done lovingly I think, and will not ruffle your plumage."[102]

He noticed the book first in an omnibus review, "Domestic Histories of the South," and then in an article-review. In each he wrote that Kennedy is "one of our favorites"; and *Horse-Shoe Robinson* is "one of our most stirring and truthful native fictions,"[103] and an "admirable characteristic narrative."[104] In dedicating *Count Julian* to Kennedy, Simms regretted that it was unworthy, but might serve as "one of the best of my own abilities, and of my respect for yours."

For Edgar Allan Poe as man and as critic Simms had mixed feelings and many reservations. Poe had brought many of his difficulties upon himself. "He is undoubtedly a man of very peculiar and very considerable genius—but is irregular and exceedingly mercurial in his temperament."[105] He was given to feuding and mystifying; he needed, Simms advised him, to "cast away those pleasures which are not worthy of your mind, and to trample those temptations underfoot, which degrade your person."[106] Moreover, as critic Poe had first noticed Simms by a "very savage attack on one of my novels"—*The Partisan*. The critical remarks on the story and the style might have been justified, although portions of the review were not just. But Poe had unfairly made his comments "rude and offensive and personal." These were grave defects, and Simms was not inclined to forget or to minimize them.[107]

Nevertheless, for Poe as creative writer he had the highest respect. After listing his grievances to Evert A. Duyckinck, Simms wrote that "He has more real imaginative power than 99 in the 100 of our poets and tale writers. His style is clear and correct, his conceptions bold and fanciful, his fancies vivid, and his taste generally good. His bolder effects are impaired by his fondness for *detail* and this hurts his criticism which is too frequently given to the analysis of the inferior points of style, making him somewhat regardless of the more noble features of the work. But, I repeat, he is a man of remarkable power."[108] In 1845 he added significantly to this estimate: Poe in his stories is "a writer of rare imaginative excellence, great intensity of mood, and a singularly mathematical directness of purpose . . . nothing more original, of their kind, has ever been given to the American reader."[109] The following year, in reviewing Poe's poetry, Simms added a larger note of praise by saying that "Some of his stories are the most remarkable specimens of the power of *intensifying* a conception of pure romance, to the exclusion of all the ordinary agents of fiction, which have been written."[110]

In his own imaginative stories Simms admitted a resemblance to those of Poe, "and partially of Hawthorne."[111] At times the latter was a "delicate, essayical prose writer," but he frequently wrote with the intensity of a poet, and he was always "quite unaffected" in his genius. Although a "tale writer, rather than a novelist . . . he has a rare and delicate fancy"; and though his range was limited, he was truthful in his delineation of character. Simms compared Hawthorne's "distribution" of light and shade with that of the ablest Italian painters, while his mind penetrated to the origin and the substance of evils. *The Scarlet Letter* had tremendous "concentrative power," but *The House of the Seven Gables* was "more truthful" to life. His domain in fiction was "peculiarly this fine one of the heart," and he entered, "with the art of Sterne, into the heart of his single captive." He was a "minute philosopher" and psychologist who lacked interest in action. *The Blithedale Romance* seemed "quite as successful" as the earlier novels: "It has all their defects, and these defects are such as seem inseparable from the author's mind. These lie chiefly in the shaping and conception of the work and in the inadequate employment of his characters."[112] Yet these were but minor blemishes, and Simms acknowledged that he had learned much from Hawthorne.

When he reviewed *The Marble Faun*, Simms not only praised the novel highly as showing "no falling off of his high powers"; he also wrote a rounded and glowing tribute to Hawthorne as author: "He is a man of genius, a man of fine original conceptions; of a taste at once delicate and masculine; of a nice blending of the sanguine and the spiritual; of exquisite sentiment; and a just recognition, along with it, of the sensuous and human. He cannot write commonplaces; and his readers, even when he may happen to fail utterly, as he rarely does, of the object at which he aims, will always, in spite of all failures, feel themselves in the keeping of one who not only thinks for himself, but will require them to do some thinking also. His genius is not of the bold and passionate order; he does not deal with men in masses, or with men in progress; hardly with men in action. In other words, he has few dramatic characteristics. But he has certain dramatic elements. He has design; he has fancy; can conceive, and enter into deep devotional moods. . . . He has the characteristic of the novelist; blending sentiment and a modified form of passion with reverie and contemplation."[113]

His opinion of Herman Melville was less clear-cut. Soon after 1840 Simms loosely allied himself with Evert Duyckinck, Cornelius Mathews, and the "Young America" movement. The members of this group or movement were almost violently advocating a distinctive American literature. Melville was Duyckinck's protégé, and Simms was genuinely fond of Duyckinck. Moreover, "Young America" was the sworn enemy of Lewis Gaylord Clark and the conservative critics, and in this period, as Perry Miller has phrased it, "the *Knickerbocker's* notices of Simms were concentrated poison, and those in the *Mirror* downright nasty."[114] Simms felt close enough to the group to write Duyckinck in 1844 that his projected *Southern and Western Magazine* would "in some measure afford us the organ we desire. Until you can get your press in N. Y. you must be content with a wing of it in Charleston."[115]

In addition, Simms apparently liked Melville and remembered him with some affection, for as late as 1867 he wrote that if he had known that Melville's brother was in Charleston, he would in spite of illness have called on Allan Melville.[116] As early as April of 1846 Simms had reviewed *Typee* enthusiastically, though he treated it as a travel book rather than as a novel: "a very curious and interesting narrative of savage life, and well deserving perusal. . . . We have every reason to believe that Mr. Melville is a veracious chronicler though it must be confessed he tells a very strange and romantic story."[117] *White Jacket* was convincing enough in its exposé of abuses in the Navy that it deserved "the equal consideration of government and people,"[118] and *Redburn* had much to commend it to the reader. But Simms thought *Mardi* a much better book; "wild, improbable and fantastic as was that allegorical production," it yet gave more proof of "real powers in reserve" than Melville's other work.[119] This was no slight concession on Simms's part, for Melville had done his best to spoil the work for Southern readers by painting "a loathsome picture of Mr. Calhoun, in the character of a slave driver drawing mixed blood and tears from the victim at every stroke of the whip."[120]

Even this qualified approval disappeared utterly when he reviewed *Moby Dick*. Although the sections on whales and whaling were "very interesting," the book itself was "sad stuff and dreary or ridiculous." In fact, the "ravings" of Captain Ahab and "those of Mr. Melville are such as would justify a *writ de lunatico* against all parties."[121] *Pierre* baffled him completely, and he confessed to his readers that he greatly feared Melville should be "put in ward," for he has gone "clean daft . . . certainly he has given us a very mad book, my masters."[122]

When he disapproved of a book, Simms had little regard for the reputation of the author. An anonymous novel, *The Swamp Steed,* revealed the writer's complete ignorance of South Carolina, as to terrain, people, and dialect. This was a defect of knowledge as well as of art.[123] Longfellow's *Kavanagh* failed for an entirely different reason: in spite of some passages of "beauty and felicity," it had only a "slight and commonplace" moral.[124] By 1845 Simms was also likely to be aroused to wrath by attacks on the South, and to damn a book for that reason alone: even his friend Catherine Maria Sedgwick, "one of our favorites—one of

those writers whom we always find it very safe to commend"
was castigated (in Simms's own words, "I shall be constrained to
reproach her gently") for her "unnecessary flings at the South."[125]

A puzzling yet amusing example of his surprisingly rare surrender to sectional prejudice came much later. In 1859 he wrote
a mediumly favorable review of John W. De Forest's *Seacliff*,
although it was weak in invention, "exception in the *dénouement*."
He implies also that he knew De Forest personally. When in 1867
he reviewed *Miss Ravenel's Conversion from Secession to Loyalty*, the infuriated Simms declared (forgetting, or deliberately
disclaiming, any previous knowledge) that it was by a writer who
"seems to have done other works, of which we know nothing."
The novel is "the embodiment of all the brutal malignity
Northern writers have ever conceived, or reported, to the slander
and misrepresentation of the South." As De Forest lacked "the
art-faculty of Mrs. Stowe," the book had in it nothing remarkable
except its "intense malignity, which has blackened every page with
a slander, and pointed every paragraph with a lie."[126]

Since he did not like Cornelius Mathews or his writings but
heartily approved his fight for an international copyright and for
an original American literature, Simms asked Evert Duyckinck
to review *Big Abel and the Little Manhattan* (1845) for his
Southern and Western Magazine.[127] He published what seemed
to him an excessively laudatory review, for the novel was "too
entirely New York" to interest those readers who were not familiar with the city: "A more qualified language in his behalf,
would not only be more just, but much more kind." When the
Knickerbocker attacked Mathews, Duyckinck counterattacked.
Simms thought that Lewis Clark deserved to be "scourged hip
and thigh. . . . But you have erred in making his assault upon
Mathews your particular text. . . . He is confessedly your
questio vexata in New York. Wilful in the employment of his
talents, rejecting wholesome counsel and quarreling with those
who bestow it, he perversely wars not less upon his own genius
than upon public opinion." Simms recognized Mathews as an
ambitious and sometimes an able writer, but his mind was essentially undramatic: "He seems fettered and frigid when his
business is to develope his story through the medium of other
agents. He does not succeed in grouping, and seems to lack the
required flexibility—the capacity to enter into the characters of
his persons, and to speak only in obedience to their necessities."[128]

Toward the younger Southern novelists Simms assumed the role of a generous but just mentor, who did not hesitate to tender advice both privately and publicly. This can be illustrated by two letters to John Esten Cooke, and two notices of his work. In July 1859 he advised the younger author to "work freely and frequently in papers which do not involve invention. Your error has been to have striven to write in fiction with as little reserve as in narrative and facts—topics. This cannot be done with safety. Fiction requires invention, more elaborate design, your whole heart as well as head; and these demand frequent pauses, when the Imagination may repose, and, looking up, catch new inspirations." Cooke scattered his energy and "divided the reader's attention among too many personages"; he was chiefly successful in "the liveliness and piquancy of the dialogue, and the saliency of feature in some of your portraits."[129]

When *Henry St. John, Gentleman* was published in 1859, Simms warned Cooke that "I find fault, as matter of course."[130] There is in Simms's notice in the *Mercury* a reasonable amount of praise for Cooke's portrayal of Virginia, for his doing justice to his section, and for his "life-like portraits"; there is qualified praise for the story as "lively, well sustained and interesting, without being deeply tragical, or intensively acting upon the imaginative and nervous systems"; there is also severe admonishment to the author: "He has done well, so far; but his sinews must be a little more seasoned by the proper exercise; his mind more patient, more deliberate, more sensible of the burden of the task, more grandly stirred within him, by the hourly growing sense of the value of his theme, so that he shall shape it with proper care, with a becoming purpose, and under a severer, sublimer design."[131] However unwelcome, this was excellent advice, though it must have seemed ironical to Cooke that it should come from William Gilmore Simms.

In his post-war reviews, Simms welcomed new or unfamiliar novelists, although he continued to distribute praise and fault-finding in what seemed to him a judicious manner. Two examples will suffice. He thought that *Dallas Galbreath,* by Rebecca Harding Davis, was a "strange compound of a good story well told, with characters that do violence to the popular conception of nature . . . in the conception of the plot she has displayed considerable tact and skill, and in her portrayings of the characters she has met in one or two instances with success."[132] More interesting is his treatment of Sidney Lanier's *Tiger-Lilies.* Since he was familiar with some of the author's "quaint, vigorous little poems," Simms expected to find the novel "sketchy, disconnected, strong, nervous, rhythmical—and we have not, on the whole, been disappointed." It was almost plotless, with little dialogue; but it was eminently suggestive, with a wealth of "illustration and poetic analogy." Sectional pride was still strong in Simms: "Southern literature may well thank Mr. Lanier for giving it a child of which it need not feel ashamed."[133]

IV

Simms's reviews, like his letters, were written hastily, with little or no revision. He intended to present fairly the intention of the author, as well as to judge his achievement, for he firmly believed that the "standards of good criticism require that the reader should glow with the same element which inspires the writer."[134] And he had thought long if not very systematically about literature. Like most nineteenth-century critics, he had discarded the idea that the universe is a harmonious machine for the concept that it is a growing organism. Likewise the literary work should grow under the hand of the novelist, but it should develop organically into a planned design.[135]

In a somewhat elaborate comparison, Simms depicts the growth of the novel as resembling the progress of a traveler taking a day's walk. He has companions; he passes through a varied landscape in variable weather; he is sometimes beguiled from the path; but toward the close of day he arrives at the object of his quest.[136] Yet all must be harmonious, in a way that actual life or history rarely shows it to be: "Hence, it is the artist only who is the true historian. It is he who gives shape to the unknown fact, —who yields relation to the scattered fragments,—who unites the parts in coherent dependency, and endows, with life and action, the otherwise motionless automata of history."[137]

Simms rarely achieved this goal in his own fiction; he was often fallible in judging the achievements of others. But he was constantly aware that such a goal existed. However imperfectly shaped and used, it gave a consistent and reasonably philosophical basis for his criticism of fiction.

V

"I Regard Poetry as the profoundest of human philosophies," wrote Simms in 1854; "poetry is the mysterious voice of the deeper nature lying in the heart, or in the depths of the great Nature spreading about and above us."[138] Poetry seemed to him "the foundation of the fine arts,"[139] and the finest expression of man's thought, his imagination, and his fancy. Many people thought of it as merely "a soothing pastime for writer and reader," and demanded little more of it than "lucid and liquid commonplaces."[140] This was a vulgar error. There might well be legitimate disagreements about the definition of poetry or the merits of a poet, but "his humanity, like his genius" must be catholic. Any writer worthy of the name drew his inspiration from the "deepest fountains of philosophy. He is not your versifier, simply. He is a thinker, a seeker, a discoverer, a creator."[141]

Poetry is "thought delivered in music . . . born of beauty";[142] it is "among the best agencies," and in some respects superior to formal religion, "to procure for us that wing which alone can lift us above the world." This did not imply vagueness, except insofar as it enabled the poet to escape from the literal: "Directness of aim, and concentration of thought do not necessarily imply the literal, and these, with Imagination and Fancy, as a decorative quality, are the whole source of power in poetry, and so of permanent reputation. Poetry is winged thought. It must be thought; this, founded upon close observation of man and nature, the moral and physical world. . . . Such, we find in Homer, Aeschylus, Milton, Dante, Shakspeare, and other great masters of the past. . . . To think and feel in poetry is the true secret."[143]

Simms had started writing poetry when he was about eight years old; although the bulk of his verse was written before he was thirty, throughout his life he continued to write new poems and to re-write and to publish his youthful verses. His real forte, he sometimes claimed, was in writing poetry instead of prose, and he was troubled and angry at his lack of recognition in this field. He wrote E. A. Duyckinck that "I flatter myself that my poetical works exhibit the highest phase of the Imaginative faculty which this country has yet exhibited, and the most philosophical in connection with it."[144] Even his youthful friend and admirer Paul Hamilton Hayne found this a gross misjudgment; when Simms fancied himself as a throw-back to the rugged Elizabethans, Hayne shuddered privately, however much he was willing to praise and defend Simms publicly.[145]

If he over-valued his poetry, Simms was certain that the so-called practical men erroneously undervalued all poetry. To be known as a poet or painter was directly harmful to a lawyer or a businessman, but this was based on a false notion of what was useful. In various articles and in a long unpublished lecture, "Poetry and the Practical," Simms developed his idea that religion and philosophy must teach "the worship of the *Ideal* as a corrective against the dangers of the *Real*."[146] Both the English and the Americans were eminently practical, but they were too much concerned with external and material conquests, too little with spiritual values (2-4).

In a discussion of the Bible and of the moral laws of God, Simms presents man as serving a kind of apprenticeship on earth before reaching a state of true goodness after death (9-14). God presents himself to man not through the Church and the Bible only, but through Nature and Art (here, specifically, poetry) as well. In phrasings reminiscent of Wordsworth and Emerson, Simms praises the daily-recurring miracles of nature, and the ability of the uncorrupted child-heart to absorb its lessons. (15-26). But men generally lack the ability to understand or to interpret. Here the poet must take over. Poetry has a minor use when it deals with man and the earth, with thoughts and moods, but at its best poetry helps us to turn from the animal and the inferior to the intellect and the divine (26-27; I, 15-18). For the poet is "the Prince of abstract ideas . . . the material is simply the medium for the expression of that imaginative truth which he possessed long before he gave shape to it in song." Paraphrasing Michelangelo, he agreed that the sculptor "beholds the statue in the rock, long before he seeks to give it outline with his chisel" (29-30). Figuratively, the poet works in the same way. Through the "Divine form of language," the poet "indicates the possible *real* to which the future may attain." Thus the abstract of today becomes the practical of tomorrow: "it is the shadow of the approaching *Reality*" (37-38).

Inspiration embodied in art strengthens the intellect, but it sustains the soul. Many people feel the need of church and priesthood for spiritual sustenance, but there are valuable and neglected auxiliaries in nature and art (47-67). For the poets were the first priests and prophets, and the "true Poet is one who brings us daily revelations of new truth, from him who is the source of all truth (70-73)." Poetry also is rich in its variety, and capable of appealing to all tastes and classes. For the unlettered, there was "Homer, singing from door to door. For the noble and the stately, the refined and lettered . . . minstrels like Tasso and

Ariosto, like Virgil and Campbell. For young Hearts, there is the earnest, and amorous Burns, and the passionate Byron; for the universal heart there is Shakspeare; Homer lights the fires of war, illuminates the wastes of history, and persuades to Fame; Wordsworth beguiles the soberer mood to contemplation, and Milton and Dante wing the Soul for Heaven with all the ardors of a Divine Enthusiasm. Enthusiasm, in fact, is the high and holy gift which the Poet imparts to Society; and enthusiasm is the great antagonist quality opposed to Self;—the vital element which informs all the nobler passions (74)."

When he enlarged the essay, Simms added an introductory section on early English poets. He began with a tribute to Chaucer as "the Father of English verse—a statesman,—an Ambassador abroad, shrewd always and sensible,—yet a Poet, with a genius at once tender and masculine—with an art that could persuade the loveliest landscapes to his canvas, yet depict, in the foreground, the homeliest aspects, true to the life, of his own rugged people; a delightful humorist, a sharp satirist, a man of keen observation and calm, discriminating judgment." Although not masters, Wyatt and Surrey were worthy followers who "refined upon the language of Chaucer." In life and in poetry, Sidney was an exemplar of "refined chivalry." But Spenser was the "first great poet after Chaucer . . . . What a rich variety, in thought and language, grace and strength, marches on, like an army, with the pomp of banners, and the joy of music, in his quaint array (I, 1-3)."

These English poets, with Gower, shaped our language. Other poets in other lands had done the same, often (as with Schiller) at a material self-sacrifice, partly because they minister to "all the wants of our nature—not as the nature of an animal,—but as the nature of a God" (III, 3). The poets have shaped language, preserved history, informed philosophy, and inspired science. Simms believed in the richness of the inner life and in the reliability of intuition; he believed in the civilizing powers of the fine arts, and especially of poetry; he believed that in this sense poetry was practical.

The self-described utilitarians were bent only on quick and immediate gains. They were short-sighted. Even of authors they demanded only something equivalent to the tyranny of trade, a rapid success commensurate to the hours of employment. In Simms's estimation, these values were false, and therefore ultimately non-utilitarian: "as the Literature of every nation constitutes its most enduring and honorable monuments, it follows that permanence and premeditation must enter largely into the spirit with which the laborer sits down to his task. The works of genius are labors always; not sports."[147] Now and then, a well-trained man might by accident achieve greatness through a casual production, but this seemed to him unlikely.

At the same time, he preferred to trust, for shorter lyrics, to impulse rather than to art. When Hayne objected to the lack of artistry in some of his works, Simms objected vigorously if not quite coherently: the lyrics "are *not* fugitives at all. They are mostly remarkable *improvisations,* refined subsequently by exquisite art—*Happy Inspiration. I object to studies of art* in a province which implies improvisation—lyrics really being bird gushes—involuntaries—unpremeditated."[148] In another letter he speaks of his lyrics as being "overflowings," and suggests that his correspondents do not understand the nature of the lyric. It may be that Hayne was more nearly right when he wrote that Simms was reluctant to undertake the onerous task of correction and revision.[149]

Yet there seems no reason to believe that Simms was not here expressing an honest opinion. W. P. Trent states dogmatically that Simms not only did not know how to write a sonnet, but did not have much idea of what a sonnet should be.[150] Unfortunately Trent mentions but does not reckon with Simms's trenchant if highly prejudiced remarks about English and Italian sonnets. Sensuous love sonnets could be written in the sinuous and flexible Italian language. But in English the strict form was a fetter, and "its uses will comport only with such grave subjects as demand severity, enjoin dignity and exhibit power and thought, and moral and will." In reviewing Hayne's *Avolio* (1860) Simms warns his friend that the love sonnets of Wyatt and Surrey are forgotten; Sidney and Milton chose the form not because of its appropriateness but because they were passionately fond of Italian letters; Shakspeare was wise enough to blend the metaphysical with the sensuous, yet his sonnets are "unlike and inferior in music, to the wonderful musical effects and exquisite felicities of his blank verse!" Of all the English writers Wordsworth has "in his political and ecclesiastical sonnets, done best of all . . . but, even in his hands, as in those of Milton, we still doubt if anything has been gained, by the thought, in the rigid form chosen for its utterance."[151]

Simms was not exactly ignorant of Italian literature; his trans-

lation of Dante's "Paolo and Francesca" episode was called by
Theodore Koch in his *Dante in America* highly creditable, and
Simms was familiar with Italian poetry and novels. But he did
not agree with Leigh Hunt and with Hayne[152] that the Italian or
"legitimate" sonnet was superior to the English, "a thing of freedom." The best of English sonnets, he thought, belonged to
what was "somewhat improperly styled the *Illegitimate* Sonnet."
As far as Simms was concerned, there were only two rules: a single leading idea, and compression into fourteen lines.

The flexible Tuscan language lent itself to an exact art form
and to the language of love; the sterner and less flexible English
did not regard "with much esteem the dexterity which delights
to multiply its fetters"; in the sonnet, as in all his other works,
he did not set much value on "pure art." Rather, he valued
moral differences: the Italians were "given mostly to themes of
tenderness, love and fanciful sentiment. But English and American Poets cannot make love in Sonnets. The very severity and
rigidity of the rule of art in the Sonnet is unfavorable to the expression of an earnest passion." Even Shakspeare's sonnets when
they deal only with love indicate how seriously they are "infected
by this weakness." But English and American poets had used the
sonnet for "sterner purposes." As it had developed in these countries, Simms believed, the sonnet was a "bolder, braver, manlier
thing than the Italian, and you cannot in all the collections of
Italy find any Sonnets to compare in thought, grandeur, dignity,
a sonorous emphasis, or masculine majesty" with those of Shakspeare, Milton, or Wordsworth.

He was more interested in content than in form. He was divided in writing poetry, he wrote R. W. Griswold, "between the
desire to appear correct, and the greater desire to be original
and true."[153] He set little store on certain of the grace notes of
poetry. Rhyme seemed to him "the mere decoration of
thought,"[154] and verse was essentially that, also. In a letter to
James Lawson, Simms defended his prose romance *The Damsel
of Darien* on the ground that it "is, indeed, a Poem."[155] His
words in The Prefatory Letter to *The Yemassee* are more moderate: the romance is the "substitute which the people of the
present day offer for the ancient epic. . . . It approximates the
poem." But neither verse nor rhyme seemed to him essential in
poetry. Unavailingly and perhaps a bit obtusely he advised
Thomas Holley Chivers to "seek for simplicity and wholeness. . . . Be manly, direct, simple, natural—be full, unaffected

and elaborate."[156] This described what Simms sought for in both the reading and writing of poetry.

He coveted fame as a writer and recognized that it could best be gained through imaginative works: "A fine song or a sonnet will make a reputation when a grave history will be forgotten. . . . Contemporaries seldom see this. They are more impressed with shows of labor and research than of invention. Were Shakspeare and Sir Thomas More now living, the latter would take rank of the former amongst all contemporaries. Yet look at the past! It is through the poets of the Hebrew; Homer and Aeschylus of the Greeks; Horace and Virgil among the Romans; Milton, Chaucer, Spenser, Shakspeare, among the English; Lope de Vega and Calderon among the Spaniards, etc., all writers of the imagination—poets simply," that later generations know and understand even the "histories of their several countries."[157] Hoping to be remembered, even if not in such august company, Simms published his poems (frequently at his own expense) in order to "put myself on record" for posterity.[158]

VI

In his early poetry Simms was most powerfully and directly influenced by Byron; in his later, by Wordsworth, "the greatest of all the tribe of contemplative poets. From 15 to 40 a man of blood enjoys Byron and Moore. After that he asks for the food of thought, and not of passion."[159] He did not consider them the greatest of English poets. Definitely ahead of them were Shakspeare, with his "universal song. . . . The mighty master-hand in his we trace"; Chaucer, who with his "healthy Muse" won respect for "native England's *tongue*"; probably Spenser, artful and mystifying, with his ability to "spiritualize the passionate, and subdue/ The wild, coarse temper of the British Muse"; and certainly Milton, a "Prophet Bard" with a "godlike voice" that allied earth to heaven.[160]

These were the giants. Even Wordsworth, with his "voice of purest thought in sweetest music,"[161] came behind them. As Simms uses the term, *contemplative* is by no means an unmixed compliment, for the "contemplative writer is usually a phlegmatic in temperament," who does not arouse the emotions as do writers like Scott and Byron who "appeal to the blood and the brain in common."[162] Wordsworth is neither a philosopher nor a philosophical poet; he is "certainly a thoughtful poet, but his reflections are not the results of laborious reasoning, but the suggestions of a meditative genius." He had no "predecessor of equal genius" in descriptive poetry. His pictures of natural scenery were at once felicitous and faithful, but through associations and analogies he allied the moral with the physical, the internal with the external. Except in the Lucy poems, there is little passion, and there is no sense of epic or dramatic action, but there are compensations: *The Excursion* has in it "more exquisite simplicity and purity of style than any approaching the same length since *Paradise Lost* was written," and *The Prelude* is "full of passages marked by his earnest sweetness, the grave delicacy of his mood, his habit of musing contemplation, and the rare philosophical simplicity which makes the analysis of his mind and writings so interesting."[163]

The Prelude seemed to him Wordsworth's finest poem. It is essentially the "biography of Wordsworth. There he has told us all it is necessary to know. . . . His great poem is the history of his own mind." Scott and Byron could be imitated because "they were more of artists," but although many had tried, no one had successfully imitated Wordsworth, for while never neglecting art, he had an individual philosophy of life: "An art may to some extent be acquired or borrowed, its tricks be learnt, but great principles must beget their own facts."[164] As a poet, Wordsworth had certain limitations that Simms recognized and pointed out, but he also thought Wordsworth easily the greatest of modern poets writing in English. It would be many years before a successor embodied in his work so many excellent qualities.[165]

Wordsworth had "done more than any other man to direct the tendencies and form the school of modern poetry," but he had been wrongly credited with being "the chief author of the cleansing process to which our English poetry had been subjected. To Cowper belongs this credit in the highest degree." It was William Cowper, not Wordsworth, who had rescued our poetry from "the sway of French taste and authority in letters," and Simms protested that both English and American critics had consistently underrated Cowper's achievement. For Cowper was a moral poet, of "admirable fancy, humor and wit," and of strong though not discursive imaginative faculties springing from a "singularly independent" mind.[166]

Simms was not belittling the value of Wordsworth's poetry or his poetic theories, but simply giving credit to an improperly neglected writer. He never doubted that Wordsworth was greater than Cowper, just as he was greater than Coleridge, who "had, perhaps, a richer and more inventive mind, a larger range of knowledge, quicker affections, and a more fiery enthusiasm. But he has left behind him no great monument to assert his unquestionable genius."[167] For Robert Southey he had at that time less regard, since in grace and beauty his poetry was inferior to Coleridge's, as in sustained and elevated poetic thought it was inferior to Wordsworth's. Much later, he praised Southey as a man, in spite of his partisanship, and wrote that "the grand and grotesque conceptions of his muse have never found a just, capable and appreciative critic."[168]

In Byron's work Simms was conscious of passion and power. Certain parts of *Childe Harold* seemed to him "noble verses . . . they stir my blood as the sound of a trumpet. The feeling of which they speak, is not only elevated, but what is more, it is natural and true."[169] But for all his attractiveness, there was in Byron and in his poetry a considerable flaw: if he had not given way to self-pity and licentiousness, "His muse had been triumphant over Time/As still she is o'er Passion."[170] In the Preface to *Donna Florida,* Simms hoped that he "might imitate the grace and exceeding felicity of expression in that unhappy performance (*Don Juan*)—its playfulness, and possibly its wit—without falling into its licentiousness of utterance and malignity of mood." Yet he felt, characteristically, that he had gone beyond imitation and achieved something original.[171]

Byron's aspirations had been greater than his performances. He was discontented with what he had done; if he had lived, he might have written far greater poems, since his "was not the vain, small spirit to be satisfied with the successes he had won."[172] Although Simms once called *Don Juan* "that book of excellently expressed commonplaces,"[173] he believed that Byron had revealed one phase of romanticism better than any other poet: his "Harold, his Manfred, nay, even his Don Juan, are full of strains whose true import is that of the stricken soul—the haunted conscience—the heart yearning for repose, and beginning to despair of hope."[174] He was a poet "of the terrific and intenser passions," but where Dante or Milton could give a scene "in a few bold touches . . . Byron has given it in details."[175]

Sir Walter Scott had none of the personal defects of Byron. As a writer of romances he stood supreme; as poet, he was like Homer in the rush and sweep of his action but he had achieved only a limited "trumpet lay of chivalry and pride."[176] This was a restricted but not a negligible achievement in *The Lady of the*

Lake and other verse romances "such as Scott has rendered so familiar to us, in that happy combination of the epic and the ballad which is destined to a long association with his peculiar genius." There could be found a model that American poets could use advantageously in treating such native legends as that of Pocahontas.[177]

Like Byron and unlike Scott, Robert Burns had noticeable personal defects. To Simms he was a man "of pride and sorrows, weak yet strong/With still a song discoursing to the heart." He was a "melancholy conqueror," a man of "capricious genius" who held mastery over his art but not over his "own irregular soul."[178] Simms used Burns to advantage through his alter-ego, the partisan-poet George Dennison, who like Burns was a writer of native melodies, rude perhaps but "sweet and simple, and withal very touching."[179] Burns had also a secondary strength: because of his desire to "make some song which would live 'for poor old Scotland's sake,' " many of his poems possessed for his readers "a sort of symbolical influence," and Burns gained added power because he spoke "in the fulness of his own soul, and from the overflowings of a burdened heart." This was an incidental value that accrued to the national poet, for his song was that of "an aroused and earnest mind," and this impassioned earnestness roused like emotions in his readers.[180]

Although in casual, unchecked quotations he sometimes confused lines by Shelley and Keats,[181] Simms after the war desired to replace his destroyed copies of their works,[182] and he included Shelley in a poem on a group of poets, characterizing him as "a changeling" who sang "Vague minstrelsies," but whose "spiritual" voice leavened the earthiness of the times.[183] By 1828 he was familiar with their work; in an otherwise damning review in the *Southern Literary Gazette* of Leigh Hunt's *Lord Byron and his Contemporaries,* the anonymous reviewer digresses to note that the "only portion of the book worth reading, is the account of Shelley and Keats—men of genius both, the latter of high promise, and untimely end." Shelley's personal frailties had not only brought him misery but ended his hopes of "high distinction as a poet." He thought better of Keats, who "had published very little, but that little is we think of a high order."[184] The next year Simms, this time clearly in his own right, praised Keats as "possessed of a high degree of promise" and stated that "In some future notice, we shall speak of him more at large."[185] If this notice was ever written, it has not been identified.

Alfred Tennyson seemed a worthy successor to Wordsworth, although inferior to the older poet. Tennyson deserved praise, for he "has the spirituality of Shelley, without his intensity, and the contemplative nature of Wordsworth, with much more enthusiasm." Except for *In Memoriam,* which tended to become monotonous, he combined artistry, subtlety, and variety.[186] But Tennyson's great popularity and the ease with which he could be imitated presented a great danger to young poets: Simms advised Charles Warren Stoddard that "You must study Tennyson less, and the earlier masters more. You should get back to Milton, Shakespeare, and Dryden."[187]

As early as July, 1848, Simms knew Robert Browning's work and admired it enough to include a stanza on him for a book of poems on poets, edited by Caroline Gilman. Although Mrs. Gilman used only the section on Scott, Simms had included verses on most of the English poets that he liked: Chaucer, Spenser, Milton, Shakespeare, Byron, Scott, Burns, Moore, Campbell, Shelley, Wordsworth, Horne, Browning, Barrett, and Tennyson, as well as a separate sonnet, "The Old Masters," on Dante, Petrarch, and Michelangelo.[188] The long poem on English poets undoubtedly is either a rough or a final form of his "Heads of the Poets"; in it, Simms groups Tennyson, Robert Browning, Elizabeth Barrett, and R. H. Horne as writers who speak "For that fresh nature, which, in daily things,/Beholds the immortal."[189] Of these, Browning, although his power of poetic utterance was inferior to his thought, was probably considered the best, for in a review in 1850 Simms described him as "no common verse-maker. He is a writer of thought and genius, of peculiar and curious powers as an artist; subtle, spiritual, and singularly fanciful, and though as yet perhaps unacknowledged, is one of the master minds of living European song. He is obscure, however, and will scarcely ever reach that degree of popularity which follows only the limpid and lucid. . . . When his peculiar phraseology shall become familiar to the ear, it will compel an admiration which is very far from general now."[190]

The English poet in the post-war years who roused his greatest interest was A. C. Swinburne. Simms was isolated from books, and on December 19, 1865, he wrote to E. A. Duyckinck to send him, among others, "a new Poem on the model of the Greek Drama, 'Somebody in Calydon,' of which I have heard loud mention."[191] Swinburne and Tennyson between them had even made long poems popular in magazines,[192] but his admiration for

Swinburne's skill was more than counterbalanced by distaste for his tone. He noted perceptively, however, that "the prurience of passion, in these poems, is of a metaphysical sort, and is, for this reason, measurably harmless." Simms concluded that some of the verses in *Poems and Ballads* must have been written when Swinburne "was drunk"; in such earlier publications as *Atalanta in Calydon* he had shown himself admirably endowed, a flexible, elastic and lucid poet "even when most lofty in his flight."[193]

Although Simms had shown a similar moral bias earlier, it may be that Swinburne had simply come too late in his life for a just appreciation. He could find virtues in Horne's *Orion* and in Phillip James Bailey's *Festus* that elude the modern reader, although he was not blind to their faults;[194] he praised Sir Henry Taylor's *Artevelde* highly and linked his name with Tennyson as a great poet, but Hammond complained justly that his long article was a non-committal synopsis with copious quotations, written hastily to fill up that number of the *Southern Quarterly*.[195] Thomas Campbell and Thomas Moore he linked as appealing to readers in "our gentler moods," but not lifting the readers beyond beguilement they "leave us, where they found us."[196] Winthrop Mackworth Praed was even more a minor poet, but he was a man of fanciful and capricious fancy, who "mingles the fantastique and the grotesque with considerable felicity." He lived in an atmosphere of rhyme, and was a spontaneous singer, "always graceful, spirited, proper in sarcasm and sentiment, full of good sense. . . . He was as near to being a real poet as possible."[197] Thomas Hood was even better in presenting the contrasting "extremes of fun and pathos . . . we have at his hands the most touching passages of sentiment, and the most quizzical bits of fun."[198]

Generally, Simms could find virtues in a poet's work to balance against the defects. A few times he was irritated or disgusted enough to write a blistering attack, without any attempt at mitigation; a representative and amusingly-phrased example is his blast at Martin Farquhar Tupper: "It is a 1,000 pities that a man who has such an 'alacrity in sinking' as Tupper, should not permit himself to subside quietly to the bottom . . . as happens frequently with a diseased oyster. . . . N. P. Willis had the honor of first fishing him up, and holding him out, limp and dripping to the American people. . . . Had he been content to rest on the laurels thus won, the Philosophy would still have kept its place on the tables of sentimental grocers and have furnished the inspiration of gushing school girls. Unfortunate Tupper! had you lived in the age of the Dunciad . . . Pope, with the instincts of genius, would have hailed you Prince of Grub-street."[199]

Simms's taste was mainly formed by nineteenth-century and Elizabethan poets. A voracious reader, he devoured the work of the major and many of the minor poets, of all periods; a constant reviewer, he commented energetically on any new editions of older poets that were sent to him. Moreover, he sprinkled allusions, quotations, and slight misquotations throughout his novels. When a very young soldier kills his first enemy, after describing his feelings, Simms added that he "looked the picture of the personification in the ode of Collins, where Fear—recoils, he knows not why,/Even at the sound (*wound*) himself hath made."[200] An egotistical, addle-pated gallant "talked poetry by the Canto and felicitated himself on the equal taste with which he enjoyed Butler and Cowley—the antipodes of English poets."[201] In his own right Simms in *Eutaw* takes a fling at "such geniuses as Pye, and Whitehead, and Warton, successively poets-laureate. We may judge readily of the sort of poets which could willingly sing the glories of the Guelphic dynasties of the Georges—first, second, or third."[202] In general, critical commentary is rare and incidental, for Simms was mainly drawing on poets for illustrative purposes.[203]

He also makes abundant use of quotations and allusions in non-fictional writing. In a single letter to James Lawson, Simms misquotes a Milton sonnet and a line from *Othello,* quotes from *Macbeth* and Samuel Johnson's "Vanity of Human Wishes" and from Milton's prose correctly, and has references to *As You Like It* and Ben Jonson.[204] He drew on Thomas Gray's "The Bard" and Oliver Goldsmith's "Elegy on the Death of a Mad Dog" with equal ease and fervor.[205] In his reviews, likewise, there are frequent comparisons and occasional critical asides. Although Wordsworth had no predecessor of equal genius, James Thomson "in his 'Seasons' had drawn admirable pictures of nature, but they were all injured by the somewhat extravagant diction of the period in which he wrote . . . they rather dazzle than please."[206] When his story "The Loves of the Driver" was attacked as vulgar and obscene, he quoted from the "Moral Poet" Alexander Pope, and noted that, along with such diverse writers as Shakspeare and Goldsmith, Pope had portrayed human beings so exactly and graphically that even he "could not have escaped" nineteenth-

century censorship.[207] His respect for Pope as a serious professional poet, and thus not kin to the artificial poetasters or gentlemanly amateurs, he imbedded in an article on copyright.[208]

Usually his comments on Shakespeare and Dryden deal with
them as dramatists rather than directly as poets. Shakespeare's
non-dramatic work, he thought, had "never yet been properly
examined . . . their analysis, from new points of view, will
probably make the reader acquainted with beauties in them
which few conceive them to possess." This analysis would also reveal that the sonnets were in essence autobiographical: "They
are more essential than all his dramas to any just idea of the moral
nature, and the temperament, of their author."[209]

Milton's *Paradise Lost* was the touchstone by which he judged
contemporary epics and religious poems. As early as 1828, he
vigorously attacked Robert Pollok's *The Course of Time* as consisting "neither of poetry nor verse," and contrasted its feebleness with the "truly Epic grandeur" of the older poem.[210] The
scheme of Robert Montgomery's *Messiah* he found vaster, more
intricate, and more detailed than Milton's, but his execution undramatic, inefficient, incoherent, and declamatory.[211] Although
Montgomery's poem was not successful artistically, it shared "the
grand defect" of most religious poems in that the author approached his subject as an artist, without inspiration. But the
great religious poet must have passions: "in the agonies of pain
or pleasure he finds utterance." In fact, the great poets, regardless
of subject, "were all of them men of griefs and agonies."[212] The
religious poets write "not as a graceful exercise of the mind . . .
but because they are forced to do so, by the struggling and
striving feeling within them. . . . Its language must be that of an
emotion so deeply aroused and enkindled, as to rise above all
ordinary forms of expression."

Of relatively modern poets, only Milton and Dante deserve to
rank with such Old Testament poets as Job and David. In
spite of the grandeur of his theme, Milton could sustain himself, as Montgomery could not: "That Milton is great, is rather
because he has not, and could not, have fallen so low as any other
human genius. That he is equal to his theme, unless in a sense
purely comparative, must be denied." This was an ideal judgment; when human and earthly standards were applied, *Paradise
Lost* was clearly the best original religious poem in English.

In a sense, Simms's judgments were personal ones. But they
were downright and honest. They were also based on wide and

reasonably careful reading. Immediacy of appeal never led him to think or write of Wordsworth as a better poet than Milton. He never sharpened and rarely troubled to define his standards, but he did have certain criteria that as critic he undeviatingly held to. With these as touchstones, he decided upon and somewhat dogmatically delivered his personal judgments. Most of these have elements of validity in them; many are just and sensible; some are, truly, perceptive.

VII

Friendships, prejudices, and enmities naturally played a greater part in Simms's treatment of American than of British poets. His allegiance was first of all to South Carolina; then to the South; finally to Philadelphia and New York. Although he became personally fond of some New Englanders and praised highly some New England writers, he seems never to have felt at home there, personally or intellectually. He was convinced that these writers possessed didactic rather than inventive powers; no mystic himself for all of his later interest in spiritualism, he believed that transcendentalism in America was mostly "balderdash, and very bad balderdash at that."[213] He would not have admitted to any prejudice; he was simply setting down the facts as they existed. Unorthodox himself, he approved of the ideas in Emerson's essays although he deprecated their "Carlyleisms"—not as underrating Carlyle, but as objecting to an American being "this or that Englishman's man." Although Emerson's essays in their content "declare a mind of his own," Simms preferred his poetry, as being "at once fresh, felicitous, and true."[214]

This was honest but in a sense qualified praise. There was no doubt in Simms's mind that William Cullen Bryant was the best of American poets. When his close friend James Lawson in 1839 wrote of "finding fault" with Bryant as a poet, Simms begged him, in terms that possibly over-stated somewhat his own beliefs, not to publish the essay: "I do not mean to say that he is faultless—for who can be?—but I must say I never met with a writer, ancient or modern—English or American so uniformly correct. Beware then, lest you suffer a difference of taste, to lead you to a false judgment. A difference of taste does not justify censure; and where you have to deal with one so perfect as Bryant, you should rather infer the things which do not please you, were not written for you, and not that they are censurable or unworthy . . . a boyish criticism of mine pronounced him the first American Poet, when, so far as my knowledge went, the judgment found no concurrence from any other quarter."[215]

In 1828 Simms had written that the *North American Review* and *American Quarterly Review* were unwise and uncritical in proclaiming Percival's "Ode to Seneca Lake" as superior to similar poems by Bryant and Byron. Percival's work is commonplace. Bryant's poems are not. He is, in fact, "justly ranked as the first of American poets" and his "chaste and beautiful productions would do honor to any age or country." In an editorial note Simms adds that Bryant's merits and Percival's demerits are equally obvious.[216]

This was written before the two writers met in 1832; later they became friends and exchanged visits; just before and during the war the friendship was broken off; afterward, they became friends again. But Simms never changed in his critical judgment. Bryant in America was doing what Wordsworth did in England; he worked from the internal and moral idea to ally it with the external and physical world of nature; he was worthy of being compared with Wordsworth, though by no means the equal of the English poet. He wrote better blank verse than Cowper. Wordsworth and Cowper were in Simms's estimation rightfully among the masters; yet he did not hesitate to link Bryant's name with either of them.[217]

Simms's warmest personal tribute was published in 1842. In this essay he talks of their friendship, describes Bryant and his way of life, and of the times indoors and out that he has heard Bryant read poetry. Yet even in this personal tribute, Simms presented what he considered a just rather than a laudatory appraisal of the poet: after noting "the exquisite polish of his poetry," Simms adds that his mind is "rather discriminating than profound; his genius is manly rather than bold, and we suspect that his fancy is somewhat enfeebled by his fastidiousness. . . . He could never become a passionate poet," partly because of a trait that deserved high praise, the "delicacy of his tastes." Simms quoted the newly-published "Antiquity of Freedom" with the comment that it "is distinguished by his usual characteristics—a calm, contemplative philosophy . . . some forcible lines; and conceptions rather bolder, in some instances, than those which usually mark Mr. Bryant's writings."[218]

Possibly Simms's finest tribute to Bryant was written in 1859, after they had disagreed politically. It is also a fine example of Simms's objectivity in judging literary works. The Richmond

Enquirer had published an editorial calling Bryant "An Inditer of Mean Doggerel." To this Simms responded vigorously: "We find Wm. Cullen Bryant referred to as one 'whose vocation it is to write poetry without the inspiration, as a poor inditer of mean doggerel.'

"Now the express purpose of the editorial is the exposure and denunciation of the political course of the New York *Evening Post* —a most laudable object. . . . Why, should the Editor of the *Enquirer* go out of his way to attack Bryant the Poet, when his sole business is with Bryant, the black Republican? Why should he make himself, at the outset of his argument, supremely ridiculous by attempting to deny the poetical claims of a man, whose fame was probably established long before his wise critic was born?"[219]

Simms was personally fond of Fitz-Greene Halleck, describing him as a genial, humorous, witty person who "never forgot the gentleman in the poet."[220] In 1845 he seemed "one of our few classics." Simms defined the characteristics of his poetry, listing "its terseness, its felicitous turns of expression, its epigrammatic points, its adroit playfulnesses." His poetry depended for appeal on the mode of expression rather than the thought expressed. Although the thoughtful poet belonged to an entirely different and higher order, Simms noted that he was only attempting to place, without disparagement, Halleck's work, "for which we have very high esteem."[221] In a review in June, 1830, he had linked Bryant and Halleck as "among the very first metrical men of the country," noting that Halleck was a graceful writer who developed his individual works "with much polish and infinite judgment."[222] But even his best poems were "soon fathomed— they have no profundity. . . . Halleck, I suspect, lacks a high moral sense, and wit and humor form no necessary constituents of the poetical character—nay, I am inclined to think that they subtract from the earnestness of purpose and design, which, as much as any thing besides, leads to the effectual accomplishment of any very elevated poetical task."[223]

Halleck was far better than Joseph Rodman Drake, whose "Culprit Fay" struck him as "fanciful not imaginative—the measure is not good and the conceits not only stale but puerile." Drake deserved only a New York reputation, but Halleck for all his faults had been badly underrated throughout the country: in his special vein he was a true if minor poet.[224]

Simms had misgivings about the value of Longfellow's work. It was "delicate, graceful, ingenious," but it was derivative, and limited by the "extreme simplicity" of his thought.[225] He considered Poe "more than half right" in accusing Longfellow of plagiarism[226] (possibly influenced by his affiliation with the "Young America" group and by his friendship with Evert Duyckinck), and as late as 1869 he still thought that Longfellow, "who stole from everybody," in his tragedies had certainly "*gazed* upon" the *Witchcraft* of Cornelius Mathews. In his fury at this supposed theft Simms admitted that Longfellow "has been clever enough as an artist, to conceal his thievings. . . . Were L. as great a Poet as he is an artist, he might take Cowper by the hand. Dante would not suffer an introduction."[227] Many of Longfellow's shorter pieces were "tasteful and pretty," but they were essentially the work of "an adroit artist" who lacked "invention."[228] Occasionally they were powerful: "The Skeleton in Armor" he described as "a spirited Norse ballad by Longfellow which is a devilish sight more like poetry than his 'Blacksmith' stuff."[229]

He did not like the longer poems. *The Song of Hiawatha* seemed to him "dreary, irredeemable nonsense," and *Evangeline*, very little better, a "comparative failure." Yet "such of his verses as appeal to the affections, are household songs throughout the land. Upon these productions, rather than upon any of his elaborate efforts, we are convinced his fame must rest.[230] In spite of his great defects, Longfellow had earned this limited fame since, in the best of his lyrics and sonnets, for "purity, grace, sweetness, the consistency of tone, the charm of manner, the delicacy of his fancy, and the melody of his strain, it would be scarce possible to find his equal among living poets, and still more difficult to assert that he has any superior."[231]

James Russell Lowell, "more of a poet and less of an artist," was perhaps better. He was vigorous, fecund with thoughts and fancies, although too subservient to Boston opinion and too much given to fugitive works.[232] But Lowell gave Simms a chance to "pepper Yankeedom," and in two reviews of *A Fable for Critics* he made the most of this opportunity, complaining that Lowell had many "flings" at the South that were "mere impertinences, not called for by his subject, but lugged in by the head and shoulders," and these exhibit in the author "a bad, malicious heart." Lowell was better in his thoughtful and sentimental than in his satirical poems, although *A Fable* had some good as well as many bad points: "It is sharp and sometimes spicy, playful and fanciful, amidst much clumsiness and cumbrousness. But the fable is feeble, the point is not apparent, and the malice much more conspicuous than the wit."[233]

Whittier he objected to as the author of "offensive abolition poems," but he admitted that although declamatory in manner, they showed energy and life. Yet his talent was didactic rather than imaginative, and best suited for the occasional ode, which he successfully made into a "fierce lyric."[234]

Simms wrote to E. A. Duyckinck as late as December 30, 1855, that "I should like to know Holmes."[235] He felt that Holmes was humane in a way that Lowell and Whittier were not. Five years later, he found *The Professor at the Breakfast Table* a book to take up frequently and with pleasure, for the Professor is "discursive, oracular, thoughtful, playful, with a mixture of fancy and philosophy." Simms would like to have his creator as a guest, "in order to enjoy the Professor's eloquence from his living mouth."[236] He likes Holmes's verse, although when he compared his own *City of the Silent* with Holmes's poem at the dedication of Pittsfield Cemetery, he thought his own work vigorous and imaginative, that of Holmes "feeble and commonplace."[237] This was not usually true. Most of Holmes's poems were "trenchant enough, but not ill-natured." Moreover, Simms had the highest respect for Holmes's technical skill: "The verse flows with great smoothness, is roughened with dexterity, so as to prevent monotony, and is full of vivacity."[238]

In 1853 Simms characterized George Henry Boker's poetry as "quaintly thoughtful and picturesque." He met Boker, liked him, and corresponded with him, although Simms's letters have not been located. Gradually he came to feel that Boker was the best writer of sonnets in the United States,[239] and in 1867 he stated sweepingly (perhaps only with sonnet-writing mainly in mind, since he was reviewing *The Book of the Sonnet*) that Boker was "the most really able, various and powerful of all the poets which the Northern States have produced."[240] This review surprised and pleased Boker, who had not expected to receive critical "justice" from such unreconstructed Southerners as Simms and Paul Hamilton Hayne. For Boker's fellow-Pennsylvanian, the "buoyant" Bayard Taylor, Simms had far less regard, although he enjoyed talking with him and reading his travel books; but Taylor's poetry exhibited neither profound emotions, nor deep thinking. It was "sweet and graceful throughout," for Taylor presented "well known sentiments in very felicitous phraseology," but it was picturesque surface poetry, excellent of its kind, but one got its full value on the first reading.[241]

Edgar Allan Poe had genius. Simms never doubted that. It was questionable, however, that Poe had wisely or completely employed his talents. Poe's mind was "curiously metaphysical and subtle," his imagination probing and daring,[242] but his genius was bizarre and he was, Simms feared, "too much the subject of his moods—not sufficiently so of principle." He found Poe's writings "always interesting," although when Poe "contended for fugitive performances" he was only rationalizing "his own short comings."[243] But critics who tried to apply literary standards applicable to Dryden or Pope misunderstood and misjudged Poe's work. He did not help the reader with moral axioms or philosophical maxims; he demanded that the reader "surrender himself to influences of pure imagination." The reader who can yield himself will find a "severe symmetry," and a remarkable intensity: as in his stories, "How intensely he can pursue, to its close, a scheme of the imagination—imagination purely—rigidly defining his principles as he goes, step by step, and maintaining to the sequel, the most systematic combinations of proprieties and dependencies." Yet if Poe seemed notable chiefly for his use of imagination and intensity, he had also as characteristic qualities the "music of the verse, the vagueness of the delineation, its mystical character, and dreamy and spiritual fancies."[244] These were good qualities, but Poe's avoidance of the concrete, with his reliance on imagination and fancy, "wings his thoughts to such superior elevations, as to render it too intensely spiritual for the ordinary reader."[245]

The fact that Poe's poems and tales constituted a remarkable contribution to American literature did not make him a good model for other writers. "You show too greatly how much Poe is in your mind," he complained to Thomas Holley Chivers. As a poet Chivers had many good qualities: poetic ardor, command of language and fluency of expression, skill in versification, delicacy of taste, and spirituality; but, like Poe, he was willful and perverse.[246] *The Lost Pleiad* (1845) had excellent poems in it, but suffered from a monotony brought on by the author's writing too subjectively of personal bereavement: "He allows the man constantly to interfere with and to thwart the objects of the poet." Too much of his work was elegiac and individual, written too immediately out of personal emotion. Chivers was too good a poet to continue on "his present erroneous career," he concluded sternly.[247] In 1852 and 1853, in a personal letter and in brief reviews, he again attempted to persuade Chivers away from subjectivity and mysticism, for "You have too much real ability to be suffered to trifle with yourself and reader."[248] Chivers was not grateful, but in his turn accused Simms of having "a perfect *contempt* for what may be called the Art of Composition."[249]

A major reason for being severe on able, gifted writers grew out of Simms's great desire for a valid American and Southern literature. His friend Cornelius Mathews had fine natural endowments; in two reviews of Mathews' poetry, Simms notes his promise and his power, but perversely Mathews "studies hard to wrong his talents" by over-indulging his liking for obscurity and a strained originality, and by refusing to master the techniques of versification.[250] H. T. Tuckerman with his "gentle, musical, and contemplative" poetry revealed a mind "more tasteful than searching"; both in his poetry and his essays Tuckerman needed "an occasional painstaking roughening of the style."[251] Poets of a limited accomplishment like Frances Sargent Osgood he was ready to accept lightly, for in her fluent and exuberant verse, "free from grave thoughts and deep philosophies," she was undoubtedly writing as well as she could.[252] It was different with Mathews and probably with Tuckerman; it was different with the remarkably gifted A. B. Meek of Alabama, who lazily preferred to remain a dilettante instead of working to become a first-rate poet.[253] Simms regretted especially the untimely death of Philip Pendleton Cooke, for though "less of the artist than Longfellow," he had "a far more active and native fancy. . . . His original ballads have all the characteristics of Froissart, and of the Ballad mongers of his day."[254]

In Southern and especially in South Carolina writers Simms sought for qualities worth praising, and he recommended a generous patronage without too much regard for literary quality, since only by encouraging young authors could the region hope to develop a literature. If a sufficient number of able young men became writers, the quality of some of their work would undoubtedly be high.[255] In the meantime, he praised whenever possible the work of older Charlestonians like William Henry Timrod and William J. Grayson.[256] Although he personally disliked and distrusted James Mathewes Legaré, he described the poems in *Orta-Undis* as "full of instances of rare felicity of

phrase, happy turns of thought, analogies equally sweet and curious, and fine moralities that crown the verse, at its close, with a
sudden surprise and beauty." Too often he had merely "caught
up the overflow of his fancy," but that was delicate and sweet.[257]
Washington Allston was a professional painter, and he had given
serious attention to aesthetics: "his acknowledged familiarity
with all those laws of taste which are equally essential to the
proper direction of poet as well as painter, will necessarily make
every syllable that he has written upon the subject of art, a word
of weight." Simms could praise the "gentle, benign, and thoughtful" man; the painter and aesthetician; and the author of the
novel *Monaldi*—from which he quoted copiously. But Allston
definitely was "not a poet in the high, perhaps the only proper
sense of the term. He was not an original thinker in verse,—not
a seer,—not inspired. His poems are rather those of the accomplished and educated gentleman,—the man of taste and purity,
of grace and sentiment, than the poet. . . . His intercourse with
the muse is not one of passion. His amours are purely
platonic."[258]

After 1850 Simms set his hopes in poetry mainly on his young
friends Henry Timrod and Paul Hamilton Hayne. Sometimes
they behaved like fractious nephews, disregarding the sound and
competent advice he gave them; Timrod in particular did not
always conceal his scornful impatience with Simms's Johnsonian
pronunciamentos on poetry, although in a letter now lost he acknowledged that "Somehow or other, you always magnetize me
on to a little strength."[259] As Hayne remembered it, there had
never been a cloud of any kind on their relationship, but Simms
in April 1857 was hurt because Hayne and John Russell, as editor
and publisher of the newly-started *Russell's Magazine,* "have
equally forgotten that such a person as myself exists. They have
both sucked the orange and neither values the skin."[260] These
were temporary irritations. For his young friends Simms had a
genuine liking and admiration.

Timrod was physically frail and morbidly sensitive. Unlike
Simms, he wrote slowly, "with great pains-taking and labour."
But he was indubitably "one of our truest and purest native
poets";[261] he was not flexible, but he was "refined and highly
polished, with fine meditative tone, and a pure and graceful
fancy."[262] Simms rather tended to underrate the intellectual
content in Timrod's poems on nature and the emotional feeling

implicit in his war poems. Timrod had genius and artistry, but he "was not passionate; he was not profound; he laboured in no field of metaphysics; he simply sang . . . with a native gift, of the things, the beauties, and the charms of nature. He belonged, in the classification of literary men, to the order that we call the contemplative." Simms admired his skill in versification and "felicitous turns of thought and expression," so that "whether he sang of his own or the loves of others, the open purity of his genius refined equally the thought which he expressed and the verse in which he clothed it."[263]

Hayne had certain virtues that Timrod lacked. Hayne was friendly and cheerful; he showed a more open-hearted admiration of Simms; in fact, of all the young South Carolina writers, Hayne became Simms's closest and dearest friend. Moreover, he was industrious, and Simms thought that "Industry will tell even in so poor a profession as literature, which is hardly a profession in so poor a world of art as ours."[264] Hayne's greatest defect was that he *"deliberately sat down to manufacture a long series of provocative and exciting events into lyrics,"* instead of writing out of inspiration, imagination, and passion. This revealed a mistake on Hayne's part as to the nature of the lyric, which should be an unpremeditated overflowing of the poet's spirit. Simms complained of this somewhat mechanical quality in Hayne's poem on poets, "The Southern Lyre," although generally it was "a very felicitous performance, chaste, graceful, fanciful, and very happily versified throughout. You have done singularly well in handling a subject, which required very nice skill, discrimination, tact, and the appreciation of effects and characteristics."[265]

But his long three-part review[266] of Hayne's *Avolio* (1860) is disappointing. He excuses himself for having postponed the review because "the popular mind alternates between a sweat and a stew!" His own mind was absorbed by politics; but seizing "a moment of respite—from political pressure," he wrote a somewhat perfunctory analysis of Hayne's work. Some praise is freely given, qualified by much heavy-handed advice. At his best Hayne "soars as well as sings. . . . He possesses, indeed, a variety of notes, some of them of large compass—all of them sweet and musical, and many of them no less vigorous and passionate than fanciful and rich." But over-use of the Fancy makes his poetry too voluptuous and ornate; and Hayne erred grievously, Simms thought, in trying to write sensuous love poems in the sonnet form. Simms preferred the longer narrative poems as being more finished and more delicately told.

In his *War Poetry of the South* (1867), Simms included practically all of the best war poems of Timrod and Hayne, with a generous selection of his own work. These represented, he was convinced, the best work done by Confederate poets. He undertook the work primarily because of the "goad of that necessity which makes money so precious to me at this moment";[267] the selecting and editing were done hastily, but even so the task entailed a heavy correspondence and a difficult job of selection. He was especially pleased to be able to present the work of many men whom he valued as friends even more highly than as poets; he went to considerable effort to see that S. Henry Dickson, J. Dickson Bruns, William J. Grayson, John Esten Cooke, John R. Thompson, Margaret Junkin Preston, James Barron Hope, James Ryder Randall, Francis O. Ticknor, A. B. Meek, and A. J. Requier were fairly represented. These were minor poets, but within rather strait limits he thought them valid and authentic versifiers, and at times truly poets, though under the stress of emotion they were "speaking out with a passion which disdains subterfuge, and through media of imagination and fancy, which are not only without reserve, but which are too coercive in their own nature, too arbitrary in their influence, to acknowledge any restraints upon that expression, which glows or weeps with emotion. . . . With this persuasion, we can also forgive the muse who, in her fervor, is sometimes forgetful of her art."[268]

Actually, it did not require war-time emotions for Simms to set fervor, power, content, and thought above artistry. The bold and striking idea was to him more important than the form in which it was expressed. As critic, he naturally favored those poets who presented ideas that he approved. Sometimes he rode his prejudices hard. Yet it was his intention always, as he wrote to H. T. Tuckerman, "to dispense just judgment," and he was pleased when a living author professed himself satisfied.[269] But an individual's satisfaction was of minor importance. What mattered was to establish an intellectual climate in which good writing would be widely and generously recognized. Believing as he did in the ultimately practical value of poetry, Simms thought such a climate essential to the health of a nation and a people. In his own time, the best way in which a critic might contribute to this development was by "putting on record," honestly and vigorously, his own personal beliefs about poets and poetry.

VIII

I hope that this survey of William Gilmore Simms's criticism of fiction and poetry has indicated clearly that he was a good but not a great critic. He wrote vigorously and provocatively, basing his ideas and judgments on what he regarded as sound common sense. Unfortunately, he wrote hurriedly, and allowed himself little or no time for revision. One result was that, like Edgar Allan Poe, he mainly hammered out his critical principles in reviews, or in articles in which the review of a book or books served as a springboard. Frequently these article-reviews present admirably his general principles; sometimes they are perfunctory, and heavily padded with quotations. Unlike Poe, he showed little interest in developing and refining a rounded aesthetic that would justify a particular kind of literature (in Poe's case, a literature suitable for magazines). Only in his effort to justify the romance, as contrasted with the novel, did Simms attempt to construct something approaching an aesthetic. Perhaps for this reason, the Preface to *The Yemassee* remains his most influential critical work.[270]

As a critic, he tried always to be genial but just. He warned his friend James Lawson "not to suffer yourself to be deceived with a dogma . . . which teaches a doctrine so unjust as to make fault finding the merit of a Critic. The merit of a Critic, like the merit of any other judge whether elected or self constituted is to see that justice is done,—not to desire to pass judgment, but to award justice. . . . In reviewing a work, you are required not merely to review the story,—if that were all that were required from the critic, there would not be a butcher's boy who could not form as good and correct an opinion as the wisest scholar; but you are to review the thousand qualities of the writer—his skill as an artist, his moral sense, his taste, his knowledge of character, of human passion, and foibles, his powers of expression, and the range and the degree of enthusiasm which is possessed by his genius. To do this effectually calls for long study of these qualities, an intimate knowledge of the writings which are similar, and corresponding sympathies with a kind of performance to which they belong. A heart susceptible of human feelings, and a mind not rendered obtuse by a particular and foreign direction in its pursuits, are also necessary to so serious a task."[271] In a concise and well-phrased definition, Simms perhaps unfortunately put one other duty (that of mentor or guide) upon the critic:

"Neither to praise nor to blame is the object of true criticism. Justly to discriminate, firmly to establish, wisely to prescribe and honestly to award—these are the true aims and criteria of criticism."[272]

Within his limits, Simms attempted to embody these critical precepts in his own reviews. He made a manful and usually successful effort to be objective in his judgments. He was generously indignant about the niggardly recognition given to James Fenimore Cooper; he disliked intensely that type of comparative criticism which was interested only in elevating one author at the expense of another, and pleaded instead for an analytic and intrinsic criticism. His fear of English intellectual domination did not cloud his estimates of English authors, past or contemporary; his desire for a national literature did not lead him, in his own judgment, to minimize the faults of American authors; his intense sectionalism did not blind him to the merits as well as the faults of the New England writers. Simms had his full share of convictions and prejudices, and he acted on them: he dissected *Uncle Tom's Cabin* with more wrath than dispassion, yet he freely admitted that Mrs. Stowe wrote with power and passion. Many of his analyses and judgments seem today well-founded and just; his over-praise of a novelist like Bulwer is readily understandable on the ground of a contemporary appeal that has largely vanished with the years. In his literary judgments he attempted always to be honest with himself and with his readers.

His critical theories often seem better than his fictional and poetic practices. Largely because of his habit of hasty writing and his dislike of revision, he frequently violated his own concepts of unity and of design, especially in the romance. It was easier to digress, to invent on the spur of the moment, and to discourse on historical matters, than it was to make or to follow a severe, carefully-planned, and artistic design.

At times he seems to ante-date Henry James in his comments on morality in art, but there is at once a curious kinship and a curious dissimilarity: when Simms declares that a writer is moral only in proportion to his truthfulness, he puts the primary emphasis on the writer's truthfulness to life, whereas James emphasizes truth in the writer's art. Clearly, Simms's ideas left much freer room for the handling of story and characters, but this freeness undoubtedly worked to his disadvantage. It is not that he was unconcerned with the problems of art; as his criticism reveals, he was concerned with these problems, but he did not set a primary value on them. Genius, inspiration, bold and original thought could more than counterbalance any defects in strict artistry. Yet he was troubled by these blemishes in his own works, and sometimes apologized for them. But he also felt that, for one of his own ardent temperament, his way of writing was best. This was rationalization, but it may also have been true.

It is unfortunate although perhaps inevitable that the one collection of his critical articles was "devoted entirely to American topics."[275] The articles for *Views and Reviews* were selected and the two volumes published in the 1840s, when Simms was most highly involved in the Nationalism controversy; the work was planned for a series called the "Library of American Books," under the general editorship of Evert A. Duyckinck, a prime mover in the "Young America" group. This gives the book a certain unity, but at the expense of a fair presentation of Simms's critical views. There is no reason to doubt that he believed everything he said here. But his anti-English feelings are not properly compensated for by his sane and appreciative comments on English writers and writing; his patriotic fervor is not balanced by his admiration for foreign, especially German, authors. It is not that the individual judgments in this collection give a warped or distorted impression. Yet the totality does. Simms was neither as narrowly nor as ignorantly prejudiced as a casual reading of *Views and Reviews* has led some literary historians to infer.

He believed that it was one function of American critics and criticism to encourage the development of a healthy native literature, but an equally valid function was to bring about a healthy intellectual climate. Such a climate would inevitably result in a healthy native literature. But it could not be established in or by ignorance. The intellectual climate he envisioned must be based on international knowledge and cosmopolitan appreciation. As a result, many of his newspaper commentaries were designed simply to "apprize" his readers of what was going on in the literary world. He did not believe this without value: when the people demanded a first-rate literature, writers would appear who would be capable of producing great poems, dramas, and novels. His better articles go beyond this. Through them also, undoubtedly, he hoped to teach his readers discrimination and judgment, but he realized that the only way to demonstrate that was by clearly stating his principles and by making just discriminations and wise judgments in his own criticism.

7

PHILIP PENDLETON COOKE
Romanticist

WHEN AN anonymous correspondent ridiculed one of his poems, Philip Pendleton Cooke opened his vigorous response with a definition: the legitimate aim of criticism, he declared, is "to point out the proper path towards excellence. A true critic effects this by gently and courteously exposing error and lauding beauties where beauties are to be found."[1] Cooke resented the discourteous tone of the communication even more than he did the unfavorable literary judgment. Only nineteen, he was already pondering questions that were to perplex him throughout his brief life. Was it possible to be, at one and the same time, an author and a gentleman? How did one reconcile gentlemanliness with the need for money and the desire for fame? These were questions that Cooke never successfully answered.[2]

One method was to give up "Poetry and verse making," for they were as barren "as a worn-out tobacco field." He was discontented with what he had written: "My standard of poetic excellence is very high, and I rarely fail to see, after the excitement of composition has passed away, the want of merit in my pieces." Moreover, he believed firmly that *the sale of a book and the reputation of its author certainly go together.* Byron had gained poetic popularity by "the humbug mystery of his bearing, and the eccentricity of his fortunes"; Washington Irving, although writing in prose, had remained poor for years; of American poets, even Bryant, "the master of them all," had "sheltered himself from starvation behind the columns of a political newspaper."[3]

Yet Cooke set a high value on poetry. His brother John Esten Cooke has noted that Philip "sought for the sweets of letters in the 'flowery pastures' of Spenser, Chaucer, (always favorites with him) and the elder poets of the language, to whom his devotion continued earnest and unchanging throughout life." The most cherished books "in his library were a fine English edition of Chaucer in fourteen volumes, and Lord Berners' Froissart, also English, in four large volumes."⁴ Cooke's finest tribute to these early poets appeared, appropriately enough, in one of his best poems, "The Power of the Bards":

> I love the verse of England,
>   Her consecrated lays,
> Which tell the faithful story
>   Of life, in ancient days.
>
> The past is barred by shadows,
>   But the minstrels march before,
> And guide us, with their music,
>   To the breathing life of yore.
>   * * * * *
> And owe we not these visions
>   Fresh to the natural eye—
> This presence in old story—
>   To the good art and high?
>
> The high art of the poet,
>   The maker of the lays?
> Doth not his magic lead us
>   Back to the ancient days?
>
> For evermore be honored
>   The voices, sweet and bold,
> That thus can charm the shadows
>   From the true life of old.⁵

Cooke was a bookish poet. As the title implies, several poems in *Froissart Ballads* were drawn directly from the French historian, and were "as faithful to the text of Froissart as the necessities of verse permitted"; two others, which he claimed as stories of his own invention, are in the same manner and tradition; his own favorite, "The Story of Ugolino," was adapted from an episode in Cary's translation of Dante's *Divine Comedy*. Even poems dealing with his other favorite subjects, love and nature, make extensive use of literary references and allusions.⁶ A translated

quatrain that applied to his own works he described as applicable
to the best work of many ancient and some modern poets:

> A certain freak has got into my head,
> Which I can't conquer for the life of me,
> Of taking up some history, little read,
> Or known, and writing it in poetry.[7]

But Cooke felt that he received literary sustenance only from
his library, and from a few men with whom he corresponded.
The *Southern Literary Messenger* accepted and praised his
poems, articles, and stories; John Pendleton Kennedy, N. B.
Tucker, and Rufus W. Griswold exhorted him to write more;
Edgar Allan Poe not only praised his work but promised to "give
your contributions a hearty welcome, and the choicest position in
the magazine."[8] Otherwise, his environment was unfavorable.
His friends were not interested in poetry, or were downright
suspicious of it. As typical of their attitude, Cooke asked of Griswold, "What do you think of a good friend of mine, a most valuable and worthy, and hardriding one, saying gravely to me a
short time ago, 'I wouldn't waste time on a damned thing like
poetry; you might make yourself, with all your sense and judgment, a useful man in settling neighborhood disputes and difficulties.' You have as much chance with such people, as a dolphin
would have, if in one of his darts he pitched in amongst the machinery of a mill. 'Philosophy would clip an angel's wings,' Keats
says, and pompous dulness would do the same. But these very
persons I have been talking about, are always ready, when the
world generally has awarded the honors of successful authorship
to any of our mad tribe, to come in and confirm the award, and
buy if not read, the popular book."
He also warned Griswold not to expect too much from his
poems: "You will find them beneath your sanguine prognostic.
They are mere narrative poems, designed for the crowd. Poetic
speculation, bold inroads upon the debatable land—'the wild
weird clime, out of space out of time'—I have not here attempted.
I *will* hereafter merge myself in the nobler atmosphere; in the
mean time I have stuck to the ordinary level, and have endeavored to write interesting stories in verse, with grace and
spirit. I repeat my fear that in writing for the cold, I have failed
to touch the quick and warm—in writing for a dozen hunting
comrades, who have been in the habit of making my verse a *post*

prandium entertainment, and never endured an audacity of thought or word, I have tamed myself out of your approbation."[9]

Although he wrote several times that in order to make money he would abandon poetry and "become a novelist," for prose was the proper weapon for a stout-minded man,[10] he disdained familiarizing himself with the practical aspects of writing. He turned over to Kennedy and Griswold the troublesome details of arranging for the publication of *Froissart Ballads,* explaining that "I am quite as ignorant as any country gentleman ever was of the business part of literature, and no doubt if my ballads are not to be printed until I (personally) induce a publisher to print them, they will be converted into gun wads first."[11]

He kept on writing poetry, perhaps as much from compulsion as from choice. In words that help to explain the defects as well as the virtues in his poetry, Cooke declared that "I detest the law. On the other hand, I love the fever-fits of composition. The music of rhythm, coming from God knows where, like the airy melody in the Tempest, tingles pleasantly in my veins and fingers; I like to build the verse cautiously, but with the excitement of a rapid *writer,* which I rein in and check; and then, we both know how glorious it is to make the gallant dash, and round off the stanza with the sonorous couplet, or with some rhyme as natural to its place as a leaf on a tree."[12]

Such comments as those quoted above, however, must be taken with a degree of caution. Cooke was by no means a literary innocent. If his highest praise goes, as it does, to the ancient minstrels and bards, to the makers of lays, it was not because he did not know the poetry of his own time. Rather, he felt more at home in an earlier age. Yet at the same time he was ready to recognize generously any literary merit that he could find. He was not a literary nationalist: "Mr. Griswold suggests many themes purely American to American poets, amongst them, revolutionary incidents, scenery, and the dark conjectures concerning the ruined cities of central America. As for the first, whatever useful speculations they may furnish to philosophy, there is no inviting poetry in our colonization, and political revolution—'unenchanted' by time as they are. As for scenery, no man can write a good poem of *descriptions.* For the ruined cities, who could cast his sympathies into so wholly unknown a world, and repeople them with living men and women? Poets must be let alone in the choice of their subjects. Force them to be patriotic—and *voila* Barlow's Columbiad."[13]

He did not care whether an author was American, English, French, or Italian; he asked only that the author's work interest him. The haze of antiquity helped, for Cooke was frequently discontented with his own prosaic time: as "The Power of the Bards" suggests, he would gladly have brought back to life the glorious age of chivalry. It is probably true, as John Allen writes, that he had "no definite critical theory, consciously employed in the process of estimating an author's qualities. Cooke's mind, it would seem, had little interest in theories in general, in critical and esthetic theories in particular. On the other hand, in dealing with the specific and the objective fact, it displayed in its maturity a vigorous good sense which illuminated whatever subject of criticism it chose to examine."[14]

II

Although Cooke dismissed his three youthful articles on English poetry as "a compilation which any one might compile," they reveal his wide reading and independent, vigorous judgment. He devoted his first article entirely to pre-Chaucerian writings, to the period when in England as in Scandinavia "the scald was as well a chronicler as a singer." Their works might be rude, but they were distinguished by "the unpruned freedom of thought and unextinguished fire of feeling, so essential to true poetry."[15] Cooke was convinced that the Saxons had minstrels long before the Norman conquest, and he divided their work into that meant to be recited or chanted, that meant to be written down, and that which was essentially improvisation. French and Italian influences softened this rude but strong early poetry, but the new emphasis on rhyme did not reduce the native love of such legendary lore as the versified stories of King Arthur and of Robin Hood.[16]

The second installment drew heavily on an article in the *Edinburgh Review,* but Cooke again did not hesitate to present his own views. He acknowledged that Chaucer properly was called "the father of English verse," but he denied Chaucer's supremacy as a "painter of characters . . . he excels in describing manners, bearing, dress, &c.—not in picturing the workings of the 'human heart.' " With little fancy and less imagination, he is minute and particular in description, and so paints a vivid picture. This same talent "for descending skillfully into particulars" gave unusual beauty to Spenser's Pastorals, and to the tragedies of

Shakespeare and Shelley: "The whole secret of Chaucer's charm is, as I have said, particularity."[17]

In discussing the ballad "Chevy Chase," Cooke enters a plea for a certain roughness in poetry. Sidney had been right in praising the ballad, but wrong in wishing it "trimmed in the gorgeous eloquence of Pindar. . . . Would the natural and manly simplicity, for which the greatest works of man are so renowned, be well exchanged for the diffuse and ornate style of a Grecian lyric poet? I think not. As for this old ballad's roughness, I think *that* rather a merit. Bating some uncouthness, I think the language really better, much better adapted to the subject than our own more polished diction could be." The obscure author has attained excellence without imitating Homer; he is "the father of English heroic poetry."[18]

Gentle and melodious, Sir Thomas Wyatt was "an Anacreon compared with his contemporaries." Surrey added more, although he too had not escaped from the early "rudeness" of English verse, but at its best his work was worthy of comparison with that of Petrarch, "perhaps the most musical of all bards." Sidney was deservedly famous as a man, less as a poet, for his verse "abounds with conceits and strained similes, and the versification is occasionally cramped. Nevertheless, many of his sonnets contain beautiful images and deep sentiment."[19]

Spenser deserved to be called "father of the English allegorical and pastoral poetry." True, he had noble predecessors, from whom he borrowed freely: in allegory, Homer, Virgil, Ariosto, and Tasso; in pastoral, Theocritus and Virgil. But Cooke argued that allegorical personages should be excluded from the drama and the epic, and all lavish embellishment from the latter: "This species of poem—the grandest of *all* species—should be superior to such embellishment." But Spenser perceived that an allegorical vein heightened pastoral poetry, and in this he "has never yet been excelled." Yet the *Faerie Queene* is even better than the pastorals; with its "elegant and sometimes magnificent beauty," with the hidden meanings under the "exquisite allegory," it proves that "Spenser as a *natural* poet" was "imaginative, bold, and even witty: as an artist, or *educated* poet, skillful, elegant, and full. His language is, for the most part, rich and expressive, his verse (remarkably various in expression) could scarcely be more melodious and pleasing."[20]

After interpreting Shakespeare's sonnets as autobiographical, and in a note objecting to the mixture of comedy and tragedy in the same play, Cooke remembers wryly that to "praise such men as Shakespeare and Milton, is like praising Hercules."[21] But his treatment of Milton is not perfunctory. Satan, especially, is a magnificent creation; he "is not like MacBeth or Lear, real in himself, literally true, and only lifted into poetry by circumstances: but he is altogether moulded in a dream of the imagination. . . . Perhaps Ariel and Caliban are as purely ideal, as the hero of Milton, and approach as nearly to him as any other fiction; but the latter is incontestably a grander formation, and a mightier agent, and moves through the perplexities of his career, with a power that defies competition." Even Dante, excellent as he is, did not have "the grasps nor the soaring power of the English poet. The images of Dante pass by like the phantasma on a wall . . . they have complexion and shape, but not flesh or blood. Milton's earthly creatures have the flesh of living beauty upon them, and shew the changes of human infirmity."[22]

Samuel Butler had at times a "refinement of thought and style frequently entwined about masses of obscurity and ridiculous vulgarity," and Waller should be called a versifier rather than a poet, for he "wrote *prose* in metre, and metre too of great polish." These were minor figures. Dryden was not, although a deficiency in taste had led him in youth to write plays in rhyme. He became an admirable critic, and in "translation, satire and lyric poetry, he was unrivalled until the coming of Pope. Indeed in the last, he has never been rivalled." Cooke based this claim on his belief that Dryden's "Song for St. Cecelia's Day" was "the greatest ode in the English language . . . an unrivalled example of lyric excellence." Dryden's logical talent showed at its best in his satire, but Pope was his superior here mainly because the older poet lacked leisure "to perfect the reasoning which enters so importantly into that species of composition." As a didactic poet Pope was supreme: "Neither Virgil nor Lucretius can in this, boast superiority. And Akenside, Armstrong, and even Boileau, fall far beneath." His translations were less happy, for "Virgil would have suited his style of genius far better than Homer."[23]

Cooke summed up his article with high praise: "Pope perfected the music and elegance of the English verse. Drawn out of chaos by old Chaucer; softened by Spenser; twisted into pliancy by Surrey; subtilized by Cowley; smoothed by Waller; strongly and beautifully modelled by Dryden;—it still wanted the finishing touch, and this, Pope gave."[24]

Cooke was less interested in the precursors of romanticism. He had regretfully passed over, he noted, poets like Herrick, Lovelace, and Swift; he warned the reader that he had no intention of treating such contemporary "bad bardlings" as Alfred Tennyson.[25] The result is a survey, more biographical than critical, that begins with James Thomson and ends with Robert Burns. Thomson was a sluggard, with a sluggard's vision of nature lulled with quietude, but "with this drowsy enchantment he mingled all the freshness of that age which, from its far distance in the past, takes upon itself the hue of far clouds." Perhaps one-half of "The Castle of Indolence" was worthy even of Spenser.[26] Edward Young was an example of primeval piety mingled with gloom. Although too heavily labored, Young's satire seemed to Cooke better than the more popular "Night Thoughts," but he admitted that both works "often display a dark, stern roughness . . . a vast and somber imagination—full of metaphor—rather metaphysical—sometimes obscure, and this rather from idea than expression."[27] After noting that William Shenstone had refined tastes, wrote prettily of fruitless love, and "had trained himself well in the art of expression—if expression can be called an art," and after acknowledging briefly that Thomas Gray was "perhaps the most learned man in Europe," Cooke regained some measure of enthusiasm in writing about Thomas Chatterton. But his admiration was for "the fiery and determined spirit" rather than for the poet: "Chatterton was not unlike Byron. The morbid misanthropy hanging unfixedly about the former—fully developed in the latter—was in both but a retort upon their fellows. Both had hearts which only detraction or cold neglect could harden into a hatred of humanity."[28]

For Scottish poetry in general, and for that of Robert Burns in particular, Cooke evinced considerable enthusiasm. Burns had successfully mingled "the spirit of *martial frolic*" with the softer tones of love; like Scott, he was much indebted to the nursery tales of childhood. Yet he was a man of pride and genius rather than of real independence, a man whose sociability hid a constitutional melancholy, a poet whose misfortune was "to want an aim." He was nonetheless a great poet. "Scotland has had an Allan Ramsay to revive the pastoral visions of Colin Clout—an earlier Drummond to transmit to posterity the *fresh philosophy* of the olden time—a Leyden to haunt the "far east countries" with the pleasant traditions of Teviotdale—an Allan Cunningham to embody the spirit of the ancient Scottish romaunt in the sturdiest language of our own day—a Hogg to fill the Ettick valleys with his 'trueful song'—a Scott to restore to the hills of Moffat and to the banks of the Annan the lance and the eye-haunting plume—a Scott to restore knight and monk, to castle and abbey, from the Skye to Melrose—a Scott to tell of old-time tales of Gallawater and by Yarrow—but Robert Burns has no master among these. The 'Robin of Ayr had the richest song of them all.' "[29]

Cooke did not continue the series. He had noted incidentally that "in the course of time" men would learn to appreciate Shelley and would place him alongside Shakespeare and Spenser, and he wondered how misguided readers could complain of Shelley's obscurity while they applauded the beauty of Cowley's odes.[30] In discussing the autobiographical nature of Shakespeare's sonnets, he digressed to add that "Byron lives in his vagrant 'Childe,' and bating some most disgusting affectation in his Corsair-Lara-Giaour. Shelley groans with his Prometheus—breathes in his Laon—and draws his own image with the life of his Helen. . . . This self-identity is not so visible in the tragedies of Byron and Shelley, for the simple reason, perhaps, that these are more the works of art—more the creatures of the brain than heart—abound more in skill than feeling."[31]

In a letter to his father, he advised his younger brothers that "light, desultory reading, except to relieve the mind when it has been over-worked, is, I think, hurtful. . . . The best poetry of men like Milton, Wordsworth &c. is full of great truths, magnificently uttered; and the pomp of numbers sometimes inflames the mind when it would go to sleep over prose."[32] John Esten Cooke wrote to Griswold that Keats, Shelley, and Coleridge were "favorites with him; not Southey or Byron. When the Ballads were published he had not seen Tennyson but his poems afterwards were favorites with him—more especially the 'Morte D'Arthur' and 'Ulysses.' "[33] However, Cooke's perceptive biographer, John D. Allen, seems to me correct in concluding that contemporary poets had very little influence on his poetry.[34]

This includes Poe. They were at least literary acquaintances from the early days of the *Southern Literary Messenger,* and some of Cooke's most discerning criticism was written about Poe's work. As early as September, 1835, he advised the publisher to value Poe "according to his merits, which are very great. I say this with deliberation, for I have been months in coming to the conclusion that he is the first genius, in his line, in Virginia. And when I say this, how many other states are included—certainly all South of us. The conversation in *Morella*—the description in *Berenice* of a mind dwelling with strained intensity upon some particular [trifling] object with which the eye meets—and the description of that Beckford of Venice, and his singular sanctum in the *Visionary*; as also the vague speculations of *Hans Phaal* upon the scenery of the moon—with its shadow-stained lakes and sombre vegetation—are compositions of great beauty."[35]

When Poe asked for his opinion of "Ligeia," Cooke replied that "I think it very fine. There is nothing *unintelligible* to my mind in the 'sequel' (or conclusion) but I am impertinent enough to think that it (the conclusion) might be mended. I of course 'took' your 'idea' throughout . . . your intent is to tell a tale of the 'mighty will' contending with and finally vanquishing Death. The struggle is vigourously described—and I appreciated every sentence as I advanced, until the Lady Ligeia takes possession of the deserted *quarters* (I write like a butcher) of the Lady Rowena. There I was shocked by a violation of the ghostly proprieties—so to speak—and wondered how the Lady Ligeia—a wandering essence—could, in quickening *the body of the Lady Rowena* (such is the idea) become suddenly the visible, bodily Ligeia. If Rowena's bodily form had been retained as a shell or case for the disembodied Lady Ligeia, and you had only become aware *gradually* that the blue Saxon eye of the 'Lady Rowena of Tremaine' grew daily darker with the peculiar, intense expression of the 'look' which had belonged to Ligeia—that a mind of grander powers, a soul of more glowing fires occupied the quickened body and gave an old familiar expression to its motions—if you had brooded and meditated upon the change until proof accumulated upon proof, making wonder certainty, and then, in the moment of some strangest of all evidence of the transition, broken out into the exclamation which ends the story—the *effect* would not have been lessened, and the 'ghostly proprieties' would, I think, have been better observed." Poe's stories of this class had all the logical plausibility that a dream has, and he added that "You *write* as I sometimes dream."[36]

Soon after this, Cooke read "Fall of the House of Usher," "William Wilson," and "Conversation of Eiros and Charmion." The latter he thought "very singular and excellent, and the skill of one small part of it unapproachable." He was doubtful that he understood the true meaning of "William Wilson": "From the 'Whispering Voice' I would apprehend that you meant the second William Wilson as an embodying of the *conscience* of the first, but I am inclined to the notion that your intention was to convey the wilder idea that every mortal of us is attended with a shadow of himself." He admired the story, but he felt happier with the "House of Usher": "the glare of the moon thro' the sundering house, and the electric gleam visible around it, I think admirably conceived." But the poem imbedded in the story, "The Haunted Palace," for some reason did not strike Cooke's fancy; he had instantly understood it "as a picture of an intellect," but he considered it "beautiful but obscure."[37]

What must have pleased Poe most, however, was Cooke's high praise of his style, "the very best among the first of living writers; and I must let you know that I regard style as something more than the mere manner of communicating ideas. 'Words are used by the wise as counters; by the foolish as coin,' is the aphorism of a person who never appreciated Jeremy Taylor or Sir Thomas Browne. You do not, to be sure, use your words as those fine old glowing rhetoricians did, as tints of the pencil—as the colours of a picture—you do not make your sentences pictures—but you mould them into an artful excellence—bestow a care which is pleasantly perceptible, and accomplish an effect which I can only characterize as the visible presentation of your ideas instead of the mere expression of them."[38]

These detailed and warm-hearted comments so impressed Poe that he requested Cooke to bring up to date the earlier memoirs by James Russell Lowell. Somewhat reluctantly, Cooke agreed, in a long and interesting letter:

"John Kennedy, talking with me about your stories, old and recent, said, 'the man's imagination is as truth-like and minutely accurate as De Foe's'—and went on to talk of your 'Descent into the Maelstrom,' 'MS. Found in a Bottle,' 'Gold Bug,' &c. I think this last the most ingenious thing I ever read. Those stories of criminal detection, 'Murders in the Rue Morgue,' &c., a prosecuting attorney in the neighborhood here declares are miraculous. I think your French friend, for the most part, fine in his deductions from over-laid and unnoticed small facts, but sometimes too minute and hair-splitting. The stories are certainly as interesting as any ever written. The 'Valdemar Case' I read in a number of your Broadway Journal last winter—as I lay in a Turkey blind, muffled to the eyes in overcoats, &c., and pronounce it without hesitation the most damnable, vraisemblable, horrible, hairlifting, shocking, ingenious chapter of fiction that any brain ever conceived, or hands traced. That gelatinous, viscous sound of man's voice!

"There never was such an idea before. That story scared me in broad day, armed with a double-barrel Tryon Turkey gun. What would it have done at midnight in some old ghostly country-house?

I have always found some one remarkable thing in your stories to haunt me long after reading them. The *teeth* in Berenice—the changing eyes of Morella—that red and glaring crack in the House of Usher—the pores of the deck in the MS. Found in a Bottle—the visible drops falling into the goblet in Ligeia, &c &c—there is always something of this sort to stick by the mind—by mine at least."[39]

The article itself is disappointing. Cooke reprinted a large part of "The Raven," calling it "a great triumph of imagination and art." The circumstances are all congruous, the phraseology admirable, musical, and apt, the rhythm exquisite. . . . The tone was wonderfully sustained, and highly appropriate to the subject. He returned briefly to "M. Valdemar's Case" as the "most truth-like representation of the impossible" ever written; and praised "The Philosophy of Composition" as "an admirable specimen of analysis." But he confessed himself unfamiliar with Poe's more recent writings, and (after quoting appreciatively from "Ligeia" and "Fall of the House of Usher") fell back on an elaborate comparison of Defoe and Poe. Poe had the earlier writer's "peculiar talent for filling up his pictures with minute life-like touches—for giving an air of remarkable naturalness and truth to whatever he paints." But there were significant differences. Defoe deals only with the factual and the homely. Poe had also a daring and wild imagination, for the "fires of a great poet are seething under those analytic and narrative powers *in which no living writer equals him.*" Cooke felt that Poe would be more popular if "he brought his singular capacity for vivid and truth-like narrative to bear on subjects nearer ordinary life, and of a more cheerful and happy character. . . . I would like to read one cheerful book made by his *invention,* with little or no aid from its twin brother *imagination* . . . a book healthy and happy throughout, and with no poetry in it at all anywhere, except a good old English 'poetic justice' in the end." Such a book would not increase Poe's reputation with the discerning few, but it would endear him to a million readers. For the moment, at least, Cooke's critical good sense seems to have deserted him.[40]

III

Poe almost certainly spurred Cooke into writing his best critical essay. For Poe had quoted three lines of a poem and called them imitative of Lovelace's "Althea." Cooke denied the charge: "If they are so, the imitation is one of the unconscious appropriations I have spoken of; I pronounce it so, on the highest authority, as the letterwriters say, for I wrote the verses myself."[41] If Cooke was completely unwilling to admit a specific indebtedness, he voluntarily acknowledged a generalized one. When a poet selected an every-day name for a character, he was likely to pick one that "some old favorite book has redeemed from common-place, and made pleasant to him." Although he does not mention specifically that the poem Poe quoted from was entitled "Emily," he obliquely asks: "What poet, for instance, ever called his heroine 'Emily,' without such pre-occupation of taste and judgment?—without taking an argument for his choice, from that fair 'Emilie,' for whose white hand the doughty heroes of Chaucer contend 'in tourney high'?"[42]

Cooke's reasonable essay might have been read with profit by Poe and Chivers. If read, it was disregarded. Yet Cooke was simply arguing for the continuity of literary thought, for the somewhat obvious fact that a modern author can not disregard completely those authors who "go back in a line that seems only to end because it fades out of view in the distance." Cooke tempered his romanticism by humanism. The first poet necessarily created his art at the same time that he created his poem. But no poet or critic could achieve the impossible task of going back "from McAdam to Adam"; he must therefore be, perhaps in spite of himself, an imitator. This, Cooke writes in one of his few remarks on nationalism, "furnishes a defence of much of our American POETRY, which the critics have censured as wanting in originality."[43]

When a poet has "one of his fever-fits of composition upon him," he may consciously or unconsciously have been excited by something he has read, rather than by something he has experienced; when he selects a verse and stanza structure which poets before him have used "as a general property," Cooke adds dryly that a perfectly new measure "would, perhaps, be a monstrosity. The rhythm is remembered and well-loved music, not perhaps consciously identified; the ideas have almost certainly been used before; his poetic phraseology, even, is imitative."[44] The man completely ignorant of poetry would hardly do anything "worth the inquiry whether it be native or borrowed." Robert Burns was not, as sometimes claimed, an exception: he "was steeped in the minstrelsy of the Scottish border." The mod-

ern poet inevitably uses "an old poetic phrase as we draw a
breath—unconscious of the use, as we are of the inhalation." Poe
himself has done this: a line from "Israfel" declares that "None
sing so wildly well," but Byron earlier in his *Bride of Abydos*
had written of a character, "He sings so wild and well." Cooke's
temperate comment has much wisdom in it: "Of course this was,
as in my own case, an unconscious appropriation—or, if conscious,
still perfectly innocent. The man who goes out of his way to
avoid such trivial imitations, is over dainty to do manly work."[45]

Griswold was as wrong in demanding nationalism as Poe was
in demanding originality. The United States had not developed
from a cultural infancy. American writers, for better or worse,
are in the English tradition: "Shakespeare is as much an American poet's ancestor, as he is an English poet's." Geographical distance and political division had not disenfranchised us of our
inheritance. A time of crisis might bring forth impassioned
poetry, but a deliberate limitation to national subjects would
"make merry work" with our poets.[46]

The same critics did not seem concerned with the originality
of poets in other times and other countries, yet these poets have
"established in their practice, a mode of appropriation, which
conveys not only a thought, or a phrase, but often the whole substance of one author's creation to the pages of another." Tyr-
whitt not only made the general statement that Chaucer wrote the
Canterbury Tales "in imitation of the Decameron of his master
Boccaccio"; he devoted thirty pages of fine type to tracing various tales to this source. Spenser had borrowed freely and directly
from Tasso, and had drawn upon Euripides, Virgil, Ovid,
and Ariosto. Shakespeare's was a "haunted domain," and in
modern times Keats had fashioned "Isabel" from one of Boccaccio's stories.[47]

But the American poet was condemned by "the over-fastidious-
ness of our critics, who damn a man for smaller departures
from originality." Why damn the reputation of a man who ex-
pects no material reward from his labor, Cooke asked pointedly,
"because he cannot unread himself to the point of primitive
ignorance." Clearly Goethe or Byron (depending on the dates of
composition) borrowed from the other in their respective
"Bride of Corinth" and "Seige of Corinth," but this borrowing
also was "proper and innocent."

Cooke admitted that direct imitation of poetic models and
manners was reprehensible. Quevedo in following Cervantes

was "an imitator in the worst sense of the word." So was Albert Pike in his imitations of Keats. The poet who works openly is justified, but "positive theft of thought and expression, accompanied by tricks of concealment, which the world brands as plagiarism, is, of course, unjustifiable." As an example of this "concealing care," Cooke puts in parallel columns a passage from Browne's *Religio Medici* and its artfully re-arranged version in D'Israeli's *Vivian Grey*. This, he declares, is plagiarism, but it ought not to be confused with general imitations of thought, music, and phraseology, or with the open appropriation of old tales as "the ground-work of new stories." The final test must be whether "good work has been done by the modern poet."[48]

In his long review of Henry Francis Cary's translation of the *Divine Comedy,* Cooke discusses the difficulties involved in turning an Italian poem into English. He does not question the value of translations, although it is unfortunate that most English-speaking people "know this greatest poet from the breaking of Virgil's harp, to the advent of Shakspeare, only through interpreters."[49] Of these, Cary was probably the best: his version was honest and faithful, and "greatly more than a bald verbal version." He had been wise to eschew rhyme, for in a long poem the despotism of rhyme inevitably led to distortion: "In our language, comparatively poor as it is in words of like final sounds, blank verse is, beyond doubt, better for purposes of translation than rhymed verse. In truth, we are inclined to believe it also a better form of expression for the greater labors of original poetry. If it loses in the charm of accordant terminations—a charm often sufficient to redeem verse of no real pith of thought—it yet places a shackle the less upon the poet, and leaves him so much the more of that freedom, without the largest possible amount of which, the most expansive genius, the most complete mastery of his art are insufficient to the achievement of the highest poetic miracles. Noble work has been done in rhyme—but not the noblest." The balcony scene in *Romeo and Juliet* puts to shame all rhyme, from the first known couplet to the "latest triumphs of Miss Barrett and Tennyson."[50]

A short poem can be successfully translated in rhyme. Cooke cites as an example one of Pushkin's poems, and notes especially that "Byron has given a rhymed translation of the story of Francesca di Rimini in the Inferno, with wonderful beauty. It far from follows that he could have soared with the same sway of wing through the hundred cantos of Hell, Purgatory, and Paradise." Partly because of Byron's example, Cooke appended to his article a rhymed translation of the story of Ugolino.[51]

But Cooke intended to discuss Dante's work rather than the merits of Carey's translation. The poetry immediately preceding did not promise much. The Provençal troubadours with their polished lyrics and their courts of love had gained great popularity and power, but they were essentially frivolous. Dante with his admirable genius changed this. The poet, Cooke thought, who "overbears all hostile influences, enters into new fields, and produces immortal poems, is entitled to that grand isolation of praise and honor, which the world justly yields to a discoverer of new lands, or of secrets in nature." Dante was comparable with Columbus not only in achievement, but also in that each pretended to draw on earlier guides when in reality they were setting "a novel and bold course." Like Columbus, Dante did not set out in ignorance. He had behind him valid and valuable experiences: a necessity in Cooke's view, for "We have a theory, that no man can write a great book until age and the rubs of a worldly warfare have matured his powers. . . . Shakespeare, Milton, Bacon, Scott, are examples fortifying our theory—and Dante is one more. The *Divina Comedia* was written in the matured age of its author, and after a life spent in action. . . . Dante writes like a man who knows men well."[52]

Cooke dissented sharply from the conventional English judgment that Milton was "Lord of the *Ideal*," and Dante "Lord of the Actual." He considered Dante "more remarkable for ideality than Milton, and quite as much as any poet that ever lived, unless we except Chaucer, pronounced, by the same review, the most earth-seeking of the actual minds in poetry." To buttress this highly original judgment, which he knew many readers would disagree with, Cooke gave his own definition: "the Poet is most highly endowed with ideality, who, in his account of things not perceived by the senses, but only imaged or pictured to the imagination, can make the picture most distinct to the comprehension of others." Many poets usually credited with ideality lack this needed distinctness of perception and portraiture— among them "Shelley, that argosy rich in freight, but winged with too much sail."[53] The forms in the Inferno "are not dim phantoms, but sharp-lined, life-like, with human eyes streaming superhuman agony." Yet this very distinctness of portraiture detracts from its terrors. The suggested horrors in Horace Walpole's *Castle of Otranto* and in the opening part of Eugene Sue's *Wandering Jew* leave something for the imagination to go to work upon. Terror must move in shadows. But Dante was concerned with something different, at once greater and more difficult, and his power to make others see his imaginary figures "in such bold clearness" makes him "one of the highest Lords of the Ideal."[54]

In fiction, Cooke was willing to accept with some reservations the conventional distinction between the romance and the novel. Works in either *genre* were likely to be ephemeral, for they both belonged to the "lighter forms of creation. Livy and Virgil remained, but most popular novels, like Bryant's gentle maiden, 'perished with the flowers.' " A few survived. Cooke listed among them "the Golden Ass of Apuleius, the Arabian nights, the Canto Novelle Antiche of the witty and inventive Italians, the Gesta Romanorum of the monks, Gil Blas, Don Quixote, and many others." He preferred the romance, and noted approvingly that these were tales of romantic adventure, rather than novels "painting manners, dealing in domestic incident, and altogether trading on humble ground. But we do not see why romances should live, and novels die; and, moreover, romance and novel must in fact partake so much of the characteristics of each other, as to make it questionable whether the lines of the critical distinction are not after all merely nominal."[55]

At the end of his list of immortal fiction, Cooke asks rhetorically, "when will the Waverley novels die?" Clearly, in his view, they were not in danger of death. Scott was his touchstone.[56] Just as Byron's verses had once driven Scott's out of fashion, so for a time it had seemed possible that Bulwer's immense popularity threatened "to dispose of his immortal prose romances." Cooke's phrasing reveals his own critical point of view: "It is somewhat humiliating to know that the author of Pelham came very near supplanting, with a large class of readers, the author of Ivanhoe. Time and truth, however, have adjusted positions; the divine Sir Walter holds the throne and pinnacle: Bulwer has receded, and holds a position far below him."[57]

In part, this was because his writings are "singularly undramatic." A great baron does not talk like an individual, flesh-and-blood individual, but like Bulwer's conception of "a great baron in general." Bulwer might be historically accurate; the talk of his characters was easy, elegant, often witty, but invariably his characters "do not talk like man the individual, but like

man the representative of a class." Even his plays suffer from this
lack of dramatic effect, in a way that the plays of Massinger
(frequently accused of wanting dramatic power) do not. In
Richelieu, the most effective parts are the long speeches of Richelieu himself, "which have more to do with rhetoric than the
drama." Cooke admits that Bulwer handles melodrama effectively,
but Cooke objected to this on critical principles.[58]

Bulwer is deficient also in that "he has not the least idea how
to make men, individuals, or armies *fight.*" Of a personal encounter in *The Last Days of Pompeii,* Cooke remarks sarcastically
after quoting the passage: "We certainly never read any where
else of so much fighting and so little execution done." His love
scenes have a highwrought "fire of passion," but Cooke doubts
their reasonableness: "The 'peculiar fires' of Bulwer are not in
Kenilworth, or the Bride of Lammermoor, but who wants more
truth and profoundity of the holy passion so dear to poets,
dear to all men, than he finds in the unhappy Countess Amy,
or poor Lucy Ashton?"

The highly-praised and popular *Last of the Barons* Cooke unhesitatingly pronounced "an unmitigated failure." It is over-
elaborate, and has too much of that finery which "is fatal to this
class of fiction. Men must talk naturally and fight manfully." In
addition, Bulwer's style is bad because it is "painfully ornate,
ambitious (a fatal fault of style), full of musical circumlocution
introduced evidently for the sake of the music, and where natural
often slovenly." Many writers, Cooke thought, had singular no-
tions about style. In his admirable writings, Dr. Channing thought
that a little obscurity added dignity and impressiveness; N. P.
Willis advised cultivating "foibles" as a means of securing individuality.[59] Cooke was convinced "that good thought requires
no trick in its expression; and that bad thought cannot be made
good by an artful envelopment in musical, fantastic, passionate,
or any other language." The requisites for writing well might
be exceedingly difficult, but the relatively simple laws he held to
be "immutable and inexorable": "Write clearly, go by the nearest way to your meaning, use words of distinct, well understood
signification, abjure ornament as a separate quality, but where
it comes as a natural grace make it welcome." Bulwer sinned
because "the good homely words of plain life, short, perhaps
rude, always strong and direct, were too coarse, too inharmonious an utterance for him." Bunyan, writing in "the language
and idioms of the English hearth-sides, and never dreaming of

style at all, has a better style than Bulwer." Jeremy Taylor's "utterance is gorgeous because his thought is gorgeous," and not because he separated "the labors of word-building as a thing distinct from thought-building." Sir Thomas Browne's style is not really "ambitious, and no matter of artful care"; it is rather a compound of his devotion to ancient things and of the poetry of his thought.[60]

For all these damning strictures, Cooke concluded that Bulwer was a man of "brilliant genius." The reader never encounters stupidity, never the barrenness of a "plain mind." With all his faults, he has "Creative power, inventiveness, a quick perception of the beautiful, a rare knowledge of certain classes of human passions and emotions, together with a singular skill in their display, great melody of phraseology, which at times is exquisite enough to make the most stubborn critic forget his censure, these and some other gifts and marks of a genius great and accomplished."[61]

Cooke tended to be suspicious of men who polished their writings too carefully. The one-book critic could not understand the Elizabethan dramatists, although their works are "the best wealth of English literature," for they "were too numerous for their slow-paced judges; they were, moreover, creations of original genius, cast in novel moulds, and possessed no points of resemblance to the ancient classic drama to give a foundation for that kind of stately eulogy which expresses itself in the Plutarchian parallel." Of these over-fastidious writers, Lord Herbert of Cherbury was "the head and front," and Joseph Addison the "perfected glory."[62] The modern author can no longer be so fastidious and slow-paced, for if he stops between labors he is forgotten: "The public instead of nibbling at sentences, swallows chapters—swallows volumes." Cooke is inclined to forgive Dumas and G. P. R. James many faults because they have written rapidly.

Dumas had responded to the "new necessities of authorship" by setting up a "kind of literary manufactory."[63] He supervised the production of his novels; probably he wrote the best parts of them. He has many merits: a curt and rapid management of details, with particularity yet without tediousness; an indomitable good sense that leads him to keep his characters natural, to limit his tragedy, and to qualify his comedy; and to keep his mind always on the story, with little moralizing or philosophical comment. If there is extravagance, it is because the "mind of Dumas is more of a fountain than a cistern."[64] By comparison, James was a tame genius.[65] All that he had written was "everlastingly respectable," although he was "sometimes guilty of the most arrant twaddle," and his trite reflective remarks Cooke found "excessively annoying." He advised the reader "to begin every chapter with the second paragraph." Also hard to forgive, even in a man who had written fifty novels, was James's use of the same incidents and the same plot in so many different books. These were venal sins. The real "proof of original sterility" in him was his failure to create striking or impressive characters. He had dealt with many of the great names in history, yet where "among his kings do we find a Coeur de Lion, among his nobles a Dunois, or Leicester, or Claverhouse, among his outlaws a Locksley or Rob Roy? The same poverty is visible in his conception and delineation of original characters." But on a lesser scale James had the art of keeping the reader interested in the narrative, and this talent, though a rare occurrence, is an absolute necessity in a "greatly successful novelist. James possesses it in remarkable degree."[66]

The younger D'Israeli seemed the greatest of living novelists, possessing "one of the most gifted and accomplished minds in the world," his *Vivian Grey,* greatest of juvenile triumphs, a "book which no future age of English letters will let die." Cooke thought that D'Israeli had "a perfect mastery of the English language." He might be said to have no style at all, for his work is free of mannerisms and peculiarities, for all his power: "No living writer equals D'Israeli in the mastery of the strength, dignity, music, and grace, of our language."[67] But his "greatest power is in his imagination." It was neither wild nor unbridled, as some critics asserted, for D'Israeli "imagines no monsters, and always imagines clearly. He runs riot—flashes—dazzles—seems to exercise no restraint upon himself—but a natural symmetry in his power guards him at every point." Although he lacked the profound knowledge of a Bacon, he possessed and made expert use of a polite universal or general knowledge. Finally, he had great dramatic power: "His passion, wit, humor, pathos, and merriment, flow from the lips of his characters, and color their action, as if nature, not a feigning novelist, had made and placed them before us." Unfortunately, he had also an "adroit knack of pilfering the stories of other writers"; even worse, he was careless in his plots; worst of all, he had presented readers with disgusting "miraculous boys." Cooke longed for a few ordinary roughneck children, and confessed that "D'Israeli has, in one or two instances, carried his sentimental weakness for supernatural boys so far as to make a fool of himself." Yet on the whole there was little to censure, and much to admire.[68]

Cooke closed with a brief survey of American novelists. Of these, James Fenimore Cooper was easily the best: "We have a multitude of various merit and kind, but he is isolated far above them." Of this multitude, some "amuse themselves with slight deeds." Foremost of these is John Pendleton Kennedy. A few "old crippled field-marshals" like James K. Paulding are "too restless to be quiet, and yet too much spoiled by long inaction for fresh campaigns." Some men are willing to hire out their literary services: "Willis is a plumed and burnished specimen of these condottieri." Cooke ranked Simms at the head of those "partisan leaders, who do fine things on a limited scale, and waste their prowess in a multiplicity of small adventures." Cornelius Mathews with his *Puffer Hopkins* was only one of many "silly drolls." There was also, he added sarcastically, the Professor Ingrahams who were intent on carrying off "the savings of servant maids," and, worst of all, the pamphleteers who made a sensation of the most recent murder or seduction.[69]

The lesser novelists were numerous, their work varied in kind and in quality. Cooper towered above them "because he is the most creative, and most dramatic of our novelists—and the only true *poet* amongst them." Cooper deserved to be called "a great original genius," for no other novelist save Scott had "conceived so many characters so well." Of these, Natty Bumppo was the best; his character was not merely presented, but was developed through incidents. This, to Cooke, is creative genius, and best manifested in *The Deerslayer* when Natty kills his first Indian. Although Cooper had wasted "time and temper in rather ridiculous libel suits," and although his European novels would "doubtless sink like lead," his sea tales and the fine Leatherstocking novels were not "perishable stuff."[70]

IV

In poetry, in fiction, and in criticism, Cooke remained a gifted amateur. As John Esten Cooke perceptively noted, "Literature with my brother was a recreation—and he would never write unless he felt the desire and could take pleasure in embodying his thoughts."[71] He was easily beguiled into digressions or into changing the structure of a story. With discerning candor he noted that interest in the love-story had warped *The Crime of*

Andrew Blair: he had intended to trace "the progress of a nature in some repects well-gifted, from a single crime to which unrestrained passions in an evil hour propelled it, to remorse and ruin. . . . I must now leave the more pleasant theme, which should have been subordinate, to give in a final scene, some necessary explanations, and an appearance of connection between the beginning and ending of my book."[72]

Although some of his best work is drawn directly from the pioneer and plantation life that he had personally known, the lore that he had heard, he turned from it apparently with relief to the more romantic and, in his view, more heroic ages of chivalry in Europe. He was interested in justifying the romance as an art-form, in fiction and in poetry, but he developed no formal theory. His theoretical remarks, in fact, are practically always digressions, suggested directly by the specific subject in hand. He did not expect to purify the public taste or change popular verdicts, but his justification for one essay may well serve to justify all his critical work: "The utterance of honest opinion," he modestly declared, "generally serves a useful purpose."[73]

8

THOMAS HOLLEY CHIVERS
Mystic

AT HIS DEATH, Chivers left in manuscript form a considerable body of literary criticism. These projected articles
and lectures are incomplete and fragmentary, but they supplement his Prefaces and his relatively few published articles.[1] When
he deals with the theory of poetry, Chivers is consistent to the
point of repetition: he uses the same epithets, phrases, and
clauses over and over. When he treats individual poets, he de-
livers downright judgments that are frequently over-enthusiastic,
sometimes dubious, and always individual. But the difficulties
implicit in his criticism are not in his ideas or judgments; rather,
they stem from his highly personal, transcendental vocabulary.

Thus, he believed that true poetry could be written only by a
divinely inspired poet. He was at once the mediator and the revelator of God: "Poets are the apostles of divine thought, who are
clothed with an authority from the Most High, to work miracles
in the minds of men"; even Christ would consider "the divinest
thing this side of heaven" to be the man who "reveals to the
World, through the medium of Art, that he is *really* and *truly*
the Viceregent of God upon the earth—a Prophet and a Poet."
Even the best is necessarily imperfect, since "the music that we
have now as well as the Poetry is only the repetition of a type
which was only, at best, but the faintest echo of that Prototype
which has never yet been distinctly heard by any man on earth."[2]

It is, nevertheless, the best we have. A deeply religious, mystical man who believed that he had seen and experienced authentic
visions, Chivers had little faith in theology or in organized reli-

gion. From the beginning God had entrusted revelation to the Prophet-Poets, for "religion is pure Poesy"; in his own time, Chivers believed, "every *true Man of God* is sincerely disgusted" with what pretends to be religion as exemplified in the Church, for "there is no such thing on earth—except that which is contained in the true worship of the *'pure in heart,'* who are the *Sons of God—the true Poets.*"[3] He was convinced that "Religion is pure Poesy—the harmoniously melodious Evolution of the oversoul of true love."[4]

Chivers put the primary emphasis on intuition. Ordinary men behold all things with natural or material eyes, while "the Poet sees them with his *internal,* or *spiritual* eyes . . . this at once elevates the Poet above the sphere of mortality."[5] Even so, celestial beauty can be only partially glimpsed here, and this "Intuitive perception . . . may be expressed either in Painting, Sculpture, Music, or Poetry—but more perfectly in Poetry . . . the reproduction of this Divine Beauty is the highest attainment of man—being that which constitutes true Poetry." For this reason, the poet is "the only Prometheus who can bring down fire from Heaven," and the "Prophets of God were called Celestial Men—that is, Poets—because they were enabled to dwell in the Celestial, or Angelic, idea . . . the difference between the Poets and every other man consists in this—namely, that he beholds every thing in the plane of the Celestial, and not in the Terrestrial light."[6]

His favorite phrase, practically always italicized, was that poets are "the *Revelators of the Divine Idea through the Beautiful,*" and that poetry is the "*crystalline revelation of the Divine Idea.*"[7] God had first spoken to man in poetry, and all true poetry was only the echo of that "First Word . . . modified by the fashions of the garments of the thoughts of those who live afterwards." In the Edenic state, man incarnated the will of God, and lyrical poetry "was the primeval dialect of the Edenic or Perfect Man." But as men have grown increasingly away from God, it has become hard to understand the images and meanings of those "who lived near Nature and God." Once the poet-prophets like David had understood the harmony which subsists between man and the external world and between man and God.[8] In later times only the poet could intuitively grasp those relations, for "Poetry is the power given by God to man of manifesting those relations. . . . It is only the susceptible, poetical, and refined mind that can see these things as they are, while others think they see them as they ought to be."[9]

The inspired writer can recognize transcendental truth and he can "convey the idea of a heavenly truth by an earthly one—that is, we may make an earthly truth the representative of a truth beyond expression. This shows the power of language. This shows that language has a higher office than to manifest the relations which subsist between us and the external world."[10] One method of doing this, he suggests, is "by glorifying sensation, which is finite, into thought, which is infinite, thereby creating an image . . . . the more palpably this thought is made manifest in the IMAGE, through Art, the more lucid will be the *Revelation of the Divine Beauty*."[11]

These revelations can be perceived only by the man who has had his eyes "couched."[12] All men are by nature divine, for "Man is the reason of God—the highest expression of God's ideal of the Beautiful in the creation. It is by realizing here on earth in its fullest extent, the two fold object—*spiritual* and *natural*—of his creation, that he can assimilate to the Angels in Heaven. As Man is the incarnation of God's reason in the world, it is impossible for him to exercise his natural faculties in harmony with the manifold beauties of the visible creation, without experiencing some of these ineffable thrills of delight which He himself felt in giving birth to them."[13] But men did not share equally in these natural faculties. There were degrees of perceptiveness and of goodness. The true poet must have "the perfectly couched eyes of an illuminated Seer"; he must have, also, inward virtues so that he can be in harmony with, and thus understand, transcendental ideas.[14] Chivers quoted with approval "the sublime words of Milton, that 'He who would write a Heroic Poem, must live the heroic life.' "[15]

This meant that the poet must write out of his own experience, and above all out of his own imagination. In his own poetry Chivers practised strenuously his theory that poetry should be self-expression. In sending a group of poems to Edgar Allan Poe, he claimed that "They were written right out of my heart, as I write everything. Poetry, with me, is the melodious expression of my very being."[16] This should be inherent in the work of other men, for he generalized from his own belief and practice when he stated dogmatically that a "true Lyric must be stricken from the Poet's Soul at a high heat. It must be a reverberation of the joyful thrills of the throbbing heart."[17] If emotion was genuine, the poem would be authentic: "whenever you see a song which is the offspring of either true Love, or bitter Sorrow—it is a true song—a legitimate child of its father—otherwise it is no true son of the soul, but a poor bastard. It is by this that you may judge of a true song—one that is truly self-revelative—for by its own potency it will burn its own way into the hearts of all those who have ever really loved or suffered."[18]

This did not mean, in his estimation, that the writer could disregard art. Ideally, the concept and the form should come into existence simultaneously: "If the Poet be a true one, the garments will be woven at the moment of the birth of the Angel of Beauty, and not afterwards. . . . The garments will then be sure to fit the form, as the form will be certain to swell out into the classic folds of the garments."[19] As Chivers' numerous revisions of his own poems testify, this rarely happened even in his own works. Also, the value that he set on art, in spite of his high praise, was ultimately secondary; it was not a satisfactory substitute for nature or passion or enthusiasm: "Art is the offspring rather than the mother."[20] Philosophically he believed that "Beauty, in its outward manifestation, is the expression of an inward formal grace—just as the body is an outward expression of the soul." In attempting to differentiate between nature and art, he found this comparison equally applicable: "There are, in every true Poem, two beauties (just as there are in the Sacred Oracles, a spiritual and a literal meaning)—an outward and inward beauty—one of Art, the other of Nature, or Passion. Now, the outward form, or Art, of a Poem, is precisely to that Poem what the body is to the soul. . . . Now, that Poem which consists in a perfect unition of these two—that is, Passion and Art—a pure body united to a pure soul—is a pure Poem; and stands in the same relation to its Author, that Man does to God. Such a Poem would be the truest Revelation of the Perfect, or Divine Man—as none but just such a man could write such a Poem."[21]

In his attempt to clarify the distinction between nature and art, Chivers divided poetry into the Gothic and the Greek. His use of the term *Greek* is clear-cut and consistent: it denominates that kind of poetry in which artistry prevails, frequently at the expense of nature or passion. *Gothic,* although not ambiguous in his usage, frequently designates the thought or passion or enthusiasm implicit in the best poetry, and at other times describes that poetry in which passion predominates. This difference between Gothic and Greek had appeared very early in man's history, for the "most ancient utterings of the God-inspired Prophets" were essentially Gothic, with the result that "While

Taste sat as umpire of the Greek Beauty, the Moral Sense governed the Hebrew mind." Yet this did not mean that the Gothic must be inartistic, for "all Art, whether the true Greek Art or not, must be that which is fortuitous—that which is coeternal with the creation of the Poetical Forms of Beauty. . . . Nor do I mean by this that the Gothic thought should not be able to mould its forms into such beauty as characterized the Greek Art, but that the expression of the soul—the manifestation of the being— the Existere of the creation must be coeternal with its Divine Esse."[22]

The Hebrews had lost more than the Greeks. After the time of Adam, the Hebrews had lost the image of the "truly Divine Man"; only a few Prophets possessed a "clairvoyant intuition into the Divine Glory," which they expressed through their poetry. But the Hebrew ideal was the image of the divine man; the Greek, that of the "perfect human, through Art—Man." Chivers thought that the ideal of beauty had been stronger in Greece than in any other nation, for they "adored the Divine Being through the mediation of the perfected human form. . . . This they manifested through the most perfect forms of art."[23]

The greatest poets had combined the Gothic and Greek element in their work, for the "true Poet is always an artist of the highest order." Art could be perfected by study, although it could "never be acquired by mere talent."[24] But art could give only the outward beauty, not the necessary fusion of passion and art. The greatest delight "which Poetry produces in the mind of every well educated man consists in the Gothic grandeur of the thought. . . . What I mean by the Gothic nature of a poem consists in the intuitive fortuitousness of its creation. . . . Now the Gothic is the true—the Natural; the Greek, the artificial, thought."[25]

Such writers as David, Solomon, Homer, Shakespeare, Milton, and Shelley had been predominantly Gothic. This quality especially characterized the writers of the Elizabethan era: "Their quaint grotesqueness is just precisely the quality which constitutes the Gothic nature of their Poetry—a quality entirely independent of any intention or foregone conclusion—therefore, intuitive—fortuitous." Poe was wrong in thinking that Tennyson wrote better poems than the Elizabethans, just as Poe was wrong in believing that a "pure Poem proper is one that is wholly destitute of a particle of passion." Chivers was convinced that Poe and Tennyson erred in writing poems "totally devoid of passion, the primum mobile of the true Poet—that Gothic fortuition which characterizes all true Poems being swallowed up in the marble statuesqueness of Greek Art." The fundamental difference was that the "Elizabethan Bards wrote out of the heart; Tennyson out of the brain."[26]

Artistry was needed, but artistic ingenuity was not enough. Poetry first of all, he believed, "consists in ideality." Using a favorite word, he describes the "artistical skill of a Poem" as the "Shekinah or visible manifestation of the divinity within. Poetry is, therefore, the perfection of literature. It is the perfected artistical symbol of the most perfect wisdom of the most exalted mind."[27]

Although he wrote to Poe that "Music and poetry are my chief delights," he seems never to have doubted that poetry was the greatest of all the arts.[28] Music represents "the *feminine,* and Poetry the *masculine* elements of expression. . . . Music is to Poetry what light is to the sun." Wagner was wrong in thinking that he had emancipated the poet from the menial relation in which he had stood to the musician. As far as the opera was concerned, the musician was dependent on the poet: since there has never been a perfect libretto, there is, "consequently, nothing like a perfect opera." Chivers regretted this, for he believed that "the union of perfect Music to perfect Poetry is the representation not only of the marriage of Earth and Heaven, but also the *crystalline Revelation of the Divine Idea.*"[29]

One possibility was to make words do the work of music. "Being is rhythm. The true revelation of this being is Melody shekinized in verse."[30] He experimented constantly with the effect of word-sounds, carrying some of them to the point that meaning practically disappears. In the same way he experimented with increasingly complex refrains, and he roundly declared that "in regard to the Refrain of a Poem, I would merely mention here, that it is not only an ornament, but an essence—a life—a vitality—an immortal soul—not a mere profane appendage, but a sacred Symbolical Ensignium—a crown of beauty, and a diamond of glory. . . . It is to a Poem precisely what Ovid says of the outward golden tire of the many-spoked wheel of the Chariot of Apollo, that makes a continual, ever-recurring Auroral chime at every revolution of the wheels, proportionate to their velocity, which is never lost."[31]

In his estimation, few American or English poets understood the proper use of rhythm, metre, and musical language: "No two things are oftener confounded than Rhythm and Metre. Metre presupposes Rhythm—for there can be no Metre without some sort of Rhythm. When applied to poetry, it may be defined to be, the musical relation, harmony, or proportion of words—for there may be rhythm in dancing without any words. Metre is the certain determinate limitations given to any Rhythm. It is therefore obvious that wherever there is Metre there is, also, Rhythm; but not because there is Rhythm that there is, also, Metre." After discussing his belief that the Greeks first used the "Satyric, or Trochaic" and his concept of the various metrical feet, Chivers added that "two kinds of Rhythm introduced in any one kind of Metre, will relieve the monotony," but this must be done in such a way "as to maintain the perfect *identity of the original Rhythm.*"[32] He was also keenly interested in discussing the proper Anglicized pronunciation of foreign words and the concomitant true or false accents, and the degree of poetic license that might be allowable for the sake of the rhythm.[33]

This emphasis on musical effect was extended so far that it became an integral part of his concept of originality. The true poet must have depth of feeling, but he must have something more: "Originality in any Poem consists in its novel combination of numbers and *not* in the unnaturalness of its manifestations—for this derogates in every sense from its originality."[34] Any versifier could imitate the old models, but Chivers claimed for himself that he did not "steal the old English forms and then send my imitations forth into the world as *something* achieved. I have too much mother-wit to use this insulting pretension."[35] He was obsessed by the spectre of plagiarism, and he made violently intemperate attacks on those he suspected of stealing his own work, and in response to mild suggestions that he might have been influenced by others. Chivers was easily driven into absurd over-statements even by friendly critics, but some of them emphasize his pre-occupation with structure: "there is nothing in which I take so much pride as in never having written a single line in imitation of another. Every line is original. If you will examine my Poems, as they *must* be examined before they can be understood, you will perceive that they are all artistically my own. Any body of moderate ideality can write a Poem by another's rhythm; but it is a task which few ever attempted to originate a style. . . . The very rhythm of my Poems cost me years of study."[36]

Since the technique was as important as the theme, it naturally followed that only a poet was qualified to be a critic of poetry: "No one but a Poet can know what *true* Poetry is. No man ever understood the *spiritual beauty* of Milton's *Paradise Lost* as well as he did himself."[37] Probably this conviction had been induced by his feeling that most critics were ignorant of the poetic art, and that "not one man in ten thousand can read a Poem correctly."[38] He recognized that in order to have great writers it was necessary to have great audiences—or, in his words, the creators must have recipients. But Chivers had a thorough-going distrust both of so-called critics and of "the popular mind . . . no people were ever yet Critics."[39] It was easier for him to conceive of great artists than it was to imagine a perceptive audience: "It is not only a difficult thing to make the music, but it is a *more* difficult thing to teach mankind that it has been made—as it is a good deal more easy to make music than to create brains."[40]

There was also little understanding of the need for a poetical language. Many people think they can write verses without any knowledge of prosody or of what constitutes "*a pure poetical language.*" In all languages some words are more beautiful than others. The true poet must know this, just as he must know the relations between vowel sounds to form musical words. There was a need also for "some conjugation of chime between the vowels and the consonants." These, with alliteration and similar devices, make up "the *Euphony of Prosody.*"[41] Only when American poets understood this euphony and admitted the necessity of using a poetical language could we expect to have great poetry. Essentially, the language he desired was based on the musical relationships of letters and of words, but as always in his definitions he leaped readily from this world to the next: it "must be a Language whose soul, *per se,* is of music . . . it must partake of the nature of the Language, of the Angels in Heaven."[42]

However essential, art by itself was not enough. Art is to poetry like wings to birds, or like body to soul—"the *Existere* of its divine *Esse.*" The creator must be an artist but he must also be a genius. True, only a perfect man, a Christ, could write a perfect poem. But a man could express through poetry what he intuitively perceived. There was one danger: "People too often mistake the *relations* of things for the *things* themselves." But writer and reader should be concerned with the psychological rather than the actual, for thus the poets can "cause to spring up in the minds of others the same emotions that live and breathe in our own."[43] Chivers never doubted the fundamental value of this revelation. Insofar as a man could achieve it, all the feelings of past, present, and future time could be represented in poetry. This might be unattainable, but the mortal poet's task is divine because the "moment that the love of poetry becomes universal, that moment will mankind become universally happy."[44]

II

According to his own account, Chivers was introduced to poetry at the age of seven, when he read William Cowper's "The Rose" in Webster's *American Spelling Book*; well over forty years later, he wrote to a correspondent that the "music of the lines . . . is still ringing in my memory now at this hour, and will forever ring there as long as I live."[45] But Cowper's influence was slight or non-existent, for Chivers approved heartily when Poe declared that his poems "partake *more* of the Chaucerian, or impulsive, than of the Cowperian, or artificial, era. This he instances not only to show the entire *originality*, but the *merits* of them."[46] His early taste was formed by writers who seemed to him more spontaneous, more inspired, and more in keeping with his age. Of the eighteenth-century poets he was most attracted to the pre-romantic Edward Young, quite possibly because in *Night Thoughts* he found some clarification of his own increasing pre-occupation with death. Several of his early poems are closely modelled after, and undoubtedly suggested by, Thomas Campbell, Charles Wolfe, Thomas Moore, and, above all, Lord Byron.[47]

If his memory is correct, his reading must have been desultory. He records that at Transylvania (1828-30) he had seen a performance of *Othello* by "Cooper, the great tragedian"; since he thought it the work of the actor, Cooper seemed to him "the greatest man that ever existed on earth." Back in Washington he read Dr. Dodd's *Beauties of Shakespeare* and apparently for the first time made the acquaintance of the author: "If the Angels in Heaven enjoy any greater delights, it is impossible for me to conceive how they do it. . . . Then I first tasted of ambrosia. Then I first drank of the nectar of the Gods—for I felt like a little God myself."[48] From that time on, he was to Chivers the "god-like Shakespeare," whose works made the building of the Pyramids a relatively insignificant accomplishment, and whose mind, "when compared with all the other great minds of the world, is as the Sun compared with the Stars."[49]

Yet his early influence on Chivers was negligible. More pertinent to his own religious interests was such a minor poem as
Robert Pollok's *The Course of Time* (1827), from which he borrowed freely; far more pertinent to his life and thought, immediately after his separation from his first wife, was the life and
the poetry of Lord Byron. It seems impossible to determine just
how early Byron became a dominant influence, but at the time
that Chivers wrote *The Path of Sorrow* he not only borrowed
many poetical devices but he clearly and deliberately suggested a
parallel between his own personal tragedy and that of Byron, as
Charles Watts has perceptively noted: "In his first volume, *The
Path of Sorrow*, Chivers pays tribute enough to Byron; while
there is no poem addressed to his first literary master, lines from
his work serve as mottoes to six of the eighteen poems, and vir-
tually every poem in the volume bears the imprint of his particular tone and subject matter."[50]

The direct influence of Byron soon waned, but Chivers never
doubted that he was one of the great poets. For Byron was an intensely personal poet who "wrote with great force. His mind was
peculiarly Lyrical, although he possessed but little originality.
No man ever had a greater horror for the shackles of pedantry
than he did. He disdained all subordination, and soared with a
free and a fiery wing."[51] As a man, Byron had been one of the
great apostles of liberty and freedom, and for this Chivers honored him poetically in "The Mighty Dead," but as a poet his
greatest achievement "is the expression of the unbridled passions
of his heart . . . one quality in his poetry distinguishes it from all
the other poetry in the world. It is that turbid fountain of sorrow
which has the power of imparting . . . the loneliness, the wretch-
edness and the apparent misfortunes of the author."[52]

Byron and Shelley had been "spiritual beacon lights to the ages
in which they lived."[53] But there was no doubt in his mind that
"the divine" Shelley, "the golden mouthed swan of Albion," was
the greater;[54] with the possible exception of Elizabeth Barrett
Browning, he was the greatest of nineteenth-century poets. It
seemed to Chivers that heavenly inspiration had "descended
upon the soul of Shelley," with the result that he "possessed precisely that grotesqueness of abandon necessary to the production
of the perfect lyric." His one defect was a lack of what Chivers
called "constructive genius." But he compensates for this by his
"forceful abandon," as well as by being "one of the most virtuous
men that ever lived. . . . Shelley professed nothing but what he

acted out and lived. He was, in the strictest sense, a practical Ethical Christian—one of God's greatest intellectual giants."[55]

Shelley was like Byron in being an apostle of liberty, but he went beyond Byron in that he also advocated divine liberty: "the difference between Byron's poetry and Shelley's consists in this, that the breathings of the former are the melancholy outbreaks of a spirit at war from disappointment, with the world; those of the latter are the pathetic expressions of a soul which panted after an *ideal of intellectual perfection*."[56] He was also quite willing to compare Shelley with greater poets, for he told Poe that "I consider him one of the greatest Poets that ever lived. . . . His Cenci I consider not inferiour, as a true Dramatic Poem, to the very best of Shakespeare's plays. In fact, in some senses it is superior to any thing that Shakespeare ever wrote."[57]

His enthusiasm for Keats, whom he also labelled as divine, was almost equally fervid: "John Keats, whom the Gods so peculiarly loved that he was taken up from the earth in early life to join them in the divine Beatitudes of Heaven. . . . He was one of the most divine souls that ever rose in England. . . . He possessed just that fortuitousness of conception—that divine instinct —which he expressed in that grotesqueness of abandon in every way necessary to the production of a great English Poet." For Keats was "the greatest Idealist" among English poets; at the same time his description of Adonis's Bower of Bliss in *Endymion* is "the most beautiful Picture ever drawn by the pencil of man or Angel."[58]

When Poe called Tennyson one of the greatest poets that ever lived, Chivers in a moment of irritation responded that "his Poems are as effeminate as a phlegmatic fat baby. He is the most perfectly Greek statuesque, if you please—in his conceptions of any man that ever lived since the days of Pericles."[59] In letters to Poe written soon afterward, Chivers moderated his language, claiming that his oral remarks were made when he was weary, but he did not change his fundamental belief that Tennyson lacked passion. "There is a finer finish—a more elaborate perfection in the Poems of Tennyson than in any Poet that ever lived," he admitted. But Tennyson was only "a lofty imitator of Shelley without a *tithe* of his force."[60] At its best, Tennyson's poetry was "the work of a man who possesses the highest insight into the divine loveliness of Beauty," but it was, unfortunately, "Art, without passion."[61] Chivers was convinced that Tennyson had never felt any deep emotions: even the language of *In Memoriam* was not that of natural grief, for he had felt no burning grief. Instead, he had submerged passionate grief "in the frozen ocean of mere sentiment," without recognizing that "the pure Elegy is the spontaneous wail of lacerated affection."[62]

For this reason Tennyson as elegist is inferior to the simple wail of Moschus, the elaborate splendor of Shelley, and the grandeur of Milton. In addition, he has here picked an unnatural and unpleasing rhyme scheme: "in listening to the response of the second and third lines, you forget that there is any such thing as a response in the fourth to the first—and consequently, the whole Euphony of the Rhyme in the Poem is lost." This was a minor defect; the major one is that which he finds in all the work: "The fact is, depth of feeling is just precisely what Tennyson wants to make him either a Song or an Elegy writer."[63]

For at least a brief period, Chivers considered Elizabeth Barrett Browning the best contemporary English poet. When John Wilson and Tennyson were suggested for the vacant laureateship, he declared flatly that Tennyson was "a million times a greater man and will dignify the office better than any man that has ever been a Laureate." But he added immediately that he preferred Mrs. Browning, "the milk-white swan of Albion, to either."[64] When he read her *Drama of Exile* he wrote an ecstatic sonnet of the effect this narrative poem had on him; in equally unrestrained prose he called her the "greatest genius of modern time—if not the greatest the world ever saw. . . . Her *Drama of Exile* is the sublimest Orphic Monument ever erected by the female mind. . . . Her peculiar idiosyncrasy is nervous exuberance of ideality. She possesses all the abandon of Shelley, with a good deal of the artistical skill of Tennyson—all those attributes of a true Poet of the highest order which Shelley did not possess and Tennyson wants, namely the constructive genius which Shelley had not, with the forceful abandon which he had; and the divine lightning which Tennyson does not have."[65]

Like many of his contemporary critics, he over-valued R. H. Horne's *Orion*. Horne lacked ideality, but he had great artistical force.[66] In maturity Chivers continued to admire Thomas Campbell as "one of the finest of the English Lyrical Poets. . . . Not that he ever invented any remarkable *combinations of rhythm,* but that the *finish* of his Art was of the Greek fastidiousness . . . rather the result of his knowledge of the Poetry of Language, than fortuitous." He thought "Hohenlinden" a model of lyrical genius, combining fervor and beauty.[67] But he had lost his taste for Tom Moore. Hazlitt was wrong in objecting to *Lalla Rookh* for being *"only some short tales"* and not a long or true epic. This in fact is its main virtue. But it failed because it was only "a poetical paraphrase" of "Persian Mythology and Oriental Travels transmuted into seductive couplets." And running through Moore's work, especially in his *Loves of the Angels,* was an "odoriferous goatism."[68]

In his own view, he was justifiably incensed when he was accused of imitating Wordsworth. For Wordsworth, like Tennyson, had "little or no passion—the *primum mobile* of the *true* Poet."[69] He substituted sentiment, with the result that although some passages are "beautifully and pathetically expressed," his poems are either didactic or metaphysical. This meant that "Wordsworth has written as little *true* Poetry, to have written as voluminously, as any man that ever lived in England, or any other country with the exception, perhaps, of Montgomery."[70]

Although he repeatedly calls Coleridge "the myriad-minded,"[71] Chivers seems to have been more interested in his criticism than in his poetry. When he collected definitions of poetry, he praised Coleridge for making pleasure the end of art, and for calling poesy "the vision and faculty divine," although he complains that Coleridge did not go far enough.[72] But Coleridge was wrong in defining poetry as the antithesis to science because poetry has nothing to do with science or with prose. Prose is "this imperfect language of mankind" which prevents us from expressing our "innate yearnings after the unattained." Prose was really "no tongue at all . . . a *true* language being none other than that of pure Poetry."[73]

He preferred the Scottish poets to the Lake poets. Scotland had produced in Robert Burns, Robert Tannahill, and John Mayne three great lyrical poets, as well as innumerable fine writers of ballads. They had "always excelled in ballad-writing, from the very fact that they never forgot to make good use of the refrain."[74] Burns especially possessed insight into "the true nature of what constitutes the perfect lyric—that is, the Art and Passion necessary to create a suitable mediator for the lucid revolution of the highest song." Critics who called them minor poets because they had not written epics did not understand the nature of poetry; the epic is "a very good thing, *in its way,* but it is no better than a lyric." It requires as much genius to write a good lyric as a good epic, and the poet who can write a large volume of perfect short poems could as easily have written an epic. Burns could have done so.[75] In the poems that he had actually written, the most obvious characteristic "is natural, artless and unsophisticated sincerity." But the artlessness was in his nature, with its patriotic and tender emotions; his poems possess "art of a high order—if not of the very highest" in his "purely *Gothic Lyrics.*"[76]

Chivers rarely hesitated to deliver positive, off-hand judgments about other poets. Robert Montgomery in *The Messiah* had written on a subject that appealed to Chivers, but he had handled the material so prosaically that he "has written as little good poetry, to have written so voluminously, as any Poet, perhaps, in England. There is a good deal of masculine force and religious energy about all he writes." But his theses were didactic and he lacked ideality, with the result that his works "betray none of that Cherubimical outpouring of enthusiasm which radiates from the spirit-stirrings of that sweet singer in the Temple, George Herbert, and which ought always to characterize devotional Poetry. Nor are they equal, in any degree, to the simple and pathetic Hymns of Wesley and Watts."[77]

When Poe called Tennyson and Horne the best poets in England in 1845, Chivers complained that he had left out Thomas Lovell Beddoes, and he later declared that Beddoes' *Fool's Tragedy* had "all the strength of Mr. Bailey's Festus without his rudeness of expression."[78] He did not care much for Scott's narrative poems, but he noted that there were many beautiful lyrics scattered among them. Leigh Hunt had tenderness but was destitute of passion.[79]

His English contemporaries interested him. Few poets of the preceding century did. He described Edward Young as "religion's Cicero," and drew on his work for headnotes to thirteen poems.[80] About Thomas Chatterton he was ecstatic. Pope and Cowley were reputed to have written poems at twelve and fifteen, but this work was inferior to Chatterton's at eleven. Also, Chatterton was self-educated, and this when rightly considered "will lift this glorious little Ganymede of God far above any other being that ever lived on the earth of the same age." Chatterton's lyric gift was proved by the two-fold beauty of his poems: "that of conception—that is, *the theme*—and also, of the *execution.*"[81]

Pope and Cowper typified the most prosaic and therefore the most objectionable kind of poets. In his judgment, "Pope was no Poet." Neither was Cowper. Chivers would not even allow that Pope was a skillful technician: his use of the caesura was monotonous, especially in his translation of the *Iliad.*[82] After admitting that Pope's "The Dying Christian to his Soul" was beautiful and lyrical, he added the stinging comment that it "is perhaps the boldest plagiarism ever perpetrated. It is the finest specimen in the English language of how beautiful a superstructure can be raised upon the basis of another man's invention."[83]

Chivers nearly always spoke of Milton in superlatives. To him, Milton "was the most Godlike child. . . . His father bestowed upon him a double amount of his spirit and blessed him with a double portion of his wisdom in making him not only an image of himself as a Poet, but a Philosopher and a Prophet. . . . Like Moses he saw God from afar."[84] Chivers imagined that he could see the "divine spirits of Milton and Dante . . . walking arm in arm among the never-ending *Fields of Bliss* amid the *Holy Paradise of God.* . . . Dante, Petrarch, Shakespeare, Milton, and Calderon were those bright shining stars in the firmament of mind, which reflected, as the stars the sun, the spirit of the Messiah." Although he at least partially contradicted the statement elsewhere, Chivers added that "*Paradise Lost* is the living witness of the deathless divinity which gave it birth. It is the sublimest epic that ever the spirit of Genius bequeathed the generations of all succeeding time."[85]

Not the least of Milton's achievements, in Chivers' estimation, was that he had developed a poetic style and rhythm peculiarly his own. He varied the pause in his blank verse, thus producing "variety in the meter"; he was always in control of his verse, which was founded on rhetoric and therefore "unlike the lofty Gothic fortuitous intuitions of Shakespeare."[86] Yet there is a certain resemblance. The versification of *Paradise Lost* is "peculiar in being the Gothic Dramatic glorified by the highest Epical Art."[87]

Chivers held that while Milton's mind was epical, his education was "dramatical." In a long comparison of *Paradise Lost* with the *Iliad,* Chivers argues that the two poets had entirely different concepts of what constitutes an epic. True, both stories were founded on a mythology, and their respective theologies were developed in each. But Coleridge was wrong in preferring *Paradise Lost* because it had greater unity; he missed the essential point that "this is no demerit to the Iliads, as they were Lyrics, so that the Iliads, when combined in one Book, may be called *Lyrical Epics.*" Chivers was, in fact, rather doubtful that a unified long epic could be pleasing in its entirety, but only in "beautiful or select passages,"[88] and he noted that Milton "touches us most nearly" in the subjective lyric at the beginning of Book III. For the very reason that it is a series of poems, the *Iliad* has a certain superiority. Homer's is the "true Epical style— Milton's not." He was satisfied that he was right in preferring only "the really poetical passages," to the whole with its inferior connecting links, and he declares grandly though perhaps unwisely that "Coleridge says differently, but who cares for that." Also, while *Paradise Lost* abounds in "many purely Epical passages," these are all "deduced from the Dramatic Style of the Elizabethan Era—that beautiful, world-illumining golden Age of English Literature."[89]

Apparently Chivers thought these reservations minor. In a sonnet he wrote that *Paradise Lost* had been "Dipt from Heaven's everlasting golden well";[90] he repeatedly praised Milton for his "matchless descriptions" in that poem and in *Comus*; he was certain that only Shakespeare had surpassed Milton in felicity of language. "What a great *Moral Poem* is Milton's *Paradise Lost!* What a great *Moral Teacher* was he! The world never produced a greater."[91]

Shakespeare also was "God-like." Milton, knowing the art of poetry, attributed Shakespeare's inelegancies to want of it, but Milton forgot the exigencies of drama and also that "the highest order of Art is not that which is the outside polish of the conception, but coeternal with it." Shakespeare made no apparent effort to attain sublimity, "yet he is the sublimest of Poets. . . . Go where you will, you will always find something that is beautiful —something wherein his worst is better than the best of other minds."[92] Chivers enjoyed quibbling over textual variants, and in tracing the derivations of disputed words to their origins, whether Greek, Hebrew, or Gothic.[93] His enthusiasm reached its highest and most rhetorical peak when he declared flatly that "the building of the Pyramids was a mere child's play when compared with the Titanic monuments which he erected for the Glory of God. What is the Chinese wall when compared with Hamlet or Antony and Cleopatra?"[94]

With two exceptions, his praise of the other Elizabethan dramatists is usually generalized. He singled out John Lyly for enthusiastic comments, calling *Emdymion* "one of the most beautiful and classical dramas ever written," and the song "Cupid and my Campaspe Played" a "perfect paragon . . . unequalled in the language, and sparkles like a diamond-studded crown. . . . Here we see the simplicity of Anacreon; the pathetic tenderness of

Simonides; the fervid and golden mellifluousness of Sappho; and the grotesqueness of abandon of Keats." Lyly was indeed "one of the sweetest singers that ever raised his clarion voice to the gates of God."[95]

He was equally enthusiastic about John Webster, and there is some evidence that he contemplated preparing a modern version of *The White Devil* for the stage.[96] Certainly he made an extensive textual comparison of the 1665 edition and the new version edited by William Hazlitt. Also, he recorded his conviction that "This Tragedy contains not only some of the loftiest learning, but, also, much of the most starry writing. It is written in the noblest Dramatic style, and is, in many parts, equal to the *Duchess of Malfi*—the Masterpiece of Tragic Composition."[97]

Although he quoted readily from well-known writers like Sir Thomas Wyatt and relatively obscure ones like Nicholas Breton, Chivers felt that of the non-dramatic writers Edmund Spenser had the most to offer, for "Reading his poetry is like going into the Bowers of Paradise before the fall—an Elysium to the Soul." English poetry before Chaucer had been rather narrative than lyrical, and essentially a part of Scandinavian poetry. The Normans through their troubadours brought in lyrical forms; Chaucer invented no new rhythmical or metrical forms, but he perfected and Anglicized the old. He was "the great old Morning Star of English Literature, in whose style the original, Gothic Narrative Poem was consummated."[98]

III

Although an ardent nationalist who wished to encourage the development of a distinctive and valid American literature,[99] Chivers rarely let this handicap him when he was discussing his fellow poets. In theory he believed that criticism should be helpful, especially to young writers, and he protested to Poe that sometimes "you seemed to me to lay aside the pruning-knife for the tomahawk, and not only to lop off the redundant limbs, but absolutely to deracinate the entire tree. In such cases there is no hope of its ever afterwards bearing fruit. . . . I have seen a little sapling transplanted before now, which had every appearance of dying, until it had undergone a gentle pruning and watering, when, to the astonishment of the Gardener, it towered above all the rest in the grove, and remained a living monument of his skill and kind attention. The same thing is true in regard to the literary world."[100] In practice, however, he could find little that was good in his contemporaries.

Except for Poe, the only American poet who really interested Chivers was Ralph Waldo Emerson. For one thing, he was convinced that "All *true* poetry is certainly transcendental," for to him transcendentalism was only another name for revelation, and was the effect of inspiration.[101] Emerson recognized this, and he was by far the "most Ideal" of any of the Northern poets; despite a certain "crudity of expression," he had "glimpses of the Dawn of a Day but only partially revealed." Such a poem as "The Mountain and the Squirrel" seemed a "*piquant* and *naive* little poem," although if Emerson displays an art in this and similar works, "it is rather the Art of Nature than the Nature of Art." But "The Humble Bee," his best poem, was a successful attempt "to blend Nature and Art." Chivers concluded that Emerson was greater as a prose writer in the sense that he has "done more *for* prose than he has done for Poetry," but nothing he has written in prose "will compare with what he has done in poetry."[102]

For Bryant, Longfellow, and Lowell he had scant regard. Chivers sympathizes when Poe lamented that he was forced to speak respectfully of Bryant even though Bryant did not know what true poetry was, and had never written any. Chivers' own unflattering judgment was that the "only thing he ever wrote that may be called *Poetry* is 'Thanatopsis,' which he stole *line for line* from the Spanish. The fact is, that he never did anything but steal—as nothing he ever wrote is original."[103]

Longfellow was far worse, because he had stolen directly from Chivers. He would admit that Longfellow was an artist, but "his passions are still rooted in his brain—not in his heart—where they ought to be." Since Longfellow does not believe that morality and human passion are compatible, how can he be a poet? Moreover, Longfellow "never creates, but writes under the firm conviction . . . that to *appropriate* is the prime wisdom." He had, among other appropriations, taken over Poe's *Raven*," transmuting "his crow-like plumage into the milky whiteness of a true Bird of Paradise." Worse, he had (like Poe) stolen from Chivers, who had written "To Allegra Florence in Heaven" in trochaic form, "the most tender, pathetic and melodious style ever invented," and the one best suited for the elegy: a fact which Chivers believed he was the first to realize and to put into practice. *Hiawatha* revealed the "power which this style exercised over the mind of

Professor Longfellow," although he had only achieved "an echo of the true voice of Melody." Chivers admitted that Longfellow might have borrowed thematic material and legendary lore from the Finnish mythology and Eddas, but he could not have found the "essentials of rhythm" in the *Kalevala,* because they are not there. Chivers rested his case on the "rhythmical idiosyncrasy" common to *Hiawatha* and his own poems.[104]

Lowell simply was not a poet. Chivers claimed that he had read and re-read *The Legend of Brittany* and "endeavored to find any traces of Poetry in it, but tried in vain." He asks rhetorically if blood can come out of a turnip, or if there is any taste in the white of an egg. There is nothing original, and the "whole volume is made up of effeminate efforts to become strong." There is only one poem worthy to be called such, and that only so in "a subordinate sense, namely on account of its expression, and that is *Rosaline.*" These poems may be called "the little end of nothing whittled out to a point."[105] When Poe praised "Rosaline," Chivers responded that it was "as palpable a plagiarism as was ever palmed off by arrogant mental mediocrity upon a too credulous Public." Poe asked what made it a plagiarism, and the reply helps to make clear Chivers' peculiar ideas about originality: "Not only in the rhythms but also the rhyming consonations. In fact, it is a plagiarism in the very chime of it."[106] Chivers returned again to the attack when he asked if it was Lowell who wrote "a book called a *Fable for the Critics?* Certainly he did. Very well then. Why should I speak against him? . . . No words of mine could do what he has done to damn himself."[107]

His comments on other poets are rarely more generous. In 1850 he noted that in New York there were "few men of real talent . . . and *not one real genius.*" Byron had written his *English Bards and Scotch Reviewers* in "a fit of spleen"; A. J. H. Duganne, "perhaps, the best poetical critic here," had written *Parnassus in Pillory* in cold blood. Mr. Duganne had mistakenly used the poetic form, but "Satire belongs to the province of prose —not poetry."[108] He quoted two lines from Joseph Rodman Drake's "Niagara," with the scathing comment that there "never was, perhaps, a more obstreperous or asinine specimen of exuberant bathos." He had no use for N. P. Willis and deprecated his criticism of Poe; in addition, "No man can put his finger on a single poem by N. P. Willis, which would authorize him to call him by the sacred name of Poet. His style had an airy fantasqueness . . . but this is only a manifestation of his extreme artificial-

ity. . . . The most of his rhythms are copies from Mrs. Hemans'
—which are also copies."[109] The best he could say for Willis, after
he heard Poe read "Unseen Spirits," was that "I am compelled to
doubt its originality. However, it is a beautiful poem."[110]

Although he wrote a four-page preface to a novel which he had
written or (more probably) contemplated writing and in which
he proclaimed that "there has never been any such thing as a
true novel—consequently, no such thing as pure delight from the
reading of one,"[111] he apparently has left no material that would
indicate much interest in that literary form. In this fragment he
notes, in fact, that all men desire happiness, but intellectual men
seek it through music or poetry. After reading Simms's play
Norman Maurice, he wrote in a personal letter that it is "the
best thing I have ever seen of yours—in fact, I am now puzzled to
know why you should ever have worn out your faculties in writing Novels."[112] He was bitter about Mrs. Stowe, "authoress of
the miserable book entitled *Uncle Tom's Cabin,*" but his basic
objections were to her anti-slavery sentiments rather than to her
insufficiency as novelist.[113] Perhaps his indifference to the novel is
traceable to this: as he indicated often, he regarded prose as an
inferior medium, useful for oratory and for defenses and explica-
tions of poetry and for dealing with the mundane world, but of
no real value when compared with poetry.

The records of his opinions of Poe are voluminous, and somewhat confusing. As a man Poe had certain aberrations which
Chivers could not condone, for he believed that Poe too often
"*subordinated* his mind [to] his body." Chivers admitted (or perhaps boasted) that he had preached "many sermons" to Poe on
the evils of drinking, but when Rufus Wilmot Griswold placed a
false and misleading emphasis on Poe's "drunkenness," Chivers
was furiously and contemptuously angry: "No man can dislike
drunkenness any more than I do; but I dislike injustice *infinitely*
more." Chivers notes that it was only "at long interims, he 'got
drunk.' . . . But independently of all this, was he not, with *all*
his foibles, greater, better, in every sense of the term—infinitely
better—than the very best of those who denounced him? Certainly
he was—inasmuch as he was infinitely above them in everything
that constitutes the *true man.*"[114]

The blemishes in Poe's life were not the results of character
but "were the results *solely* of circumstances." Griswold and
other narrow-minded commentators might try to make him out

"the incarnate Fiend," but they erred grievously: "Mr. Poe was not a monster—no demon—but rather an Angel—a fallen Angel if you please—but no monster."[115] Since Poe was human, he yielded at times to bodily temptations. Thus Chivers records that Poe confessed he was carrying on "the d---dst amour you ever knew a fellow to be in in all your life," and was desperately anxious to conceal it from his wife. But his physical lapses were less important than his disregarding "the Real for the Ideal," forgetting or not realizing that a "Poet should not go out of this world for the enjoyment and realization of his Ideals—for his Ideal should sphere within his Actual—but he should so temper them that that which is earthly should assume the far-up beauty of the heavenly."[116]

But Poe's greatest defect as poet was his false idea of the content of great poetry. Chivers disagreed violently when Poe declared flatly that "Passion has nothing to do with pure Poetry; for every drop of passion that you infuse into any Poem just so far do you materialize, deteriorate and render it no-Poem."[117] Chivers believed instead that pure poetry should be and is the embodiment of "the poet's purest passions," whereas Poe "always wrote as though all Poetry consisted more in the Poetry of the language, than in the passions of the heart to be expressed through that language."[118] Poe erred when he "subordinated intuition to pure art," just as he erred when he "made the God-created freeborn Passion a slave to Art." One of Poe's "unaccountable deficiencies was, his utter inability to see that any work, to be perfect—or even to *approach* perfection,—must be the result of an equal blending of Art and Passion—that is, the highest Passion united with the most exalted Art—the passion moulding the Art." The result was that too often his poems "are creatures of marble in a world of frozen music."[119]

In spite of this cardinal defect, Poe possessed genius, in a very high if not in the highest degree. Chivers gives his own definition of what constitutes a genius: "It is the sum total of all those qualities which go to make up true greatness; the power, within the human soul, to do that which constitutes all that we can conceive of the highest intelligences in Heaven; that peculiar characteristic which contradistinguishes one mind from every other; the ability to do what no other man can do, the faculty to reveal, in an unmistakable Synthesis, the Analysis of the divine Loveliness; the capability to bring down Heaven upon earth—to lift earth up into Heaven."[120]

With characteristic overstatement, Chivers asserted that Poe "possessed a higher genius than Plato,—a loftier talent than Pythagoras."[121] But where he pinpoints what seemed to him Poe's weakness as a poet, Chivers is vague about Poe's strength. Frequently Chivers refers to Poe as a fallen angel, not as one sent to earth "on some Divine Mission of use, but as an exile out of Heaven"; nonetheless, he was able to "ray off some of his divine lightnings for the dark midnight of this world. . . . Because the tongue that he spoke was not of this world but of Heaven. So it is with all great men—with every true Genius."[122]

It would seem that Chivers thought of himself as pre-eminently a Gothic poet; certainly he thought of Poe as pre-eminently a Greek poet. His comments on individual poems emphasize this limitation in his friend's work: "To Helen" seemed to him a "beautiful specimen of versification—particularly for a man of his age, but it is totally devoid of passion, the primum mobile of the true poet—that Gothic fortuition which characterizes all true Poems being swallowed up entirely in the marble statuesqueness of Greek Art"; "Ulalume" possessed a "Greek classical Olympian sombreness not only artistically wonderful, but mellifluously enchanting"; "Israfel" was "not only the most etherial—least passionate—but comes up *more to his own Ideal* of the Art— (which he contended consisted in being *wholly passionless*) than any that he ever wrote. In many senses, it is a truly remarkable production—being not only an Ariel in its physiology, but, in its psychology an Aeolian Harp. Ullalume [*sic*] is Nectar mixed with Ambrosia—this is the Bread of Heaven."[123]

As a writer of tales, Poe seemed to Chivers to remain essentially a poet. All of them "appear to me to be the faithful records of some peculiar phase of his own being, or mental rapture, at the time of his composition." From approximately seventy, Chivers selected "Eleonora" and "Shadow" for reprinting in his biography of Poe "not only because they are the most wonderful specimens of psychological Literature in the whole wide world of inspiration; but because they are the most perfect revelation of what he considered the *true* nature of the Tale proper."

"Eleonora" had also the virtue of being a "most beautiful unique as well as graphically true—although highly idealized—record of his early love for his wife." It seemed to Chivers to possess "all the novel charms of a Poem proper—if indeed, it may not be considered a Prose-Poem of the highest order—equal not only in originality of conception, but in artistical conception, to

the very best of Ossian's Poems." Chivers indicated that he
thought this the best of all Poe's creative work; he judged it "a
Classic of the highest order—the Gothic thought being wrought
out into the most enchanting beauty by an Art equal to that
which characterized the best Poems of the Periclean Age of
Graecian Glory. This is what constitutes its classicism—although,
as in all lofty productions—the creations of a true inspiration—the
Art is the offspring rather than the mother, of fortuitousness. Not
so with all Poe's productions—particularly his Poems—wherein we
can recognize how far he subordinated intuition to pure Art."

"Shadow" also was a "revelation of his own lofty Ideals of
Beauty—a Beauty, indeed, enveloped in darkness—a darkness that
unfolds to us, as it were, the very loveliness that it, at first blush,
appears to hide—bursting upon us, not in a flood of glory—as a
less skill-ful Artist would have made it—but in fitful and enchanting glimpses, like the revelation of a Divine Light from
Heaven. In this consisted the wonderful, if not supernatural, Art
of Poe. . . . This constituted his originality as a Tale writer."[124]

For Poe as critic, Chivers had almost unbounded admiration.
Perhaps the superlative among many superlatives was his statement that Poe was one of "the greatest—if not *the* very greatest
Critic that ever lived."[125] He made one complaint about Poe's
critical practice in dealing with authors: he did not like it when,
as he wrote in a letter, *"you tomahawk people."*[126] But he at
least partially retracted this judgment when he later wrote that
"It was the firm belief of the asinine *bon-homie* that he delighted
in torturing an Author; but nothing is farther from the truth—his
whole severity consisting in a clairvoyant intuition into the merits
or demerits of his work."[127] Poe had also a gift for explication:
"I can read a Poem with greater delight after your criticism than
before."[128]

Chivers had one major reservation about Poe's poetic theory:
his belief that "pure Poetry consisted in Artistical passionless expression."[129] Here, Poe seemed clearly wrong. Otherwise, he
paid ungrudging tribute to Poe as theorist: "Your conception of
the uses, or excellence, of Poetry is the loftiest I have seen. . . . I
consider your definition of Poetry far superior to Lord Bacon's—although I consider him one of the greatest men that ever
existed."[130] In a letter to a Georgia editor, Chivers significantly
extended his estimate of Poe when he wrote that no "more perfect gentleman existed. He is not only one of the best Critics,
but one of the most versatile and accomplished scholars in the

world." Poe's critical theories and his practice were based, in Chivers's estimation, not on ignorance but on comprehensive knowledge, and they pleased him mightily.[131]

The accusation that in his poetry Chivers was an imitator or at least a follower of Poe did not please him—in fact, he re-acted to the charge so violently that he ceased to be the critic and became almost irresponsible in his own charges and denials. He believed that many poets, including Poe, had levied heavily upon his "To Allegra Florence in Heaven." When critics after his death praised Poe's originality, Chivers responded in a generalized and temperate article. Universal imitation of a poem is *"prima facie* evidence of its excellence." But the imitation he refers to is not that of ideas. He again defines his idea of originality: "There is a vast difference between a Poem whose rhythm is written after a model, and one that is entirely original. What I mean by an original rhythm is one that is not only *not* to be found in any of the English rhythms, but no where else. . . . It is *more* than difficult to create one that *does* not appear any where." Byron, Southey, Moore, and many other English poets were content to write in other men's rhythms, and American poets mainly copied the English. Several American poets had appropriated Chivers's measures. Among these was Poe, whose "Raven" was directly indebted to "Allegra Florence." He acknowledged that "Mr. Poe was a very great genius. . . . But he would never go to the trouble to invent."[132]

It was the remarks in reviews and letters, after the publication of his *Eonchs of Ruby* (1851), that infuriated Chivers. When A. J. H. Duganne, in reviewing the volume, praised the book but advised the author to eschew "Tennysonian mysticism and Wordsworthian attempts at milk-and-water simplicity" and noted that "much of the matter . . . seems but the reflex of Poe," Chivers wrote him the following day a letter compounded of appreciation and anger. His work was not borrowed or plagiaristic; instead, "There is not a single Poem in that whole Volume imitative of either Wordsworth, Tennyson, or Poe. . . . Poe stole every thing that is worth any thing from me. This I thought you *knew* perfectly well. . . . I never read any thing of Wordsworth that pleased me. Tennyson is an Epicurean Philologist. Poe stole all his '*Raven*' from me; but was the greatest Poetical Critic that ever existed. This I will prove to you, if you will call and see me."[133]

When Simms wrote that "You show too greatly how much Poe

is in your mind," and advised, "Give him up as a model and as a guide," Chivers warned him sharply that "you must disabuse your mind" of misconceptions. Believing himself to be a Gothic poet and Poe a Greek, he believed that it was the inspired poet who could teach the artistic one, for his own poems "in that Volume are all original—my own—not only in conception but in execution. There is not a Poem in that book modeled, as you suppose, upon anything that Poe ever wrote." He does not except "The Vigil in Aiden," even though he notes that it "was founded upon Poe himself"; instead, he claims that all the poems are original works of art, including their rhythms and ornaments, and he adds grandiloquently, "I am the Southern man who taught Mr. Poe all these things."[134]

Temperately enough, Chivers had claimed in the *Georgia Citizen* that "The Raven" was derived from "Allegra Florence," and had printed parallel passages as proof.[135] Yet critics continued ignorantly or wrongheadedly to praise Poe for the originality of his poetic style. In reviews of *Virginalia* (1853), critics again charged Chivers with imitation.[136] One perceptive reviewer in *Waverley Magazine* praised the way in which "the author gives himself up to his thoughts . . . the verses before us prove that the essence of poetry is Passion." Perhaps even more important to Chivers was his praise of their originality: "every one must concede to Dr. Chivers the merit of imitating no one."[137]

These must have been welcome words, and probably encouraged Chivers to renew his claim. His "Origin of Poe's Raven" (published July 30, 1853, under the pseudonym Fiat Justitia) undertook to prove that Chivers had first used trochaic tetrameter, catalectic, in elegiac verse; rather incidentally, he also asserted that he had first used the refrain "nevermore" in "Lament on the Death of my Mother."[138] This drew two replies that were published: one, amusingly enough, accusing Chivers of being a Northerner who was jealous of a Southern writer; the other, by the poet Henry S. Cornwell, citing earlier uses of "nevermore" and disparaging Chivers' claims about metrical originality.[139] Chivers responded, although he made no attempt to answer analytically; rather, he lashed out with insulting remarks about "the *thickness* of the skull" of his antagonist.[140] As the debate continued, Chivers resorted to a second pseudonym, "Felix Forresti," and he continued to advance his claim until Moses Dow refused to publish any more of his articles. In the final one, Chivers promised *Waverley* readers a "lucid exposition of all the manifold resemblances between the two poems" in the biography of Poe that he was preparing (an exposition that, if ever written, apparently has been lost); and he added the new and otherwise unsubstantiated claim that "It was not until after we had accused him of having derived it, soul and body, from the poem 'To Allegra Florence in Heaven' that he wrote the *concession article* entitled 'The Philosophy of Composition.' "[141]

An intemperate article that Dow rejected, "The Mastix," denies that Chivers was indebted in any way to Poe or Shelley, and emphasizes again the importance of sound: "It is the melody of a Poem which gives it a glory. This melody is entirely dependent on the rhythm. If that be deficient, the Poem is not a perfect work of Art." Poe in his borrowings had recognized this, but to cover his tracks, divert himself, and puzzle readers he had invented "a mode of scansion" that had no rhythm at all. Chivers repeats his claim that "no person ever used the purely Trochaic Rhythm for an Elegiac Poem before myself." He was, in the main, re-hashing in a violent tone old arguments that had long festered in his mind. Yet in this diatribe he paused to pay tribute to "The Raven." As a poem, it is "Lyrical-Epic. The style, simple-ornate. No kind of Poem can be better adapted to the development of Genius."[142]

Chivers felt that his own rightful claims had been unfairly denied and sometimes ridiculed. He presented his case, not persuasively but with the evident intent of bludgeoning his detractors into submission. In the process, he hurt only himself. It is significant, however, that in his most unrestrained articles he never denied what he considered to be the true genius of Edgar Allan Poe.

IV

Chivers's criticism is fragmentary. Although he planned to write several books of criticism[143] and to deliver a coordinated series of lectures on literature,[144] he apparently never completed any of these projects. Only a few prefaces and articles were published during his lifetime. He got no catharsis from his efforts. The extant manuscripts indicate that he returned again and again to the same critical problems, without ever putting into final form his ideas and beliefs. This explains the disjointed nature of his criticism, for his views and judgments are reasonably consistent. It perhaps explains also the frequent repetition of phrases and sentences, as well as of ideas.

It is a highly personal and somewhat eccentric criticism. Yet it is based on a wide-ranging knowledge, for Chivers read voraciously not only in English but in Hebrew, Greek, Latin, French, Italian, and Spanish. His youthful training in medicine influenced his poetry heavily, but except for an occasional medical phrase it seems to have had no influence on his criticism. His steadily-held interest in poetry, drama, music, philosophy, and religion control and illuminate his criticism. But he employed the fruits of his reading mainly to bolster or buttress his own beliefs. In a sense, his reading was as personal and subjective as his poetry or his criticism or his religious beliefs.

No doubt his theories are in part rationalizations of his practice. They also reflect his temperament. Chivers firmly believed that he was both a passionate and an inspired poet; he had no gift whatever for self-criticism, and in turn only a mild talent for revision. He reproached Simms for having "a perfect *contempt* for what may be called the *Art of Composition*,"[145] but his own emphasis on the superiority of the Gothic poet over the Greek indicates the subsidiary value that he placed on art. The primary function of the poet was to be a mediator between God and man, to be a "Revelator of the Divine Idea" through the true and the beautiful poem. Always his criticism is securely based on his unorthodox, highly personal, and deeply-felt religion.

9

WILLIAM J. GRAYSON
Neo-Classicist

WHEN William J. Grayson in 1863 wrote his autobiography, he devoted one chapter to literature.[1] No doubt this seemed a reasonable proportion to a man who had spent his life as a distinguished lawyer, state legislator, Congressman, Collector of Customs at Charleston, and plantation owner. Much of the material in this particular chapter is lifted directly from his one critical essay, "What Is Poetry?"[2] He was an old man before he turned to critical and creative writing, mainly because "my calling had left me"; as might be expected, his literary work has more sociological than literary value.

Yet as critic Grayson has a definite if minor value. He was a die-hard adherent of Neo-Classicism in a Romantic age, and he is easily the most vigorous and most persuasive of these unconverted literary reactionaries. Grayson makes no bones about it: "My select friends are not of the new schools. I adhere to the old masters and their followers. I believe in Dryden and Pope."[3]

In 1854 he wrote his first book length poem, *The Hireling and the Slave*.[4] Its main purpose was to contrast the humaneness of slavery with the inhumanity of the factory system; it is confessedly a didactic and argumentative poem. There was a secondary reason. Grayson noted that he had tried to give new interest to a trite subject "by throwing the remarks offered into verse. I have done so, not only for the reason assigned, but with the additional purpose of offering some variety to the poetic forms that are almost universally prevalent. The Poetry of the day is, for the most part, subtle and transcendental in its character. Every sentiment, re-

185

flection, or description is wrought into elaborate modes of expression, from remote and fanciful analogies. The responses of the Muses have become as mystical, and sometimes as obscure, as those of more ancient oracles, and disdain the older and homelier forms of English verse." Quite deliberately, then, and in part as an "experiment on the public taste," Grayson wrote his poem in couplets, in a plain and downright style. He believed that the "school of Dryden and Pope is not entirely forgotten. May we not imitate the poetry of Queen Anne's time as well as the tables and chairs? The common measure of that period, applied to a didactic subject, may diversify the dishes presented to the public."[5] This was plainer fare, but he hoped it would be welcome.

Although he thought Horace the best of all writers of criticism, Grayson considered himself a follower of "that sturdy old master of vigorous common sense," Samuel Johnson.[6] But in his critical essay he takes an oblique approach, at least in the beginning. He does not directly attack Romanticism, or defend Neo-Classicism; instead, he asks a generalized question as to the nature of poetry. In his autobiography he is blunter: Coleridge beclouded every issue that he touched; Wordsworth's use of nature was essentially mechanical; Shelley's sentiments were emptily metaphysical; Keats busied himself with renovating "pagan deities" and Southey with Hindu "mythological monsters." The result was a "transcendental oracular school" of poetry, that denied the realities of nature and human nature: "The sin of modern poetry consists in exaggeration of sentiment, of passion, of description, of everything. It seeks to be sublime and becomes inflated. It strives to be deep and is obscure only. It strains after the new and the wonderful and sinks into the grotesque and unintelligible. The modern poet finds the field of thought occupied and is driven to shifts and expedients."[7]

Even in the published essay, he objected to the idea that poets are persons set apart from ordinary mortals. It was natural that poets should do this, for every man desires to "magnify his calling." Therefore the poet claims that the Muse "inspires his song. He never opens his lips without supplicating her aid. Homer invokes her to sing the wrath of his hero and its dire evils to the Grecian host. Virgil supplicates all the divinities of earth and heaven to help him while he instructs the husbandman in the science of sowing and reaping, of planting the vine and olive, of managing bees and cattle. Milton asks the Heavenly Muse's aid when he essays things unattempted yet in *prose or rhyme*. It is a divinity always that sings, the poet is the instrument only. He himself has about him something which is divine."[8]

This is all very well, comments Grayson dryly, as long as no one is fooled by the words. But orators and philosophers had not helped matters any: the orators had declared that while other artists were dependent on learning, practice, and perseverance, "the Poet derives his power from nature alone, he is self-dependent; there breathes through his soul a certain divine spirit, the peculiar gifts of the Gods."[9] No hero is truly a hero until his exploits have been celebrated in poetry. And when Plato "banished the poets from his ideal republic, it was, perhaps, an indirect compliment to the seductive powers of their art which overshadowed the Philosopher's less alluring dreams and visions." But one at least equal to Plato "does all honor" to poetry. Lord Bacon had given a noble "sketch of the limits and purposes of poetry" in his *Advancement of Learning;* he had also properly rebuked those "unworthy votaries" by whom poetry "has been sometimes degraded."[10]

Grayson resumes his dry tone when he observes that these commendations by poets, orators, and philosophers do no harm "if they are received with a discreet and proper spirit." Grayson readily acknowledged that the purpose and the result of good poetry was indeed noble, although he had weighty doubts about the theory of inspiration.[11] What infuriated him was the modern critics like William Bowles and William Wordsworth (and, I suspect, in Charleston, his young friends Henry Timrod and Paul Hamilton Hayne) who would rule out of the domain of poetry all verse that did not fit their pre-conceived ideas. The modern critics would make poetry into "an indefinable something, which is neither prose nor verse. . . . Poetry becomes prose and prose becomes poetry. The confusion of ideas and language is endless, and we talk of prose poems and poetic prose, as if those terms were not as incongruous as the phrases, round square and oblong circle."[12]

What Grayson particularly objected to was the prevalent idea that "certain classes of poets are no poets at all." Thus James Hannay thought that satirists should be excluded from "the precincts of Parnassus" because they did not understand that satire is not a fit subject for poetry. When he is thus forced to exclude Juvenal, Horace, Dryden, and Churchill, the arrogant and ignorant critic should have realized that "the absurdity of the conclusion proves the falsity of the theory."[13]

In attempting to defend the validity of various types of poetry, Grayson drew (a bit ironically) on Wordsworth. Unlike Sir Walter Scott, Wordsworth was niggardly in his praise of other poets, but he was "always ready to defend his own." When an American admirer objected to his "Idiot Boy," Wordsworth replied: "You begin what you say upon the 'Idiot Boy' with the observation that nothing is a fit subject for poetry which does not please. But here follows a question: Does not please whom? Some have little knowledge of natural imagery and, of course, little relish for it; some are disgusted by the very mention of the words pastoral poetry, sheep or shepherds; some cannot tolerate a poem with a ghost or any supernatural agency in it . . . . please whom or what? I answer, human nature; as it has been and will be. And where are we to find the best measure of this? I answer, from within."[14]

This was indeed magnificent grist for Grayson's literary mill. Wordsworth had replaced objective standards with subjective judgments. But Wordsworth had no monopoly (although he seemed to think he had) on an understanding of human nature. Because understanding and tastes differ, we have a great variety in the poetry of different nations, even in England and the United States; poetry for that reason assumes "a diversity of forms, applies itself to all subjects, addresses itself to all minds." But one poem will not please all readers: the individual poet may be limited, but poetry must be "multiform in shape and character." There is, naturally and unavoidably, diversity of tastes; there must also be variety in poetry: "If there are 'Idiot Boys' there must be 'Londons' and 'Rapes of the Lock,' and 'Elegies in Country Church Yards.' If we have Wordsworths, we must have Virgils and Popes also."[15]

Grayson in one respect was quite liberal. If the modern critics would allow that the poetry he admired really was poetry, he would at least state fairly the claims of the Romantic poets. Ossian had once been "almost universally admired," although Dr. Johnson treated his "ghostly creations" scornfully. The ancient ballads were now accepted (although Grayson boggled over men who "fought upon their stumps" after their "legs were smitten off"), but Grayson had his doubts about Coleridge's "Ancient Mariner," which he rather satirically called "the wonder of ballads." In a passage that ridicules as vehemently as Dr. Johnson ever did, Grayson insists that "the glittering eye, instead of fixing the guest, would assuredly have led him to run away or call for help from the nearest police officer." Coleridge had erred in his timing: "after the festival, when being filled with wine and wassail, the maudlin carouser would have been a fit, and perhaps a willing auditor, to the lunatic old Salt."[16]

Grayson was equally unwilling to give credence to some of Coleridge's more ecstatic remarks on Shakespeare. Grayson himself admired Shakespeare's plays greatly, but when Coleridge remarked that it was as impossible "to displace advantageously a single word in his poetry as it is to push a stone from one of the pyramids," Grayson evidently felt that he could only fall back on irony: "commentators have been pushing these words out and in, with their pens, for more than a hundred years." Even Shakespeare was not sacrosanct from criticism: Voltaire considered him a "barbarous violator of the unities," and Byron and Rogers were "cold in their devotions to the Bard of Avon."[17]

"No writer writes to all minds." That, essentially, was Grayson's thesis. He knew that he was fighting a rearguard battle; he was the Marshal Ney of the retreat from Russia. But he too was undaunted. He did not hesitate to counterattack into the enemy's territory. He was insisting that no writer writes to all minds. Wordsworth could find nothing worthy of remark in Samuel Johnson's "Vanity of Human Wishes," but Scott was emotionally moved every time that he read it. Coleridge preferred Collins to Gray—a judgment that Grayson disputed sharply, adding that "if such chimeras as the Mariner or Abyssinian Maid had presented themselves to Gray's pure taste, he would have run away from them in horror and disgust." Even more sharply, Grayson declared that "Tennyson's last poem, which, to some readers, is Tennyson's 'Maud,' to others is Tennyson's 'Maudlin.' "[18]

Wordsworth deserved more respect: he had been "unduly deprecated . . . unreasonably praised." But Grayson's dislike for Wordsworth was almost pathological. In words that may infuriate but will probably entertain modern readers, Grayson roundly declares: "He was a sort of verse making machine all his life. He lived to manufacture verses. His morning and evening walks were taken to levy poetical blackmail from every stock and stone, every shrub and flower, every bird and butterfly.—The daisy that to Peter Bell was a daisy and nothing more, was to Wordsworth a very different and much more important object—it was a peg to hang verses upon." Wordsworth, to Grayson, was intent only on using nature for poetical purposes. A pebble was important only if there were a stanza underneath; even a bench had somehow to produce a stanza: "If he visited a river it was made to rhyme. If he returned to its banks it was forced to do double duty. . . . He wrote with a sort of malice prepense. He walked to make verses. He travelled to make verses. . . . He looked on nature as a kind of poetical milch cow, which he was never tired of milking." Where Burns stumbled upon a daffodil or daisy, Wordsworth hunted for them, to turn a verse; where Burns wrote from the heart, Wordsworth wrote from "the eye and the head."[19]

Just as there should be and must be many kinds of poetry, there is also room for poets of varying merits. Grayson enters a plea for the minor poet. The slopes of Parnassus are pleasantly wooded; it is "resonant with melodies and harmonies various as the songs of birds. . . . The great masters of song alone may occupy the summit, but every thicket and dell and bosky bourne from side to side, has its attendant melody. Let them all be enjoyed according to the hearer's taste." There is room also for every variety of subject-matter: one makes nature his subject; another delineates the passions; yet another may array his "moral teachings in sonorous and attractive verse"; or, like Juvenal and Horace, "scourge the vices of their times" in satire. The point is, all are poets. Any theory that excludes one group or the other is simply an incomplete theory based on narrow and peculiar standards.[20]

As an essential part of his defense, Grayson essayed a definition of poetry. It is simple enough, and down-to-earth: a work written in metrical form is a poem. The nature of the thoughts expressed has nothing to do with it. "It is not beauty of imagery, nor play of fancy, nor creative power of imagination, nor expression of emotions or passions, nor delineation of character, nor force, refinement or purity of language, that constitutes the *distinctive* quality of poetry. All these elements are shared with prose." Milton's "Tractate on Education" has beauty of imagery, but is not a poem; and where "in poetry shall we find invention, fancy, imagination, more abundantly exhibited than in the writings of Defoe or Fielding, or Scott or Dickens? And yet, unless it be metaphorically only or to sustain a theory, no one calls Tom Jones or Robinson Crusoe or Ivanhoe a poem."[21]

Coleridge gave a false emphasis when he defined prose as "words in their best order," and poetry as the "best words in the best order." Grayson was confident of that: "If he had made the distinction to consist in the order, and not in the words, it would be nearer the truth. For certainly the 'best words' are as fully the property of fine passages in prose as they are of poetry. It is in the order, then, and not in the words, that the point of distinction is to be found."[22]

Poetry is "nothing more than one of the grand divisions of articulate sounds. . . . There are but two." It is sufficient, then, to define poetry as "the expression, by words, of thought or emotion, in conformity with metrical and rhythmical laws." This alone separates the divisions, for poetry and prose are "co-extensive with the limits of human thought and expression. . . . It is true that there are subjects more suitable to one mode of expression than the other, and it would indicate a want of taste and judgment to mistake in the use of the one or the other as the topic may require." But this error in judgment would not impugn the validity of the distinction. Lucretius, for instance, "may have been injudicious in expounding the doctrines of Epictetus in any other form than prose; but no one ever doubts that his work is a poem." *Paradise Lost* is a poem in totality, and not alternate passages of prose and poetry; a translation of the *Iliad* may be either, but it can not be both.[23]

Grayson refuses to accept any distinction between poetry and verse. The individual poem may be excellent or good or mediocre or bad; it may even, justly, be termed prosaic. The critic has wide latitude of censure: "When from asking whether a book is a poem, we turn to examine into its merits, the whole province of inquiry is changed." Confusion arises when figurative expressions (like calling a man an ass, or effeminate) are applied to a category, rather than to the merit, of a work. The chat at a corner, the talk of a laborer, the slang in a pot house are prose; even doggerel and extemporized stanzas are not: "A bad poem is still a poem, the most excellent prose is still prose, and the landmarks must remain undisturbed by the conflicting parties."

Grayson did not feel that this denigrated either language or poetry: "Language is a divine art, and of this divine art the poets are masters of the highest form. . . . Homer paints with a word. Virgil's style or diction is inimitable. To Horace belongs the *curiosa felicitas* of words. In Milton and Shakespeare, according to Coleridge, you cannot alter a word without spoiling a line." These represent the best, but the distance between doggerel and *Comus* is no greater than the distance between slang and Burke's orations.[24]

In two sonnets, Grayson gives a fairly romantic picture of the purposes of objective and subjective poetry. Through the subjective, our natures can be "etherealized above the dust and noise/Of earth's low thought"; through the objective, poetic melodies can "impart new charms to nature," both by beautiful descriptions and by delineations of great deeds.[25] Poetry can exalt our joys, in bridal hall or national victory, in thanksgiving for bounteous harvest or in saintly devotions: whatever the purpose, "the voice of song imparts/A brighter smile to every bliss on earth." In a third sonnet, Grayson has the poet receiving his reward in the "Visions of beauty, and the life and light/ Of hope, and love, and joy, thy melodies impart."[26] If these quotations and paraphrases indicate that Grayson's sonnets have slight value as literature, they indicate also that the neo-classic critic was at times caught up in the current of Romanticism.[27]

Grayson's taste was formed by Latin and especially by English Neo-classic poetry. He sturdily defended the entire wide realm of poetry, but his essential purpose was to justify the kind that he himself liked. His salty prose is not always convincing, but it continues to be readable.

10

HENRY TIMROD
Traditionalist

TIMROD's prose and verse are closely related. They reveal the same intense, disciplined mind, the narrow range of interests, and a constant preoccupation with aesthetic and ethical and strictly poetic problems. Much of his early criticism was cast in verse; with one exception, his essays discuss the ontology of poetry. Although he worked as tutor and newspaper editor during most of his adult life, these jobs were a means to living. His justification, his reason for being, was in his poetry. Even in the harshest days of war and reconstruction, of poverty and illness, he continued to write: his best poem is a product of these years.

The war gave depth to his thought, intensity to his feelings. His note of melancholy was wrenched into the deeper, more abiding note of tragedy. The poems become dramatic contrasts. He retained his earlier concepts of nature and mind and soul; against these he set the blood and hatred of war. He found his individual theme late in his short life and he wrote only a few poems on it; but his earlier verse and his critical ideas combined to give him the technical equipment needed for an authentic final achievement.

Timrod made three formal attempts to define the nature of poetry. Indirectly through other poems, essays, and editorials he revealed in glancing allusions or brief, considered statements his preoccupation with this problem. His basic ideas did not change. The later presentations do not contradict the earlier; rather, they show the full development of his thought, and the final form of a tenable, rounded aesthetic of poetry.[1]

A protecting cloak of fiction and of poetic convention is thrown around his first attempt. "A Vision of Poesy" is cast in verse; the protagonist is an anonymous fictional character. But the sentiments spoken by him and to him are the beliefs of Henry Timrod; in thought, although not in fact, the work is autobiographical.

"A Vision of Poesy" is the product of youth; it is, Hayne notes, marred "by a too evident lack of harmony and unity of parts, proceeding from the fact that the narrative was composed in sections, and after the lapse of periods so long between the different *bouts* of composition, that much of the original fervor of both conception and execution must have evaporated." The underlying concept is clear enough. Timrod is presenting the subjective sources of poetry; or, in Hayne's phrase, "the true laws which underlie and determine the noblest uses of the poetical faculty."[2]

The protagonist as a youth had more than ordinary sensibility. Strange portents had marked his birth; afterward, the child had seemed withdrawn, and frightened his parents by a strange far look and by "brief snatches of mysterious rhymes."[3] He is conscious of uncomprehended mysteries, of an intuitive understanding which he cannot order with thought, and of strange emanations from natural phenomena. He is troubled by dreams and disturbed by thoughts that alike elude his grasp. One night when he has gone in solitude to a favorite nook deep in the woods, a spirit appears to him—or seems to appear. She is the angel of Poesy, and she reveals the high mission of the true poet.

The task of Poesy is closely related to that of religion, though definitely subordinate to this "mightier Power." She helps to keep the world spiritually "forever fresh and young";[4] to arouse in men the nobler emotions and desires; to "turn life's tasteless waters into wine"; and to inspire poets to seek as much knowledge as men can learn, and to translate that knowledge so that ordinary men can understand it. But Poesy can only "sow the germ which buds in human art." The poet himself determines the result. If he is, as poet, worthy, he must be pure and consecrated; he must belong "to the whole wide world." Timrod deliberately reverses the famous statement of Keats on beauty and truth: the poet must be "assured that Truth alone/ Is Beauty." Mindful of this, he sings not merely for himself, or of his own subjective thoughts and longings; he sings for those who grope and wonder, and can not sing.

Timrod breaks off the fable to comment directly on the inability of the poet to present his full concept. The idea had seemed alive "to the Poet's hope within my heart," but as it became an actuality, the concept lost its semblance of life.[5]

The third section of "A Vision of Poesy" describes a man grown old while yet in the prime of life, a poet who has largely failed because, misunderstanding the sources of art, he has yielded to a morbid subjectivity. This concern with self, partly brought on by the scorn of the world and by the disdain of the woman he loved, had vitiated his poetic accomplishment. He returns home to die. But the angel of Poesy appears to console him. Although the fault of hidden selfishness had marred his verse, he had been scornful of specious falsehood, and he had uttered "Truths that for man might else have slumbered long." This ingrown morbidity had prevented his attaining full stature, for the great poet "spheres worlds in himself." He must be concerned with the mysteries of his own soul and mind, but "on the surface of his song these lie/ As shadows, not as darkness": he makes use of the personal light to help clarify the general darkness.[6]

Timrod points the contrast between partial achievement and completeness. A complete poem is an ethical poem; it not only functions within itself, it acts upon the world to make for positive good. His terms are romantic, and his words often abstract. As a poem, "A Vision of Poesy" is uneven, frequently unconvincing, and at best achieves only a limited success. As a vehicle for his critical theories, it is less persuasive than his essay, "A Theory of Poetry."

Several writers have suggested that Timrod in this poem was greatly influenced by Shelley's "Alastor."[7] Since Timrod's immature work seems a beginning yet also an integral part of his critical theory, and is so treated here, it is useful to compare the two poems.

Both Shelley and Timrod write of an idealistic young poet who finds tragedy rather than a fulfillment of genius; in each poem, the young man broods in solitude upon the majesty and mystery of nature. The resemblances are circumstantial, not spiritual. Alastor is essentially Shelleyan, or Byronic. He is dedicated to poetry, to earth, to nature. But in his quest of the spirit of poetry he left an "alienated home/ To seek strange truths in undiscovered lands"; he has pursued "Nature's most secret steps" in strange and far-off places, and in the "awful ruins of the days of old."[8] It is essentially a traveler's concept of nature, not a mystic's; the revelation that he could never hope to find at home might somehow come to him in Arabia or Ethiopia or the Arctic. Although Shelley states the opposite, Alastor apparently seeks understanding through experience, not through contemplation. Timrod's young poet has an entirely different concept of nature. He is more Wordsworthian than Shelleyan, although he lacks Wordsworth's certitude and spiritual rapport with nature. It is the Wordsworthian mystical comprehension that he seeks. For that, he goes deep into the woods and takes as teachers the leaves, the trees, the stars, the sky, and the wind. He depends upon intuitive reverie, rapt contemplation, and revelation;[9] he seeks them in the familiar solitude of his own region instead of in the wanderings of Alastor.

Each poem uses a dream symbol. But Alastor's is a simple dream of a maid who typifies the spirit of poesy. Her voice "was like the voice of his own soul." She represents the unattainable perfection that he yearned for.[10] She is an oriental goddess or houri for whom Alastor feels a physical as well as mental passion; having known her in a dream, he can never be satisfied with the earthly love that a woman can give. His wanderings become wilder, more frantic: seemingly, the ideal unattainable in life might somehow be attained in death. The anonymous poet in "A Vision of Poesy" does not have the sensation of "shuddering limbs and . . . gasping breath"; he is not, in fact, quite certain whether he has in his solitude dreamed of a maiden, or been visited by a spirit: " 'Here was it that I saw, or dreamed I saw,/ I know not which, that shape of love and light.' "[11]

However briefly, Alastor possessed the maid who personified poetry; in Timrod's vision, Poesy remains aloof and remote. She will not give the young poet full knowledge of the mysteries, but only so much as a mortal can know. Even then, she limits her promise severely. She gives the fire and genius, but the "true bard is his own only Fate."[12] The poet fails in Timrod's version through his own human faults, and not through a vain quest after the unattainable. He too has known solitude, brought on him by the scorn of a material world and the scorn of a beautiful woman. But Poesy, while she comforts him, places the blame directly on him; he has grown too enwrapped in his own thoughts, and heeded too little the cares and aspirations of other people.

Timrod's concept of the ideal has little relation to Shelley's. Alastor sought a perfection that had, except in the strikingly physical personification of poesy as a woman, no concern with the things or people of this world; he sought it by romantic, concretely geographical wanderings. In his Preface, Shelley notes that "The Poet's self-centred seclusion was avenged by the furies of an irresistible passion pursuing him to speedy ruin."[13] But Alastor is self-centered before his dream, as well as afterward; and the dream itself encourages this egoism and leads him to destruction. Timrod's poet fails, at least in part, because he forgets or ignores the nobility of his vision. He has had his moments of insight and of accomplishment. He has been "A priest, and not a victim at the shrine."[14] His work has had positive value; it leads to loneliness and sorrow, but not to ruin.

In death, as in life, these imaginary poets present basic differences that are more important than their superficial resemblances. Shelley set out to write an allegorical tragedy; Timrod sought to give meaning to a poet's life through a complex vision. Even the machinery and forms of the poems differ. Timrod may have found in "Alastor" a suggestion that kindled his poetic imagination; but Timrod's philosophy was too far removed from Shelley's for this suggestion to do more than start him on his way.

In other respects, Timrod's resemblance to Shelley is slight.[15] Each believed in the nobility and the mystical power of poetry; each man was integrally a part of the romantic movement. Timrod had read Shelley's "A Defence of Poetry," and twice he quotes approvingly, but inaccurately, the definition of poetry as "the record of the best and happiest moments of the happiest and best minds."[16] These words had impressed Timrod as truth; he was in full agreement. But the extent of his disagreement with Shelley's ideas is most apparent in their respective treatment of inspiration. In the paragraph preceding his definition, Shelley had identified poetry as something divine, and the poem as supernally inspired: "I appeal to the greatest poets of the present day, whether it is not an error to assert that the finest passages of poetry are produced by labour and study. The toil and the delay recommended by critics can be justly interpreted to mean no more than a careful observation of the inspired moments, and an artificial connexion of the spaces between their suggestions by the intertexture of conventional expressions."[17]

Without mentioning Shelley's words and probably without considering them worth a rejoinder, Timrod contradicts this theory of art. He insists on making a clean and sharp distinction between the subjective essence of poetry and the objective, tangible poem.[18] This distinction governs his treatment of inspiration. He felt that a poet's mind had to be stimulated, roused, in-

spired. The stimulation might come from within, through a
chance day-dream or dazzling thought; it might come after long
contemplation of some natural or human phenomenon; the spark
might be kindled by some external pretty face or casual word. In
his college days, "Every pretty girl's face acted upon me like an
inspiration";[19] in his greatest poetry, the tragedy of war served
as a more powerful stimulus. But this inspiration, whatever its
cause, acted upon the mind of the poet, taking hold of his imagination or being played upon by his fancy. There was a mystical
quality involved; the poet differed from the ordinary man principally in his being able to express this inspiration: "The ground
of the poetic character is more than ordinary sensibility."[20]

When he presented his idea of inspiration through the objectifying medium of poetry, Timrod emphasized the mystical
concept. His youthful poet not only gets a sense of mystery from
the trees, skies, and winds, he also murmurs rhymes which he
does not himself understand, and feels dull, clinging memories of
a mystic tongue and a once-clear comprehension.[21] Inspiration,
embodied in the form of the angel of Poesy, rouses, troubles, and
perplexes his soul, and drives his mind on to such knowledge as
mortals can attain; she is the light of the poetic imagination. Yet
even in this romantic concept, Timrod allows to inspiration only
the function of beginning the poetic process. The poet's reach depends upon himself. He alone can govern his poem, and he must
do it through his own knowledge and technique.[22]

When he spoke more prosaically, in his own person, Timrod
shied away from defining inspiration. He knew, for himself, that
it existed, but he knew also that it had limits. In trying to prove
that the sonnet was no more artificial than other forms of verse,
he stated flatly that "If the poet have his hour of inspiration
(though we are so sick of the cant of which this word has been
the fruitful source, that we dislike to use it) it is not during the
act of composition. A distinction must be made between the moment when the great thought first breaks upon the mind . . . and
the hour of patient and elaborate execution. It is in the conception only that the poet is the *vates*. In the labor of putting that
conception into words, he is simply the artist."[23] Otherwise, the
poet would be merely an improvisator, and "perhaps, poetry
would be no better than what improvisations usually are."

This antipathy to inspiration as a substitute for art may have
led to Timrod's writing a defence of the sonnet. It seems more
probable that the work was the outgrowth of a heated argument,

or of some bit of reading that aroused his mind. Hayne suggests that admiration for Wordsworth was responsible, and that Timrod is defending the form "against the assaults of a large body of depreciators with admirable skill and effect."[24] Whatever the cause, the ideas expressed are Timrod's, and they help to adumbrate his mind.

The essay begins uncompromisingly. There is, first, an aristocratic disdain of popular taste. The sonnet "has never been a popular form of verse"; it is never likely to be. But the popularity and comprehension of a poet's work rarely begin with the multitude. A few cultivated persons understand and explain his work; gradually, after these explanations seep downward, his verses may become popular. In the essay, Timrod makes no attempt to reconcile this doctrine with his belief that the poet must speak what men dimly feel but can not say for themselves.

He is emphasizing the artistry that a completed poem should have. The sonnet is artificial only as all forms of verse are artificial; that it is one of the more difficult forms means that it presents a greater challenge to the artist. The enforced condensation requires him to order his thought before he writes, to discard the irrelevant and to concentrate on "one leading idea, around which the others are grouped for purposes of illustration only." Since great poetry had been written in the sonnet form, Timrod, a traditionalist, believed that the form was good: the particular result depended upon the individual poet.

In defending the sonnet, Timrod was dealing only with the tangible or objectified form. He was not attempting to define poetry; he was simply arguing the validity of one type. His next essay is an attempt to distinguish between the poem and poetry. It is a defence of his concept of poetry, written in answer to a direct attack. Both essays are entitled "What is Poetry?" The first is by William J. Grayson; the second is by Timrod.[25]

The disagreement, at least superficially, was one of definition. Grayson was a neo-classicist, Timrod a romantic. Grayson was inclined to answer his question by considering the form; Timrod, by considering the essence or principle of poetry. The argument is in no sense a new one. Aristotle attempted to differentiate between essence and form, at a time when the word *poetry* included practically all imaginative writing; with the delimitation of the word in English usage, and with no accepted word to signify the older, larger concept, confusion still results. When the scientist Joseph LeConte discussed the nature of poetry, he began by carefully considering the dual nature of the term. The form is verse. In essence, prose addresses only the emotions and the understanding; poetry addresses also the imagination and the aesthetic sense. There can be no clear line of demarcation: although lacking the form, much prose is in essence poetry; and much verse, despite its formal quality, is not poetry.[26]

Grayson allows only the single meaning. Paraphrasing Dr. Johnson, he declares poetry to be "rythmical composition and a poet, one who composes in measure." The peculiar quality of poetry is in the form of arranging words, without regard to the ideas expressed. All other definitions lead to confusion. To him the terms *prose poems* and *poetic prose* seemed "as incongruous as the phrases, round square and oblong circle." Such phrases were simply a "mystical jargon of rapturous superlatives" freely used by the "transcendental oracular school" of Coleridge and his followers. They sought to give to poetry qualities that poetry did not have. An example of this was in Coleridge's defining poetry "as the proper antithesis not of prose but of science. What more is this than to insist on using words contrary to their common acceptation? According to general usage, is not art the proper antithesis of science?" Also, is it not enough to be a good poet, when poetry itself "is the noblest, most refined, pointed and energetic of the two modes by which among all people, thought and emotion are expressed by language"?

By Grayson's standards, all verse is poetry. A casual bit of doggerel belongs to the genre as surely as the finest work of Milton or Shakespeare. Once this is allowed, the province of inquiry changes: from asking what it is, we turn to an examination of the quality of a poem. Here, figurative language may be used effectively, but the labelling of a poem as prosy does not mean that the work is prose; it means simply that the writer was a clumsy poet. The intrinsic merit can be judged, but the simple and clear distinction between poetry and prose must remain steadfast.

Grayson's essay infuriated Timrod. He objected particularly to the "illogical confusion of the ideas conveyed by the terms *poem,* and *poetry*," which Grayson had used as identical in reference. A poem is objective, tangible, a thing complete within itself; poetry is subjective, an essence or feeling rather than a definable reality. Then the antithesis to prose becomes, properly, metre; if this is recognized, the question ceases to be how to distinguish poetry from prose, and becomes an inquiry into "those operations of the human faculties, which, when *incarnated* in language, are generally recognized as poetry."

A part of the definition, therefore, turns on the character of the poet. He must have "a more than ordinary sensibility," and out of this characteristic must come a "medium of strong emotion" which can fuse and transform the objects and thoughts which are the material of poetry. From this powerfully emotional imagination there comes naturally a language which differs from the language of prose. The poet's words are sensuous, picturesque, and impassioned; they are short and concrete. Although the thought may be abstract, the poetic expression of that thought must have life, form, and color. Abstract words make the verse prosaic, until the work "no longer calls up the image which it expresses; it merely suggests the thought which it stands for." The poet is not content with words that convey the meaning; he seeks also the most beautiful, in sound and in association, so that his words will "challenge a slight attention to themselves."[27]

The form is important, but it is not all-inclusive. Timrod is willing to admit that "there may be such a thing as a prose-poem." Yet he admits it reluctantly. Concentrated, heightened thought and emotion find their natural and proper expression in verse. In a long poem, certain parts will inevitably be merely skillful verse, but the artistry of the writer must so fuse these passages with the impassioned poetry that the entire work will be an organic whole.

As criticism, the essay suffers from being a rebuttal as well as an affirmation. The lines of the argument had been drawn in unshaded black and white by another man; they outraged Timrod's sense of the philosophical and the mystical, which he felt to be at the heart of poetry; but the narrow matter-of-factness of the preceding argument made a reasoned answer difficult. He was forced to deny rather than to disprove. The most valuable part of his reply is in the place that he could most tangibly take hold of his adversary's dicta: in the matter of poetic language. Significantly, here, Timrod is on the side of Dante, and not of Wordsworth. He declares that words in themselves have beauty and euphony and concreteness; in this, he answers Grayson convincingly.

In his longest and best essay, "A Theory of Poetry,"[28] Timrod develops and completes his earlier attempts at definition. After dismissing briefly Grayson's essay, he considers Poe's dogmatic statements that a long poem is a contradiction in terms and that the poetical sentiment is derived only from the sense of the beautiful.

In response to the first dictum, Timrod presents two answers. One has to do with the reading of poetry. Although a psychal excitement is necessarily transient, it does not follow that poetry must be read in that mood. In fact, the reading of the greatest poetry "is characterized . . . by a thoughtful sublimity and the matured and almost inexhaustible strength of a healthy intellect." Granted this quality of mind, the reader need not complete a poem at one sitting to preserve its unity of effect. If he reads the first book of *Paradise Lost,* he will bring to the second and third books all the impressions of his former reading; he will feel a deeper richness as he continues. The mind will be conscious of the vast unity of the poem, so that "its grand purport and harmonious proportions become more and more clearly apparent."[29]

The length of a poem has nothing to do with its excellence. Only the author can know how long a poem should be; and only through "the ordeal of criticism" can the author's success or failure be determined. Timrod admits that he is inclined to consider Dante's *Divine Comedy* as three distinct poems, and Spenser's *Faërie Queene* a succession of poems. The character of the poem and the intention of the poet may be responsible for a lack of unity. But the poet, if he has artistry enough, can impose order and secure unity. Not all of his poem will in the subjective sense be genuine poetry; parts of it will inevitably be verse, but "these parts may be raised so far above the ordinary level of prose by skillful verse as to preserve the general harmony of the poem and materially to insure its unity as a work of art."[30]

With Poe's theory that poetry was limited in subject to "the sense of the beautiful," Timrod dissented vigorously. He was willing to grant the validity of this kind of poetry, and even to admit that Poe had "fixed with some definiteness one phase of its merely subjective manifestation. It is, indeed, to the inspiration which lies in the ethereal, the remote and the unknown, that the world owes some of its sweetest poems; and the poetry of words has never so strange a fascination as when it seems to suggest more than it utters."[31]

But to admit the validity of the kind was not to accept this kind as the only, or even the highest, poetry. Literature is not independent of life, or of truth. The creation of beauty is a sufficient aim for a writer; it is not the highest or noblest aim. For the greatest poetry, two other elements must be added: "these

are *power* when it is developed in some noble shape, and *truth*
—whether abstract or not—when it affects the common heart of
mankind. For the suggestion of these two additional principles, I
suppose I ought to say that I am indebted to Hunt; but I cannot
help adding that I had fixed upon the same trinity of elements
long before I became acquainted with his delightful book on
Imagination and Fancy. It is then in the feelings awakened by
certain moods of the mind when we stand in the presence of
Truth, Power, and Beauty, that I recognize what we all agree to
call Poetry."[32]

He was willing to divide poets into two classes, "differing essentially in their several characters. The one class desires only to
utter musically its own peculiar feelings, thoughts, sentiments, or
passion, without regard to their truth, or falsehood, their morality
or their want of morality, but in simple reference to their
poetical effect. The other class with more poetry at its command
than the first, regards Poetry simply as the minister—the highest
minister indeed but still only the minister—of Truth, and refuses to address itself to the sense of the Beautiful alone. The
former class is content only to create Beauty, and writes such
poems as the Raven of Poe, or the Corsair of Byron. The latter
class aims to create Beauty also, but it desires at the same time to
mould this Beauty into the shape of a temple dedicated to Truth.
It is to this class we owe the authorship of such poems as the
Paradise Lost of Milton, the lines on Tintern Abbey, and the
Excursion of Wordsworth, and the In Memoriam of Tennyson.
The former class can afford to write brief and faultless poems because its end is a narrow one; the latter class is forced to demand
an ampler field, because it is influenced by a vaster purpose."[33]

Essentially, Timrod was an ethical critic. He did not propose
to limit its scope, but he was convinced that the greatest poetry
must have an ethical content. Poe had attempted to reduce the
many and varied sources of poetry to a single element, beauty.
There are other, equally valid sources: particularly, power and
truth. A poem need not be philosophical, but it can embody
philosophy; every poet has the right "to make his art the vehicle
of great moral and philosophical lessons."

Some miscellaneous ideas garnered from letters, editorials, and
poems help to round out Timrod's poetic theory. One concerns
standards of poetry. He required a high level of performance of
himself; since his mind was not easily malleable, he found it
hard to excuse poor work in others. Even brotherly affection

could not lead him to pardon bad poetry: "Sissie has been sending me several sheets of her nonsense. Poor girl! She has very little to amuse her, and I found it hard to tell her the truth about them. But of all things in the world, I think a poetaster the most contemptible; and to save myself the discredit of having one for a sister, I have written to her, treating her versicles without mercy."[34] This brutal letter has not survived, and there is no record of his sister's verses.

Soon after he assumed the editorship of the *Daily South Carolinian,* Timrod wrote an editorial, "To our Poetical Contributors." This was a public performance; also, it may be, Timrod had mellowed somewhat in his opinion of mere versifiers. Whatever the reason, he begins mildly. But the concluding sentences are, under their politeness, as uncompromising as words can well be:

We have a heart to sympathise with all lovers of poetry, not excepting those who are incompetent to appreciate it critically, and who, in consequence, sometimes, mistake its weeds for its flowers. The instinct which leads all men to delight in the musical expression of sentiment is a divine one, and we may not despise it even where its action happens to be vitiated by defects of judgment and taste. Such, indeed, is our reverence for that instinct, that we are inclined to accord some respect even to the writer of bad verse. Indifferent rhyme may occasionally be the offspring of genuine feeling, for poetry is an art in which no one can excel without genius and cultivation. Where, then, the offender has the excuse of natural emotion, we think he ought to be treated with great gentleness. Yet, at the same time, we would advise all in whom the *aura divina* is wanting, to suppress their productions, however unaffected may have been the impulse which led to these compositions. There is no necessity of giving to the public verses, the only merit of which is in the source from which they spring. With regard to the poetical criminal whose inspiration is vanity alone, we have no mercy for him whatever. There ought to be a pillory for the punishment of every evil-doer of this stamp.

We may as well state at the outset, that the standard upon which we have fixed, and by which we shall measure all poetical contributions to our columns, is high, and that to that standard we shall adhere, without reference to any other considerations than those of merit or demerit. While there are in the English language so many exquisite poems not very well known, we shall prefer to give selections from these, or even from authors who, however familiar, can never lose their perennial freshness, than to afflict our critical readers with such effusions as, in the corner of some newspapers, appear under the head of original verse.[35]

One who reads today the poetry that Timrod included may feel that he frequently relaxed his standards. But he was publishing, or quite often reprinting, the work of people whom he knew personally. In addition to his own and some of his father's work, Timrod used many poems by his friends: Hayne, Simms, Bruns, and Requier; several by two men—Harry Lyndon Flash and James Ryder Randall—whom he had met in his days as war correspondent; a poem by Thomas Bailey Aldrich and part of one by Whittier; and quotations from many English poets. He felt himself unduly handicapped: he could not pay for original contributions, and he did not himself receive the papers that came to the office. Even his opportunity to clip and reprint was limited.

A few technical remarks are interesting. In a letter to Hayne, Timrod writes that he has "the right poet's inclination to plunge at once *in medias res.*" In another letter, Timrod defends himself against dogmatic remarks by James Wood Davidson; after reading Davidson's criticism of his poetry, Timrod wrote indignantly to Hayne:

Did you mark what the fellow says about the use of *my* & *thy* before vowels? "A well established principle of euphony demands the use of mine & thine. ["] One would think that Mr. Davidson must have scrutinized closely all the great masters, and found this rule invariably observed" [*sic*] I turn to Tennyson (Talking Oak) and read "And even into *my in*most ring" (D. objects to ["] thy inmost heart"). Again, "Then Close and dark *my arms* I spread"—"Showering thy gleanèd wealth into *my open* breast" &c, &c. I could quote a half dozen similar instances. Even this fool's favorite Poe has "My Mother, *my own* Mother who died early." The truth is, of course, that this rule is not, like similar rules in Greek & French, imperative in English. The poet has the privilege of using either form as his ear dictates. Mr. Davidson has no ear, and therefore he cannot understand that if I had crunched together so many *ns* as I would have done if I had written "in thine unmingled scorn," so far from consulting the laws of euphony, I should have been guilty of a cacophony. But you know these things as well as I.

To the same friend, he wrote his opinion of prize-poems in general, and specifically of one that Hayne had just published. His criticism is mild, yet exact:

I received your prize poem this morning—thank you for sending it. It is a very noble production indeed—quite worthy of the crown—but may I be so frank as to tell you that its excellence seems to me rather rhetorical than poetical. This fault, however, belongs to all prize-poems,—to mine, I think, in a far greater degree than your own. The poet cannot draw his purest and subtlest strains except from his own unremunerated heart.[36]

These are direct statements. Ideas embodied in poems are indirect: they represent the poet speaking dramatically, and not necessarily in his own person. Yet, if evaluated with reasonable caution, the thought in many poems can be read as a valuable extension of his remarks in prose. In varying forms but with the same core of meaning, basic ideas that troubled his mind appear and re-appear.

One is partially objective. The values of the world seemed to him material values; those of poetry were ethical, spiritual, and aesthetic. He could find no way to reconcile these opposites. Yet if poetry is to have meaning for the world, the values of poetry must be accepted by it. Otherwise, a man's poetry became a private possession, and there was little reason for him to put his thought into an objectified form.[37]

Although the period in which he lived was in his estimation less materialistic than the eighteenth century, it felt little need for intellectual and spiritual knowledge. Sometimes the very structure of the world appeared to make this structure of society inevitable: since men were bound to matter, space, and time, then "Communion with the spirit land / Died with the last inventions." It was a prosaic day, in which the world falsified its dreams.[38]

The poem "Youth and Manhood" combines this feeling of the world's indifference with the poet's sense of being aloof, and therefore removed. But he suspects that his youth is a reason for his inhabiting a freer, loftier region: the men who toil and plod may have simply, in the endless strife, lost faith with youth. With a young man's arrogant prayer, Timrod closes his poem:

> If the same toil which indurates the hand
> > Must steel the heart,
> Till, in the wonders of the ideal land,
> > It have no part;
>
> Oh! take me hence! I would no longer stay
> > Beneath the sky;
> Give me to chant one pure and deathless lay,
> > And let me die![39]

The desire for death may have been rhetorical; the feeling which permeates the poem was real. It intensified rather than lessened. When he asked himself, or possibly was asked in such a way that he could not shake the query from his mind, why he did not write more poetry, his feeling about the indifference to that art breaks forth: "the world, in its worldliness, does not miss / What a poet sings." But the writer in objectifying his thought has somehow cast it away from him. Thus the thought, dream, or fancy loses its personal application.[40]

Closely related to this is his feeling that some truths are better left unsaid, that "Too broad a daylight wraps us all." Perhaps Timrod was half-ashamed of the mystical part of his thoughts, and hesitant about voicing them too plainly. He believed that there were impenetrable mysteries, which could be intuitively known and in part understood; he felt that richness was lost when too much was explained. Apparently uncertain in his own beliefs, he knew only that introspection lost much when it was forced into the semi-reality of words.[41]

Another phase of his dissatisfaction is most clearly stated in the poem "Retirement." In a dramatic soliloquy, the poet advises a friend that a lonely house awaits them; there the two can build "A wall of quiet thought, and gentle books / Betwixt us and the hard and bitter world." In that retreat, they can shut out unpleasant news, and dally with peaceful thoughts and feelings. Another form of his discontent shows in passages that express an inability to loose his thoughts and at the same time to order and discipline them. The dim monotones of an embryonic poem bewilder his brain "With a specious and cunning appearance of thought / I seem to be catching but never have caught."

He felt, also, that men did not understand or value meditation. If a man worked, even though he labored only at the paltry trade of sonnet-writing, he should have tangible results to show. Men accustomed to a "busy vacancy" had no patience with a man's lying fallow, with simply observing and thinking: he was an idler, and to be sneered at.[42]

These troubled expressions are too much a part of his mind to be disregarded. His dissatisfaction with his completed work is a compound of many elements.[43] He could occasionally profess an aristocratic disdain of the world's opinion;[44] beyond question, he had a low opinion of mass intelligence. Yet a private art intended for the few seemed to him an imperfect and largely useless art. The poet had a function to perform: to translate for this mass-mind the aspirations and thoughts which, otherwise, it could never grasp.[45] The poet was minister of truth, power, and beauty; he was a responsible agent, performing a function that no other agent could perform.[46]

This may be at the heart of Timrod's discontent. He was confident of his poetic power, yet, judging from his early poems, it seemed to him a power without adequate direction or control. His work was too much abstracted from reality, both within itself and in its audience. It was not enough to write graceful love lyrics or give voice to his personal feelings. In that manner, the poet could find relief for his own impatient spirit; but he had not, as artist, attained full manhood.[47]

If this reading of his work is correct, Timrod until 1860 was a poet in search of a theme. Before that time, he found many themes, and he wrote good poems on some of them. But only infrequently did such a poem satisfy him. His concept was noble; in comparison, his performance was inadequate. So he was influenced heavily and directly by the writers he most admired, while he was painfully working out for himself the passage from their ideas to his own.

The war gave him a theme. Timrod was ready for it, with a technique that had become individual to himself, and capable of translating this matter of poetry into poetry itself. Whether rightly or wrongly, he felt that in his theme he had found common ground with his people, that he was giving expression to what they dimly felt. In this poetry the direct and sometimes embarrassing evidences of indebtedness disappear; his thought had grown strong enough to absorb the earlier influences and to transmute them until they became an integral part of his own thought.

The finest and clearest expression of that thought is not in the early (and factually erroneous) paeans to a coming victory.[48] It is rooted in tragedy. In victory as in defeat, the tragedy would remain; and it would be almost equally pitiless for victor and vanquished. Against this tragedy of men Timrod sets the eternal quality of nature with its inherent peacefulness; and he sets against it, also, the faith of human beings. With this sombre awareness of death there came also, in 1865, the personal tragedy of the death of his only son. The man who wrote "Spring," "Christmas," "A Mother's Wail," and the final "Ode" had experienced universal emotions.

These poems are not, in the technical sense, major poems, and

Timrod is not a major poet. But in them Timrod has magnificent-ly embodied his concept of poetry. When he was simply voicing in restrained and powerful verse the emotions that had become a part of him, he was an authentic poet.

II

A vast amount of Southern intellectual energy was expended, in the years 1830-1860, in presenting arguments and pleas for a regional intellectual independence. These partisan efforts to create a literary nationalism brought little in the way of tangible results. If the discussion was unprofitable, the problem itself was painful, engrossing, and apparently inescapable.[49]

To this forensic arena of bitterness and vexation, Timrod came late.[50] By 1859 the South was almost unified in its opposition to the North. The easy, popular thing to do was to throw hard verbal bricks at Boston and New York. Timrod does his share of this, but he does not absolve his own region of blame or responsibil-ity. The Southern author is "the Pariah of modern literature" because he is caught between hostility and contempt abroad and scornful indifference at home: "It is the settled conviction of the North that genius is indigenous there, and flourishes only in a Northern atmosphere. It is the equally firm conviction of the South that genius—literary genius, at least—is an exotic that will not flower on a Southern soil."

Timrod reserves his sharpest thrusts for Southerners. Native writers are neglected because literature is considered an epicurean amusement, and because readers prefer the classical and neo-classical to the modern romantic authors. The writer himself is not esteemed in a land where taste is archaic and judgment is uninformed. Timrod never doubted the superiority of nineteenth-century writing; he was troubled only that readers and teach-ers seemed frequently to prefer Pope to Wordsworth, and remained oblivious to "that most important revolution in imag-inative literature . . . which took place a little more than half a century ago." The men who brought about that revolution had introduced a mystical element into verse, which distinguished it from earlier kinds, and into criticism an analysis which deduced its laws from nature and truth rather than from the authority of particular writers.

Equally provincial and almost equally harmful was the current demand from another group for a superficial "Southernism in literature." It closely resembled the earlier demand for "Americanism in literature," and each meant only that "an author should confine himself in the choice of his subjects to the scenery, the history, and the traditions" of his own section or country. Without any qualification, Timrod labelled this a false and narrow criterion by which to judge of true nationality. It is in the handling of a subject, and not in the subject itself, that the characteristics of a writer are revealed, and "he alone, who, in a style evolved from his own individual genius, speaks the thoughts and feelings of his own deep heart, can be a truly national genius." To such a writer, the circumscription of subjects was foolish and unfortunate. The author must have the right to choose according to his own needs and taste; that he would not thereby lose his nationality was easily proved by the Roman plays of Shakespeare and the French novels of Scott.[51]

In January, 1864, Timrod began to write a series of editorials that continue and in part repeat his essay, "Literature in the South." The war, he thinks, has brought about one improvement: the blockade has cut off the supply of English and Northern books, and thus has forced Southerners to read native works. In turn, Southern authors, awake "to the fact that they have at last an audience," have been writing vigorously, and with enough ability to indicate "that a new era of intellectual energy is dawning upon us." These books and the best of the literary magazines and papers show "the national mind struggling to find fit and original expression." If there is much imitation and many indifferent books, there is also evidence that Southern literature is beginning to "trust to its native strength alone."[52]

Although he favored an independence of foreign models and asked for a literature that would reflect and reveal the Southern mind,[53] Timrod did not want a local color literature. He rephrases his earlier concept: "There is but one way to be a truly national writer, and that is by being a truly original writer. . . . the man of original genius draws his matter from the depth of his own being; and the national character, in which, as a unit of the nation, he shares, finds its utterance through him."

Timrod also considers the parallel demand for a national song. Most songs of this kind he thinks worthless from a literary point of view. "The Star-Spangled Banner" and "Rule Britannia" gained popularity through their effective refrains, and not through any merit as poetry; with the exception of "Maryland My Maryland," no Southern song attained even that type of popularity. Since people do not choose their songs on the basis of poetic merit, the poets are not to blame. Timrod lists four things as necessary to the success of a national song: "Its verse must run glibly on the tongue; it must contain somewhere, either in a stanza or in a refrain, a sentiment, tersely and musically expressed, which appeals to some favorite pride, prejudice, or passion of the people; it must be married to an effective, but not complicated air, and it must be aided by such a collocation of accidents as may not be computed." The poet even of genius cannot control all of these elements; the Confederacy possessed no writers equal to the task of expressing "the whole great soul of a nation within the compass of a few simple and melodious verses." But the task was worth attempting, and he hoped that writers would, in the effort, "find inspiration enough to draw forth the utmost capacity of their genius."[54]

He was not optimistic. The turbulence and excitement of war might be excellent as a period of germination. but not as a period of growth. Yet the intense emotion which prevents a poet from writing well at the time may give strength and character to his thought. After a period of meditation, which could come only with the return of peace, Southern writers might be able to write great poems.[55]

The editorials themselves suffer from this lack of tranquillity. On August 25, 1864, Timrod described his work to Hayne: "I have not written a line of verse for a twelve-month. All the poetry in my Nature has been fagged out of me I fear. I work very hard,—besides writing the leaders of the paper I often descend into the local column, as you must have noticed by such articles as *Literary Pranks, Arsenal Hill,* and the *Troubles of a Midsummer Night.* My object is to show that a poet can drudge as well [as] a duller man, and therefore I don't complain."[56] It was one thing to drudge uncomplainingly, and presumably Timrod was equal to that task; it was quite another under the circumstances to write with strength and intelligence. Even dwarf essays require a sustained thought that Timrod often seemed unable to give to them.[57]

III

Few writers have ever indicated so precisely the major influences upon their art as Timrod did. He expressed frequently and quite frankly his indebtedness to Wordsworth; he praised the work of Milton and of Tennyson; and he is said to have com-

pleted a metrical translation of the poems of Catullus.[58] Although
he knew the works of many other poets, these four influenced him
most directly and immediately. Hayne notes that "his reading
was more exact than varied. His unerring critical tact rejected the
false and meretricious; but for authors of his deliberate choice,
his affection daily increased."[59]

First in his affection was Wordsworth. In the morning of his
career, writes his close friend Hayne, "Timrod looked up to
Wordsworth as poetical guide and exemplar."[60] Wordsworth
seemed not only his personal mentor, but the guiding spirit of
poetry in his time: "The poet who first taught the few simple but
grand and impressive truths which have blossomed into the poetic
harvest of the nineteenth century was Wordsworth. . . . When he
began to write, it was with the purpose of embodying in all the
poetic forms at his command the two truths of which the poets
and readers of his time seemed to him completely incognizant.
These were, first, that the materials and stimulants of poetry
might be found in the commonest things about us; and second, behind the sights, sounds, and hues of external nature there is
'something more than meets the senses, something undefined and
unutterable which must be felt and perceived by the soul' in its
moments of rapt contemplation. This latter feeling it is that constitutes the chief originality of Wordsworth." In Timrod's estimation, this feeling did not appear in Shakespeare or his contemporaries, in Milton or his followers, in Dryden, Pope, Thomson,
or Cowper. But it "has been caught up and shadowed forth" by
every poet from Byron to Tennyson.

Timrod was especially distressed that few teachers of literature
recognized that any change had taken place. Rhetorically he
asked: "Is it not a fact, of which we may feel not unreasonably
ashamed, that a student may pass four years under these mislead-
ers of youth, and yet remain ignorant of that most important
revolution in imaginative literature—to us of the present day the
most important of all literary revolutions—which took place a
little more than half a century ago. The influence of the new spiritual philosophy in producing a change from a sensuous to a
super-sensuous poetry, the vast difference between the school represented by Wordsworth, and the school represented by Pope,
the introduction of that mystical element into our verse which
distinguishes it from the verse of the age of Shakespeare, the
theory of that analytical criticism which examines a work of art

'from the heart outwards, not from the surface inwards!' and which deduces its laws from nature and truth, not from the practice of particular writers; these surely are subjects which, in an institution devoted to the purpose of education, may not be overlooked without censure."[61]

An individual adumbration of this feeling or idea appears in Timrod's poetry. He felt himself to be in the tradition of Coleridge in criticism, and of Wordsworth in poetry.[62] When a correspondent suggested to him that his poem "Katie" was Byronic in tone, Timrod answered that the resemblance was "merely a *verbal* one," and that the particular couplet under discussion is "made the text of a train of sentiment which is much more *Wordsworthian* than Byronic in its character."[63]

This admitted influence permeates his work in the decade 1850-60. The need for dealing with common and human things is emphasized by the angel of Poesy in the "Vision";[64] it is explicitly stated by Timrod in a sonnet on poetry:

> POET! if on a lasting fame be bent
> Thy unperturbing hopes, thou will not roam
> Too far from thine own happy heart and home;
> Cling to the lowly earth, and be content!
> So shall thy name be dear to many a heart;
> So shall the noblest truths by thee be taught;
> The flower and fruit of wholesome human thought
> Bless the sweet labors of thy gentle art.
> The brightest stars are nearest to the earth,
> And we may track the mighty sun above,
> Even by the shadow of a slender flower.
> Always, O bard, humility is power!
> And thou mayst draw from matters of the hearth
> Truths wide as nations, and as deep as love.[65]

This was not a plea for a limited provincialism. Rather, it represents his belief that universality could be secured through the method of handling immediate and well-known objects, and through giving a new richness to ordinary things.

The major influence of Wordsworth is to be found in Timrod's concept of nature. Although he knew the classical poets and drew intellectual sustenance from them, he spoke truly of having "fed my muse with English song/Until her feeble wing grew strong."[66] In particular it had fed upon the intuitive, contemplative mysticism of the romantic poets. That his own concept of nature deviated from Wordsworth's somewhat, he consciously realized; but he knew likewise that he had started from Wordsworth's premise.

Both men are conscious of spiritual qualities no longer understood; instead of setting this consciousness in the period before birth and in early childhood, Timrod feels that he must some time, some where, have existed in a finer and more sensitive form:

> O mother! somewhere on this lovely earth
> I lived, and understood that mystic tongue,
> But, for some reason, to my second birth
> Only the dullest memories have clung.[67]

For both poets, these memories can best be stimulated by nature.

In Timrod's view, nature can provide an ethical basis for poetry; she is so bountiful that her lessons "may be gathered from the very dust we tread beneath our feet."[68] He admits that it is possible to disregard truth and yet to write good poetry, by concentrating on subjective beauty. Even in attaining this narrc end, nature can help the writer. Timrod grants readily that there need be no moral shut within the bosom of the rose; equally, that poems may be judged, without regard to morality, in "simple reference to their poetical effect." The contemplative or philosophical poet is "influenced by a vaster purpose . . . [he] aims to create beauty also, but . . . desires at the same time to mould this beauty into the shape of a temple dedicated to Truth." Beauty is implicit, but is made to serve a loftier end: in Milton, to justify God's ways to man; in Wordsworth, to give meaning to natural phenomena and richness to familiar things.

Timrod tried to accept Wordsworth's view of a beneficent, all-healing, wisdom-bestowing nature. It represented to him a tenable ideal and a way to contentment. But his own unquiet spirit and his first-hand observation frequently contradicted the words of the older poet. He recommended a study of Wordsworth to Rachel Lyons, in significant words: "I am quite sure that nobody could devote a month or many months to that grand old bard, without being made wiser and better. I myself would be a far happier man if I could follow his teaching, rather than my own dark and perturbed spirit."[69] This happiness he could never attain.

In "The Summer Bower," Timrod describes a secret covert, deep in the woods, that he had often gone to when depressed by grief or distressed by joy. There, usually, he "found the calm

I looked for, or returned/Strong with the quiet rapture in my soul." One day, "most sick in mind," he sought this tranquil place, but he found there no comfort for vain repinings, sickly sentiments, or inconclusive sorrows. Nature had sympathy and medicinal virtue for human suffering, but only "In her own way and with a just reserve"; for a certain kind of introspective suffering—a kind that Timrod knew only too well—nature had no balm:

> But for the pains, the fever, and the fret
> Engendered of a weak, unquiet heart,
> She hath no solace; and who seeks her when
> These be the troubles over which he moans,
> Reads in her unreplying lineaments
> Rebukes, that, to the guilty consciousness,
> Strike like contempt.[70]

The fault was in himself, he thought, and not in nature.

As poet Timrod was scrupulously honest with himself. He could not use material that had not become a part of his being, no matter what powerful sanction that material might have. What he could do was convict himself of lacking philosophy and understanding. In an article written immediately after Timrod's death, William Gilmore Simms traces this lack of certainty to a lack of profundity: "He labored in no field of metaphysics; he simply sang . . . with a native gift, of the things, the beauties, and the charms of nature. He belonged, in the classification of literary men, to the order that we call the contemplative; and without the deeper studies and aims of Wordsworth, he yet belonged to his school. . . . The fields, the wayside, the evening twilight, stars and moon, and faint warblings of the birds in green thickets—these were the attractions for his muse. These he meditated in song and sonnet, and his songs emulated all the gentle intuition of nature."[71]

Simms had only a partial understanding of Timrod. The qualities he describes are profusely scattered through the poems: Timrod was observant, with a quick eye and retentive mind; he wrote many descriptive passages that are accurate and beautiful. The external properties of nature provided a suitable poetic framework. In his best work, the function of nature was more fundamental, more integral, than decoration or the kind of intuition that Simms described. Nature typified the best aspects of life; it hinted at things about which man could only guess. When war came, this peaceful, eternal force contrasted with man's in-humanity and shortsightedness.

Although less pervasive, the influence of Tennyson was equally direct. Timrod's friends in Charleston first detected that influence in his poem "The Arctic Voyager";[72] since Timrod borrowed obviously and freely from Tennyson's "Ulysses" in thought and in structure, detection was easy and inevitable. Even more directly derived from "Ulysses" is the beginning of "Lines to R. L.": "That which we are and shall be is made up/Of what we have been."[73] Timrod develops this idea through the entire poem, in a manner individual enough; he is writing to a young lady, and his mood is removed from that of "Ulysses." Perhaps he wished deliberately to call Tennyson's poem to the reader's mind, for contrast. The borrowing is too plain not to be intentional.

Timrod liked the dramatic soliloquy. He used the form effec-tively in such poems as "A Dramatic Fragment," "The Summer Bower," and "A Rhapsody of a Southern Winter Night." From Tennyson, also, Timrod adapted the form of "Break, Break, Break" for his own poem, "Hark to the Shouting Wind," al-though he makes subtle and interesting changes both in the metrics and the idea.

This general indebtedness to Tennyson, likewise, was openly stated in "A Theory of Poetry"; in fact, Timrod implies that he was aware of it earlier than Hayne was. In treating Poe's theory of poetry, Timrod notes that it leads inevitably to the conclusion that Tennyson is the noblest poet who ever lived, and also to the conclusion that Poe is second only to Tennyson. After acquitting Poe of any petty vanity, Timrod adds: "I yield to few, and only to that extravagant few who would put him over the head of Mil-ton himself, in my admiration of Poe, and I yield to none in a love which is almost a worship of Tennyson, with whose poems I have been familiar from boyhood, and whom I yet continue to study with ceaseless profit and pleasure. But I can by no means consent to regard him as the first of Poets." Tennyson's accom-plishment is broader and finer than Poe's theory would provide for: his "large nature touches Poe on the one side and Words-worth on the other."

His most striking comment on Tennyson reveals that Timrod was conscious of a softness and immaturity in some poems. He had met a young lady who seemed passionately fond of poetry, but who had "not yet got beyond the period which goes into ecsta-sies over Locksley Hall, and into sleep over *In Memoriam*."[74]

Timrod's copy of Tennyson has survived, but there is little to be learned from a study of his light markings. The pocket-size volume, now re-bound, is badly worn and the opening pages have been lost; on the fly-leaf, Timrod's wife has written: "This volume of Tennyson belonged to Henry Timrod. He carried it constantly, for many, many years."[75] But any significant notes were made elsewhere: with the exception of his Catullus, Timrod did not annotate his books.

That he considered Milton superior to Tennyson and possibly even to Wordsworth is made clear in "A Theory of Poetry." Timrod's analysis of *Paradise Lost* is based on close study of the poem. But it is difficult to find in his work such unmistakable echoes as can be found of Wordsworth and Tennyson. Technically, he took from Milton the extended simile, and it retained its place after the influence of Tennyson had been so completely absorbed that it disappears. In "The Cotton Boll," the lines beginning "As men who labor in that mine / Of Cornwall" indicate how completely he had made this poetic device his own.[76]

The influence of Browning is slight, and readily apparent in only one poem, "Praeceptor Amat." Here the resemblance is one of form rather than of thought: Timrod employs the couplet in a manner similar to that of "My Last Duchess," and the poem is a dramatic monologue rather than a soliloquy. But Timrod's whimsical story of the emotions of a tutor seems frequently to embody the mannerisms and verbal obscurities of Browning for the effect of parody. It seems evident, from his remarks in "A Theory of Poetry," that Timrod considered himself well acquainted with the works of Robert and Elizabeth Barrett Browning, but that his admiration had been partly checked by some over-enthusiastic admirers. A theory of poetry could be drawn from their practice, he notes; but it would exclude many other excellent poets. The application of this doctrine was the work of their followers. In 1866 he complains of Davidson's "*niaiseries* in regard to Wordsworth and Mrs. Browning."[77]

The influence of Shelley has been previously treated. That of Keats appears to be negligible, although certain personal similarities in the lives of the two men have called forth unconvincing comparisons of their work.[78]

The poems in Timrod's *Autographic Relics*,[79] mainly written in the 1840's, reveal a marked indebtedness to the lyrics of Byron[80] and the lyrics and Anacreontics of Moore. This was a transitory influence, but in Timrod's youth it was a strong one.

Although he published in 1857 a poem strongly reminiscent of Moore, he indicated in the same magazine a realization of Moore's superficiality.[81]

Timrod's early liking for James Thomson lasted longer than his fondness for Moore. One of his earliest poems (dated 1843), has beside it a note, "Written in a blank leaf of Thompson's Castle of Indolence"; the nine-line poem makes a comparison between the English poet's dream country, where he "created a fancied realm," and the "sad reality" of a Carolina school room.[82] Thomson's handling of nature seemed too matter-of-fact for Timrod to rate him as a truly significant poet: he had concentrated too much on description, and neglected the symbolic meaning.[83]

Timrod's knowledge of Chaucer may have been slight. Once, in celebrating the flower that he loved so well, Timrod mentions that a daisy called to mind that these were "Chaucer's favorites, little pink-tipped stars."[84]

Timrod's highest tribute to Spenser was embodied in an editorial attacking England for her pretended neutrality: "there are few of us so free from the strong spell of her great literature as to be able to hate her without considerable reluctance." In contrast to England's materialism, one remembers "the ethereal enchantments of SPENSER, and in recalling that he too, that mystic wanderer into fairyland, was one of her children, we are well nigh seduced into believing that a land which has given birth to so divine a creature cannot be organically affected by a vice so inconsistent with the character of its offspring."[85] This admiration for Spenser's work may indicate that the Elizabethan poet had not become a favorite until late in life. Hayne suggests, however, that the metrical form of "A Vision of Poesy" is "that employed by Shakspeare in his *'Venus and Adonis,'* by Spenser in his 'Astrophel,' and Cowley in his least ambiguous verses."[86]

The songs of Burns Timrod praises mildly; he notes that they have become a folk possession—possibly after they had been talked about and drawn to general attention by a few discerning men.[87] In an editorial on the appropriateness of the names of the months, he calls the Scottish poet as witness: "We have Burns' authority for asserting that 'November chill blows loud with angry sough.' "[88] Timrod's work belongs in a later tradition, and Burns influenced him only as his songs had become a part of a larger current of thought.

Timrod used Shakespeare's works freely and with evident familiarity. But this use is primarily as a source of allusions that would not require explanation. When he was competing in a contest that seemed to require references to dramatic characters, he employed brief descriptions and personifications of Lear, Hamlet, Juliet, and Miranda;[89] when he sought a fit and concluding epithet to express his sense of indebtedness to England, he wrote "Shakespeare's England."[90] His liking for Shakespeare may have been inherited. His father had, in his boyhood, read the plays by moonlight, and had considered Shakespeare "his favorite companion."[91]

Shakespeare was used, once, as justification. In a letter to Hayne, Timrod objects bitterly to Simms' describing him as indolent and on one occasion reading a "yellow-covered novel. Now I remember the occasion very well. I was really sick with a most painful malady—a *stricture,* but I didn't tell him that—and I was reading Shakspeare. I have not read ten novels in as many years, and I never read trash, not even Mr. Simms."[92]

When Timrod was dying, two lines from Shakespeare troubled him with their haunting precision. He wondered at first if he could not will himself to live;[93] but the next day he quoted Milton's "Death reigns triumphant," and, after that, he "asked me if I remembered the lines from Shakespeare's King John, he had quoted to me on our last walk on the meadow back of Mrs. Stack's house. These lines commence—

> And none of you will bid the winter come
> And thrust his icy fingers in my maw,

etc. and alludes to the fearful consuming internal fires from which the dying Monarch suffered. He said I little thought I should suffer from what in reading those lines had caused me so much horror."[94] This is graphic testimony to the power that Shakespeare's lines could wield on his thought.

That he knew something of Shakespeare's contemporaries Timrod reveals in the course of a letter to Hayne, lambasting "this 'milk & water' Dennis of Southern criticism," James Wood Davidson. Dekker's lines "about Christ's being 'the first true gentleman that ever breathed,' had never fallen on Mr. Davidson's ear. By-the-way, Mr. Simms has in more than one place attributed that passage to Middleton. I have assured him over and over again that he was mistaken, but to no purpose. Please show him, when you next meet, the passage in the last scene of the 1st Part of 'The Honest Whore.' "[95]

Although he wrote many love lyrics, he does not seem to have been drawn into the cavalier or metaphysical tradition. One sonnet has the old and well-worn poetic idea that Marvell expresses magnificently in "To His Coy Mistress"; a few lines, especially, remind one of that earlier poem:

> So everywhere on earth,
> This foothold where we stand with slipping feet,
> The unsubstantial and substantial meet,
> And we are fooled until made wise by time.[96]

But the metaphysical style was not intellectually in fashion. Timrod's poetry seems nearer to it than does the poetry of most of his contemporaries. Hayne, who disliked such intellectual daring, writes that "A Cry to Arms" contains "one of the few palpable conceits I can recall, which would seem not merely admissible, but charming."[97]

Timrod seems equally removed from the cavalier tradition. He makes only a casual reference to Suckling; otherwise, his knowledge of these poets must be by assumption only, and any indebtedness must be proved by rather doubtful parallels.[98]

That he was fundamentally religious is made clear in many poems and letters. His fondness for the Hebrew stories and characters in the Bible led naturally in his poetry to references and allusions; two poems, in fact, depend largely upon such extended reference for body and meaning.[99] These poems reveal only a knowledge and use of easily available, well-known material. It may be, subjectively, that Timrod made a close association between the Bible and poetry, but hesitated to put this idea into writing. In a paragraph which he wrote and then deleted, Timrod identifies the spirit of poetry as second only to that of religion: "The sentiment of poetry as it thus developed in the mind is the very ground on which (apart from Revelation) we base our hopes of immortality & this fact should make it the next sacred thing to the great chart of Salvation."[100] Although he discarded the statement as part of his address, Timrod undoubtedly believed it to be truth.

Any reconstruction of Timrod's reading must necessarily be incomplete. As a rule, his references are casual and suggestive, but the samplings indicate a rather exact knowledge of English poetry, and a wider acquaintance than Hayne implies. Some of his estimates of authors and his side remarks have a penetrating incisiveness, though they are incomplete and at best give only a partial picture.

In his essays, Timrod quotes from many sources. In addition

to those already noted, he lifted illustrative bits from such writers as Francis Bacon,[101] Charles Lamb, Matthew Arnold, Arthur Henry Hallam, John Sterling, Henry Taylor, and Aubrey de Vere. He expressed great admiration for Coleridge, whom he called the noblest critic that ever lived, and he quoted or paraphrased both from the prose and the poetry. Since Timrod's own work was frequently appearing in them, he must have been familiar with the diverse material in the *Southern Literary Messenger* and *Russell's Magazine*. It seems probable that he was also well acquainted with the easily available English and Northern magazines.[102] His quotations and remarks display only that knowledge for which he had an immediate use.

Thus, a hasty answer to a sister's question gives his opinion of the work of Charlotte Brontë: "I have not time to write a criticism of Villette; but I agree with most people that it is inferiour to Jane Eyre. It is by no means a bread and butter thing however." He comments briefly on the naturalness of the characters, but thinks the "conclusion of the book is a specimen of claptrap unworthy of the author of Jane Eyre. . . . You have heard me admire Miss Brontë's skill in sky- and weather-painting. There are many such pictures in this book; but their style is more ambitious than those in Jane Eyre and Shirley—they are less simple, sketchy, and graphic, and I don't like them half so well. However, the moonlight scene in the park is magnificent."[103] Timrod's opinion of Charlotte's sisters remains unknown.

Hayne's belief that Timrod read with more exactness than variety is partially borne out by Timrod's frank statement that an outside stimulus was responsible for his reading Ovid and Persius.[104] Yet in the war and post-war years there is another side to the picture. Books were scarce, and difficult to obtain. In December of 1861 he wrote that "the camp is *life*," and that there were "No new books, no reviews, no appetizing critiques, no literary correspondence, no intellectual intelligence of any kind!"[105] He continued to feel a need for books and magazines, but mainly he did without them. Even his position as an editor did not help much, as he explained to Hayne: "You are aware that it is the rule of all papers and periodicals that the books which are sent to be noticed are the perquisites of him who criticizes them. Having 'noticed' one or two books, and finding that Fontaine took possession of them notwithstanding, I reminded him of the rule, when he said that for the future then, he would notice the books himself. One pleasant consequence of this is that his wretched criticisms are credited to me by the public, while all my leaders are attributed to him."[106]

This desire for new books became more acute. Timrod felt himself out of the current of intellectual thought; he expressed this discontent to his more fortunate friend, and incidentally gives an excellent criticism of Augusta Evans Wilson:

I have read (skippingly) St. Elmo. Somebody lent it to my wife— I could not have got it otherwise—for nobody sends me books or magazines, and of course I can't purchase them. I have yet to see Jane [sic] Ingelow, Swinburne,[107] and Robert Buchanan—each of whom I long to be acquainted with. Nor have I read a line of Simm's [sic] Serial—nor laid my eyes upon a single number of the "Old Guard."

I quite agree with you with regard to St. Elmo, and the character of Miss Evan's [sic] talents. I met her, you know, in Mobile—took tea with her several evenings in succession. She talks well, but pedantically now and then; though not so pedantically as she writes. She has very peculiar, but very false and shallow opinions about poetry and poets.[108]

Later in the month, Timrod again wrote to Hayne, expressing eagerness over a possible visit to Copse Hill. In addition to the 'aromatic pine-land atmosphere" and the "happy prospect of your own society," Timrod adds that he is also tempted because "you speak of the publishers sending you their *new books!* You can afford to put up with what Mr. Simms really appears to consider appetizing fare, so unctuously does he refer to it (I mean 'hog and hominy') if, mean time, instead of having your imagination starved, it (or she?) is free to wander in fresh literary pastures."[109]

In less than a week, according to Hayne, Timrod was at Copse Hill, for a "month's sojourn." The two men sauntered through the pine forest, rested on the hillsides, and talked literature. In August the visit was repeated. Hayne consolidates his account of the two visits, but he describes Timrod as apostrophizing "twilight in the language of Wordsworth's sonnet," quoting the Elizabethan dramatist John Ford and wondering if perhaps he was quoting Fletcher, memorizing a ballad by Jean Ingelow, and reading Robert Buchanan. In talking about his desire to live to be *"fifty* or fifty-five," Timrod commented on the picture of old age given in Charles Reade's *It is Never too Late to Mend.*[110]

Timrod wrote to his sister Emily that "Hayne has plenty of

new books—I suffer from an *embarras de richesses*. It is hard to tell which to begin first. I distract by insane attempts to read all at once."[111]

The extent of Timrod's knowledge of classical poetry is difficult to estimate. His friends thought him deeply if not widely read; Hayne writes that while Aeschylus revolted him, he was charmed by Sophocles, revelled in "the elegant art of Virgil," and never wearied of Horace and Catullus. J. P. K. Bryan goes even farther, and finds a direct indebtedness to Catullus: "At times there is 'the easy elegance of Catullus,' always his delight, and a metrical translation of whose poems he had completed."[112]

If it ever existed in fact, the translation has disappeared. W. A. Courtenay could not locate it, although he believed that Timrod not only had completed the work but had also had it set in type, in the same manner as the poems for an English edition. When he asked Mrs. Lloyd for the proof sheets of this translation, he got what is possibly the final answer: "I cannot recall that he commenced a metrical version of Catullus, but I have no doubt but that he contemplated doing it at some time . . . . I am sure it was never begun." However, she admits in another letter that "I did not preserve all Henry's papers," so her disclaimer is not conclusive.[113]

It is impossible without vague guesswork to trace a direct indebtedness in Timrod's original poetry to that of Catullus. There are similarities of tone and manner, but there is, also, the possibility that these are traceable to an English intermediary.[114] Of Timrod's direct knowledge, no doubt exists. His copy of Catullus is available, and is extensively annotated; it lends support to the statements that Timrod either translated or intended to translate the poems, for it is the only one of his extant books that shows numerous notes and markings. Yet these may reveal only a student's transcription from lectures or commentaries. Timrod's notes indicate an interest in poetic metaphor, in idiomatic expression, in variant readings suggested by commentaries, and in identifying persons and places, especially the Greek and Latin synonyms for the same name.[115]

On the flyleaf, Timrod has quoted lines of poetry from Ovid, Martial, and François Maynard (in French). They indicate that Timrod considered Catullus' life more virtuous than his writings; the Martial runs, "Lasciva est nobis pagina, vita proba est." And the French verse notes that if the author's pen is evil, his life is decorous. Presumably these quotations seemed appropriate: it may be that Timrod felt some justification or palliation was needed for the more licentious passages.

His copies of Tibullus, Propertius, Cornelius Nepos, and Statius[116] have survived, but they contribute little that is significant beyond the record of his ownership. In spite of the quotation from Ovid on the flyleaf of Catullus, Timrod did not read the entire poem until 1866. In a letter to Hayne, he attacks James Wood Davidson's critical acumen and classical scholarship; to prove that Davidson's knowledge was faulty, he cites a personal experience: "I borrowed from him not long ago a copy of Ovid's Metamorphoses, of which I had hitherto only read fragments in the original. He told me that he had only glanced into it himself and spoke of the difficulty of the Latin. I took the book home and found it perfectly easy Latin for very ordinary scholarship. I read it through with little more trouble than so much English."[117]

A year later, in again commenting on Davidson's ignorance, Timrod gives a little more information on his own reading: "Of Horace he literally knows nothing. I have tried him with several other authors—but he seems to be familiar with none of them. The other day he spoke in raptures of Persius. I had not then read Persius, but curious to see D's taste, I went to the library and glanced over his Satires."[118] From the lack of enthusiasm implicit in this statement, a glance was apparently enough.

Though he used "Aglaus," the name of a Greek pastoral poet, as an early pseudonym, and though he was certainly conversant with Greek literature, there are no indications of its effect upon him. In "Praeceptor Amat," he manages to use a Greek phrase cleverly enough that it fits naturally into the mock-pedantic context, and into the rhyme as well as the rhythm.[119] Likewise, one can only guess at his knowledge of German. His father was proud of his German descent (the name was originally Dimroth), and served as Captain of the German Fusiliers during the Seminole War. The one tangible result of this German blood is a translation, "Song of Mignon," from the *Wilhelm Meister* of Goethe. Apparently Timrod did not consider it worth publishing; Simms thought poorly of it.[120]

A few times Timrod mentions his interest in French. He wrote his sister that his pronunciation was considered "elegant," and he occasionally employs a French phrase in his correspondence.[121] His extant copy of Rousseau's *La Nouvelle Héloëse* has no marginal comments;[122] he does not mention the French author in any known letter, or remark on Rousseau's treatment of nature. Yet when he wanted it, Timrod found an apt quotation in French to describe Catullus.

There is a strong and pleasant temptation for any writer on Timrod to play up a father's influence. Every account of William Henry Timrod portrays him as attractive, studious, and independent, an excellent bookbinder who was proud of his craftsmanship, a good citizen and soldier, and an affectionate husband and parent. Although the local newspaper frequently mentioned his name in connection with the activities of the Fusiliers and the German Friendly Society, he clipped for his Daybook only the annual announcement of the officers of the Charleston Library Society; these show him a director from 1827 to 1829.[123] He talked well about literature, and attracted to him the ablest men in Charleston. If his poetry was definitely minor and frequently derivative, it had also a firm craftsmanship and occasional excellence.

In 1814, William Henry Timrod published his one book, *Poems, on Various Subjects*.[124] In his maturer days, he was ashamed of this youthful work, and regretted the publication.[125] Later verses were published in local magazines, and four of them appear in *The Charleston Book* (1845). This work reveals that William Timrod had read Moore and Byron; it shows a maturer mind and a better command of verse. That Henry was pleased with his father's poems is easily proved: in 1864, he re-printed several in the *Daily South Carolinian*.

The elder Timrod died on July 28, 1838, when Henry was ten years old. Any personal influence was very early in Henry's life, and cannot be traced in his poetry. Simms, who knew both father and son, fancied that there was a general resemblance, but he suggests nothing more: Henry's "genius was, in some degree, inherited. His father—William H. Timrod—was a poet before him. . . . He wrote freely and frequently. He published a volume of poems in Charleston, some fifty years ago, the general characteristics of which somewhat resembled those of his son. He, too, was a lover of nature, and his poems were meant frequently to illustrate her phases."[126]

It would also be pleasant, but I believe equally impossible, to find evidence of direct indebtedness to the Charleston writers of his day. The men who with Hugh Swinton Legaré wrote the distinguished papers in the *Southern Review* were no longer active, but the group that congregated at Russell's Bookshop and Simms' town house had wit and intelligence. Simms, James Mathewes Legaré, S. Henry Dickson, John Dickson Bruns, and several others wrote capable and occasionally distinguished verse; Petigru, Grayson, Russell, and similar men had taste and energetic opinions. To them all, literature was alive. These doctors, lawyers, merchants, and writers talked heatedly yet intelligently of books and ideas; they had magazines at hand to publish their shorter work when, and if, they got around to putting it on paper.[127]

To the younger men, this intellectual atmosphere was bracing. They considered themselves an integral part of an active group, working in the tradition of English poetry yet contributing something new and individual. Timrod, Hayne and Bruns, the classicists John della Torre and Basil L. Gildersleeve, and other young men talked freely with each other; undoubtedly, each profited by the criticism of the others.[128] Inevitably, the tension of increasing bitterness directed their thoughts from literature to immediate political and economic problems; the war itself disrupted their lives. Each writer was forced to develop his powers alone, and under difficulties.

Timrod knew an intellectual and personal loneliness. Physical weakness prevented him from taking an active part in the war. These personal deprivations are not expressed in his poems, but they helped to add intensity and strength to his work. Only through his writing could he become identified with the thought and emotion of his region. This, at least, he achieved. His opportunity for meditation, for development, for an expression in poetry of his own critical ideals, was cut short by poverty and death.

11

PAUL HAMILTON HAYNE
Eclecticist

F ROM CHILDHOOD until his death Paul Hamilton Hayne was a wide-ranging, voracious reader. He was brought up in a bookish atmosphere by a mother who encouraged not only the reading but the writing of poetry. In "To My Mother" he indicates that he began writing verse early in youth, and that his mother was sympathetic and encouraging about this "earliest rhyme":

> Thou did'st not taunt my fledgling song,
>   Nor view its flight with scorning:
> "The bird," thou said, "grown fleet and strong,
>   Might yet outsoar the morning!"

He remembered also exchanging early ballads of stirring adventures and sanguinary catastrophes with his classmate Henry Timrod, another precocious writer of verse.[1] By 1845, the fifteen-year-old Hayne was publishing verses in the Charleston *Courier* under the pseudonym Alphaeus; soon afterward, so prolific was his output, he took as a second literary name Basil Ormond. With him, reading and writing went hand in hand.

The normal youthful inclination to like most of the books he read Hayne carried into maturity. As he grew older the range of his reading widened from romance and poetry to include nonfiction: in youth Burton's *Anatomy of Melancholy* became "my *Vade Mecum*," but it was only one of many books that enthralled him. Apparently this tolerance did not extend to legal books. After graduating from the College of Charleston in 1850, he read law in James L. Petigru's office and was admitted to the bar. He soon abandoned this uncongenial occupation for literature and, rather incidentally, journalism.[2]

Because he liked to write about books and found that by doing so he could acquire them free, Hayne began writing literary notices and reviews for Charleston newspapers. A few years earlier, Poe had used magazine book reviews as a medium through which to hammer out, refine, and develop his philosophical ideas on literature: he made the best of his reviews springboards into literary criticism. Hayne as a rule was content with the book in hand, and only mildly concerned with general critical principles. His aim was to read intelligently and to give his own impressions of book and author, with ample quotations to illustrate his points. Since he was an intelligent reader with a wide background, his remarks frequently have considerable value; since he enjoyed most books, he frequently communicated his enthusiasm and appreciation to his readers; since he judged by personal taste rather than by strict aesthetic or philosophical standards, he became essentially an eclectic critic.

Presumably Hayne would have disagreed with this estimate. He thought criticism in his age superior to that of former times because it "has now been elaborated into a *science* of comprehensive inductions and profound analysis"; as proof, he cites the superiority of Coleridge's Shakespeare criticism over Johnson's or Pope's.[3] But Hayne's own method ran to a few generalizations, a summary, and extensive quotations: generally he attempted to give the flavor of the book rather than to judge it. This tendency to use the scissors generously Hayne defended with some justice in a letter to John Esten Cooke, concerning the editorial practices of the *Southern Field and Fireside*: "When, for example, I have been at the trouble of reading a book carefully, to extract its *'cream'* Mr. [William W.] Mann nullifies my labor by omitting the most important *extracts;* simply because, he doesn't think I have a right to charge for them!!! *You* know that the labor of *compressing* the thoughts of others is *harder* than original composition."[4]

No doubt Hayne also felt that his literary standards were sufficiently high. There are occasional slashing attacks. *The Discovery of Sir John Franklin* by the Georgia writer J. A. Turner is dismissed as a "volume of versicles . . . devoid of every essential of true poetry."[5] However harsh it may be, this judgment seems objectively rendered, but the most astringent of Hayne's

remarks usually have a personal or moral basis, or a national or
sectional bias. In 1852 he was offended when a British reviewer
attacked Longfellow, Bryant, and Poe. Superciliously the reviewer had noted that a poem may be written "in a masterly manner,"
yet be worthless even if it pleases the ear and the taste. It may be
original, yet still be worthless. Hayne denominated this narrow
critical creed as bad and vicious. The application was even
worse, when the reviewer called Longfellow's "Psalm of Life"
a piece of "pretentious, unprofitable, anti-Christian trash." Hayne
defended it as a pure, noble, Christian poem. The reviewer noted
that every idea in "Thanatopsis" could be found "somewhere or
other in Shakespeare, or Wordsworth, or Young," and that Bryant's poem was worthy only of being compared with the work of
Samuel Rogers. This indicated a total misunderstanding of
"Thanatopsis," which rightly should be compared with Gray's
"Elegy." Hayne was pleased with the mild but deserved praise of
Thomas Buchanan Read; on the other hand, the praise of Poe
was so feeble that "the intended compliment degenerates into
farce." Any perceptive reader should have recognized that "The
Raven" is a "weird, but powerful production," and that it is,
with few notable exceptions, "The most purely original poem in
the English language."[6]

When he thought his friends neglected or misrepresented, he
leaped eagerly to their defence. Thus Charles A. Dana as editor
of the *Household Book of Poetry* was "lamentably incompetent,"
rejecting good poems and including bad ones on the basis of personal caprice rather than of sound editorial standards. If his
choice from English poets seemed haphazard (omitting Skelton,
Lodge, Donne, Swift, Young, and Crabbe, but including Byron),
his American selections were largely dictated by prejudice, for no
Southern poets were included. This neglect of the South and
especially of Simms infuriated Hayne, and he noted flatly that
Simms's "fame rests upon the solid foundation of real and indisputable merit."[7]

For a similar reason, Hayne was bitter about the critical preten-
sions of such Southern editors as Howard Caldwell and John Wilson Overall: "Caldwell is a man in whom I have *no confidence
whatever.*—He has conceived the *bitterest* enmity against Simms,
because the *latter* reviewed *his poems* in 'Russell' with a touch of
severity . . . . Caldwell is assisted by an obscure literary adven-
turer, who edits the lighter department of the N. Orleans 'True
Delta' . . . *he too* is incensed against Simms, because a poem by

Jno Wilson Overall, entitled '*The Death of Mirabeau*' was noticed contemptuously in the *So Quarterly Review*."[8] These men,
with James Wood Davidson (described by Hayne as "that dogmatic and arrant ass"),[9] represented the enemy at home, as Dana
represented him in the North. Hayne felt himself spokesman
for an unjustly neglected group and he never hesitated to speak
out vigorously in its behalf.

His tendency to judge poetry on moral grounds is more am-
biguously phrased. He was never happy in dealing with Byron,
whose work apparently did not belong in a book intended for
family reading; yet he had no inclination to minimize Byron's
poetic abilities: Frances Anne Kemble's *Poems* are "characterized
by a morbid, Byronic sadness, without the grace, fervor and passion which go so far to redeem the vicious school of art which
Lord Byron inaugurated." He was fascinated yet repelled especially by Childe Harold, with its "picturesque episodes, and that
fierce, consuming fire of genius, which . . . despite its blasphemy,
selfishness, and egoism, make it one of the most fascinating works
ever produced by man."[10]

No such ambivalence was forced upon him in dealing with
the "mobocratic" Walt Whitman: in 1860 he wrote to his friend
and fellow-editor John R. Thompson that "The *comparative*
success of his work demonstrates the lowness both of *morals &
taste* among even the better class of readers, & critics at the
North." This judgment Hayne never felt any inclination to
change, for he did not like free verse ("that fantastic, & monstrous style of metrical architecture") any better than he liked
Whitman's statements about sex: "his ideas when comprehensive,
being filthy and revolting; and the whole atmosphere of his
writings a vague, nebulous haze, composed in about equal proportions of feculence and falsehood."*[11]

Yet he preferred to find in books qualities that he could honestly praise. Theoretically he believed in strict and universal
literary standards, in a cosmopolitan and international tone, in
judging a work entirely on its own merits without regard to

---

* Hayne himself did not escape the charge of being guilty of "moral offenses," by
the editor of the Columbia *Daily Southern Light*, for a two-part article in *Russell's*
on Nell Gwynn. Hayne, evidently fascinated by Peter Cunningham's biography,
wrote that it was useless to approach this period from the point of view of a moralist; to be entertained and perhaps instructed by the humors of that period "we must
resolutely shut our eyes to the folly and wickedness which universally prevailed."
In a later issue of *Russell's*, Hayne vigorously rebutted these charges of moral laxity
in his own writing (*Russell's*, II [February 1858], 466).

its place or time of origin. No doubt he thought that he consistently employed such standards. But there were direct and indirect pressures that he probably never recognized. He was a child of his century, a thorough-going if slightly belated Romantic; his taste and his intellect were shaped by his own time. This carried with it an abiding interest in certain earlier periods, and a distrust of anything that smacked of neo-classicism. With this there was combined Hayne's emotional feeling: his friendships were many, and warmly partisan; he might in private letters admit the literary deficiencies of a friend, but he rarely admitted them publicly.[12]

Henry Timrod was his closest friend, and Timrod as person or as poet could do no wrong. Hayne generously conceded that his friend was the better poet: "Timrod possesses more ability, (native, & acquired)," he wrote to R. H. Stoddard in 1860, "than *all* the other *young* poets of the *South,* placed together. For *myself,* (loving the man as I would a *brother*)—, *his* successes are *my* successes."[13] In *Russell's* Hayne was equally unreserved: Timrod's forthcoming book would add luster to the individual and to literature; the poems came from an imagination "not only subtle and delicate, but vigorous," and revealed a truly imaginative poet who would gain permanent fame through the faculty of imagination; who in "A Vision of Poesy" had already written an American classic.[14] Two years later, when he published "My Mother Land," Hayne added in a footnote that it had been written before Timrod's "Carolina" appeared: he "would not otherwise have been so presumptuous as to select a theme, already treated with a force, power, and spirit, which indeed render Mr. Timrod's claims to the Laureateship among Southern poets, as clear to the general public, as they have been long indisputable in the eyes of those admitted to his more intimate friendship and regard."[15]

After Timrod's death, Hayne tried unceasingly to get his friend's collected poems published; when a volume of his own appeared, he wrote to Mrs. Timrod: "Heaven is my witness when I declare that I would—rather, a hundred times over, have brought out Timrod's book than mine." When Stoddard rated Timrod the best Southern poet and placed Hayne second, Hayne wrote to Margaret Junkin Preston: "what he says of Timrod I cordially agree to. Never, for one instant, have I failed in acknowledging his superiority."[16]

In various poetic tributes and in the biographical memoir prefixed to Timrod's *Poems* (1873), Hayne testified open-heartedly, without trace of envy or jealousy, to his belief in Timrod's greatness. If his praise sometimes overshoots the mark (as when he proclaimed Timrod one of the six best writers of blank verse in English),[17] he was trying to make up for undue neglect by other critics and to gain attention for work he sincerely admired—and much can surely be forgiven when motivated by such openhearted friendship and admiration.

His personal and critical feelings toward William Gilmore Simms were mixed. In some ways the relationship between them parallels that of uncle and nephew, with the younger man occasionally showing impatience for the elder's Johnsonian arrogance and sometimes revealing even in print a dubiety about his literary achievement. Such instances were rare. That Hayne both loved and admired Simms, in spite of some reservations, he makes abundantly clear.

A typically frank admission of Simms's defects was made late in life, in a letter to Bayard Taylor: Simms, self-confident and arrogant, with "his 'war-paint on' . . . would 'mouth' now & then, upon the subject [of his literary ability] after the fashion of 'Ancient Pistol' . . . you ought to have seen how bravely Simms held up *after the war* . . . he was grand in those days . . . . As a national *literary power,* (proper) he is just *nil*; but the subtler influence of his example, cannot die!"[18]

That far he would go, privately, in balancing the human good with the bad. He also admitted publicly some defects. When W. P. Trent believed that Hayne "wrote reverently and lovingly of Simms in 'Russell's,' " he must have glided over Hayne's longest and most ambitious reviews, must have read very hastily even Hayne's long, semi-official poetic tribute read to aid the Simms Memorial Fund, and the nostalgic reminiscences that Hayne in 1885 contributed to the *Southern Bivouac*: "That Simms was essentially a poet, that he possessed force, feeling, imagination, an active fancy, and a not unmusical ear, I hold to be unquestionable, but his prodigious faculty of verse-making, amounting to improvisation, led to great diffuseness, and a fatal neglect of the '*labor limae.*' " It is true that Hayne unfailingly though not without qualifications praised Simms's romances and stories, for he believed them worthy: Trent adds that his praise was given "well and honestly," and that it was not the "puffery of a clicque," but a striving for "the advancement of their art, and especially the art of their section."[19]

In fact, Hayne begins his review of Simms's poetry by noting that "clicquism is the curse of our literature," and that Simms has suffered because with great independence of spirit he has stayed aloof from these pushing groups; he concludes by noting warily that if his judgments have been too lenient, those of other critics have been too harsh. In between, he compares Simms's poetry with that of the Elizabethan dramatists in its "directness of diction, its abrupt audacity and defiance of conventional trammels, its compressed vigor." If Hayne's comparisons are pitched too high, he was careful to select those qualities for which his friend could be justly lauded: other praise-worthy characteristics were "richness and force of thought, affluence of expression, a versatile range and breadth of sympathy, a comprehensive imagination." With numerous quotations Hayne illustrates the variety and richness of Simms's poetry, but he adds that there are serious blemishes: "Occasional great diffuseness," "verbal mannerisms," and worst of all an "apparently invincible repugnance to the distasteful duty of correction."[20]

Clearly Hayne believed that Simms as lyric poet had vigor and strength, but lacked artistry. When he turned to the dramatic works he likewise qualified his praise, and in addition used the essay to express his dislike of "the commonplaces" of his own time. In *Norman Maurice* Simms had attempted to mould the unmalleable material of everyday life into an original American tragedy. But romance, Hayne thought, "dwells mostly in the Past . . . the tragic drama, approaching the universal in comprehensiveness, and dealing with grand passions upon the amplest stage, partake of many of the best traits of the romance proper." For that reason, "no attempt *can be* more difficult than the attempt to elevate the ordinary phases of political and social life, in our time, to the grave dignity of tragedy." In spite of scenes that are "almost Bathos," Simms had written an impressive tragedy, although a better tragedy could have been written out of "more plastic material."[21]

It was pleasanter and possibly more effective to quote favorable notices that had appeared in Northern magazines. When the New York *Literary World* described *Norman Maurice* as a production of great originality, force, and beauty, *Russell's* reprinted the critique—a practice that Hayne as editor consistently followed. It had the advantage of giving Simms and other Southern authors the attention that Hayne felt they deserved, while absolving the editor from the necessity of pointing out defects in their work.[22]

The literary Charleston that Hayne knew in the 1850s had many writers, but only Simms, Timrod, and Hayne himself can be called professional, even in the sense of being primarily interested in writing. To most of his friends writing was an avocation definitely second to law or medicine or farming. In editorials Hayne encouraged them to write more: such men, by helping to create a favorable intellectual climate, would improve the public taste and at the same time gratify their own self-esteem.[23] As editor, he published their articles and poems, frequently with a brief but encouraging commentary. One such article, William J. Grayson's "What is Poetry?", must have offended Hayne's critical sensibilities, for it glorified Pope and neo-classicism while wittily denigrating Coleridge and Wordsworth.[24] But Grayson, he wrote to Theodore B. Kingsbury, editor of the North Carolina *Leisure Hour,* is "one of my dearest personal friends . . . shy & modest. His poems, so far, have not rec'd. the attention at the South which they deserve." Although he published Timrod's devastating rebuttal and undoubtedly agreed with Timrod's praise of Wordsworth, Hayne continued to publish and evidently to value Grayson's work. As critic he was equally encouraging. When Grayson's book-length poem *The Country* appeared, Hayne wrote: "In melodious verse he sings the praises of country life . . . the thought is clear, the allusions palpable, the sentiments natural to a cultivated mind, the descriptions picturesque, and the moral admirable."[25]

Sometimes he was forced to dissent from the opinions of his friends. When Judge George S. Bryan in a published oration on "The Character of the Poet" held that Robert Burns "is the truest and intensest of poets . . . the greatest of poets," partly because he held himself aloof from the world, thus like all poets exercising "a divine office," and upholding "the cause of truth even when his conduct deserves her censure," Hayne dissented vigorously on the general proposition and the specific judgment: not only is Burns not a first-class poet but "the most exalted of the Poets have borne themselves bravely and gallantly in the strife of *actual* life: Shakespeare, Milton, Dante, the grand triumvirate of modern Bards, were not only 'in the world,' but in a certain and most significant sense '*of* the world.' "[26]

Open disagreement of this kind is unusual. Hayne preferred the gracefully-worded tribute: the poet James Mathewes Legaré had "a pure taste and delicate perception of the beautiful."[27] Sometimes it was possible to glide over what one did not approve.

Although ostensibly reviewing the Writings of Hugh Swinton Legaré, Hayne barely touches the critical essays with their strong classical bias and their distaste for romantic subjectivism: these show "the author's capabilities in a somewhat less exacting department of literature and thought" than the ones on law and on classical subjects. Hayne could appreciate Legaré's liking of the Elizabethan drama and Greek literature, but he was undoubtedly suspicious of a critic who considered Byron the most important of English Romantic poets; so he concentrated on Legaré's biography to the neglect of his writing.[28]

This tolerant attitude, this tendency to concentrate on the good and overlook the bad, Hayne extended to all his friends, anywhere—and he considered a friend any person with whom he corresponded with fair regularity, whether he had met that person or not. So he found ready words of encouragement for a host of minor writers, and after the war for the promising beginner, Sidney Lanier, although he lost some of his enthusiasm when Lanier turned to national themes. Nonetheless a "purer, gentler, nobler spirit of American literary men never existed on earth; and in this spirit he wrote his poetry." Hayne recognized that Lanier was attempting to speak as a major poet, whether he was succeeding or not.[29]

It was easier to praise Francis O. Ticknor as a spirited lyrist par excellence of the War, and to write a graceful introduction to his collected poems.[30] Yet he tried also to be just. Of his friend A. B. Meek's poems he could say favorably that "they contain abundant evidence of talent, and are, many of them, musical and vigorous," but unfortunately they "exhibit a general lack of artistic 'last-finish.' "[31] It was also easy enough, when dealing with John R. Thompson's academic *Poesy: an Essay in Rhyme,* to label it "just in thought, and singularly graceful and musical in rhyme."[32] But he was baffled when the Georgia poet and mystic Thomas Holley Chivers sent him for review *A Paean of Glory for the Heroes of Freedom,* and he expressed his bewilderment frankly: "The most curious part of the performance is the evident earnestness of spirit in which the author set about competing with *Bombastes Furiosa* . . . . Dr. Chivers deserves to be considered the Founder of a new, striking School of Art in Poetry. Read his Preface, after which, if you retain sufficient equanimity to proceed, make his acquaintance as a Poet! We cannot advise however this last piece of temerity, unless indeed you are naturally very strong headed!"[33] True, Hayne was dealing with one of

Chivers' weakest performances, but there is little reason to think that he would have liked the best of Chivers.

His attitude toward Poe indicates that admiration for the artist was tempered by pity and some distrust for the man. In 1859 he objected to several attempts to prove Poe "a much-injured, and long-suffering lamb," yet on one of his trips north Hayne made a pilgrimage to Poe's grave.[34] Poe's ideas on poetry, if not always perfect, were always philosophical; and his revision of "Lenore" and "The Valley of Unrest" Hayne used as a text to prove the value of revision both of ideas and words even by a poet-genius.[35] But more fascinating even than Poe's work was the peculiar dichotomy of his being: in Hayne's poetic tribute "Two mighty spirits dwell in him: One, a wild demon. . . . One, a fair angel." In a letter accompanying the poem he added that "With all his faults, Edgar Poe possessed *original genius*."[36] This is not an echo of Hayne's complaints about Byron, in whose poems as in his life he detected morbidity and unwholesomeness; rather, Hayne approves of Poe's work while retaining doubts about him as a person. Thus he honored the writer although he had reservations about the man.

Poe had left the South; Hayne at times was tempted to do the same. If he was distressed by the commonplaceness of life in nineteenth-century America, he was more immediately distressed by the indifference of Southerners to writers and to literature. He had met something worse than savage opposition, he wrote to Kingsbury in 1858: "systematic neglect, & that terrible species of coldness which embodies itself in quiet sneers. . . . The So. literary man must necessarily feel that he occupies a wrong position."[37] Two years later, after James Russell Lowell in favorably reviewing his book of poems *Avolio* suggested that the young poet was working in an "atmosphere uncongenial to letters," Hayne reluctantly admitted the charge: "I have partially confessed to the justice of your remark in regard to the *unliterary character* of the Southern people . . . to a young literary aspirant, it is very hard to know that his *very profession* is looked upon with contempt. . . . You will not deem me unpatriotic, or false to my people, & section, in making *such* a confession."[38] The same complaint appears and re-appears in post-war letters. In a typical example, he wrote Bayard Taylor in 1875 to "thank the beneficent Gods who appointed *your* birth-place northward of the 'great line'!"[39]

Partly because of this sense of neglect, partly because of his genial friendliness, Hayne treasured his Northern friends and correspondents. In the 1850s he met many of these writers; from that time on he was as ready to defend them against English attacks as he was to defend Southern writers against Northern attacks. Perhaps his closest friend in Boston was the critic Edwin Percy Whipple, who (he wrote Stoddard in 1855) "has been a sort of father to me. I am told that he has reviewed me in *Graham* with great good nature, & kindly interest. He is not only the acutest critic, but one of the most estimable of men." He made this estimate more explicit, and indicated his own views on criticism, in a letter to the Virginian Margaret Junkin Preston: "Whipple is the one Northern Critic I know of broad, Catholic views on art,—a man who—whatever his political opinions,—always judges a poem, story, or essay on aesthetic grounds solely." To him Hayne dedicated in a prefatory sonnet his book *Avolio,* and in *Russell's* he frequently quoted with approval excerpts from Whipple's essays.[40]

In an 1870 letter Hayne calls an unidentified correspondent "the *first poetic artist* in America." This might well be any one of four men: William Cullen Bryant, Henry Wadsworth Longfellow, John Greenleaf Whittier, or James Russell Lowell.[41] Hayne liked and admired the men and their work. Perhaps the strongest expression of personal literary esteem is to be found in an 1877 letter to Bryant, with its salutation and opening sentence: "*My Dear & Honored Master;*—Indeed you have been '*My Master*' in all *important* matters of *Poetic art, & Study* for many years!"[42] To him Bryant was a "great and true Poet!—our Wordsworth of America." But he also wrote in more general terms that "to my mind Lowell is *the* poet of America. He possesses a *compactness* of creative imagination, a breadth of view, & a wealth of expressive phraseology *none* of the others can *begin* to rival."[43] He knew many of Lowell's poems by heart, and liked to recite them—but that was also true of the works of several poets whom even Hayne considered indisputably minor. Also, in an 1874 letter to Longfellow, Hayne wrote that "More than a year ago, the idea occurred to me of composing *three* brief Poems upon our chief American Poets; *namely, yourself, Bryant, & Whittier. Two* of these have now been completed, the second to Whittier; and *now* I venture to enclose for examination, the verses dedicated to your honored *self*. They can claim *one* merit—a profound sincerity."[44]

Although he doubted that *Hiawatha* could be rightly called an

American poem and felt that the unrelieved hexameter line of *The Courtship of Miles Standish* was cumbersome and monotonous,[45] these were relatively minor defects in one whose work had delighted "the world with music as full of *perfect* art, as of a divine *hope, & a faith in all things good, pure and noble! Your* poetry elevates the spirit, and makes strong the heart, instead of merely charming the *fancy,* and then leaving one in the twilight of scepticism, as to the existence even of a *Hereafter!* Recent poetry is the poetry of *Doubt;*—look at Morris, Rossetti, Swinburne!"[46] These positive affirmations were qualities that Hayne valued, and he praised Whittier in much the same terms: "You are a *good* no less than a *gifted* man!—& the consolation of knowing that your *Muse* has elevated and consoled *thousands, ought* to bring the most *soothing* peace to your declining days."[47] So Hayne sent his honest if overwrought poetic tributes to Longfellow and Whittier, feeling that they had succeeded in accomplishing poetically what he most desired as poet to do: "The older I grow, the more truly I yearn to come near and to rouse the great heart of humanity. The more I desire to elevate, comfort and console the lives of my fellow creatures. I long to illustrate the Beautiful, and to sing of the Ideal in its loftiest phases, to bind the broken heart, to stimulate the despondent spirit. . . ."[48]

Emerson, a divinely-inspired seer, also had done that, though in a different way. To the charge that Emerson was cold, Hayne retorted by quoting "Threnody" and claiming that "sometimes the cold philosopher *does* give place in his works to the profoundly sympathizing man," and touches the heart.[49] But Dr. Oliver Wendell Holmes, a personal friend, got much higher praise: when an English magazine mildly commended *The Autocrat of the Breakfast Table* but suggested the author give up writing poetry, Hayne retorted fiercely that the *Autocrat* was "the wisest and wittiest book which has graced the literature of Europe or America for many years. . . . since the death of Thomas Hood, probably no poet who writes in the English language has arisen, possessed of the humour, pathos, and catholic sentiment of Dr. Holmes, expressed at all times in sparkling and harmonious verse." These sweepingly partisan sentences are characteristic Hayne over-statements when his dander was up at what seemed to him an unjust attack. After noting a similarly unfair attack on Longfellow, Hayne wonders plaintively when English reviewers will realize that every American author who "adds anything true and permanent to the literature which belongs to us both, does as much for the glory of England, as for the glory of his own country."[50]

Hayne was equally generous in commenting on the work of older and younger writers. Fitz-Greene Halleck had written poems characterized by "pleasing fancy, and a free and graceful diction"; his "Marco-Bozzaris" was a "memorable achievement." Thomas Bailey Aldrich was a "poet of great richness of fancy and peculiar grace of art and feeling,"[51] and Celia Thaxter a woman of "exquisite genius."[52] Now and then he wields a sharp-bladed knife, once describing a volume of Julia Ward Howe's poems as "morbid and mewling nonsense,"[53] but even the stresses of war and reconstruction did not for long estrange him from his New England friends.

Amicable relations with the thorny Richard Henry Stoddard were difficult to maintain, but in spite of barks and growls, and occasional critical bites at his own poetry, Hayne kept up a friendship frequently strained by Stoddard's proclivity for giving "unnecessary offence" (one witty example: of Hayne's friend, the young poet Edgar Fawcett, Stoddard asked, "Won't somebody please turn this Fawcett off?").[54] There is no doubt that Hayne greatly over-valued Stoddard's poetry, but the editor's efforts to secure unpublished poems for *Russell's* indicates the sincerity of the feeling; he was enormously pleased when Stoddard agreed to be listed as "a regular contributor to my Magazine," and in most unbusinesslike fashion suggested that Stoddard *"make your own terms"* for a long poem. Hayne added that "your verses touch me nearly—there is real genius in them. . . . I like your style both of Art, & of Thought."[55] In the first issue of *Russell's* he described Stoddard's *Songs of Summer* as "distinguished by consummate grace of diction, a rare sensuous fancy, and an exquisite sweetness and melody of rhythm"; in the final number, in what is possibly the strangest of all Hayne's critical aberrations, he selects as the six most adept writers of blank verse in English (excluding dramatic poets) Milton, Keats, Tennyson, Arnold, Stoddard, and Timrod.[56]

His comments on George Henry Boker are more moderate, and not undeserved. With perhaps unintentionally faint praise Hayne called him *"the* dramatist of the country," especially commending *Francesca da Rimini* for its profound insight into character, and Boker himself for his "fluent imagination" and "remarkable constructive power." That he had also great admiration for Boker's

sonnets is attested by his own sonnet to Boker, who has filled with
sweetness and glorious strength "that slandered song/ We term
the Sonnet."[57] With rather less justification he rhapsodizes over
Bayard Taylor's *Poems of the Orient,* especially "The Desert
Hymn to the Sun ("Surely there is inspiration in *that*"). Yet
Hayne's many letters and the laudatory but not undiscriminating
article that he wrote after Taylor's death attests that he sincerely
valued Taylor as man and writer.[58]

In 1875 he read E. C. Stedman's *Victorian Poets* and was im-
pelled to write him a letter of "admiration . . . a free-will offering; as sincere as sincerity itself." He thanks Stedman for the
"*rare* instruction, the *keen* delight" the book with its "philosophic
insight" has given him. Incidentally he adds that "Many of your
poems too, have greatly charmed me. Chief among them . . . the
narrative poem of '*The Blameless Prince,*' " which he never read
without "a moisture of the eyes, and a 'sweet pain' at heart."
This tribute began a letter-friendship that in his enforced isolation
at Copse Hill was balm to Hayne's spirit.[59]

II

One of Hayne's unrealized desires was to visit England, partly
because it was the home of his ancestors ("There lived my sires,
whose sacred dust is there"),[60] but even more because he recognized that his mind and art had been largely fashioned by English
writers. The literature of England was as much a part of his
heritage as that of America, and infinitely richer. True, the greatest influence on him, the men he valued most highly, were men
of his own century: Shakespeare, Milton, and Dante made up
the "grand triumvirate of modern poets," but it was Wordsworth
and Tennyson who quickened his poetic imagination. He seems,
in fact, to have come rather late and then not too appreciatively
to a systematic reading of English poetry, for in 1855 he wrote to
Stoddard: "I have reviewed our English Poets from Chaucer on
down, i.e., I have read such authors as may be considered the
Representatives of different periods, & schools. I believe the
study has been instructive; but I have waded thro. a great deal
of dull stuff, & am amazed at the quantity of inanity which once
passed with the Public as genuine inspiration."[61] Although he
changed or at least tempered this opinion as he read more of the
early poetry, he expressed enthusiasm mainly for modern writers
—and he wrote voluminously about them.

Clearly Wordsworth and Tennyson came first. Wordsworth was "the great contemplative poet" of the nineteenth century;[62] Tennyson, "the noblest *Singer* of our Century," and "this consummate artist, this most ethereally imaginative of singers." These are superlatives that Hayne somewhat qualifies, but never really changes.[63]

In a thoughtful and appreciative essay, partly inspired by reading an attack by Francis Jeffrey, Hayne presents "a glance at the characteristics" of Wordsworth's genius. Hayne regrets the controversy that Wordsworth's theory of diction aroused: Wordsworth would have been wiser to let his poems speak for themselves. Actually both his theory and his poetry are founded on a belief in "the inherent beauty both of the spiritual and material worlds," as this beauty appeared to a "nature . . . pre-eminently subjective." Despite his universal sympathies, Wordsworth sometimes voiced extreme views and wrote puerile poems, misled by the "fanaticism of the great Reformer" desirous of purifying the spirit as well as the diction of poetry. Before him, only Cowper felt anything of this spirit; the others followed Pope, but lacked his sense, wit, and art. Wordsworth changed that: he is "the interpreter of the Spirit, not in its passion and activities, but its serene contemplation and holy trust"; he sees the meaning behind the externals of nature, and "may be said to have inaugurated a new era in philosophy as well as in poetry."[64]

Since he considered Coleridge the father of modern criticism and the criticism of his day superior to former times, Hayne frequently levied tribute on the English critic for support and for illustrative quotations. The charge that Coleridge was "a mere purposeless theorizer" especially aroused his ire, although in one instance he characteristically offered as rebuttal the "keen, subtle, but most lucid logic" in De Quincey's estimate of Coleridge's performances.[65]

Although Scott was the supreme novelist, "who knew man & life, as few since Shakespeare have known them," Hayne is surprisingly mild in saying of a new edition of Scott's poems that they "will appeal. . . . Nor are they destitute of high intrinsic merit." Possibly as he grew older he liked them better; at any rate, when his own narrative poems were attacked as "too antiquated" in style Hayne blamed not himself but "the present *fantastic taste*, which *denies* poetic merit to Macaulay's 'Lays'; & sneers at *Walter Scott's Homeric* narratives in verse."[66]

For the *Southern Field and Fireside* Hayne wrote in 1860 a

series of papers, "The Whittington Club; or Dialogues upon Literature." The comment was sweetened by being dressed in story form, with several men agreeing or disagreeing about the same author, the purpose being "to enliven his comments upon books by presenting the natural, unstudied action of different minds." Despite this slight fictional disguise, the ideas are Hayne's. He begins with praise of Byron, Keats, and Shelley, here minimizing his own doubts about Byron's wholesomeness and later qualifying his otherwise high praise of Keats by noting that he was "eminently sensuous."[67] But it was the attacks on Shelley that led Hayne not only to prose defenses (his work reveals scepticism, but "nothing of ribaldry or bitterness"), but inspired one of his best sonnets. In it Hayne presented a man maligned, although "A soul whose charities were wide as heaven, / whose deeds, if not his doctrines, were divine."[68]

Hayne also was attracted to the poetry and criticism of Leigh Hunt, sneered at as a cockney, but "respected even by Coleridge, & beloved, even by Keats." As poet, Hunt united "the best elements of the sensuous and the spiritual. . . . His poetry does not pretend to be of the highest kind, yet it is all but perfect in its way . . . a light, and sparkling, yet potent cordial."[69]

Hunt he admired as an "invincible and delightful author," but in some ways he felt more powerfully drawn to a relative failure, Hartley Coleridge. Although lacking his father's genius, Hartley had many excellent qualities; his sonnets in particular are "subtle, thoughtful, artistic compositions—gravely imaginative, and with a cast, now and then, of that metaphysical perception" which had been his father's outstanding quality. But Hartley was inescapably a minor poet because *"He lacked a great central purpose in art, precisely as he lacked a great central purpose in life."*[70] For him Hayne felt more than a literary kinship: when Kingsbury praised Hayne's sonnets in the *Leisure Hour,* Hayne thanked him but notes that he is more successful with sonnets than with long poems "because I have not the persistent strength of wing, or of will, to venture boldly upon more sustained flights!, because I lack as Hartley Coleridge lacked, 'a great central purpose in art.' " This sense of kinship, this fascinated concern with the younger Coleridge's achievements and his failures, led Hayne in 1866 to publish an article on Hartley in *Scott's Magazine,* and in 1880 to expand it into a two-part article for the *South Atlantic.*[71]

It is Tennyson's influence, however, that is most immediately apparent in Hayne's verse. In Timrod's first book Hayne had noted "unconscious imitation" of Tennyson, but the echoes and overtones ring far more clearly in his own lines. Hayne too was probably unconscious of any imitation, though he might well have argued that "this consummate artist" was indeed a worthy model. In reviewing *Idylls of the King* in 1859 he noted approvingly that Tennyson's work has received "the all but universal applause of the literary world," although Rufus Griswold might mistakenly place him among the third-rate poets of the age. In refuting Griswold, Hayne rated the *Idylls* as the "*great imaginative poem of the century,*" and "the most carefully elaborated of all the author's productions, except his 'In Memoriam.' " In his enthusiasm and indignation Hayne likens the work to "the rough grandeur" and the "rugged force" of Homer's epic—a comparison that however mistaken in judgment, leaves no doubt concerning Hayne's opinion.[72]

Tennyson's poetry was always distinguished for "clearness of design, diction, imagination, metaphor, and allusion," but Robert Browning could justly be charged with obscurity.[73] Hayne corresponded with Swinburne and in poetry added with what seems undue poetic license that "Not since proud Marlowe poured his potent song . . . Has England hearkened to so sweet a strain."[74] For Arnold as a theorist of poetry he had great esteem, but in his poetry he did little in the way of "illustrating the doctrine for which he argues"; in fact, Arnold in his shorter pieces "has written some atrocious stuff. . . . His larger poems, however, possess very great merit."[75] If Arnold's pessimism somewhat repelled him, the "brave lyrist" Jean Ingelow,[76] the devoted sweet singer Elizabeth Browning, and the blind English poet Philip Bourke Marston fitted his taste more exactly.[77] So did R. H. Horne,[78] and so at first did William Morris, whose *Earthly Paradise* seemed "one of the most marvelous achievements of Modern days."[79] But Hayne cooled somewhat when he was accused of plagiarizing or at least imitating Morris. Although Hayne noted that "The Wife of Brittany" was based on Chaucer's "Franklin's Tale," his friends Whipple and Taylor compared it favorably with Morris's work. This was pleasant enough, but other critics thought his "Vengeance of the Goddess Diana" so derivative that Hayne wrote an indignant footnote: "In a volume of comparatively youthful verses [1860], the above poem appeared under the title of '*Avolio; a legend of the island of Cos.*' The original narrative has now been carefully rewritten and amended and upwards of a hundred and fifty lines of entirely new matter has been added thereto. So far as we know, the only poet who has celebrated this significant and beautiful tradition, is William Morris, in the first section of whose 'Earthly Paradise' there is a story (called 'The Lady of the Land') founded upon some of its more obvious and popular incidents. Since Morris's wonderful tales were not published until 1868, we can, at least, assert the humble claim of precedence in the poetical treatment of *this* legend."[80]

Although he recommended in his sonnet "Freshness of Poetic Perception" that poets look directly "in a weed's heart, the carved leaves of corn/ The spear-like grass," Hayne based many of his own poems on stories or legends. Several of these, he himself noted, came from nineteenth century writers rather than the older originals: for example, to "Glaucus the Thessalian" he adds a note, "the elements of this story are to be found in Appollonius Rhodius, and Leigh Hunt has embodied them in a graceful prose legend," and to "Widderin's Race" that "The incidents of the following sketch will be found in 'The Recollections of Geoffrey Hamlin,' by Henry Kingsley."[81]

Yet some poems, like "The Wife of Brittany," reveal that Hayne had studied the older English poets closely, especially Chaucer and the Elizabethan dramatists. For *Russell's* he started a series of essays intended "to embody in a popular form some account of their lives, incorporated with brief critical remarks upon their works and genius." His preliminary gleanings are rather slim from the mystery and morality plays, and from Kyd, Nash, Peele, and Greene. Lyly's *Euphues* he called "the most absurd work in the English language," but his classical dramas are praised for "general elegance of treatment, and polish of style"; Hayne quotes from *Endymion* and praises "Cupid and my Campaspe." Marlowe, however, kindled his enthusiasm: "the first of those grand and permanent lights in our dramatic firmament. . . . The informing genius of Marlowe's work is Titanic, rude, unhallowed POWER! His 'mighty line' rolls impetuously onward, reckless of offense, and turbulent with the rush of haughty, defiant thought." Marlowe's work is "distinguished by a prodigality of power, a wealth of illustration, and a fertile richness of diction."[82] These qualities place Marlowe as dramatist second only to "the many-sided character of the highest poetical genius," Shakespeare.[83] But the projected papers were "brought to an abrupt close—at least for the *present*—on account of the sickness of the author"—and though he planned to return to the subject, and to write a series "of articles on the old, & least known of the *British Poets*," he never worked systematically on either project.[84] It is perhaps as well. Hayne was an intelligent and enthusiastic reader, but in no sense a scholar. His remarks might be interesting but would hardly be of enduring value.

III

Although he bewailed his lack of "wing, or of will," Hayne was at his best in short poems, especially sonnets. His facile mind needed the discipline of a strict form and a fixed stopping-place. In addition to writing quatorzains, Simms, Timrod, and Hayne evidently discussed at length the nature and scope of the sonnet, for in 1857 the younger men published articles on it, and the following year Simms proclaimed it "the best medium for the moral and contemplative utterance in verse."[85] Timrod and Hayne agree that the sonnet should be, in Hayne's phrase, the "expression of a single cardinal thought," that it is "an artificial structure," and that the strictness of the form can be of advantage to the writer. Hayne goes beyond his friends, however, in stressing the advantages of the regular or "Petrarcan model."

Hayne begins the Preface to his *Sonnets and Other Poems* (1857) by citing Dr. Johnson's dislike of the sonnet, and claiming that Wordsworth had demonstrated the absurdity of Johnson's criticism: "Wordsworth has proved that the English Sonnet, in capable hands, may be moulded into the most unique, harmonious, and dignified of Lyrics." But it is not for those who depend on the "gush of genius," since it requires "finish and completeness" and conscientious workmanship: "The nicest balance and adjustment of phrases, a fastidious deference to language, and rhythm are essential to guard against epigrammatism on the one hand, and superfluity on the other."

Regrettably, English sonneteers have preferred to write irregular sonnets: Hayne adds that many of his own sonnets are "not strictly LEGITIMATE" because of "a too hasty, though by no means unconditional acceptance of the heresy of Coleridge, who at one time asserted 'that writers of Sonnets were at liberty to consult their own convenience both in the choice of metre and the disposition of rhymes.' " The Italian system of restricted rhymes is preferable. But in one respect Hayne feels the earlier model a bad one: "The law which divides the Italian Sonnet into four arbitrary parts each, to some extent complete, *per se,* is the one particular in which the Legitimate model is at war with the 'genius of our language.' A rigid adherence to this rule gives to the English poem an air of formality, and didacticism *in structure,* against which the superior flexibility of words, and capacity of graceful inversion are sufficient to provide in the Italian. Even Wordsworth has recognized the force of this objection."[86]

Hayne again discussed the sonnet, but not in a form that he intended for publication, in 1867. Leigh Hunt had edited with a lengthy introduction an anthology of English and European sonnets. For the American edition S. Adams Lee persuaded Hayne and Boker to select appropriate American sonnets, and write the introduction for this part. Although the initials S.A.L. are signed to it and Boker wrote at least the paragraphs on Hayne, most of the work of selecting the poems and of writing the introduction was done by Hayne. Lee may have been satisfied with the result. Boker was not, and Hayne was so dissatisfied that he wrote in his own copy: "This crude essay was never designed for publication, it was merely written to furnish Lee with certain NOTES, which I presumed he would properly arrange. In its present form, nothing could be feebler. All that Lee has done, is to make big sentences of rather small ideas; and to add some absurd notes."[87]

For all its imperfections, the essay has some pertinence. It extends without basically changing our knowledge of Hayne as a critic.

As in the Preface to *Sonnets,* Hayne again distinguishes between legitimate and illegitimate sonnets, and indicates his strong preference for the legitimate. He also laments the paucity of good sonnets in America, but our poets were unwilling to do the amount of revising and polishing required; they were content to addresss the mass of uncultivated readers; and young poets, too much under Poe's influence, preferred "metrical mechanism" and "architectural eccentricities" in their verse.

Although he praised Longfellow's as generally legitimate and "admirable specimens," his sonnets are weakened by the "too frequent desire to illustrate by material images and comparisons what is abstract in thought and emotion." Even though Boker was his collaborator, it seems surprising that Hayne rated his sonnets above Longfellow's, calling him flatly the greatest American sonneteer. Written "in accordance with the established Italian rule," they "remind us of Wyatt, Sidney, and Spenser" with their "air of devoted self-abnegation and abstraction, half-sensuous, half-metaphysical; their terse verbal felicities." Bryant's sonnets are "delicate and beautiful," while Lowell's reveal "extreme sensibility to moral and spiritual beauty; imagination not so bright in its coloring, as clear, defined, harmonious in its outlines; and finally, in their mechanical construction, a degree of care and scholarly construction."

Chief of the illegitimate sonneteers was Jones Very, with his "deeply devotional" tone, in spite of his following Donne: "he could not, in many respects, have chosen a worse master" since he was already inclined to a vague mysticism and to obscurity. In some ways Simms was better, "the most original and salient of the irregular sonneteers," with his chief merit in the character of his thought: "strong, suggestive, and perspicuous. A rugged and impetuous power, and, where the topic admits it, a passionate intensity of feeling, rising almost into vehemence, leaves the author no time to consider the 'proprieties of verse'; he rushes on with the energy of an improvisatore . . yet many of his sonnets are complete and 'rounded,' possessing a fine metrical balance, and leaving consequently little to desire in reference to their construction."

For Tuckerman and Aldrich there is mild commendation; for Stoddard, a writer of "exquisite lyrics," somewhat more; and brief but ardent comments on Timrod and his "rare poetic gifts." There is, also, what Hayne evidently regarded as a charitable treatment of feminine sonnet-writers, with the admission that the sonnet "has not been especially 'glorified' by our countrywomen."

In general, the Preface is uncritical, but it does not represent Hayne unfairly. As usual, he sought those qualities which he could praise, and in the main found them.[88]

IV

Aristocratic and conservative by birth, training, and temperament, Hayne had no abiding faith in the Jeffersonian concept of democracy. Distrusting mass judgment, he preferred the idea of a Greek democracy as promulgated by Calhoun. Equally he doubted the literary taste and judgment of most readers. The fact that the *Leisure Hour* was conducted with "taste, ability, and judicious care," that it set out to be "independent and intellectual," would be a "serious drawback to [its] general success." A writer, like a magazine, profited if he threw in some equivocal

matter, a little blackguardism, and even a bit of wickedness.[89]
This essentially moral and aristocratic attitude he stated positively in a letter to Longfellow: "for my part, I can perceive no
valid reason why a *Poet,* however passionately intense his genius . . . should not be a Christian, and a gentleman."[90]

Yet the only remedy was a higher general culture, and the best
method of raising the general standard was by introducing readers
to good books through appreciative yet percipient criticism. This
was especially true in the United States, for a new society gives
little encouragement to art and literature. It is concerned mainly
with the so-called "practical." Hayne might doubt the validity of
the public taste in his own day, but he never discounted the ultimate value of the arts: in the long view, "the most practical
faculty" even in a young country is that of "the creative imagination." In the meantime, it was the artist who deserved sympathetic
treatment, from critics and from fellow-artists.[91]

Believing this, Hayne had little patience with arrogant, fault-
finding criticism, with the type of professional critic (described
in his poem "In the Studio") who views "art-work all askance"
and quickly gauges "in a shallow pate" the work of a lifetime.[92]
For poetry the only reliable critic was a practicing poet. Of Stedman's essays on the Victorian poets he stated flatly that "Only a
Poet could have written them," and in a letter to Stoddard was
even more explicit: "Let Poets be the Judges of eath other—With
all their proverbial irritability they are, when above the chances
of jealousy, the only true Critics of such works of Art as are
founded upon the higher processes of the Imagination."[93] In his
correspondence he played many variations on this theme.

Allied to it is his idea of the kinship through art of men of
letters, another recurrent theme: "There is a bond of sympathy
among literary men," he wrote Bayard Taylor in 1859, "extend-
ing from the *least* to the *greatest*," and he notes specifically that
when one writer derives instruction and pleasure from another,
he should acknowledge the debt.[94] Hayne tried to do so, in his
reviews and by writing directly to poets whose work he had enjoyed; isolated, he yet wanted desperately to feel and be part of
what he considered a literary brotherhood.

V

Hayne himself published only a few mediocre stories, but as
editor and critic he commented perceptively on many nine-

teenth-century novels; he helped, especially as editor and reviewer of *Russell's Magazine* (1857-60), to form the reading taste of the Southeast. Essentially his method was a simple one: to read a novel intelligently and appreciatively, then to bring out salient facts about the book in such a way that readers might know whether or not they wished to read or even to buy it. He had no philosophy of fiction, no formulated set of aesthetic or philosophical principles, but he set a high value on good novels and considered it a definite advance in critical taste that "Works of fiction are no longer viewed as *ephemera*, wherewith to relieve the monotony of a summer's noon, or a winter's evening by the fire, but as productions which, if worthily wrought out, demand for their due appreciation, a certain portion of the care and study, originally employed in their conception."[95]

Although he tried to indicate what the author had intended to do and how well he had succeeded in doing it, mainly he tried to communicate his own feelings about the book. But he usually opened a novel hoping and expecting to get pleasure from it, for "Of all things (next to good poetry) I *do* enjoy a clever novel; and pity profoundly the poor devil that does not!"[96]

His taste was formed by nineteenth century fiction. He admired Goldsmith greatly, and was familiar enough with *Tristram Shandy* to write allusively to Longfellow about desiring to swear that he was "tempted to relieve my mind after the fashion of 'the *Army* in *Flanders*.'" These were exceptions. That he had little enthusiasm for most eighteenth century fiction he made clear in a letter to Bayard Taylor: "I think of [Thomas] Gray stretched on his sofa before a comfortable fire, and devouring the last popular fiction, as the very acme, the *summum bonum* of half mortal, & half sensuous happiness." But Gray had relatively poor stuff to read: "what would have been his feelings over 'Copperfield,' 'Pickwick,' 'Ivanhoe,' 'Middlemarch' &c."[97]

The authors of these works were to him the best of all novelists writing in English. He had grown up on Defoe, Scott, and Froissart, but it did not occur to him then that *Robinson Crusoe* was a novel: "I believed as firmly in the existence of *Crusoe* and his man *Friday*, as I did in my own."[98] Even a boy knew that Scott was writing fiction, but he was "the 'great Wizard,' who knew man & life, as few since Shakespeare have known them." He never doubted Scott's greatness; as late as 1874, an item which confirmed his belief that William Dean Howells was often "radically wrong in his artistic, & literary conclusions" was his "remarking superciliously *apropos* an edition of the Waverly Novels, that 'he supposes (!!) W. Scott may be considered a *man of genius.*' "⁹⁹ As reviewer he dealt only with reprints of Scott, but if he noticed them briefly, it was also with what he considered a proper and deserved enthusiasm, for he considered Scott's mind, except for Shakespeare's, "the healthiest and most wholesome in English literature."¹⁰⁰

George Eliot's work seemed equally wholesome. Although he wondered about the identity of the author, Hayne in 1859 called *Adam Bede* "one of the most meritorious and successful fictions of the day." He liked all her novels and approved of the moral sense always implicit and often explicit in them; but he was in no doubt in 1872 about her best work: "What a treat was *Middlemarch!* . . . It represents Geo. Eliot's genius in its ripest and richest maturity! . . . *Middlemarch* must take its place at once beside the *classics* of the English tongue."¹⁰¹

His admiration for Dickens (the third of his triumvirate of great English novelists) had begun much earlier, and lasted throughout his life. In his letters Hayne frequently uses Scott or Dickens characters for illustrative purposes: the hero in one of his poems has been somewhat touched up because in life he had too much of Scott's Dalgetty in him; Louis Godey, the "good natured proprietor" of the *Lady's Book,* always reminded him of the brothers Cheeryble in *Nicholas Nickleby*; and Sam Weller's father in *Pickwick Papers* provides perfect ammunition for humorous commentary to a friend who is courting a widow.¹⁰² Clearly characters in the novels of Scott and Dickens seemed more real to him than any other fictional characters, more vitally alive than many of the people he met. But the superlative tribute to Dickens is that the English writer can be forgiven his harsh treatment of the United States simply because he is Dickens.¹⁰³

For Thackeray he had considerably less enthusiasm. Thackeray's work, Hayne wrote in "The Whitington Club" papers published in *Southern Field and Fireside* in 1860, is disconnected and diffuse, especially in *The Virginians*; moreover, Thackeray has become embittered, and that attitude spoils much of his work. On the credit side is Hayne's belief that no novelist had better understood women.¹⁰⁴ Yet Hayne apparently thought Bulwer-Lytton the better writer: after noting that "Thackeray is now up and Bulwer-Lytton down," Hayne adds that while they are not comparable as writers, he is confident of the lasting quality of Bulwer's reputation—with the implication, of course, that he has less faith in Thackeray's. Evidently this was a displeasing heresy to many readers, for a month later Hayne protested that he had not intended to condemn Thackeray: "To magnify the reputation of one great man by depreciating the powers of another, is more than 'simply ridiculous'—it is a *moral* as well as a *critical* misdemeanor." For all this ambiguity of judgment, he continued to read Thackeray, and when commenting on his own poverty he remarked that "like Philip in Thackeray's latest novel, I rather glory in my broken boots."[105]

He never doubted that Bulwer-Lytton was a great novelist, speaking "profound truth, embodied in striking, vigorous, bitter words," but Hayne was profoundly disturbed by Bulwer's matrimonial difficulties. Without attempting to judge whether or not Bulwer was in the wrong, Hayne quotes in *Russell's* a scathing attack by his friend E. P. Whipple on Lady Bulwer's fictional exposé, *The World and his Wife,* and an equally bitter attack that had appeared in the London *Critic.* But if Bulwer's life had elements of dubiety in it, his attempt in his novels to give body and reality to abstract truth was strikingly successful. Hayne had a strong preference for the fundamentally ethical novel, and Bulwer at base was, he thought, ethical.[106]

The same feeling played a large part in his judgment of other novelists. Although Charles Kingsley's novels have "many blemishes of characterization," Hayne approves highly of the moral tone that "pervades the body of his narrative with a clear, fluent, unobtrusive persuasiveness." He also employs Kingsley as a weapon against the inferiority of public taste: he "is too little of an egotist, too wholly a Christian gentleman, and . . . too eminently an artist, ever to be popular with the masses; and his boldness in speculation, and uncompromising hatred of conventional sophistry and falsehood, daringly and bitterly expressed, are not calculated to render him a favorite." Yet as editor Hayne published in the next issue (May 1857) of *Russell's* a scathing review of *Two Years Ago* by a former admirer, Sue Petigru King: "We are willing to look upon him as sincere, but we shall never forgive Charles Kingsley for making himself absurd—for writing such pages of silliness and mawkish sentiment."[107]

His significant comments on Charlotte Brontë indicate the high esteem in which he held her work: she had "exploded the conventional notion of novelists that personal beauty is essential to awaken interest in their characters. Thereby she accomplished much for art, and more for the dignity and truthfulness of human nature." She was at her best not as a novelist in the strict sense of that word, for her work was too analytical to have much movement, plot, or even complicated incidents: "As an intellectual and moral anatomist, Miss Brontë has no superior. True, the scope of her observation was limited; she depicts but few characters . . . but what she attempts to portray is portrayed with a fidelity, clearness, and profound sagacity, unattainable by mere *talent,* however perfect in culture, or exalted in degree."[108]

George Borrow's appeal is diametrically the opposite, for his appeal was primarily personal, to an extent that *Lavengo* and *The Romany Rye* seem "utterly destitute of artistic method, and unity of plan." Yet, though only incidentally a novelist and his works as stories "both failures," Borrow was "an eccentric but vigorous writer . . . entertaining even in his vagaries." If his heterodox and audacious opinions frequently offend the reader, his "shrewd and *pungent* work" is sure to arouse "a sort of pugnacious interest."[109] A comparably spirited writer, Charles Lever, had lost in one respect as he gained in another: "The careless exuberance of style, and spirit" that had added to the charm of his earlier work had in *The Fortunes of Glencore* "given place to thoughtful, often profound observation, a more comprehensive sense of art, and a style of matured vigor, perspicuity, and elegance."[110]

A novel that at once attracted and repelled Hayne because of its subject-matter was the anonymous *Ernest Carroll, or Artist-Life in Italy* (1859). Extravagant in plot, anecdotal in manner, it was interesting because of its comments on writers. The chapter on Ruskin he found "disgraceful": whether Ruskin's theories are right or wrong, he is "a vigorous and picturesque writer of English" who does not deserve to be "coarsely denounced and abused." The author's complimentary remarks about Longfellow, Holmes, and Lowell are quoted approvingly, but the judgment that Emerson "plays round the head, but never reaches the heart" is only partially true: "sometimes the cold philosopher *does* give place in his works to the profoundly sympathising man."[111]

But the best novel that year, in fact "one of the best that has come under our notice for some time past," was Anthony Trollope's *The Bertrams.* Trollope's handling of plot and motivation is at times faulty: in *The Bertrams* no sufficient cause is shown for a suicide, which "seems to us a great fault, but it is the only one we have to censure in the book." Such a defect can easily be forgiven when "the characters are all strongly painted . . .

the reflections are just and profound; the knowledge of life individual and rational, minutely exact; and the tragic power of
the author is decided." He found in Trollope an unusual freshness: "the author thinks for himself and reminds you of no one
else";—he portrays life and people strictly according to what
he has himself observed and not "from the reflections of Dickens,
or Thackeray, or Reade."[112]

This implies a higher opinion of Charles Reade than Hayne
customarily expressed. For Reade had a "certain sharp, shrewd
sarcastic faculty of observation," and with it a willingness to draw
some very ugly characters, but he was not an "original thinker"
and for all his apparent boldness he belonged as novelist to a
school "essentially conventional." His "ingenious plots" and
"inimitable dialogue" somewhat redeem his tendency to melodrama, to stories that are often sensational and sometimes "spas-
modic." At least he is never dull, for he "would rather be para-
doxical than tedious." Yet the good qualities prevailed over the
bad: "With all his faults, we look upon Mr. Reade as a writer of
sterling merit." Later, however, he thought Reade guilty of
"a stupendous piece of conceit, & folly" in his method of defending *Griffith Gaunt,* although the *"notoriety* gained by the work
will make its author's fortune."[113]

After the war Hayne started and kept up a friendly correspondence with Wilkie Collins and William Black, but the novel which
impressed him most was by Thomas Hardy. In January 1875 he
wrote to Bayard Taylor: "have you chanced to read an English
work . . . . 'Far from the Madding Crowd'. . . . If not, procure
it! The pictures of English rural scenery and rural humors are
inimitable. Upon my soul, I have laughed over some of the dialogues in this book as I seldom found myself laughing, except
over the extravagances of Falstaff. . . . One can exclaim with
Squeers, as he pinched the fat haunch of his promising Wackford,
'here's richness'!"[114]

There was less richness to be found in American novels, but
more than English critics were willing to allow. Paulding's novels
and satires were "full of quaint humour and clever characterization."[115] Hayne considered Hawthorne our best novelist, and took
delight in vigorously defending his work against foreign animad-
versions: when an Englishman called him "the American writer
of *pretty stories,*" Hayne described the unperceptive judge as
"some critical 'Muddle-head.'" Clearly *The Scarlet Letter* was
his best book. When Hayne was both troubled and fascinated

by the charges of adultery against Henry Ward Beecher, the natural comparison was with that impressive novel; "Arthur Dimmesdale, in Hawthorne's *'Scarlet Letter'*, has been dragged out of the realm of fiction, and compared, or contrasted with him. A *contrast* it merely *ought to be*; for the Puritan Clergyman gives one the idea of a soul, not merely *troubled,* but *absolutely eaten into (cancer-like),* by an ever-present torturing *Remorse,* the intense agony of which *forces* him, at last, to grovel down in dust and ashes, at the moment of his *supreme worldly* triumph."[116]

Hayne would have liked to put his close friend and mentor first, for though Simms had been like "a father" to him, "I yet enjoyed the most unrestrained social & literary communion with him." He could not conscientiously do so. It was easier to praise Simms as novelist than as poet, for "his *true Genius* was . . . conspicuous in the more characteristic of his novels & romances." But Simms had not had "leisure to cultivate the finer amenities of *Art* in composition,"[117] and Hayne was uneasily aware that "Simms's genius *never had fair play. . . .* A really *great author* (whether in *prose* or verse) Simms *emphatically was not,* and there is no use in maintaining so fulsome a proposition. But his *talents* were splendid, and his whole life seems to me noble." Hayne recognized that his friend's books were "too carelessly written" to have much chance to endure, and he regretted it, for "I loved him with all my heart."[118]

The temptation to over-praise him was great. With some justification Hayne believed that Simms had never received the literary recognition he deserved, regionally or nationally. He took keen delight, therefore, in quoting laudatory remarks and notices, especially from Northern magazines; he undoubtedly believed this to be the most effective way of enhancing his friend's reputation. Yet his own reviews are relatively restrained. In 1857 he hailed the revised version of *Charlemont* as "characteristic . . . one of the very best," but noted that it needed to be read in conjunction with *Beauchampe*. Hayne writes admiringly of Simms's vividness in sketching the locale and of his skill in characterization, but most of the review consists of a resumé of the story, with ample quotations.[119]

The Cassique of Kiawah deserved and got better treatment: "Were this tale destined to be Mr. Simms's last, we scarcely think it would be possible for him to produce a work which more fittingly closes, in a high artistic sense, the brilliant series of his

Carolina novels. All of the author's characteristic powers of invention, narrative, dramatic effect and picturesque description, are happily combined in this story."[120] Later in 1859, however, Hayne intimates that, for all the excellences of *The Cassique* and the earlier romances, Simms is inferior to Cooper: he is gratified "that the *two* novelists in this country (Wm. Gilmore Simms and Jno. Esten Cooke), upon whose shoulders the mantle of the American Scott (Fenimore Cooper), has fallen, belong to the South."[121]

Hayne published Cooke's *Estcourt* serially in *Russell's,* agreeing to pay $300.00 for it but discovering to his distress and embarrassment that the magazine could actually pay only $50.00. Although Hayne offered to be personally responsible, Cooke declined. Even this incident did not affect their close friendship, or Hayne's belief that Cooke ranked second only to Simms among Southern novelists: "I have read '*Henry St. John*' with the most *vivid interest, & delight,*" he wrote Cooke in 1859, calling it "*one* of your very *best,* & a noble historical novel beyond doubt." In the December 1859 *Russell's* he was equally enthusiastic: Cooke is "a truly bold, free and vigorous writer, of picturesque power, keen observation, and rarely delicate sensibilities"; moreover, he knows that "a plot" is "only a succinct phrase to express *that harmoniousness of general conception,* whereby the separate details are brought into close union."[122]

After the war he continued to read Cooke's work "with avidity" but perhaps with some envy: "No man in America can show a fuller record! Novels, essays, biographies, histories, miscellaneous tales, poems, &c &c—flow from your brain with a magic facility." But praise of Cooke's post-war romances seems natural and inevitable, for Hayne liked the author, the genre, and above all the defence of the South.[123]

In 1859 he thought exceedingly well of John W. De Forest, "a man of keen observation, an humorist, and something of a philosopher," and of his novel, *Sea-Cliff.* Although a little too melodramatic towards the conclusion, it has "a vivid, sustained, almost painful interest, which hurries the reader uninterruptedly to the solution of the mystery with which the story terminates. The author exhibits rare ingenuity in his manner of veiling the secret of Mrs. Westerfelt's life to the last, whilst his pictures of individual characters are graphic and strongly drawn."[124]

Hayne lost enthusiasm for De Forest completely when in 1867 he read *Miss Ravenel's Conversion from Secession to Loyalty.*

The author had had abundant opportunity, as Hayne knew personally, to become acquainted with the South, and thus to present a fair picture. Instead, he had presented "a brutal and one-sided caricature" of a defeated section, with the result that the book was immensely popular in the North. Hayne noted that he had "perused the work with unusual care. It is written no doubt with great cleverness, in a style lively, graceful, and piquant"; yet the man "must be blind indeed" not to recognize that its "peculiar success" is not because of artistic merit, but of a choice and handling of subject-matter that "pleased Yankeedom." What, asks Hayne indignantly, shall we say of one who heaps "epithets of the foulest reproach" upon his own country, and, though he closes ironically with "expressions of universal philanthropy," nonetheless dances "as it were, a moral war-dance of jubilation around the quivering and mangled remains"? Nearly twenty years later, however, he was more charitable; in writing about *Russell's* and his own desire to publish the work of Northern authors, he wrote: "I remember De Forest, who sent me an inimitable sketch, brimming over with fun, entitled 'The Smartville Ram Speculation.' "[125]

Since Hayne started a novel with the expectation of enjoying it, his criticism is usually genial. Occasionally he was roused to ire. He ridiculed Fanny Fern's style, and dismissed T. S. Arthur's *The Two Merchants* as a work "calculated to stir the bile of the best-natured critic on earth." When Maria Jourdan Westmoreland's *Heart-Hungry* (1872) was described as showing "wonderful artistic promise," Hayne was moved to angry protest: it is a *"spurious,* disgusting abortion, in the shape of a Novel."[126] His most effective protest against this type of work appeared in 1874. "Literature at the South: The Fungus School" is a satirical article on Southern novelists who without talent or genius get ahead by puffery, cliquism, and "claquement," until "the unlucky masses are stunned, if not into admiration, at least into acquiescence: they find it 'quite the thing' to have read Mrs. Duck-a-love's 'pathetic and passionate romance, that marvelous revelation of a woman's famishing heart,' or Mrs. General Aristotle Brown's 'profound philosophic novel, in which metaphysical acumen and clear comprehension of the knottiest social problems of our time are combined with dramatic capabilities seldom equalled, and never surpassed, in the literature of the present or any other age.' If any reader a trifle more enlightened or less partial than his fellow-townsmen, should upon pe-

rusal discover Mrs. Duck-a-love's 'romance' to be an illustration
rather of bosh than beauty, and Mrs. General Aristotle Brown's
'philosophic novel' an exponent of effervescing commonplace,
with much fizz, fussiness and froth, and the smallest conceivable
undercurrent of good sense or suggestive thought," the perceptive
reader had better keep this knowledge to himself. Yet the
Southern man of letters, Hayne adds, must speak out because
these fungi schools are "most harmful to the countries or communities in which for the time they flourish. Wrong standards of taste or notaste are set up. The first essential principles
of art are wholly ignored." These schools are "begot of ignorance
upon presumption," but they flourish until "the literary future of
our unfortunate South would appear to be as dark almost as her
political."

Ironically, when Hayne turned to a living novelist, he proved
as soft-minded as any of the critics he attacked. Using some of the
critical clichés he had just deplored, Hayne praises *A Daugher of
Bohemia* by Christian Reid (the pseudonym of Frances Christine
Fisher Tiernan) to a degree that, however unintentionally, his
remarks seem to have a satirical tone.[127]

Since his taste in fiction had been mainly formed by Scott and
Dickens, Hayne found little to admire in post-war American
fiction. Like his friend John Esten Cooke he preferred the outmoded romance even though he knew it was outmoded. Late in
life he wrote that "I read again & again" the best of Scott's novels,
and he derived great enjoyment from them.[128] That was
more than he could say of most modern novels. Friendship for
Bayard Taylor may have caused him to approach *Joseph and His
Friend* favorably, and almost certainly influenced his estimate, in
a letter to the author: "You have taken a simple, country vil-
age, & its surroundings, & woven a narrative out of them which has
all the fidelity of Flemish art, with an atmosphere of idealization
which softens the literalness of detail, and harmonizes the
whole picture. Of your female characters, Lucy I think is perfect
(artistically). She realizes Wordsworth's hackneyed, but im
mortal lines about the woman 'not too good for human nature's
daily food'. . . . Joseph, his mind, temperament, trials, & gradual
development of thought, & purpose—is a noble conception, very
carefully, & with close psychological probings, carried out to a
legitimate end."[129]

Ordinarily he did not care for psychological novels. He preferred that novels have "a plot, more or less elaborate, objective

characterization, and dramatic action." Disregard of these essential qualities, and over-elaborateness of style led him to dismiss Henry James as finical: "Tens of thousands now believe that there is but *one* Divinity, or potent inspirer of art in Fiction, and that Mr. Henry James is his prophet. This deity is 'Aesthetic Realism'—this art should have for its motto the Knife-Grinder's exclamation, 'Story! God bless your honor, I have none to tell.' "

Angrily, or at least irritably, Hayne objected to what he regarded as William Dean Howells' excessive over-praise of James, especially as a stylist: " 'listen, *ami lecteur,* to Mr. Howells' revelation to a grateful world touching his idolized James, at whose feet he prostrated himself years ago, and where, 'crouched upon the marrow-bones of his soul' (Fanny Fern, I thank thee for that phrase!) he has remained ever since in the most pathetic posture of oriental and ecstatic devotion." That Howells considered the style of James better than that of any other novelist was bad enough, but the main cause of Hayne's irritation stemmed from the attacks on his own favorites: "we can readily fancy the disgust of these gentlemen [James and Howells] at the bare mention of the names of such uncivilized antiques as Simms and Cooper."[130]

He tried to like the novels of William Dean Howells and was mildly pleased with *A Foregone Conclusion,* but Howells as novelist with his new realism was helping to level down our culture; Howells as critic spoke doubtfully, "with an air of hesitating reluctance, of languid supercilious concession," of Scott's genius while devoting "columns of half qualified condemnation to such awful 'bosh' as young [Julian] Hawthorne's 'Idolatry' "; worst of all, Howells as editor consistently rejected most of the poems that Hayne submitted.[131]

For Joel Chandler Harris he had only praise: "His genius, especially in the delineation of the negro character, is absolute." His virulent dislike of George Washington Cable was based not on Cable's fiction but his essays. Cable's statements about the Civil War and the Negro seemed to Hayne downright traitorous; he poured forth his hatred in a series of letters to the equally bitter Louisiana historian Charles Gayarré.[132] For Hayne did not like the "New South," and he would not admit that the Old South had been wrong. Neither was he prepared to admit that pre-war writing had been poor. In a warmly reminiscent essay about old days and old authors in Charleston he entered a vigorous protest: "That a considerable number of vigorous and brilliant authors—some of genius even—have risen among us since the close of the civil war is a subject for cordial congratulation; but surely it is not necessary to the establishment or increase of their fame that a class of servile paragraphists . . . should profess to find the whole department of Southern *ante-bellum* literature a desert of antiquated rubbish."[133]

This was meant to be a defence of his friends, but it was at least indirectly a defence of Hayne himself. Although he lived until 1886, his mind was formed in the days that he so fondly remembered. Even the poetry written late in life seems to belong to that earlier era; the best of his critical prose had been written then. If ante-bellum literature was only antiquated rubbish, so was his own writing. It is not surprising that he turned with distaste from Howells and Cable to the more congenial company of Simms and Cooke, of Dickens and George Eliot, and especially of Sir Walter Scott.

NOTES

1. JEFFERSON

1. Letter to Jonathan Boucher, in *The Writings of George Washington,* edited by John C. Fitzpatrick (1931), III, 36. Washington wrote, however, that had Jack Custis "begun, or rather pursued his Study of the Greek Language, I would have thought it no bad acquisition." In analyzing Washington's character, Jefferson noted that his education had been limited to "reading, writing and common arithmetic, to which he added surveying at a later date. His time was employed in action chiefly, reading a little, and that only in agriculture and English history" (*The Writings of Thomas Jefferson,* edited by A. A. Lipscomb and A. E. Bergh, 1904, XIV, 49-50; hereafter cited as Lipscomb, *Writings*). Whenever possible, I have preferred to quote from the more reliable *Papers of Thomas Jefferson,* now being edited by Julian Parks Boyd; hereafter cited as Boyd, *Papers.* I have also quoted a few items from Paul Leicester Ford's *The Works of Thomas Jefferson* (1904-05). For background material, I have found the biographies by Marie Kimball, Dumas Malone, Gilbert Chinard, and Albert Jay Nock especially helpful. Two very useful studies have been Eleanor D. Berman's *Thomas Jefferson Among the Arts* and Karl Lehman's *Thomas Jefferson: American Humanist.*

2. Boyd, *Papers,* I, 96-101. Charles McPherson relayed this request to the supposed translator James McPherson, who of course refused since there were no originals. Jefferson's enthusiasm for Ossian was so high at this time (1773) that he asserted in the letter: "I am not ashamed to own that I think this rude bard of the North the greatest Poet that has ever existed." The Marquis de Chastellux in his *Travels in North America* (London 1787, II, 45-46) describes an Ossianic evening at Monticello in 1782.

3. *The Works of John Adams* (1850), II, 513-14n.

4. Lipscomb, *Writings,* XVIII, 168-70.

5. "Autobiography," Lipscomb, *Writings* I, 91-92. The best account I have seen is in Marie Kimball's *Jefferson: War and Peace,* 259-305. For his comments to James Madison about his efforts to prevent publication, see Boyd, *Papers,* IX, 264-71, with an illuminating editorial note; for his difficulties with the English publisher John Stockdale, see the index to volumes 7-12. Jefferson's remarks in a letter to George Wythe (Aug. 13, 1786; Boyd, *Papers,* X, 243) are characteristic: "Your wishes, which are laws to me, will justify my destining a copy for you. Otherwise I should as soon have thought of sending you a horn-book; for there is

no truth there that is not familiar to you, and its errors I should hardly have proposed to treat you with."

6. Letter to Dr. Joseph Priestley, Lipscomb, *Writings*, X, 146-47. In 1819 (Lipscomb, *Writings*, XV, 208-09) he elaborated somewhat on this: "The utilities we derive from the remains of the Greek and Latin languages are, first, as models of pure taste in writing. . . . Second, among the values of classical learning, I estimate the luxury of reading the Greek and Roman authors in all the beauties of their originals." Jefferson distrusted translations: "I make it a rule never to read translations where I can read the original" (Lipscomb, *Writings*, IX, 280).

7. *The Literary Bible of Thomas Jefferson*, edited by Gilbert Chinard (1928), esp. 6-8. Chinard's Introduction is quite valuable.

8. Lipscomb, *Writings*, XVIII, 448. In Paris in 1786, he prepared for Madame de Tott a "Short Greek Prosody," for the purpose of studying with her "the rythm of Homer." (Boyd, *Papers*, X, 553-54).

9. "Autobiography," Lipscomb, *Writings*, I, 5. See also William Wirt's *Patrick Henry*, 60, for Jefferson's recollections of this speech. Jefferson did not trust Henry, for "he was the laziest man in reading I ever saw" (I, 12), and on occasion "all tongue without either head or heart" (Boyd, *Papers*, VI, 205). But he did not question "the poetical fancy of Mr. Henry, his sublime imagination, his lofty and overwhelming diction" (Lipscomb, *Writings*, I, 55).

10. Lipscomb, *Writings*, XV, 353. Livy, Sallust, and Tacitus were essentially historians rather than orators; Jefferson seems here and elsewhere to be recommending the set speeches which they wrote and put into the mouths of eminent historical characters. But Jefferson considered them speeches, and in addition "preeminent specimens of logic, taste, and that sententious brevity which, using not a word to spare, leaves not a moment for inattention to the hearer" (XVI, 30). Jefferson did pay one unhesitating tribute to sheer oratory: "I knew much the great Ontasseté, the warrior and orator of the Cherokees. . . . I was in his camp when he made his great farewell oration to his people the evening of his departure for England. The moon was in full splendor, and to her he seemed to address himself in his prayers for his own safety on the voyage, and that of his people during his absence; his sounding voice, distinct articulation, animated action and the solemn silence of his people at their several fires, filled me with awe and veneration, although I did not understand a word he uttered" (XIII, 160).

11. Lipscomb, *Writings*, XII, 343. Jefferson listed Cicero among "the most esteemed of the sects of ancient philosophy, or of their individuals; particularly Pythagoras, Socrates, Epicurus, Cicero, Epictetus, Seneca, Antoninus" (X, 381-82).

12. Chinard, 9-11, 82-109. Of the many articles on this subject, I have found most useful Louis B. Wright's "Jefferson and the Classics," *Proceedings of the American Philosophical Society*, 87 (July 1943), 223-34.

13. Lipscomb, *Writings*, XIV, 144-51. He believed that the "laws of nature [which] have withheld from us the means of physical knowledge of the country of spirits and revelation has, for reasons unknown to us, chosen to leave us in the dark as we were. When I was young I was fond of the speculations which seemed to promise some insight into that hidden country, but observing at length that they left me in the same ignorance in which they had found me, I have for many years ceased to read or to think concerning them, and have reposed my head on that pillow of ignorance which a benevolent creator has made so soft for us, knowing how much we should be forced to use it" (X, 299).

14. Lipscomb, *Writings*, XII, 437. See also XIII, 393. There are twelve quotations in Chinard, *Literary Bible*, 118-21, and Epode 2 on 184-87. Of this, Chinard discerningly writes (32): "Mere picturesqueness had little attraction for him. He was not dreaming of a remote past and far away lands. In his natural dispositions there was nothing exotic, and he deliberately swept away from his notes every-

thing that was unusual, strange, and we could almost say un-American. Nothing is more striking in this respect than his treatment of Horace's second epode: *O beatus ille qui procul negotiis.* . . . Jefferson did not change a word of it; but simply by omitting every detail that was purely Roman he succeeded in lifting out of time this picture of Roman farm life and in changing it into a description fitting exactly America of the colonial days. Priapus and Silvanus have been eliminated from the garden. Snaring rabbits or migratory cranes are pleasures that a young man who never went out without his gun would hardly appreciate: moreover it would not be good sportsmanship, so these lines were not transcribed. The farmer's wife may well prepare for her tired husband a simple meal but wild sorrel, mallow, kid meat, or even olives would not appear on the menu, and out they went. Thus the sturdy Appulian ploughman and his good wife lost their local characteristics, the Roman farm became similar to a Southern plantation and the slaves of the household could be mistaken for American Negroes playing in the yard after the day's work is done."

15. Lipscomb, *Writings*, XV, 220. See also X, 382-83. In this letter to Dr. Benjamin Rush, Jefferson notes that Jesus, "like Socrates and Epictetus, wrote nothing himself." Seneca divided his philosophy into ten parts: seven relate to ourselves; two relate to others; one relates to the government of the world. Cicero had eleven: five respect ourselves, the others are divided.

16. Boyd, *Papers*, X, 75; XII, 128, 161. Possibly the most interesting of Jefferson's several letters on ancient and modern Greek pronunciation is the one to John Adams (Lipscomb, *Writings*, XV, 181-85). Jefferson had given in to the modern practice generally, but against the suggestion that Greek be read by accent instead of quantity, "I raise both my hands. What becomes of the sublime measure of Homer, the full sounding rhythm of Demosthenes, if, abandoning quantity, you chop it up by accent? . . . And what becomes of the art of prosody?" See also Lipscomb, *Writings*, XV, 480-90.

17. Boyd, *Papers*, X, 553-54. Poetry in turn gave indispensable clues to the correct pronunciation of Greek and Latin: "if I meet with the word *praeteritos* in Latin prose and want to know how the Romans pronounced it, I search for it in some poet and find it in the line of Virgil, '*O mihi praeteritos referat si Jupiter annos!*' where it is evident that *prae* is long and *te* short in direct opposition to the pronunciation which we often hear." (Lipscomb, *Writings*, XVIII, 416).

18. Letter to Robert Skipwith, Aug. 3, 1771, in Boyd, *Papers*, I, 76-81. The list runs heavily to plays and poems by English authors; apparently Skipwith did not read foreign languages readily, for most of the non-English works specify a translated edition. Thus, *Don Quixote* and *Gil Blas* are listed as by Smollett; the third and fourth items on the list are Pope's *Iliad* and *Odyssey;* the fifth Dryden's *Virgil.* Jefferson and John Adams made a pilgrimage to Stratford and cut a chip off one of Shakespeare's chairs (Dumas Malone, II, 60).

19. Respectively, Boyd, *Papers*, VI, 196; XII, 15; VI, 374. The poem has sometimes been mistakenly described as an original poem by Jefferson.

20. Lipscomb, *Writings*, XV, 166. The only foreign language that Jefferson recommended for a young lady was French; it "is an indispensable part of education for both sexes."

21. In a letter to his nephew, Peter Carr (Boyd, *Papers*, XII, 14-19), he does not recommend Italian because "I fear the learning this language will confound your French and Spanish. Being all of them degenerated dialects of the Latin, they are apt to mix in conversation. I have never seen a person speaking the three languages who did not mix them. It is a delightful language, but late events have rendered the Spanish more useful. . . . Our future connections with Spain and Spanish America will render the language a valuable acquisition. The ancient history of a great part of America too is written in that language." The reading list enclosed with his letter was intended for a young law student, but

it includes a generous amount of poetry and plays: "Homer, Milton, Ossian, Shakespeare, Aeschylus, Sophocles, Euripides, Metastasio, Theocritus, and Anacreon." He admitted that of the standard foreign languages Greek would be the least useful for a lawyer, but never doubted that "the classical languages are a solid basis for most, and an ornament to all the sciences (Lipscomb, *Writings*, VI, 190; XV, 211). But languages should be studied in youth; after that, "the endeavor to attain them would be a great misemployment of time" (Lipscomb, *Writings*, XV, 209).

22. Boyd, *Papers*, VIII, 405-08; quotation on 407. Much of this reading was to be done in Carr's spare time, after he had allowed a sufficient amount for walking and hunting; Jefferson advised that these vacant hours be divided "into three portions. Give the principal to history, the other two, which should be shorter, to Philosophy and Poetry." As in the letter cited in note 21, Jefferson writes that for "a public man," a knowledge of French and Spanish is invaluable. A surprising omission is the name of Lord Bolingbroke. Extracts from his work fill pp. 40-71 of *The Literary Bible*; in a comparison of Bolingbroke and Thomas Paine (Lipscomb, *Writings*, XV, 305) he wrote: "They were alike in making bitter enemies of the priests and pharisees of their days. Both were honest men; both advocates of human liberty. . . . Lord Bolingbroke's on the other hand, is a style of the highest order. The lofty rhythmical full-flowing eloquence of Cicero. Periods of just measure, their members proportioned, their close full and round. His conceptions, too, are bold and strong, his diction copious, polished and commanding as his subject. His writings are certainly the finest samples in the English language, of the eloquence proper for the Senate. His political tracts are safe reading for the most timid religionist, his philosophical, for those who are not afraid to trust their reason with discussions of right and wrong (Jan. 19, 1821; Lipscomb, *Writings*, XV, 305). In a somewhat similar letter, originally prepared for Bernard Moore about 1765 and sent to John Minor in 1814 (Ford Edition, XI, 420-26), Jefferson insisted that for a lawyer "an acquaintance with the Latin and French languages is absolutely necessary." A law student should also read "the best of the poets, epic, didactic, dramatic, pastoral, lyric, etc. But among these Shakespeare must be singled out by one who wishes to learn the full powers of the English language." Under criticism he recommended Lord Kames and the *Edinburgh Review*; under rhetoric, Blair; and under oratory, Demosthenes and Cicero. Because Jefferson greatly admired the Scottish "common-sense philosophers," he suggested often that young Virginians be sent to the University of Edinburgh, and recommended George Tucker for a Professorship at the University of Virginia partly because Tucker was an exponent of their philosophy. Jefferson's own critical theories seem to have been independently formed, and only slightly influenced by their literary theories.

23. Ford edition, VIII, 65. That he probably did not read the poem is indicated by the fact that in January, 1808, Jefferson sent a very formal note of thanks to Barlow for *The Columbiad*, but added that he would reserve the reading of it until after he retired as President (Lipscomb, *Writings*, XI, 430). As early as 1787, Barlow had sent Jefferson a copy of his poem, *The Vision of Columbus* (Boyd, *Papers*, XI, 473).

24. See the quotations in *The Literary Bible of Thomas Jefferson* and in "Thoughts on English Prosody"; also M. J. Herzberg, "Thomas Jefferson as a Man of Letters," *South Atlantic Quarterly*, XIII (Oct. 1914) 310-27. The Scrapbook in the University of Virginia Library has been adequately described by John W. Wayland under the misleading title, "The Poetical Tastes of Thomas Jefferson," *Sewanee Review*, XVIII (July 1910), 283-99. There are 420 poems clipped from newspapers; undoubtedly many of them were sent by correspondents. A few poems are about Jefferson, Washington, and John Adams. Most of them deal with patriotic or political themes, with emphasis on liberty and national freedom. Some

are satirical, especially on the Embargo. One, surprisingly, is an Ode by H. J. Pye, British Poet Laureate, praising King George III. There are eighteen poems on Ireland, in addition to ten by Tom Moore (one of these written in Norfolk and with the Dismal Swamp as setting). Moore is identified as "the celebrated translator of Anacreon." There are two poems by Joel Barlow; one by Thomas Paine; two by Robert Treat Paine, Jr.; one by James Montgomery; one by Robert Burns; three by Robert Southey; and one, "Paper," attributed to Benjamin Franklin. There is an excerpt, also, from Thomas Sackville's *Mirror for Magistrates* (1559), glorifying the dignity of man regardless of his rank; in the margin Jefferson wrote: "As good now as when it was written." Most of the poems are anonymous. The selections seem to me, with a few exceptions, to represent Jefferson's political rather than his poetic interests.

25. For evidence that this long draft was completed by Nov. 1786, but probably never sent to Chastellux, see Boyd, *Papers*, X, 498-99. In a letter which also was probably never sent, Jefferson noted that "I began with the design of converting you to my opinion that the arrangement of long and short syllables into regular feet constituted the harmony of English verse; I ended by discovering that you were right in denying that proposition. The next object was to find out the real circumstance which gives harmony to English poetry and laws to those who made it." In the process of elaborating his own thought, Jefferson probably owed something to the critical writings of Lord Kames, but without much direct drawing on critical authorities. "Thoughts on English Prosody" has been reprinted in Lipscomb, *Writings*, XVIII, 414-51, but without any attempt to put the somewhat disordered manuscript in the Library of Congress into proper order.

26. Lipscomb, *Writings*, XVIII, 414, 416. Thanking a French friend for a description of "the tragedy of the unfortunate Louis XVI," Jefferson wrote: "I say nothing of style, not doubting its merit, and conscious I am no judge of it in a foreign language. I believe it impossible in any but our native tongue, to be so thoroughly sensible of the delicacy of style, which constitutes an essential merit in poetical composition, as to criticize them with correctness" (XII, 244).

27. Lipscomb, *Writings*, XVIII, 418, 421. The one exception is that "the whole army of monosyllables" may be accented or not, at the poet's pleasure. But the English poets had a good precedent: "The Greeks and Romans in like manner had a number of syllables which might in any situation be pronounced long or short without offending the ear. They had others which they could make long or short by changing their position. These were of great avail to the poets." Jefferson quotes examples from English and Greek to prove his point (419-20). One line puzzled him: "God save great Washington" he thought had to be "triple verse, but the accent is on the first syllable of the foot instead of the third," but since it was unique he dismissed it from consideration because " a single example cannot form a class" (428-29). He also presents examples of elision and of synecphonesis, noting that the slight but pleasing variation in the latter may be more agreeable than "actual elision" (429-31).

28. The strength of the accent might be divided "into four shades by these marks "" "" " ' the greater number of marks denoting the strongest examples." After giving numerous examples, he notes: "No two persons will accent the same passage alike. No person but a real adept would accent it twice alike" (437-38). Probably only Garrick ever drew the full tone out of the poetry of Shakespeare.

29. Lipscomb, *Writings*, XVIII, 441-42. The poet "does not depend on the printer to give a character to his work. He has studied the human ear." But a line "takes its denomination from the shortest regular intervals," so that some lines printed as having seven feet are "no more than an alternate verse of four and of three feet" (445). Jefferson frequently uses *verse* as synonymous with *line*.

30. Lipscomb, *Writings*, XVIII, 446-47. His test was a pragmatic one: "What proves the excellence of blank verse is that the taste lasts longer than that for

rhyme." *Paradise Lost* was so "truly poetical" that Milton, when "enveloped in all the pomp and majesty of his subject . . . sometimes even throws off the restraint of the regular pause." The pauses are "constantly drowned by the majesty of the rhythm and sense." But when Milton servilely copies Moses, he fails because he has not changed Genesis into his own poetry.

31. "An Essay on the Anglo-Saxon and Modern Dialects of the English Language," in Lipscomb, *Writings*, XVIII, 361-411; quotations on 363. The essay was prefaced by a letter, dated Oct. 30, 1798, to Herbert Croft, an Englishman who was preparing an etymological dictionary; these were originally published in 1851, by order of the Board of Trustees of the University of Virginia.

32. Lipscomb, *Writings*, XVIII, 386. Writing to John Adams, Jefferson noted that a few weeks would be sufficient "to give such instruction in the etymologies of our language as may satisfy ordinary students, while more time would be requisite for those who should propose to attain a critical knowledge of it" (XV, 270).

33. *Ibid.*, 365-67. Dr. Johnson had hampered rather than helped in the understanding of the English language: "besides the want of precision in his definitions, and of accurate distinction in passing from one shade of meaning to another of the same word, [he] is most objectionable in his derivations. From a want probably of intimacy with our own language while in the Anglo-Saxon form and type, and of its kindred languages of the North, he has a constant leaning towards Greek and Latin for English etymol." (361).

34. Lipscomb, *Writings*, XVIII, 367-75. Orthography also presented difficulties: the word *many* was spelled in twenty different ways. Since the Anglo-Saxon writers "each followed arbitrarily his own mode of combining the letters," the modern work should establish uniformity "with the orthography of the present dialect, as established by usage."

35. *Ibid.*, 377-82. He felt the same way about prosody; see note 27.

36. *Ibid.*, XVI, 42-44. As a young lawyer, Jefferson had made "extracts from the Anglo-Saxon laws, the sources of the common law" (I, 217). These notes, Jefferson adds, "I wrote in the original for my own satisfaction."

37. *Ibid.*, 390. As noted above, Jefferson stated frequently that languages should be learned in youth, when the memory was flexible; later, it was an unprofitable employment of time (XV, 209).

38. Lipscomb, *Writings*, XVI, 107, and XIII, 61, respectively.

39. Lipscomb, *Writings*, XIII, 160; partly quoted in note 10. Logan's speech is quoted (or, to be exact, slightly misquoted) in *Notes on Virginia*, in Lipscomb, II, 89, from the manuscript in the Library of Congress; technically, this is not a speech, but a message sent to Lord Dunmore (see Jefferson's free use of the term earlier in the comments on Livy, Sallust, and Tacitus). On the speech of Cornplanter, see XIV, 138. That Jefferson thought highly of Logan's speech is indicated when he called it "worthily standing in a line with those of Scipio and Hannibal in Livy, and of Cato and Caesar in Sallust" (138). I suspect that here there is a philosophical, possibly a moral, attitude of considerable importance in treating Jefferson's attitude toward oratory: he preferred the written to the oral speech, because the written demanded sense, conciseness, and exactness. This distinction was suggested to me by Frederick W. Haberman of the University of Wisconsin and by Bower Aly of the University of Missouri.

40. Lipscomb, *Writings*, II, 140-41. Important also was the origin of the Indians: "The question whether the Indians of America have emigrated from another continent is still undecided. Their vague and imperfect traditions can satisfy no mind on that subject. . . . Very early in life, therefore, I formed a vocabulary of such objects as, being present everywhere, would probably have a name in every language." Jefferson then asked Dr. John Sibley's help in securing vocabularies of the

Indians of the Old Southwest (1805, XI, 79-80). In 1806 he asked Levett Harris to secure for him Pallas's *Vocabularies* [sic] *compares des langues de toute la terre:* Pallas had selected 130 words, Jefferson 250; and seventy-three of the words were the same, "and therefore will enable us, by a comparison of languages, to make the inquiry so long desired, as to the probability of a common origin between the people of color of the two continents"—Asia and America (1806, XI, 102-103). He reviewed the four-volume set in 1807 (XI, 177), but apparently was disappointed in his comparisons, although in 1817 he recommended to P. S. Duponceau (then at work on the subject; Jefferson sent him "the remains of my Indian vocabularies") that he consult the "great works of Pallas" (XV, 158).

41. Lipscomb, *Writings*, VII, 267; X, 161-62; X, 192-93, respectively. However, he intended to let "the world search for affinities between these and the languages of Europe and Asia."

42. *Ibid.*, XV, 5, 158. Lewis "was furnished with a number of printed vocabularies of the same words and forms I had used, with blank spaces for the Indian words."

43. *Ibid.*, XII, 312-13. Thus matter-of-factly does Jefferson relate his loss and his disappointment. One sentence in the letter hints at his feeling: "Perhaps I may make another attempt to collect, although I am too old to make much progress in it." But what could be done to help others, he would do: he sent to Dr. B. S. Barton the surviving vocabulary of the Pani tribe (XV, 313); he encouraged another correspondent to continue with a study of the Cherokee language (XVI, 107-109); he attempted to locate, and to get published, the papers of Captain Lewis (XV, 4-8; XIX, 225-26); and to the Philosophical Society, he offered "the remains of my collection," since these would be "worth incorporation with a larger work" (XV, 153).

44. Lipscomb, *Writings*, II, 141.

45. Lipscomb, *Writings*, XVI, 109. Writing to Dr. Peter Wilson, Professor of Languages at Columbia, Jefferson again emphasizes this difference: of the words he had collected, "I am certain more than half of them differed as radically, each from every other, as the Greek, the Latin, and Icelandic. And even of those which seemed to be derived from the same radix, the departure was such that the tribes speaking them could not probably understand each other. Single words, or two or three together, might perhaps be understood, but not a whole sentence of any extent or construction" (XVI, 402) .

46. Lipscomb, *Writings*, XVI, 108. It was for the Indians that Jefferson first started his book of extracts from the New Testament: "The Philosophy of Jesus of Nazareth." Under the title he wrote (XX, 18, after the Bibliography): "Extracted from the account of his life and doctrines as given by Matthew, Mark, Luke, and John. Being an abridgement of the New Testament for the use of the Indians, unembarrassed with matters of fact or faith beyond the level of their comprehensions." Later he expanded this. The work has been given various titles, but in Jefferson's handwriting on the title-page it is called "The Life and Morals of Jesus of Nazareth Extracted Textually from the Gospels in Greek, Latin, French & English" (in four parallel columns). He omitted the miracles, but wrote in 1803 (about the time he started the book) that he considered "the moral precepts of Jesus as more pure, correct and sublime than those of the ancient philosophers" (X, 376). The Lipscomb edition has an excellent introduction on the development of this so-called "Jefferson Bible," and a photostatic reproduction of it in vol. XX. Jefferson frequently discussed his approach to religion; the best examples are in letters to Peter Carr, Dr. Joseph Priestley, and John Adams.

47. Lipscomb, *Writings*, XIII, 156-61, 246-49. In these letters to John Adams, Jefferson complained that, since Adair's kink was in believing the Indians descended from the Jews, he "makes them talk Hebrew" (157, 246).

48. Lipscomb, *Writings*, II, 203-07; quotation on 207. In this plan for the education of boys, in *Notes on Virginia*, Jefferson adds that "the reading in the first stage . . . will be chiefly historical."

49. Lipscomb, *Writings*, XVIII, 148-49.

50. Lipscomb, *Writings*, XIV, 172. Jefferson complained to Wirt: "Had Judge Marshall taken half your pains in sifting and scrutinizing facts, he would not have given to the world, as true history, a false copy of a record under his eyes. [John Daly] Burke again has copied him, and being a second writer on the spot, doubles the credit of the copy."

51. Lipscomb, *Writings*, XII, 405-06. There was no general history of England that could be recommended: "The elegant one of Hume seems intended to disguise and discredit the good principles of the government, and is so plausible and pleasing in its manner, as to instil its errors and heresies insensibly into the minds of unwary readers" (XI, 223).

52. Lipscomb, *Writings*, XII, 199-201. For a comparison of Hamilton and John Adams as men and politicians, see his letter to Dr. Benjamin Rush (Jan. 16, 1811; XIII, 1-9): "Mr. Adams was honest as a politician, as well as a man; Hamilton honest as a man, but, as a politician, believing in the necessity of either force or corruption to govern men" (4). Yet Jefferson and Hamilton had served together in the Cabinet for four years: "We had indeed no personal dissensions. Each of us, perhaps, thought well of the other as a man, but as politicians it was impossible for two men to be of more opposite principles" (XII, 351).

53. Lipscomb, *Writings*, XIV, 343; XVII, 400-03. In a letter to John Adams (June 15, 1813; XIII, 256), Jefferson gives his most temperate judgment of Marshall's work, and his own attitude: "As to myself, I shall take no part in any discussions. I leave others to judge of what I have done, and to give me exactly that place which they shall think I have occupied. Marshall has written libels on one side; others, I suppose, will be written on the other side; and the world will sift both and separate the truth as well as they can. . . . About facts you and I cannot differ; because truth is our mutual guide."

54. Lipscomb, *Writings*, I, 84; XVIII, 306-07 and 326-27. Members of his own party had been "too careless of our future reputation, while our Tories will omit nothing to place us in the wrong. . . . It is the sum of individual knowledge which is to make up the whole truth, and to give its correct current through future time" (XV, 420-21) .

55. Lipscomb, *Writings*, XIV, 456-58; 62-63; XIII, 13; XII, 408. A particular objection to Montesquieu's work was that "his predilection for monarchy, and the English monarchy in particular, has done mischief everywhere" (XII, 414).

56. Lipscomb, *Writings*, XIV, 162-72 and 335-42. The final quotation is from Paul L. Ford's edition, XII, 35-36. Of Wirt's style, Jefferson wrote to the author: "I think some passages of the former sheets too flowery for the sober taste of history. It will please young readers in it's [sic] present form, but to the order it would give more pleasure and confidence to have some exuberances lightly pruned. I say lightly, because your style is naturally rich and captivating, and would suffer, if submitted to the rasp of a rude hand" (Letter to Wirt, Sept. 29, 1816).

57. Lipscomb, *Writings*, XIV, 294-95.

2. LEGARÉ

1. Linda Rhea, *Hugh Swinton Legaré*, 80-82, 85, 94-95. This is the standard biography of Legaré, and is factually reliable. Although the *Southern Review* was started by a group of Charlestonians, most of the editorial work and the writing was done by Stephen Elliott, Sr. (until his death in 1830); Stephen Elliott, Jr.; and Legaré. From Brussels, Nov. 21, 1853, Legaré wrote in a letter to his friend

Alfred Huger that he had been "saddled" with the *Southern Review*, "as if it had been an hereditary estate." Local pride was heavily involved: "I wrote as an American, and, especially, as a Carolinian" (*Writings of Hugh Swinton Legaré*, Charleston, 1845, I, 224. Hereafter cited as *Writings*.).

2. See especially an anonymous article, "Sketch of the Character of the Hon. Hugh S. Legaré," *Southern Quarterly Review*, IV (October, 1843), 348-62; and William C. Preston's *Eulogy on Hugh Swinton Legaré*, American Pamphlet Series No. 5; Nov. 7, 1843; Charleston, 1843. These accounts were by personal friends. So is the "Biographical Notice" by E. W. J. (probably Johnson), prefixed to *Writings*. For a recent and interesting comment on Legaré as orator, see William G. Carleton's "The Celebrity Cult a Century Ago" in *The Georgia Review*, XIV (Summer 1960), 133-42. Although Legaré was undoubtedly influenced by the Scottish school of "common-sense philosophers" (see William Charvat's *Origins of American Critical Thought*), he seems to have been more influenced by A. W. Schlegel and by Coleridge. I have lifted a few items from my earlier article, "Legaré and Grayson: Types of Classical Influences on Ante-Bellum Critics," in *Segments of Southern Thought*.

3. See, for an example of extreme romanticism, the later chapter, "Thomas Holley Chivers as a Literary Critic." A. B. Meek of Alabama called the sonnet "poetry in a pillory." The Charlestonian William Crafts in his *Miscellaneous Writings* declared that we claimed as heritage only the literary productions "anterior to the American Revolution"; a voyage across the Atlantic could not disinherit us from our heritage in the English language—Shakespeare, Milton, and Pope—but we wanted no part in the "licentiousness of Byron" or the "milk and water of Wordsworth" or even in the novels of Scott.

4. William P. Trent, *William Gilmore Simms*, 45, made one of his usual free-wheeling generalizations when he wrote that Charleston gentlemen "were still living, in imagination at least, in the time of Horace. If they had come down the centuries at all, they had certainly stopped at another Augustan age,—that of Pope and Addison." The articles in the *Southern Review* indicate quite the contrary, but Trent was not interested in Legaré, and was bored by the *Southern Review* (51-52; 55-57). Most of the contributors were heavily influenced by Lord Kames, Hugh Blair, and other Scottish philosophers.

5. James Hamilton, "Novels—Devereux," *Southern Review*, IV (November 1829), 369-405 (hereafter cited as *S R*). Hamilton prefaces his review of Bulwer's novel with a survey of English fiction, which owed "its origin to the numbers of the Spectator." The legitimate novel was created by Fielding, "first of his class"; Scott is the best of the historical group.

6. Reviewing Scott's *Fair Maid of Perth*, Legaré made a typical introductory comment: "we forget that our readers are not supposed to be acquainted with the subject, and we now proceed to give them a more particular account of it" (*S R*, II, 218). William Elliott in his review of *Anne of Geierstein* devotes eight consecutive pages to an excerpt, to prove Scott's "descriptive power" (*S R*, IV, 505-12).

7. *Writings*, II, 432-33.

8. *Writings*, II, 341.

9. *Writings*, II, 25. On p. 37, he argues that scientific knowledge may be harmful to poetry, "which delights in wonders and prodigies—which seeks out its subjects where it catches its loftiest inspirations, in fabulous periods, in a heroic or feudal age, among argonauts and demi-gods, or pilgrims and crusaders."

10. He wrote from Brussels to his sister Mary (Aug. 24, 1835; *Writings*, I, 243): "the idea of reviving the Southern Review seems to me perfectly visionary. I would not do again what I did for it before for any compensation."

11. These articles are reprinted in *Writings*, I, 367-558. For his pride in his accomplishment, see *Writings*, I, 224, 243.

12. *S R*, I, 1-49; *Writings*, II, 5-51. Citations to reprinted articles will be made to *Writings*.

13. *Writings*, II, 16-17.

14. *Writings*, II, 18-19. German scholars are "the most impartial, precisely because they are most conversant with universal literature"; French the least, because classical learning perished during the Revolution. Literature also had declined: "Where are the successors of Boileau and Racine, of Fenelon and La Bruyère?"

15. *Writings*, II, 22-23.

16. *Writings*, II, 23-24.

17. *Writings*, II, 33.

18. *Writings*, II, 34.

19. *Writings*, II, 426-27. In comparing *Manfred* with the *Eumenides*, Legaré develops this idea: "The *spirit* of Manfred is strictly modern or romantic. The air of abstract reflection, the moral musing, the pensive woe, which pervade it, are a contrast to the sensible imagery and the lively personification of the Greek play. Yet its *frame and structure* are strictly 'classical'. Byron, in all his dramatic compositions, professed to copy after the Greek models,—as much so as Milton in the Samson Agonistes. But, besides discarding the chorus, he has not in other respects approached those models as closely as Milton" (*S R*, II, 440).

20. *Writings*, II, 428-29. In *S R*, I, 444, he digressed to note that "such a book as Ossian's poems (which we take to be a specimen of the genuine Romantic) would have been regarded at Athens as an instance of absolute monstrosity. A people accustomed to ask for the reason of every thing, would have seen in the vagueness, obscurity, and bombast of this pretended Celtic Epic only the effusions of a melancholy madness."

21. *Writings*, II, 38-39. Even good translations do not "supersede the necessity of studying the originals." Thus, "Pope's *imitations* of Horace are better translations than his Iliad. They are just what Horace would have done in English."

22. *Writings*, II, 43-44. It is so flexible that it is equally suited to a historian like Xenophon as to "the light and jocund numbers of Anacreon." Greek is comparable with Algebra, "another specimen of a language or arrangement of signs perfect in its kind."

23. *Writings*, II, 44. In I, 431, he notes that the Homeric poems present truly the moral standards of the Greeks; they are "true to nature in this, as in everything else."

24. *Writings*, I, 116. To understand the Greek ideal of excellence, a study of antique sculpture was necessary: "Sophocles always occurs to us when we think of the Apollo and *vice versa*."

25. *Writings*, L, 205-06. In this letter to I. E. Holmes, Legaré discusses proper interpretations of lines by Sophocles and Euripides.

26. *Writings*, II, 84. "Roman Literature" appeared in *S R*, I, 358-410; in *Writings*, II, 52-101.

27. *Writings*, I, 40. Legaré's admiration is somewhat mixed; in II, 42, he remarked that in the theater "Aristophanes, in verses, which, by the confession of all critics, were never surpassed in energy and spirit, in Attic purity and the most exquisite modulations of harmony, is holding up Socrates—the wisest of mankind—to the contempt and ridicule of the mob."

28. *Writings*, II, 79-80.

29. *Writings*, II, 82-83. He does not consider the writers of the Augustan Age, or afterwards.

30. *Writings*, II, 52-53, 55. The Romans had been wrong in depending on translations: "Imagine Dante and Ariosto to have confined themselves to a bare translation of the celebrated poems of antiquity, or to have attempted the same subjects in a close and studied imitation."

31. *Writings*, II, 70, 73, 87.

32. *Writings*, 8-8, 93-94. Catullus's "amatory poetry is less tender than that of Tibullus—and less gay and *gallant* than that of Ovid—but it is more simple, more cordial, more voluptuous than either."

33. *Writings*, II, 96, 100.

34. *Writings*, I, 382-83. See also I, 134-35 and 234-35. Here, counseling a would-be lawyer, Legaré writes: "Don't neglect Latin. It is easy to acquire a thorough knowledge of it."

35. Horace especially was an enthusiastic "admirer of the Greek models . . . a poet who has celebrated the genius of Pindar in a strain not unworthy of his own matchless lyre" (*Writings*, II, 70).

36. *Writings*, II, 101. See also II, 56. Legaré wrote for the *New York Review* a long article on "The Origin, History and Influence of Roman Legislation"; it is reprinted in *Writings*, I, 502-58.

37. *Writings*, II, 8. This is an aside; Legaré was discussing the origins of language, including "a grave disquisition, in Dante's *Tractate de Vulgari Eloquio*," to prove that Adam spoke Hebrew.

38. *Writings*, II, 54-55. Legaré's article, "Early Spanish Ballads," appeared in S R V, 62-99; reprinted in *Writings*, II, 299-333. Part of their appeal is through the use of Christian subjects, the "most venerable and captivating, and imposing in the history of modern society."

39. *Writings*, II, 348-50. Legaré's article, "Sir Philip Sidney's Miscellanies," appeared in *S R*, V, 295-318; reprinted in *Writings*, II, 334-55. Quoting Milton and Wordsworth as a means of praising Dante is a typical literary device of Legaré's. On 363, he describes Petrarch as "rather a pet with us."

40. *Writings*, II, 299-300. In Brussels, when his eyes were troubling him, Legaré had his Spanish valet read *Gil Blas* to him (I, 5-6).

41. *Writings*, II, 304. Legaré does not mention the Nibelungenlied, possibly because he did not then know German and distrusted translations.

42. *Writings*, II, 333.

43. *Writings*, II, 19. Even so, he could admire individual works, for he writes in a footnote: "See Racine's preface to Iphigénie, which does as much honor to the judgment and candor of the author, as the tragedy itself does to his genius." In an oration on the American Revolution, he translates from Racine: "to fear God, and to know no other fear" (*Writings*, I, 261). Dr. Rhea has described (50-51) Legaré's pleasure in the contemporary French theater.

44. *S R*, II, 454-55, in a review of Robert Pollok's *The Course of Time*. Athalie he calls "the noblest specimen of the classic drama" in modern times. Legaré frequently levied on Molière for apt quotations.

45. *S R*, II, 292, in a review of Robert Montgomery's *Omnipresence of the Deity*.

46. *Writings*, II, 19.

47. *Writings*, II, 424n.

48. In a letter to T. W. White of the *Southern Literary Messenger*, May 10, 1838; partially quoted in Rhea, 163-64. In *Writings*, I, 128, Legaré describes a visit to Voltaire's study at Potsdam. He especially noted that all the classic works were in French translations.

49. *Writings*, I, 500.

50. See, respectively, *Writings*, II, 387-88; I, 499-500; II, 401-02.

51. *Writings*, I, 129, 131.

52. *Writings*, I, 145.

53. *Writings*, I, 103, 114-16.

54. *Writings*, I, 125-26. Robert Henry had a long article "Goethe's Wilhelm Meister" in *S R*, III, 353-85. He begins: "This is a novel of striking interest and great power: confessedly the work of no ordinary genius."

55. *Writings*, II, 382. Legaré also quotes at length (435-37) Goethe's statement

that in *Manfred* Byron "has taken my Faustus to himself," and Byron's disavowal of Goethe's influence.

56. *Writings*, II, 410. Legaré's two articles, "Lord Byron's Character and Writings," and "Byron's Letters and Journals," appeared in S R, V, 463-522, and VII, 1-42; they are reprinted in *Writings*, II, 356-448. Legaré thought poorly of Tom Moore, regarding him as a dependent rather than as a friend of Byron's (*Writings*, II, 366-70), although he incidentally quotes some "fine lines" by Moore (402) and admits that he is a distinguished poet (357).

57. *Writings*, II, 358; see also 366. In *Writings*, I, 29-30, Legaré objected to "a *memorandum* book of Lord Byron, in which he lampoons and ridicules poor Rogers in a frightful manner . . . what a heartless, hypocritical scoundrel Byron was."

58. *Writings*, II, 375-78. Pride and vanity were Byron's ruin, for he lacked the "sublime, rational, imperturbable self-esteem" that Milton had. Byron's "morbid and jealous vanity" was more like Rousseau's (384-87).

59. *Writings*, II, 410. One reason is that his muse "is inspired by, and inspires, nothing but despair" (381).

60. *Writings*, II, 359-61. His heroines are mistresses rather than wives, but they at least remain true to love's vows. Maturin's *Melmoth* presents "an *exaggeration* . . . of Byron's ideal love, in the passion of Imalee for the preternatural Wanderer" (402-04).

61. *Writings*, II, 362. Legaré blamed Byron's failure as an orator on the "languid, monotonous and somniferous" atmosphere of the House of Lords (366).

62. *Writings*, II, 412.

63. *Writings*, II, 423.

64. *Writings*, II, 426-28. Schlegel's "main object is to account for the simplicity of the Greek drama, and its close adherence to the three unities, as well as the rigid exclusion from it of everything comic and incongruous, on principles which shall explain the difference between that style and the complicated and irregular plots and tragi-comic mixtures of Calderon and Shakespeare, without supposing any inferiority in the latter." Since Schlegel thought that "the genius of modern times is *essentially* different from that of the Greeks," modern works required "a structure totally distinct" from classical works.

65. *Writings*, II, 437.

66. *Writings*, II, 437-38. Legaré had objected (424) to the "general tone of emphasis and exaggeration" in *Childe Harold*. In his article on William Crafts, Legaré complained that "Lord Byron with his Beppos' and Juans' has done infinite mischief in the rhyming world. . . . Nothing is so easy as to rival the noble poet in his slip-shod, zig-zag, desultory style, and doggerel versification—but nothing is more difficult than to pour out with such perfect *nonchalance*, strains of the most beautiful poetry, and sallies of incomparable wit. . . . these works bear the same relation to Childe Harold, for instance, or the Corsair, as the conversation of a great orator (who happens to excel in conversation) to his harangues before public assemblies on solemn occasions" (*Writings*, II, 155-56).

67. *Writings*, II, 440-41. Goethe, he noted (439), had been fascinated by "Manfred's character and situation."

68. *Writings*, II, 441-43. Manfred's conscience was made of stern stuff, for Byron "was not a man to make a book of sentimental raving à la Kotzebue."

69. *Writings*, II, 424.

70. *Writings*, II, 32.

71. *Southern Review*, II, 216-17. Legaré's review of *The Fair Maid of Perth* (216-63) was not reprinted in his *Writings*.

72. *Writings*, II, 377-78.

73. Legaré's review appeared in S R, II, 290-302; not reprinted in *Writings*.

74. S R, II, 290-93.

75. *S R*, II, 454-70; not reprinted in *Writings*.

76. *S R*, II, 462-65.

77. *S R*, II, 455.

78. *Writings*, II, 407.

79. *S R*, II, 457. See also *Writings*, II, 407: Byron had addressed himself more to the feelings, Milton more to the imagination, of mankind.

80. *S R*, II, 457-58. Some of Milton's shorter poems possessed equal power. When in Brussels he read a French translation of a book by Adam Mickiewitz on Polish martyrs and on barbarities ordered by the victorious Russian Czar, he noted: "Milton's sonnet on the massacre in Piedmont was in my mind the whole time" (*Writings*, I, 33).

81. *S R*, II, 458. Young's book was worth "committing to memory for the purpose of apt quotation." In *Writings*, II, 382, Legaré wrote: "Young's Night Thoughts are the counterpart of Byron's poetry. But we need not say that they differ as widely in their results, as Christianity and Atheism." Young sees hope and a final victory in Heaven; Byron's "only refuge from despair is desperation."

82. *S R*, II, 459.

83. *Writings*, II, 407-08. He elaborated on the idea in *S R*, II, 291-92: "Compare the first part of Thomson's Castle of Indolence (which nothing can surpass) with his Seasons, which are liable to the same criticism as this poem of Mr. Montgomery [bombast and mawkish sentimentality]—or Campbell's Hohenlinden, etc., with his 'Pleasures of Hope,' and the difference alluded to will soon be perceived." Campbell's poem has been "fully as much praised as it deserves to be."

84. *Writings*, II, 301.

85. *Writings*, II, 338.

86. His review, "Sir Philip Sidney's Miscellanies," appeared in *S R*, V, 295-318; reprinted in *Writings*, II, 334-55.

87. *Writings*, II, 341. Milton, also defending poetry against Puritanism, although a Puritan, "maintained the same opinions, and uttered them with incomparably greater power, in his own gorgeous and magnificent prose" (339).

88. *Writings*, II, 353, 355. Before quoting one poem Legaré notes: "The following pair of kisses would not be out of place in Joannes Secundus. They are not quite so burning as those which the amorous bard of Verona snatched from Lesbia's lips to give to immortality in song."

89. *S R*, II, 468. See also *Writings*, II, 333.

90. Respectively, *Writings*, II, 354; I, 243; Charleston *Courier*, Feb. 24, 1832; *Writings*, II, 430.

91. *Writings*, II, 336.

92. The review *"Craft's Fugitive Writings,"* appeared in *S R*, I, 503-29; reprinted in *Writings*, II, 142-65. Rather oddly, Legaré pays no attention to Crafts' indebtedness to Pope, both in "The Raciad" and in "Sullivan's Island," although noting Crafts' indebtedness to Byron.

93. *S R*, I ,443-45. Legaré's review was published in *S R*, I, 442-57; not reprinted in *Writings*.

94. *S R*, I, 446-47. Legaré makes some excuse for the beginner, but he qualifies: "the rudest beginnings of the work by a great master, excite more curiosity than the master-pieces of inferior artists."

95. *S R*, I, 457.

96. *Writings*, I, 18.

97. *S R*, VIII, 433. Legaré's review appears, 443-62; not reprinted in *Writings*. That Legaré did not over-estimate Bryant's poetry is indicated (444) by his writing: "We do not see why the author might not produce something worthy to be *classed*, at least, with Gertrude of Wyoming, and the Deserted Village. We do not mean to intimate that, from these specimens, we are ready to compare Mr. Bryant with Campbell or Goldsmith—but we think that he would most excel in that

class of poems to which the beautiful productions just mentioned belong—and we have no doubt that his excellence in that kind would be of no ordinary stamp."

98. *S R*, VIII, 445. However, Bryant lacked completely "that more various, elevated, powerful and imaginative diction—itself a *creation*, and the most dazzling of poetical creations—such as we read in Pindar and the Greek tragedians, especially Aeschylus—such as we see in many parts of Shakspear, and in almost every line of Milton."

99. *S R*, II, 460: "There are also several sonnets—or rather, as the author himself avows—short poems in fourteen lines, not fashioned upon the strict Italian model, consecrated as it has been by all the grandeur and energy, as well as the beauty of genius—is after all, perhaps, essentially barbarous. Yet we candidly profess our decided partiality for it . . . more than any other kind of poetry, it abhors mediocrity. The general reason assigned by Horace in the well known *dict*, applies to it more strongly than to any other kind of poetry. It is artificial, and therefore, frigid, unless it be redeemed by surpassing excellence. . . . We love Petrarch and his sonnets—bad as the taste of many of them is—and all the world has been awakened by those of Milton and Filicaja. Mr. Bryant's, besides their wanting the legitimate form, are not master-pieces in other respects. Still they are very good."

100. *S R*, VIII, 462.

101. *Writings*, II, 358-59.

102. *Writings*, II, 373-74. For this stunting of Legaré's legs, usually attributed to an inoculation for smallpox, see Rhea, 2-4. His friend E. W. J. in *Writings*, I, VIII, noted: "while his chest, bust and head became those of a very fine *torso*, his members remained those of a very short man." In his review of Scott's *Fair Maid of Perth* (*S R*, II, 241), Legaré treats the same topic: "In general, those who have not experienced similar misfortunes, are unable to conceive the mortification, and even the madness which they may occasion, when the temper of the sufferer happens to be an irritable one. Lord Byron's sensibility on this subject is well known, and Sir Walter Scott saw into the very bottom of the human heart, when he drew The Black Dwarf—a character, however, which has generally been considered, we believe, as altogether extravagant and monstrous."

103. *S R*, II, 217, 262. William Elliott, in his review of *Anne of Geierstein* (*S R*, IV, 498-522), is equally enthusiastic: he congratulates "the reading public, on the pleasure they have shared with us" in this book—even though it is not Scott at his very best. Both Cooper and Bulwer are followers but "not servile copyists" of Scott. Cooper had the advantage of a region unknown previously to fiction, and "a power and felicity equal to Smollett" in his ocean stories. Bulwer is superior in "his conception of female character." But in Scott the power "extends throughout the whole circle" (520-22).

104. Legaré's review appeared in *S R*, V, 207-26; not reprinted in *Writings*.

105. *S R*, V, 207.

106. *S R*, V, 212.

107. *S R*, V, 219-20. Legaré's exact words are a good bit stronger: it is "painful to revert from this, to the frigid management by which the American novelist has tamed down this admirable subject."

108. *S R*, V, 223-24. Legaré, a lover of puns, objected that the play upon the name Miantonimoh for "my Antony Mow" is stupid; if intended for a definition it "betrays too much ignorance of Indians and their customs for a borderer."

109. *S R*, V, 382-99. The review of Copper's *The Bravo* (*S R*, VIII; 382-99) has usually been ascribed to Legaré. I believe this ascription to be erroneous. The reviewer reveals a personal familiarity with Venice; Dr. Rhea writes (61) that Legaré did not get to Italy. More important: the reviewer claims that it "was our happy fortune to wander with the author through many of the favourite scenes of Italy, and hence we can both appreciate and vouch for his glowing descriptions"

(397). Fortunately, this review is mainly concerned with political conditions in Venice and in the South (again not in accord with Legaré's position); it does not change in any way his criticism of Cooper as novelist.

110. In *S R*, III, 467-507; reprinted in *Writings*, II, 180-215. Actually, the Bulwer review stops on p. 205; a separate review of George Croly's *Tales of the Great St. Bernard* is then printed.

111. *Writings*, II, 180, 185.

112. *Writings*, II, 186-87. Legaré notes that it is too easy "to slide into exaggeration" on the side of heroic virtues: "we have always felt dissatisfied with the heroes of Metastasio and Alfieri on this account. Their conduct is rather *too* godlike—their language, although they say only what they are going to do or have done in fact, swells into rhodomontade and extravagance—they are so very Roman, that they cease to have human feelings, or to excite human sympathy."

113. *Writings*, II, 188.

114. *Writings*, II, 203-04. Legaré added that the author introduced the readers to Burke, Johnson, Goldsmith, and Garrick—"but the author has not made much of it; as, indeed, what author could? or what fiction come up to the naked truth as it is revealed in the invaluable Omnium Gatherum of that first of biographers and of boobies, the incomparable Bozzy?" Legaré also asks sarcastically if a fashionble dinner by candle-light makes one taste "the pleasures of a true 'Cotter's Saturday Night.'"

115. *Writings*, II, 187. Legaré also wrote a perfunctory review of Bulwer's book of poems (*S R*, VII, 192-213); he dismissed *The Siamese Twins* as a "wretched failure. . . . It is inconceivable how so clever a writer as the author of 'Pelham' should . . . have failed so utterly." The poems are platitudinous; they are "Weary, *flat*, unprofitable." He also notes that Bulwer is safe from being like Lord Byron, at least in poetic genius. And when Bulwer pleads that he is dealing only with imaginary persons, "Horace and good sense have settled that matter long ago." The title piece is jejune and disgusting; the minor poems in better taste, but no better than any talented college boy could write.

116. *Writings*, II, 206.

117. *S R*, II, 218.

118. *Writings*, II, 70-71. See also 26, especially for a quotation from Milton on earlier literary critics.

119. *Writings*, II, 94. Martial ascribes to Catullus "an unrivalled superiority in the epigram."

120. See, for one example, *Writings*, II, 426-28. It is rather surprising that Legaré in his wide reading states (I, 130) that before 1835 he had never read Samuel Johnson's *Lives of the Poets*: "Dr. Johnson is a horribly bad writer. His artificial periods and his pomposity of phrase to express the baldest common-place, are insupportable to me. Yet his criticism, in every thing that does not soar above a certain height, is usually very sensible. For the sublime or the pathetic, he had neither soul nor ear to comprehend them. Nothing can be more unworthy of the mighty theme, than his way of treating Milton, except his superficial notes on Shakespeare. From his praise of Pope's Homer as a *translation*—his significant insinuation that the best scholars have more pleasure in reading the 'blind old man,' so perverted, (the translation is a good *English* poem, *but*—) than in his own matchless verse,—and his absurd remarks on 'Samson Agonistes' and Greek tragedy —I shrewdly suspect the Doctor was no Greek scholar at all . . . he is in his true element when he speaks of Dryden,—Milton was above his pitch. He had not as much heart as head, and not as much soul as heart, and is *never* either very original or very profound."

121. *Writings*, II, 168. At the beginning of this review, "Travels of the Duke of Saxe-Weimar," Legaré expresses his great admiration for German scholarship. This admiration has been noted previously.

122. *Writings,* II, 411.

123. *Writings,* II, 26. In this statement, he was probably revealing the direct or indirect influence of the Scottish philosophers. But it was also Legaré's personal conviction.

124. See *S R,* II, 216, 291.

3. WILDE

1. Edward L. Tucker, *Richard Henry Wilde: Life and Selected Works* (Ph.D. dissertation, University of Georgia, 1957). This is indispensable for any study of Wilde's life and works. It includes all his known poetry except *Hesperia* (1867), and a generous selection of his letters and other prose. Of continuing value is Anthony Barclay's *Wilde's Summer Rose: or the Lament of the Captive. An Authentic Account of the Origin, Mystery, and Explanation of Hon. R. H. Wilde's Alleged Plagiarism,* 1871. For useful articles by Aubrey Starke and Nathalia Wright, see Tucker's excellent bibliography. I am indebted to Miss Wright for making various of Wilde's letters available to me.

2. By Luis de Camoëns; *Southern Literary Messenger,* I (Dec. 1834), 186; published in the *Chronicle* under the pseudonym "Surrey." Francisco de Lemene's "Dialogue" appeared in the *Southern Literary Messenger,* I (Feb. 1835), 318. Wilde had translated other poems by this time; they are in the Wilde Collection, Library of Congress, and also given in Tucker's work. The incomplete manuscripts of the *Life and Times of Dante, with Sketches of the State of Florence, and of his Friends and Enemies,* and of *Specimens of the Italian Lyric Poets* are in the Library of Congress.

3. Preface, *Dante:* "The Author to the Reader." Wilde had desired to use the Medicean archives for his *Tasso,* but permission came too late. He was engaged in translating Italian lyrical poems, with biographical introductions, when contradictions in the biographies of Dante bothered him. He embarked on both tasks, and was fascinated: "Once engaged in historical and antiquarian researches, those accustomed to them will readily believe how soon they entirely absorbed me."

4. *Tasso,* I, 7. Wilde wrote no introduction, but begins abruptly: "There is scarcely any poet whose life excites a more profound and melancholy interest." Wilde's legalistic approach is indicated (7-8) by his statement that "Truth is discovered by a close analysis of circumstantial evidence, and doubt remains only where a sufficient knowledge of minute facts, or sufficient skill and patience in comparing them, is wanting."

5. *Tasso,* II, 268, 270; Wilde insists (I, 10) that "it is the authority of Torquato himself which is intended to be quoted, for the purpose of solving all difficulties: and enough, it is imagined, may be gathered from his own pen to afford grounds of satisfactory belief, or at least of plausible conjecture." Wilde hoped "to settle all controversies, as far as possible, by the authority of the poet himself" (1, 16).

6. *Tasso,* I, 10, 12-13. He quotes Ugo Foscoli: "what we call imagination is little more than strong feelings and vivid recollections." Wilde reprints many of Tasso's poems to prove his points; he gives his own English translation in the text, the original Italian in a footnote.

7. Introduction to Petrarch selections, *Italian Lyric Poets.* Part of this was printed in Rufus Griswold's *Prose Writers of America* (1847), and in various magazines.

8. *Tasso,* II, 122. On 119, Wilde doubts that heresy caused Tasso's troubles: "If heresy was his offence, why was he not sent to the prison of the inquisition, not the hospital of the poor and insane?" Introduction to Boccaccio selections, in *Italian Lyric Poets.*

9. *Hesperia* (1867), V. Before quoting "the only Italian rhymes I ever ventured to compose," Wilde wrote: "*True* poetry is never written but in the tongue of our mother and our nurse. I call Milton's Italian sonnets to witness" (311). The

book is dedicated to La Signora Marchesa Manfredina di Cosenza. She has been identified as Mrs. Ellen Adair White Beatty and as the Marchesa Mary Bartolommei. Both figure in *Hesperia*, and the disguised Marchesa in the dedication may be a composite.

10. *Hesperia*, 5-7. In his extensive notes Wilde frequently quotes from travellers and historians who have described places or events that he uses in his poem. But he was convinced that "in this our day and land/All that is written perishes" (9); as yet, "We have no poetry" (220). In addition to history and legend, there must also be an audience: "When there are none to love, hear, blame, or praise,/What God or man or statue utters lays" (223).

11. July 15, 1843. Given in full in Tucker, 541-45. Wilde somewhat begs the question also when he writes: "With respect to your powers for prose works of fiction, it would be impertinent in me to say a word more, after the very conclusive expression of Public Opinion in your favor."

12. *Hesperia*, 8. Wilde was convinced his own original poetry would not last: "This lay shall fade like all that went before/While poppies and not laurels crown my head" (220).

13. *Hesperia*, 231. As this indicates, Wilde had no use for the "noble savage" ideal, in life or literature.

14. Aug. 11, 1842, Aug. 10, 1845, and March 15, 1846 (Letters in possession of Miss Nathalia Wright, University of Tennessee). As early as 1841, he wrote to Charles Sumner: "I find it *impossible* to proceed with what I began in Italy" (Harvard). In the Dedication and in the Notes on *Hesperia*, he writes of his love for Italy; and he dedicated the *Dante*: "To the People of Italy this life of their National Poet is humbly inscribed by their friend the Author." In *Hesperia* (Canto IV, Stanza XII, 173) he wrote: "My Italy! although of thine not born . . . Thy child in heart I am."

15. Nov. 1, 1842; in New York Public Library. Simms had heard Wilde read from his *Dante*, and, possibly in an attempt to prod Wilde into completing it, reported it as nearly ready for publication (*Southern and Western Monthly*, II (Aug. 1845), 144). In Dec. 1845, Simms wrote to E. A. Duyckinck that Wilde "speaks despondingly of the work—probably lacks impulse; and might be driven to the task by application" (Simms *Letters*, II, 123).

16. March 7, 1845; in Boston Public Library; in Tucker, 546-50. This same feeling is also expressed in another letter to Griswold, Nov. 6, 1843, in BPL. Wilde refused to send additional material for his biography, "being entirely absorbed by the weightier matters of the law."

17. Letter to Simms, July 15, 1843; see n. 11. To the Editor of the *Knickerbocker*, XVIII (Dec. 1841), 523-29, he wrote an indignant letter on nationalism generally; on literature and on cheap books, he stated: "While our press teems with republications of the flimsiest English reproductions; books which look as if they had been written by contract at so much the thousand superficial feet, Washington Irving it is understood has had lying by him for some time a most valuable MSS., whose publication is deferred because there is no adequate security for literary property." Wilde at this time was interested in securing a copyright for his *Tasso*.

18. Letter to Simms, July 15, 1843. Wilde also comments on the need for revision: "if a due reward for your labours ensured you all the leisure for that careful and frequent revision and improvement which any very high degree of perfection in every art requires."

19. *Tasso*, I, 140-41. See also his letter to James K. Paulding (April 20, 1836; given in Tucker, 512-17; printed in *Knickerbocker*, VIII (Oct. 1836), 447-54), in which he describes his examination of alleged newly-discovered Tasso documents. In a letter of Sept. 15, 1839, Wilde asked Charles Sumner to make enquiries about documents in Ferrara, Padua, and Venice (Harvard University Library).

20. Nov. 24, 1839 (Harvard University Library). In "The Author to the Reader,"

Dante, he noted that the Medicean Archives "to my heated imagination appeared an unexplored region."

21. Letter to William Preston, Aug. 11, 1842 (Duke University Library); in the *Knickerbocker,* XVIII (Dec. 1841), 523-29, as introduction to his translation of an article on the sculptor Hiram Powers, by A. A. Migliarini, he wrote that "every spark of genius exhibited in the beautiful creations of the mind should be carefully fanned and cherished. . . . If we fail in according to our artists due praise, it is often because our commendation is misdirected and excessive, the result of inexperience and national vanity, while any deficiency of patronage is to be attributed to the haste, impatience, and instability of our business-like existence." Because Americans distrusted their own artistic judgment and discrimination, "our government have employed foreign artists of little reputation to the exclusion of our own, in reality far their superiors; and the supposed advantage of cheap literature, but in truth the interest of a few publishers who live by literary piracy, is considered a sufficient objection to international copy-right." We should employ "the best native sculptors"—especially Horatio Greenough, Powers, Thomas Crawford and S. V. Clevenger. The failure to support native writers also arises from self-distrust: "while we laud ourselves to the skies, it is generally without any very great reliance on our own opinions, and with a secret admiration of every thing foreign." In *Hesperia* (Canto IV, Stanza XCVIII) he writes of an American sculptor: "Not Angelo's nor Donatello's skill/In folds more graceful human form could twine." On 328, Wilde writes simply: "Hiram Powers."

22. Thus he wrote to John Pendleton Kennedy, then in Congress (May 4, 1842; Peabody Institute, Baltimore): "If you make a report on international copy-right, send me one. . . . I don't see very clearly why literary piracy is to be the only one, practiced and approved by Christian nations. Perhaps letters being an invention of the Devil with the help of Dr. Faustus, they are properly left to his protection. . . . If literary piracy were confined to a few publishers, the trade would be worth following. But unhappily in all illicit trades there are small rogues who prey upon the greater. A cheap edition is pirated by one still cheaper, and that again by the cheapest, and the last by another cheaper than the cheapest, until amid new degrees of comparison, quartos dwindle down to newspapers, and dishonesty has no profit left. . . . When all the world turns robbers no one can subsist on robbery." In the cited letter to Simms, he calls such publishers "pirates" who "would fain persuade us, they publish almost gratuitously, for the pure love of the 'Dear People' and *steal* from Charity only."

23. Tucker gives a letter to the Governor of Georgia (518-22; Oct. 23, 1836; manuscript in Telamon Cuyler Collection, University of Georgia Library) listing some of the more valuable items in Count Bouterlin's library of more than 20,000 volumes. According to the Augusta *Chronicle,* Feb. 25, 1836, he had written to Congress, and the matter was discussed (*Senate Journal,* Feb. 19, March 14, and June 4, 1836); since Congress had "failed to authorize the purchase . . . I address myself to you in the hope that your state may be prevailed upon to buy it."

24. Letter to Mrs. Rebecca Tiernan Somerville, Jan. 31, 1842; in Tucker, 529-31. To Hiram Powers he wrote (Aug. 11, 1842; letter in possession of Miss Nathalia Wright) about volume I of his manuscript *Dante:* "The pains bestowed upon it would be incredible to any one who had not modelled Eve. Not a line but has been written fifteen to twenty times over. . . . I build upon it my hopes of 'being remembered in my line'. . . . Labor is not to be spared therefore, for no excellence was ever attained without it."

25. One of his best sonnets is "To Lord Byron," who as poet soars "on eagles' pinions"; it was first printed in the *Southern Literary Messenger,* Nov. 1834. In *Hesperia,* 311, he notes that the last line of Canto IV, Stanza II, 168, is Byron's: "This heavenliest hour of heaven is worthiest thee." It is given in quotation marks. In the same stanza he notes that Dante, "copied oft,/But still unrivalled," had

also praised evening. He turned into verse a passage from Moore's *Life of Byron* (Tucker, 377); his general indebtedness to Moore is apparent in many poems. In *Hesperia*, 237, his fine line, "All that is bright and beautiful must fade" was suggested by two lines by Tasso; the first six lines of Canto IV "are an imitation of Dante's beautiful and well-known opening of Canto VIII, of the Purgatorio" (310); Stanza XLV and the first line of XLVI in Canto I "are imitated from the Italian sonnet of Giulio Bussi,—'Che sei tu Gloria' " (242). These are typical; there are others scattered throughout the Notes.

26. He quoted to Simms, and used also, as a preliminary note to *Hesperia*, Goethe's statement that "the poet wishing to speak out a manifold world, uses the story of a famous personage as a thread on which he may string what he pleases. Even so are Gil Blas and the Odyssey constructed." Since he was using himself as the thread, Wilde in *Hesperia* changed the phrase to "some personage."

27. Letters to Simms and Kennedy previously cited; in a letter to Simms, Nov. 1, 1842, he calls William A. Caruthers "Friend Caruthers." See the section in Tucker, "Literary Friends," 173-78. Of the Northern writers, Paulding was his closest friend; of the Southern, Simms. Wilde wrote that he was flattered when Simms dedicated *Castle Dismal* (1844) to him. The letter to Paulding appeared in the *Knickerbocker*, VIII (Oct. 1836), 447-54, with the title, "Secret History of Tasso."

28. *Hesperia*, Canto III, Stanza XX, 123. On 298, Wilde notes Cooper's use in his novel, *The Wept of Wish-ton-wish*, of the story of the expatriate regicides Goffe and Whalley.

4. INTENT OF THE HUMORISTS

1. Franklin J. Meine, *Tall Tales of the Southwest*, XVI. I am indebted to Mr. Meine for many courtesies and much helpful information.

2. Preface, *The Big Bear of Arkansas and Other Sketches, Illustrative of Characters and Incidents in the South and South-West* (1845). An excellent anthology edited by Porter. Porter again emphasized the importance of character and incident in Southern humor in the Preface to his anthology, *A Quarter Race in Kentucky* (1846).

3. Quoted in Meine, XVIII.

4. New York *Mirror*, VIII (Dec. 18, 1830), 191.

5. Constance Rourke, *American Humor*, 52-53. This is one of the indispenable works on Southern humor, along with Meine's, Henry Watterson's *Oddities in Southern Life and Character*, Walter Blair's *Native American Humor*, and Bernard DeVoto's *Mark Twain's America*.

6. John Neal, "Story-Telling," New York *Mirror*, XVI (April 6, 1839), 321; quoted in Blair, 321. An excellent account of oral story-telling by one of the Southern humorists is in Richard Malcolm Johnston's "Middle Georgia in Rural Life," *Century*, XLIII (March 1892), 739-40.

7. Preface, *Narrative of the Life of David Crockett of West Tennessee* (1834). For Crockett in folklore, and for his collaborators, see Constance Rourke, *Davy Crockett* (1934).

8. *Southern Literary Messenger*, VI (July 1840), 573.

9. Longstreet, *Georgia Scenes* (1835, 1840), Preface, 178, 208; O. P. Fitzgerald, *Judge Longstreet* (1891), 164-66. Longstreet emphasized "Georgia language" (72) and "Georgia Humor" (200), but he set the time of his stories back to "the first fifty years of our republic."

10. *Georgia Scenes*, 47. However, as DeVoto has noted, it was not the author but the publisher that in the 1867 edition changed "sons o' bitches" to "critters." This is near the end of "The Gander Pulling." The standard biography is John Donald Wade's *Augustus Baldwin Longstreet* (1924).

11. Edgar Allan Poe, *Southern Literary Messenger,* II (March 1836), 287. Poe noted that of "geese and ganders he is the La Bruyère, and of good-for-nothing horses, the Rouchefoucault."

12. William Gilmore Simms, *Views and Reviews,* II, 177-79. But in the tall tale, he notes in "How Sharp Snaffles Got his Capital and Wife," the "bald and naked truth" is discreditable, and he has a story-teller justify a literal beginning: "The truth's nothing but a peg in the wall that I hangs the lie upon."

13. Prefaces, *Major Jones's Courtship* (1843) and *Major Jones's Sketches of Travel* (1847); Preface, *Major Jones's Chronicles of Pineville* (1845). Thompson claims that such characters are "not often found in books, or anywhere else, indeed, except in just such places as 'Pineville,' Georgia."

14. Preface to the 1872 edition of *Major Jones's Courtship.* Both in prefatory notes and in a letter to Salem Dutcher (Oct. 16, 1866), Thompson notes that the book simply developed: "I had originally no plot or plan for the letters which finally grew into a sort of narrative."

15. In the Savannah *Morning News,* March 9, 1871, Thompson wrote: "Dr G. W. Bagby continues his ridiculous 'History of the Waw.' Right here, we want to protest against this sort of thing." The quotation follows. The malapropism noted here is in Letter XII.

16. Preface, *Major Jones's Chronicles of Pineville.*

17. Joseph G. Baldwin, *Flush Times In Alabama and Mississippi* (1853), V. Baldwin also records that "the scheme of the articles he believes to be original in design and execution." As Walter Blair has noted (67), the more Western humorists like T. B. Thorpe and John S. Robb were equally concerned with local subjects, character, scenery, and setting.

18. Johnson J. Hooper, Ch. I, *Some Adventures of Captain Simon Suggs* (1845). Hooper also emphasizes the informal nature of his writing: "If what was designed, chiefly, to amuse a community unpretending in its tastes, shall amuse the Great Public, the writer will, of course, be gratified."

19. Richard Malcolm Johnston in *The Critic,* XII (March 17, 1888), 126. He also believed that a writer should take "the utmost pains in the study of naturalness, and that an artist can create interesting concretes only if he can re-enact scenes from human life." He rephrases much of this in his *Autobiography,* 73-74.

20. Preface, *The Primes and their Neighbors* (1891). Johnston also wrote that well-educated men were so fond of dialect that they "preferred it often, not only when in sportive moods, but when incensed by resentment."

21. *Autobiography* (1900), 71, and Preface, *Mr. Absalom Billingslea* (1881). See also Preface, *Dukesborough Tales* (1871), and the beginning of "The Goosepond School." Johnston notes that in "*Dukesborough* the author has preserved his memoirs of Powelton, a small village in Hancock County, Georgia, near which is his birthplace" (1892 edition).

22. See W. Stanley Hoole, *Alias Simon Suggs: The Life and Times of Johnson Jones Hooper* (1952), 181 and 249. This is the standard biography of Hooper.

5. INTENT OF THE NOVELISTS

1. See my monograph, *William Gilmore Simms as a Literary Critic* (1960). However, the more pertinent ideas are in the essay on Simms included in this book.

2. "To the Reader," in *The Valley of Shenandoah; or, Memoirs of the Graysons* (1824; published anonymously). The author concludes the novel (II, 320) by asserting his own right: "And thus, gentle reader, you may see, in this true, but melancholy history, something of the life and manners which prevailed twenty-five or thirty years ago, in Virginia, and especially in that part of it which is called the Valley of Shenandoah." Jay B. Hubbell has given an excellent account of it (*The*

South in American Literature, 252): "This melodramatic story is told with many circumstantial details that savor of realism rather than romance. The background of plantation life, partly in the Tidewater but chiefly in the Valley, is faithfully described. There are excellent descriptions of barbecues, details from life, country-court proceedings. There is even a description of the auctioning off of the Grayson slaves—a scene that would be difficult to parallel in any other novel by a Southern writer. There is, finally, a remarkable contrast of the German and the Scotch-Irish settlers of the Valley. No other novel of Virginia includes so many typical aspects of the life of the state. There is no attempt to cast a halo over plantation life, no attempt to conceal unpleasant realities. Tucker had no part in the building up of the romantic plantation tradition."

Tucker's novel was carelessly constructed and hastily written, but he was by no means ignorant of literary theory, as Robin Colin McLean has ably demonstrated in his *George Tucker: Moral Philosopher and Man of Letters* (1961); for McLean's discussion of *The Valley of Shenandoah,* see 75-89. McLean thinks that "*The Valley,* more than anything else Tucker ever wrote, fulfilled his requirements that good history acquaint man with 'the progress of society and the arts of civilization; with the advancement and decline of literature, laws, manners, and commerce,'" (79; quoted from Tucker's "Discourse on American Literature," *S L M*, IV (1838), 85.) But Tucker is chiefly important as philosopher and aesthetician, and as the foremost advocate in the South of the ideas of the Scottish school of Common-sense Philosophy, especially Lord Kames and Hugh Blair, and his disagreement with the theories of David Hume and Thomas Brown. McLean has done a first-rate job in relating Tucker's philosophy to that of the Scottish philosophers.

In a monograph on Poe, I plan to treat at some length Tucker's theory that great poetry cannot be didactic, that "the strength and beauty of all metaphysical experience have their foundation in our pleasures and pains—those having the greatest effect which refer to our liveliest emotions." As a result, it is the duty of the poet "to awaken our sympathy by giving touching natural exhibitions of human passions and sentiments" (quoted by McLean, 134, from Tucker's unpublished "Lectures on Rhetoric and Belles Letters," IX and XXXIX, deposited in the University of Virginia Library).

3. *The Partisan Leader* (1836; the title-page has the fictitious date 1856), published under the pseudonym Edward William Sidney; the pseudonymous author wrote in a dedication that "The part I bore in the transactions which form the subject of the following narrative, is my voucher for its authenticity." Throughout, the book keeps the tone of a factual historical memoir, even in the most melodramatic incidents. Montrose J. Moses, *The Literature of the South,* 253, called it "a text-book of rebellion in disguise." See pages 106 and 273, in the excellent edition prepared by Carl Bridenbaugh (1933). Tucker's *George Balcombe* (1836), a novel told in the first person, has some realistic descriptions of life in Missouri and Virginia, but is a conventional melodrama about a suppressed will. Tucker was strongly influenced by Scott and Cooper, and by Godwin's *Caleb Williams.* The book is remarkable for its large number of literary allusions and quotations: two dogs are named from *Orlando Furioso* "Gryphon, the white, and Aquillant, the black" (8); among the authors levied upon are St. Luke, Shakespeare, Dryden, Pope, Crabbe, Wordsworth, Byron, Burns, Scott, Cowper, Shenstone, and Halleck. Tucker twice gives footnotes to attest to his factual accuracy: on II, 229, about accuracy with a pistol; and on II, 89, in connection with Daniel Boone and the location of lands: "The reader is assured that this account is given (excepting names, which are not remembered) exactly as the writer received it from an eye-witness of unquestioned veracity."

4. The most useful and reliable work is Charles H. Bohner's newly-published

John Pendleton Kennedy: Gentleman from Baltimore (1961), 31-46; see also Edward M. Gwathmey, *John Pendleton Kennedy* (1931), 20-21, 30, 59-62; Henry T. Tuckerman, *Life of John Pendleton Kennedy* (Vol. X of Kennedy's *Collected Works,* 1871) 48, 60-61, 108-13. Jay B. Hubbell in *The South in American Literature* gives excellent brief accounts of the lives and works of both Tuckers, Kennedy, Caruthers, and Cooke; Alexander Cowie in *The Rise of the American Novel,* stimulating and sound treatments of Kennedy, Caruthers, and Cooke. Hubbell's edition of *Swallow Barn* and Ernest E. Leisy's of *Horse-Shoe Robinson* are textually reliable and have useful introductions and bibliographies.

5. Kennedy dedicated *Swallow Barn* to Wirt: "some years ago, you carelessly sat down and wrote a little book, [*The British Spy,* 1803] which has, doubtless, surprised yourself by the rapidity with which it has risen to be a classic in our country. I have sat down as carelessly, to a like undertaking, but stand sadly in want of the wings that have borne your name to an enviable eminence." He dedicated *Horse-Shoe Robinson* to Irving for having "furnished our idle craft an argument to justify our vocation. You have convinced our wise ones at home that a man may sometimes write a volume without losing his character—and have shown to the incredulous abroad, that an American book may be richly worth the reading." But his intimate friendship with Irving developed after the writing of *Swallow Barn* (see the many letters given in full or in part in Tuckerman).

6. To this list probably should be added *Letters from Virginia, Translated from the French* (Baltimore, 1816). I agree with Dr. Hubbell (250) that this book is by George Tucker. Defoe may also have influenced him; he wrote his God-son: "Old Robinson Crusoe I want you to know very well, for he is a fine fellow and an old friend of mine" (Tuckerman, 213).

7. "Preface" in *Swallow Barn* (in J. B. Hubbell's edition, 1929), 5, to the first or 1832 edition. To the 1852 edition, Kennedy added a longer note, "A Word in Advance, from the Author to the Reader." The original preface is signed by Mark Littleton, the narrator and ostensible author.

8. *Swallow Barn,* 5. "In a Word in Advance," 10, he adds: "I wish it to be noted that *Swallow Barn* is not a novel. I confess this in advance, although I may lose by it. It was begun on the plan of a series of detached sketches linked together by the hooks and eyes of a traveler's notes; and although the narrative does run into some by-paths of personal adventure, it has still preserved its desultory, sketchy character to the last. It is, therefore, utterly inartistic in plot and structure."

9. *Swallow Barn,* 189. In "A Word in Advance," 8-10, he emphasizes that he had written truthfully of country life in Virginia: "Presenting, as I make bold to say, a faithful picture of the people, the modes of life, and the scenery of a region full of attraction, and exhibiting the lights and shades of its society with the truthfulness of a painter who has studied his subject on the spot," Kennedy feels that his sketches may "reasonably claim their accuracy of delineation to be set off as an extenuation for any want of skill or defect of finish."

10. His kinsman John Esten Cooke, reviewing Tuckerman's *Life* in *Appletons' Journal,* X (Aug., 1873), 205, complained that Tuckerman did not present him as being "most remarkable as a social companion and *raconteur,*" and comments at length on Kennedy's skill as a story-teller. Quoted in Gwathmey, 147-48; see also 102-03. However, Kennedy has several illuminating comments on style. In 1813 he wrote what he considered a spirited article on "The Volunteers of Baltimore" for a local newspaper; when a comrade showed no enthusiasm for it, Kennedy wryly observed in his Autobiographical Sketch: "I have learned since that fine writing falls on the business world like water on a duck's back" (Tuckerman, 67) . In a letter evidently to his god-son Bryan (who had sent him an article), Kennedy wrote: "I have another remark to make in regard to your style. It is too distressingly *intense.* What new caprice has taken hold of you? You formerly wrote in a

fine, clear, transparent style, that was particularly good; but recently you have so bedevilled and bemystified and transcendentalized your style with such cracking of heart-strings, subjectivity of emotion, and with such penetration into mystical mill-stones, and are in such evident tortures from unnatural retention of great, walloping sentimentalities, that require great walloping words to deliver them, that I sometimes don't know you. Pray write like J. P. K. [Bryan], and let Walter Savage Landor and De Quincey go their own gait, without having you at their heels" (Tuckerman, 276-77).

11. Kennedy, "A Legend of Maryland," *Atlantic Monthly*, VI (July 1860), 29. Leisy suggests (XXVI) that he was influenced by Scott and Macaulay. He was a close personal friend of William H. Prescott's, and in 1856 wrote him: "Without meaning any disparagement of its history, I think Philip the Second much the best romance of our times" (Tuckerman, 371). There is also a close resemblance to the prefatory matter in Irving's *Knickerbocker's History of New York*.

12. In Ernest E. Leisy's excellent edition, 1937, the 1835 Preface is on 11; the 1850 Introduction, 5-10. For a pleasant account of his relations with Cooper, see his Journal in Tuckerman, 365-67. His friendships with Thackeray, N. P. Willis, and other authors, and his aid to Poe, are discussed there, 363-89.

13. *Horse-Shoe Robinson*, 11. Reviewing it in the *Southern Quarterly Review*, N.S. VI (July, 1852), 203-20, Simms in a "most friendly spirit" attacked Kennedy on historical details and "upon certain points of your Historical Summary" (*Letters*, III, 183). One passage which especially offended Simms was the beginning of Ch. XII, 127, where Kennedy wrote that, except perhaps for Georgia, South Carolina possessed the largest number of people "tainted with disaffection" and little attached to the union. In an 1852 letter to Simms (Tuckerman, 371-72), Kennedy wrote: "I have given a little personal attention in the introduction to this adventure which is a true history of my acquaintance with my hero."

14. See Leisy, XXII-XXIII. In his Autobiographical Sketch (Tuckerman, 48) Kennedy writes of his "admiration of 'Tristram Shandy' and the 'Sentimental Journey'. . . . I wrote a great many things in what I thought the same vein—the pages filled with dashes, and an imitation of that eccentric transition, and the parentheses, and the personal conjuration of the reader, which are to be found in all of Sterne's works." On 60-61, Kennedy describes his relish for Dryden's prose works, as well as some of his reading of Latin authors. Unfortunately he later burned practically all of this juvenile writing (62-63). His love for the Play-House (keeping the terminology of Addison, Johnson, and Goldsmith, in preference to the newer word Theatre) is nostalgically described, 91-97. A confirmed Anglophile, he drew upon *Ivanhoe* when he hoped that American troops would go to the aid of England if it were "in danger of being seized upon . . . by a horde of Front de Boeufs, De Bois Guilberts, and Malvoisins."

15. *Rob of the Bowl*, Preface and Chapter I, which are largely a description of his personal attempt to relate his research to the historical and geographical background. In the development of character, however, Kennedy preferred that the person "should speak for himself, rather than leave his merits to be certified" by the author (*Rob of the Bowl*, 19). The best account of Kennedy's use of history for fictional purposes is in Charles H. Bohner's *John Pendleton Kennedy*, 101-11.

16. Caruthers, "A Lecture, Delivered before the Georgia Historical Society, at the Unitarian Church, in Savannah," 1843, 26-28. This 36-page pamphlet had the title, "The History and Progress of Civilization with Regard to this Country." (Hereafter cited as "A Lecture"). By omitting to consider poets at all, Caruthers argued that between Johnson and Scott the English had only Monk Lewis, Radcliffe, Burney, and Edgeworth; our writers (Brown, Cooper, Irving, and Sedgwick) —"compare favorably with theirs." Caruthers also argued that the expensiveness of books in England and their cheapness in the United States (a book costing

$5.00 in England could be bought for 25¢ here) worked to the advantage of English authors: "We have the foreign article so cheap that no one can afford it at home." He also lamented the lack of national enthusiasm in literature, although we were "obedient to the magic wand of a Scott, a Southey, or a Byron."

Indispensable for any study of Caruthers' work is Curtis Carroll Davis's *Chronicler of the Cavaliers: A Life of the Virginia Novelist Dr. William A. Caruthers*, 1953—a thorough and excellent biography. (Hereafter cited as Davis.) For Davis's specialized articles, see his bibliography.

17. Introduction, *The Knights of the Horse-Shoe*, 1845. In less personal terms, he made the same point in "A Lecture."

18. Caruthers, *The Cavaliers of Virginia* (1834), 179-80; *Knights*, 213, 266 (A. L. Burt edition). In "A Lecture," 16, Caruthers noted that Bacon had "overturned the Colonial government . . . a century before the battle of Lexington."

19. "Addenda," *The Kentuckian in New York, or the Adventures of Three Southerns*, 1834, II, 218-19. Caruthers put forth the *Kentuckian* with the "intention of betraying" his readers "into a smile of good-humour with us." His concluding sentence on 217 reads: "And now, gentle reader, we will take a gentle leave of you, hoping that you have not been altogether displeased with the adventures of the Kentuckian and the Southerns."

20. *Kentuckian*, I, 181. See Davis, 98-129.

21. *Kentuckian*, II, 10-12, 104, and Addenda. Davis, 91, quotes Caruthers in 1841 on Paulding: "Though we were politically opposed to each other, we had been personal & literary friends for years, used to meet together at the coteries of the Harpers—published books together. . . ." Davis assumes that the two men collaborated, but it probably means that both were published by Harper.

22. Addenda to *The Kentuckian*; Caruthers also indicates that he had planned to call the book *The Recluse of Jamestown, a Tale of the Early Cavaliers of Virginia*. As published, the sub-title accurately and descriptively reads, *An Historical Romance of the Old Dominion*. On I, 3, he emphasizes this: "The romance of history pertains to no human annals more strikingly than to the early settlement of Virginia. The mind of the reader at once reverts to the names of Raleigh, Smith, and Pocahontas. The traveller's memory pictures in a moment the ivy-mantled ruins of old Jamestown."

23. *Cavaliers*, I, 222 n. and 127; for examples of footnotes, I, 35, 87, 179. For his deviations from historical fact, see Davis, esp. 136-42 and 147-62. In painting Bacon as an early and noble democratic leader, Caruthers was simply accepting contemporary historical belief.

24. "A Pair of Critics," Richmond *Compiler*, April 18, 1835. The adverse reviews had appeared in the Richmond *Whig*, the *Literary Journal*, and the *Southern Literary Messenger*. For details, see Davis, 183-90.

25. "Excerpts from the Portfolio of an Old Novelist," *Family Companion and Ladies Mirror*, II (April, May, June), 56-57, 79-80, 173; quotations on 56, 79. This helps to explain, adds Caruthers (II, 79) "why ours is such a novel-reading age." Literature can also ease the pain of those thwarted in love (*Kentuckian*, I, 9-10).

26. *Family Companion*, II, 173, 80.

27. *Family Companion*, II, 56-57, 79-80. In "A Lecture," 27, Caruthers declared that Scott, "the great wizard of Abbotsford, monopolized the whole ground and revolutionized the world" of fiction.

28. *Family Companion*, II, 57. Caruthers adds: "It is equally true that some master mind of the age in which he lives, may clothe a hero of infamous principles in all the alluring colors of virtue and morality, and thus confound the demarcations of right and wrong—of virtue and vice . . . some Byron-mad fool might make the thing yet more ridiculous by adopting old Judas into the family of heroes." All readers are indebted to Scott, G. P. R. James, Sedgwick, and Edge-

worth for the "purity of morals with which they have invested their principal characters."

29. The original manuscript was destroyed when his house and papers burned before 1841. *The Knights* had been promised in the Addenda to *The Cavaliers*. Caruthers explained the difficulty of preparing it for serial publication in the *Magnolia* (Jan.-Oct., 1841): "I have pruned it [before book publication] as carefully as my professional pursuits would allow. . . . I was shocked when I came to reread it carefully myself. The fact is I used to dash off my supply for the magazine, with the press almost standing waiting for me" (quoted in Davis, 202-03).

30. See the Introduction and the last two pages of *The Knights of the Horse-Shoe* (1845), and Davis, 214, 216-27.

31. "The Ruins of Jamestown," *Magnolia*, III (Jan., 1841), 14-15. The same nostalgic delight in antiquarianism appears in the Introduction to *The Knights*.

32. Quoted in John O. Beaty; *John Esten Cooke, Virginian*, 1922. Dr. Beaty gives no references, and his bibliography is incomplete, but this is the only available biography, and many of his critical estimates are first-rate. Cooke wrote the article on Washington Irving for Appleton's *New American Cyclopedia*.

33. *Southern Literary Messenger*, XXII (July, 1856), 68-72; *Henry St. John, Gentleman* (1859), VII-VIII. This quarrel with the formal historians was a continuing one with Cooke: in 1883, as in 1859, "To understand the history of the country it is therefore necessary to study the Virginia and New England of the seventeenth and eighteenth centuries." But to do this with understanding, the "fancied dignity of history must be lost sight of. The student must come in contact with the actual Virginians; discover their habits and prejudices; how they dressed and amused themselves . . . see them at church" (*Virginia: A History of the People*, 1883, IV-V). Cooke's justification of his type of history is almost identical with his justification of the historical romance.

34. Cooke, *Poe as a Literary Critic*, edited with an Introduction and Notes by N. Bryllion Fagin, 1946, 6. The kindly Cooke was repelled by what seemed to him "some of the fiercest and most savage, and most unfair literary criticism ever published in America" (1-2). He felt that Poe's "wonderful genius as a weird poet, and story teller, has dazzled everybody" (4). Cook lists some of his better poems and stories, and judges that "For a wondrous power of analysis, a weird and strange fancy, and a startling combination of the supernatural and the matter-of-fact, they are probably unsurpassed, if indeed they have been equalled by any other writer in any country" (4-5). But as critic Poe "searches for weak points in every writer," and his work abounds in personal sneers; also, he does not hesitate to contradict his own published judgments (6-9). Cooke concluded that Poe should have confined himself to poetry and fiction, but he "descended into the valley to busy himself with the petty spites and rivalries of the hour, as a literary critic. He chose this character of a severe critic and assailed everybody. It is only fair that he should be criticized in turn, as a critic." Never once does Cooke show any comprehension of Poe's aesthetic, his concept of criticism, or his basis of judgment.

35. Beaty, 23-24. Beaty notes (101) that even "during the war he was never bitter against McClellan, Meade, or Grant, just as in peace he still upon every occasion assailed the brutality of Sheridan and Pope."

36. "To the Reader," in *Leather-Stocking and Silk*, (1853), 5; Beaty, 33-37, with a quotation from Cooke: "The story was suggested by my father's account of old Hunter John Myers, whom he had known." Beaty also lists several personal experiences that Cooke used, but emphasized his indebtedness to Irving and Cooper. In a somewhat similar but far weaker book, *The Last of the Foresters; or Humors on the Border* (1885), Cooke desired only to provide "innocent entertainment" by depicting the "traits of life and manners" in an unfamiliar and picturesque region (Preface, V).

37. Preface, *The Virginia Comedians* (1854), 5-9. Cooke was modest about his own achievement: "The summits of Art rise to view often as the poor writer passes onward; but only the Titans—Shakespeare and the rest—can scale them."

38. *Virginia Comedians,* 8-9. In his very sketchy treatment of creative writing (*Virginia,* 494-98), Cooke concludes: "If no great original genius has arisen to put the lion's paw on Virginia letters, many writers of admirable attainments and solid merit have produced works which have instructed and improved their generation; and to instruct and improve is better than to amuse. Whatever may be the true rank of the literature, it possesses a distinct character. It may be said of it with truth that it is notable for its respect for good morals and manners; that it is nowhere offensive to delicacy or piety; or endeavors to instill a belief in what ought not to be believed." Cooke glanced briefly at Elizabethan literature (10-11; Shakespeare was the master teacher in an age when few could read); at the earliest Virginia writers, 133-40; and at colonial writing, 358-64. William Byrd was "a man of brilliant wit, of high culture, and the richest humor, a Virginian of Virginians," even though his work "sparkles all over with wit and the broadest humor, much too broad and comic indeed for a drawing-room table in the nineteenth century. But it is a virile and healthy book." He thought that "Virginia fiction may be said to have begun" with the novels of Caruthers; Tucker's *Partisan Leader* was a "work of very curious interest" (495-96). Cooke barely notices poetry, although he and John R. Thompson had done enough work on an anthology that *Southern Field and Firside,* I (March 17, 1960), 341, noticed it as though it were completed: they are "the editors of a volume entitled 'The Poets and Poetry of the South,' soon to be issued by Darby and Jackson, of New York." Presumably the war stopped work on the book, and Cooke and Thompson never returned to it.

39. Prologue, *Virginia Comedians,* 13-16. In the Preface to the 1883 edition, Cooke admitted that he could not give the work that "nice finish which is the cameo-work of literature." Beaty suggests (45, 23-24) that the elaborate paraphernalia was suggested by Carlyle's *Sartor Resartus,* but this pseudo-editorial apparatus was a commonplace in the historical romance.

40. *Henry St. John, Gentleman,* IX-XI, 285. In the Epilogue, 488-89, he adds: "I wished my pages to embody, if that were possible, some of the secret influences which bore on great events—to paint the humble and unnoticed source of the great stream of revolution. . . . To paint, too, the gallant youths and lovely maidens—their gay love encounters, in the old, old days. . . ." Beaty quotes (69-70) from an article by the somewhat more realistic George W. Bagby in the Richmond *Whig,* entitled "Unkind but Complete Destruction of John Esten Cooke, Novelist." Bagby wrote: "I now come to the most profuse and abandoned novelist of them all, to wit, Effingham Cooke. . . . I am about to demolish him. I shall do so by preferring against him two charges, both entirely true, and of so grave a nature that no man, and particularly no novelist, can live under the weight of them. . . . Mr. Cooke's eyes are in the back of his head. . . . They are also afflicted with a pair of rose-colored glasses of enormous magnifying powers." Bagby attacks the glorification of past times and people at the expense of the present: "I marvel much that such a set of homely, selfish, money-loving cheats as we are, should have descended from such remarkably fine parents. No doubt it is very good noveling, but I swear it is wretched physiology."

41. He did not hesitate also to use devices worn threadbare by other novelists: for example, in spite of the ridicule heaped upon G. P. R. James for opening so many books with a solitary horseman at sunset, Cooke as late as 1877 used this device in the first chapter of *Canolles.*

42. *The Youth of Jefferson,* 1854. See Beaty, 48-49. Cooke wrote the article on

Jefferson in Appleton's *New American Cyclopedia;* he also wrote articles on Madison, Marshall, Monroe, and four of the Lee family.

43. Beaty, 38-39. Cooke not only used a theatrical company in *The Virginia Comedians;* he also uses an amateur theatrical performance effectively in *Leather-Stocking and Silk.*

44. See Beaty, 23-25, 33, 136-37. Beaty notes that a short interview resulted in "Thackeray and his 'People'," "A Talk with Thackeray," "An Hour with Thackeray," and other articles.

45. See Beaty, 73-109; Preface, *Hilt to Hilt,* 7-10. In a non-fiction work, *Wearing of the Gray,* Cooke admits the lightness of these war romances: "The trifling species will come first. . . . But then will come the better order of things, when writers like Walter Scott will conscientiously collect the real facts, and make some new 'Waverley' or 'Legend of Montrose'." Cooke hopes to provide material for the good novelists ("One of Stuart's Escapes"). George Cary Eggleston has recorded a conversation that helps to explain Cooke's failure as a Civil War novelist: "I wasn't born to be a soldier. . . . I can stand bullets and shells and all that, without flinching, just as any man must if he has any manhood in him; and as for hardships and starvation, why, a man who has self-control can endure them when duty demands it, but I never liked the business of war. Gold lace on my coat always made me feel as if I were a child tricked out in red and yellow calico with turkey feathers in my headgear to add to the gorgeousness. There is nothing intellectual about fighting. It is fit work for brutes and brutish men. And in modern war, where men are organized in masses and converted into insensate machines, there is really nothing heroic or romantic or in any way calculated to appeal to the imagination" (quoted in Beaty, 109). So Cooke stuck mainly with partisan bands, guerilla actions, cavalry raids, and individual exploits.

46. *The Heir of Graymount,* 1870. See Beaty, 121-28.

47. Quoted in Beaty, 128. *Canolles* may seem equally melodramatic to the reader, but did not to Cooke: the characters might seem phantoms to the reader, but to him they "are rather real personages of flesh and blood" (269).

48. *My Lady Pokahontas,* 1885. See Beaty for the romance between John Smith and Pocahontas. Cooke only claims in the Preface that the book seems "to give the details of events and incidents briefly indicated in the contemporary chronicles," but that the historical statements "are often minutely corroborated by the great original American authority, the 'Generall Historie of Virginia, New England, and the Summer Isles.'" Yet in this late period he did not give up his claims as a romancer; *Canolles,* a story of the Revolutionary War in Virginia, "aims to present rather a series of pictures and portraits than to record historic events" (32); also to set a high value on the dramatic story: "let us not forget, what seems about to be forgotten at the present time, that this dramatic interest is a legitimate and most important element of compositions aiming to delineate the fortunes as well as the characters of men and women. When not forgotten it is denied, and we are told that metaphysical analysis and subtle apothegm are the true material with which the best fiction should be built. Is that so certain? Do not Shakespeare, Fielding, Scott and all the masters tell us stories? The story is the canvas meant to catch the mind and bear along the vessel; in the hold you may stow away, if you choose, the wealth of Ophir and Golconda" (64-65). Cooke's tendency to address the reader directly did not decrease with age. Remembering the great popularity in Virginia during the war of Victor Hugo's *Les Miserables* and the punning use of the title made by the Confederate soldiers, Cooke called one chapter in *Mohun* "Lee's Miserables"; this was reprinted as a "grim piece of humor" in the *Banner of the South,* Oct. 31, 1868.

49. Quoted in Beaty, 161-62. Beaty adds: "Strange as it may seem, the very fact that Cooke had never discarded the romantic tradition, led him to be regarded as a pioneer in the romantic revival which was headed by Stevenson."

50. Kennedy, *Swallow Barn*, 8-9. With the country aping the city, "the whole surface of society is exhibiting the traces of a process by which it is likely to be rubbed down, in time, to one level and varnished with the same gloss. It may thus finally arrive at a comfortable insipidity of character which may not be willingly reckoned as altogether a due compensation for the loss of that rough but pleasant flavor which belonged to it in its earlier era."

6. SIMMS

1. C. Hugh Holman, "The Status of Simms," in *American Quarterly*, X (July, 1958), 181-85. Quotation on p. 183.

2. *Letters*, I, 271. He wrote to James Henry Hammond in 1847 that "my income from Literature which in 1835 was $6000 per annum, is scarce $1500 now, owing to the operation of cheap reprints which pay publishers and printers profits only and yield the author little or nothing."

3. *Letters*, V. 409, for this and following quotation. See also Bradsher, *Mathew Carey*, 96. Simms's *History of South Carolina* continued to be used for several decades.

4. *Letters*, V, 409.

5. *Letters*, III, 388.

6. This and the immediately following quotations are taken from Alexander Cowie's first-rate edition of *The Yemassee* (1937), pp. 3-7. C. Hugh Holman has also edited, with a valuable introduction, *The Yemassee* (1961).

7. *Letters*, III, 412.

8. Simms, "The Writings of James Fenimore Cooper," in *Views and Reviews*, 210-11. First published in *The Magnolia*, NS I (Sept. 1842), 129-39. Simms's belief in inspiration as a major factor in artistic creativity was stated frequently. He believed that an author "may create, but he cannot control. It is upon this very condition that he is permitted to create. The Being, once filled with the breath of life, and having made his appearance on the stage of human action, must thenceforward conform to necessities over which the author exercises no authority" (*Vasconselos*, 366).

9. Introduction, *The Partisan*, VII. In a plea for the supernatural (*The Wigwam and the Cabin*, 2-3), Simms wrote: "Our story-tellers are so resolute to deal in the real, the actual only, that they venture on no subjects the details of which are not equally vulgar and susceptible of proof. . . . I very much doubt whether the poet, the painter, the sculptor, or the romancer, ever yet lived, who had not some strong bias—a leaning, at least,—to a belief in the wonders of the invisible world. Certainly, the higher orders of poets and painters, those who create and invent, must have a strong taint of the superstitious in their composition."

10. *Letters*, I, 54. In *The Golden Christmas*, 154, Simms places a higher value on characterization than his own fictional practice might seem to warrant: "The artist does not make events; they make themselves. They belong to the characterization. The author make the character. If this be made to act consistently,—and this is the great necessity in all works of fiction—events flow from its action necessarily, and one naturally evolves another, till the whole action is complete. Here is the whole secret of the novelist." In "Modern Prose Fiction" (*SQR*, XV, 44; April, 1849) he notes: "To seem like truth was, still, as it has ever been, in every age, the object of fiction."

11. *Confession*, 8-9.

12. See, for example, *Richard Hurdis*, 10, and especially *Mellichampe*, 6: In defending bringing "the vulgar and the vicious mind" into the story, Simms declares that "I am persuaded that vulgarity and crime must always preponderate—dreadfully preponderate—in the great majority during a period of war."

13. *Letters*, I, 67. In his appreciative essay, "Weems, the Biographer and Historian" (*Views and Reviews*, II, 137), he noted that Weems exercised the "privilege of the old Historians" in "putting speeches into the mouths of his heroes . . . this deceived nobody. The deception was a very innocent one; for, it so happened, that his parties, thus furnished with speech, invariably talked like Weems himself."

14. *Mellichampe*, 2, for this and following quotation.

15. *Katherine Walton*, 474.

16. *Mellichampe*, 3. Simms has a parenthetical reference to the true story in *Katherine Walton*, 279.

17. *Richard Hurdis*, 401n. In the Advertisement, 10-11, Simms emphasizes the fact that he had written out of direct personal knowledge: "I knew Stuart, the captor of Murrell, personally . . . some of my scenes, and several of my persons were sketched from personal observation . . . the facts here employed are beyond question." In the Dedication to *The Wigwam and the Cabin* he similarly asserts (pp. 4-5): "I have seen the life—have *lived* it— and much of my material is the result of a very early personal experience."

18. *SQR*, XXIV (July 1853), 218. For a full account of Simms's handling of *Uncle Tom's Cabin*, see S.P.C. Duvall, "W. G. Simms's Review of Mrs. Stowe," *American Literature*, 30 (March, 1958), 107-17.

19. *SQR*, XXIV, 217. Simms frequently described his own novels as dramas. In a notice of *Love Me Little, Love Me Long* ("Literary Docket," Charleston *Mercury*, June 21, 1859), Simms thought Charles Reade had borrowed "too many of his tastes and habits from the stage. The modern novel is, in truth, dramatic in its character, and has thus done more than anything besides to unseat the drama in the popular affection."

20. See *Eutaw*, 116, 117.

21. *Richard Hurdis*, 11-12. See also p. 72: "Let me unfold the doings of others, necessarily connected with my own, which are proper to be made known to the reader in this place, though only known to me long after their occurrence."

22. For one example, see *Eutaw*, 339-40.

23. *Letters*, I, 63. This lack of personal familiarity might also be a psychological handicap. In a "Lorris" Letter, Charleston *Mercury*, Dec. 29, 1859, he thought G P. R. James' *Ticonderoga* not among his "happiest efforts," for in his first attempt to employ American materials, James "seems to have lacked confidence in his *American* resources." Similarly, when Cooper turned to Europe for literary material, he by no means failed but the stories were "inferior in interest—there was less felicitous display of scenery, and, as the author was less confident of his knowledge, much of the description was vague, and the characters, framed under hurried glimpses and imperfect observation, were necessarily formal and frigid, wanting in earnestness and life, slow in action, and feeble in will and purpose" (*Views and Reviews*, I, 225). In the Preface (vi) to *Count Julian*, Simms indicated that he might have erred ("with the view of obtaining novelty in my material") in trying to deal with the unfamiliar: "An author, to whom the *locale* of his action is so very important (as it is with me) to the spirit of his narrative, is perhaps always more happy in his achievements when he looks at home." See also his comments to J. P. Kennedy, *Letters*, II, 159-60.

24. *Views and Reviews*, I, 42-43. In explaining what he had attempted to do in his semi-fictional treatment of the Huguenots in Florida, Simms noted that "It is by raising the tone of the history, warming it with the hues of fancy, and making it dramatic by the continued exercise of art, rather than by any actual violation of

its recorded facts, that I have endeavored to awaken interest." He had attempted "to supply, from the *probable*, the *apparent* deficiencies of the *actual*" (*The Lily and the Totem*, v).

25. *Views and Reviews*, I, 23-25. See also *Letters*, V, 399-400. Re-surveying the subject in two articles, "American Resources in Fiction" (*Southern Society*, Nov. 9, 1867, and Dec. 7, 1867), Simms notes that various phases of early American history are becoming more suitable for art as the details fade with time. But we are too impatient, forgetting that it took a thousand years of national growth to produce a Shakespeare. The true builder or creator will appear in time: "the true Prospero, with his rod of divination, will drive Caliban to his cave, and release Ariel from his oak."

26. *SQR*, XVII (July, 1850), 318.

27. *Vasconselos*, I.

28. *Letters*, II, 264-65. He objected particularly to such scientific historians as Barthold Niebuhr: "It is not our purpose to disparage the learned ingenuity, the keen and vigilant judgment, the great industry, the vast erudition and sleepless research of this coldly inquisitive man,—yet, what a wreck has he made of the imposing structure of ancient history, as it comes to us from the hands of ancient art. . . . We prefer one Livy to a cloud of such witnesses as M. Niebuhr" (*Views and Reviews*, I, 23n).

29. *Letters*, IV, 181. In a discussion of Byron's work, however, he noted that a man writes best about "one's self, one's country, and one's religion," for then he writes out of "the fulness of his own soul" (*Views and Reviews*, I, 38-39). See also *Count Julian*, vi-vii.

30. *Magnolia*, NS I (Dec., 1842), 329.

31. *Views and Reviews*, I, 212. For following quotations, 214; 215-16.

32. *Letters*, IV, 589. See also IV, 580.

33. *Mellichampe*, 4-5. Raymond C. Palmer, *The Prose Fiction Theories of William Gilmore Simms* (Unpub. Dissertation, Indiana University, 1946), 41, notes that "Simms nowhere makes a concise definition of his meaning of design," and gave it major importance only in "Modern Prose Fiction" (*SQR, XV* [April, 1845], 41-83). But he adds: "*Design* is used in this paper because Simms employs it more often than other words of similar meaning, such as "*imagination, creative imagination, constructive imagination, concept*, and *fabric*. . . . The design is composed of two parts: the purpose of the artist in creating his work of art and the over-all plan by which he means to carry out his purpose." For Palmer's discussion of design, see pp. 41-45. Alexander Cowie, Introduction, *The Yemassee*, xxiv, prefers the word *invention*.

34. *Letters*, III, 242n. Simms admitted (*The Wigwam and The Cabin*, 4) that he found it "much easier to invent a new story than to repair the defects of an old one."

35. *Views and Reviews*, I, 218.

36. *SQR*, XV (April, 1849), 74-75. In the Introduction to *Confession*, p. 7, he noted that "The work grew beneath his hands to a size far exceeding his original purpose. . . . A work so growing, without design, may be strictly legitimate, as the natural progress of the author's mind to the solution of his problem, yet fail in every essential, as a work of interest for the reader, or even of art. The mere logical array of facts, distribution and arrangement of the proper relations of parties and events—all these, however well done, may yet constitute no more claim to art than may be urged in behalf of a well-put law argument."

37. *Letters*, IV, 168, 191n.

38. *Letters*, II, 308. This would preclude digressions, but would not preclude moral or philosophical commentary by the author, who will "strive to rise from his mere narrative—he will pause in the analysis of character—he will linger in

contemplation of the beautiful and noble, and will strive to persuade, or compel, his reader to linger and enjoy it also." "Bulwer's Genius and Writings," *Magnolia,* NS I (Dec., 1842), 331.

39. *Letters,* I, 316.

40. *Letters,* V, 207.

41. *Letters,* I, 400. In *Confession,* 124, although speaking through a fictional character, he strikingly phrased this belief: "The genius that suffers itself to be fettered by the *precise,* will perhaps learn how to polish marble, but will never make it live, and will certainly never live very long itself."

42. *Letters,* II, 528.

43. *SQR,* XVII (July, 1850), 360.

44. *Magnolia,* NS I (Dec., 1842) , 331-32.

45. *Idem.*

46. Preface, *The Partisan,* viii.

47. Quotations in this paragraph are from *The Magnolia,* NS I (July, 1842), 51-52.

48. *SQR,* XV (April, 1849), 41-83. Very late in life, he again stated this belief, in "The Cub of the Panther," *The Old Guard* (1869), VII, 815: Tell "the whole *truth,* and nothing but the truth; 'nothing extenuate,' and 'nothing set down in malice'; and the moral grows inevitable. It is always present in the perfect fiction."

49. Advertisement, *Mellichampe,* 5-6.

50. *Letters,* I, 255-57. Also in *The Magnolia,* III (Aug., 1841), 376-80.

51. *Letters,* I, 265. Also in *The Magnolia;* see above note.

52. *Letters,* I, 258-59.

53. Cowie, Introduction, *The Yemassee,* xxiii-xxv.

54. *SQR,* XV (April, 1849), 72-73. Simms frequently emphasized the need for "naturalness": "what is fiction, but the nice adaptation, by an artist, of certain ordinary occurrences in life, to a natural and probable conclusion. . . . The naturalness must be that of life as it is shown in such picturesque situations as are probable—seemingly real—and such as the artist has chosen for his guide. . . . We require as close reasoning, and deductions as logically drawn, in tale and novel, as in a case at law or in equity. . . . What we show must not only be the truth, but it must also seem like the truth" (*The Wigwam and the Cabin,* 71-72).

55. See, in order named, *SQR* (April, 1849), XV, 83; *Letters,* I, 154; *Views and Reviews,* I, 213-14, and II, 151.

56. *Views and Reviews,* I, 215.

57. *Ibid.,* I, 33. In the published version of "The Moral Character of Hamlet" (*Orion,* IV, 89) he states flatly that *The Fair Maid of Perth* is "the most *artistical,* beyond comparison, of any of the romances of its author." But in the later revised and unpublished manuscript in the Charles Carroll Simms collection in the South Caroliniana Library, he modified his earlier high praise to "one of the most ingenious of the many wondrous legends of the author."

58. W. P. Trent, *William Gilmore Simms,* 7; quoted from Hayne's article in the *Southern Bivouac,* NS I (Oct., 1885), 261.

59. See particularly chs. XXI-XXII and XLV.

60. *Views and Reviews,* I, 223 and II, 161, 175.

61. *Views and Reviews,* II, 161-62, 175. Quotations in following paragraph from pp. 174, 175, and 165, in that order.

62. *SQR,* NS IX (Jan., 1854), 224-28. In *Views and Reviews,* II, 159-60, he declares roundly: "There is something decidedly unfriendly to art, in the present popular mode of writing for *serial* publication. . . . The author soon becomes indifferent to all general proportions in his work,—to all symmetry of outline,—all compactness of plan and execution. He uses irrelevant matter,—forgets or neglects his main purpose,—yields to frequent changes of plan—to frequent weariness,—and,

satisfied in the preparation of a few spirited sketches, such as may keep attention wakeful,—becomes heartily indifferent to consistency of tone, harmony of parts and colour, uniformity of execution, or appropriate finish and denouement. The winding up of plots, framed in this manner, is usually feeble and defective. . . . It is the fault of the whole tribe,—Dickens, Ainsworth, and the rest."

63. *SQR*, XV (April, 1849), 270.

64. On *Hard Times*, a "Lorris" Letter, Charleston *Mercury*, Dec. 29, 1854; *SQR*, XIX (April, 1851), 568. Reviewing *A Tale of Two Cities* in the Charleston *Mercury*, May 9, 1860, Simms wrote that "Mr. Dickens cannot make a dull book, though he may sometimes lead his readers into the long-drawn-out meshes of a tedious one." Simms thought it "less artist-like" and "less profound and unique, than his average performances—still the interest of the reader is maintained throughout."

65. *SQR*, XIX (Jan., 1851), 74-100.

66. *SQR*, XIX (April, 1851), 559.

67. Review of *The Newcomes* in Charleston *Mercury*, Feb. 26, 1856.

68. Charleston *Mercury*, Jan. 5, 1860.

69. *Views and Reviews*, II, 168.

70. Charleston *Mercury*, Jan. 5, 1860.

71. *SQR*, NS VII (April, 1853), 515, 521-22; VIII (July, 1853), 266. In the Charleston *Mercury*, Jan. 5, 1860, Simms wrote that Thackeray's "stories are all excellent specimens of mental joinery and construction. The parts fit beautifully. . . . Symmetry, propriety, a nice adaptation of means to ends; perfect fitness of action to character, and of character to plan; keen insight of the social moral; a judgment that rarely errs in the proper sentiment for his parties, or proper person for his agent; or a proper *denouement* for his piece; these are among his chief excellences as an author of fiction."

72. *Magnolia*, NS I (Dec., 1842), 329-45.

73. *Ibid.*, 329.

74. *Letters*, II, 227.

75. *SQR*, NS VIII (July, 1853), 266; *Magnolia*, NS I (Dec., 1842), 332. As early as 1829, Simms had praised *The Disowned* and *Pelham* (*Southern Literary Gazette*, I, Feb., 1829, 321-23): "The author writes well, and is evidently a man of first rate genius. . . . We think the conception of character over-charged and extravagant, but the execution excellent." After the war, Simms wrote brief notices of various reprints of Bulwer's works. *Ernest Maltravers* had survived thirty years; it was a good minor novel, but not "entitled to rank in the same category with a production like the 'Wilhelm Meister' of the great German author" (Charleston *Courier*, June 9, 1868).

76. *SQR*, VII (April, 1845), 312-49. Quotation on p. 348.

77. *Ibid.*, 344-45.

78. *SQR*, XV (April, 1849), 70-72. Simms adds, however, that while Lever's later novels show a greater mastery of construction and design, they have less vigor than his earlier work.

79. *Views and Reviews*, II, 164. In the Jan., 1852, *SQR* (NS V, 263) he complained also of monotony: "crime is committed, the innocent is accused, and is only saved, at the last minute, by the guilty man turning up. The action and interest in seven out of ten of his tales have hinged upon this single condition." But James' novels were always "readable."

80. *SQR*, NS VII (April 1853), 515. As early as July, 1842 (*Magnolia*, NS I, 53-56) Simms had called James a "most prolific writer" and "as a mere *raconteur*," about the best in England. Even then, Simms was complaining that James' works were alike. He had succeeded in imitating Scott "only in one of the attributes of that great intellect:—In warming the interest of his reader in the progress of the history."

81. *Letters,* III, 425 n.

82. *Letters,* IV, 73-74. The notice referred to in Simms's letter to James was a brief review in the Charleston *Mercury,* July 3, 1858, of *Lord Montagu's Page.*

83. *SQR,* XV (April, 1849), 41-83. See especially p. 75. Simms objected vigorously to the sentimental and immoral novels of Lamartine and George Sand—perverted work that had been heavily influenced, like so much of French fiction, by the bad but powerful work of Rousseau. See *SQR,* XVII (July, 1850), 355-69. In the *Southern Patriot,* Oct. 8, 1845, he complained that Sue's *Wandering Jew* contained "an insidious, and only partially disguised attack on the rites of marriage," and attributed a good part of his popularity in America to his "vigorous crusade against Roman Catholicism, especially the Jesuits." Dumas, amazingly, in spite of interesting parts and good points, sometimes allowed "his historical material to fetter his prerogatives as a romancer. . . . To write a really good historical romance, the author should be careful to make his chronicles subordinate to his persons—to use history sparingly, and only as tributary to the main object of developing individual character, under striking conditions, and with a view to the finest dramatic effects" (Charleston *Mercury,* Feb. 3, 1855).

84. Respectively, "Goethe's Essays on Art," *Southern and Western Magazine,* II (Dec., 1845), 423-24 and the *Correspondence Between Schiller and Goethe,* 424; *Southern Literary Gazette,* I (March, 1829) , 384-85; *SQR,* XX (July, 1851), 248. In *SLG,* he quotes the "admirable analysis of the character of 'Hamlet' " from the novel. In 1851 he praised Carlyle's translation highly, and lamented that there was no good American edition of Goethe's works.

85. *Southern and Western,* II (Nov., 1845), 357-58.

86. *SQR,* XV, (April, 1849), 78; XVII (April, 1850), 255; NS VIII (July, 1853), 267.

87. *SQR,* XIX (April, 1851) , 548; *Letters,* III, 109. In an obituary notice of Charlotte Brontë, Charleston *Mercury,* May 1, 1855, he again praised her highly as a writer of fiction.

88. "Literary Docket," Charleston *Mercury,* June 22, 1859; Charleston *Courier,* April 13, 1869. Writing on *Phineas Finn,* Simms notes that it "is not liable to objections sometimes urged, that of giving false views of life and characters."

89. Respectively, Charleston *Mercury,* May 20, 1859; Charleston *Mercury,* Oct. 3, 1860; Charleston *Courier,* Aug. 31, 1866. Here Simms complains that in all her novels there is "a residue of unpleasantness." Briefly noticing a reprint of *Romola* (Charleston *Courier,* Nov. 11, 1869), Simms attributes its success to "exquisite characterization" rather than to the "dramatic nature of the incident," although he adds that it is "full of beauty."

90. *Views and Reviews,* I, 216-22.

91. *Ibid.,* 212, 225.

92. *SQR,* XVI (Oct., 1849), 269-70. In "A Chat in a Symposium," *Cosmopolitan,* I, 19-21, Simms and his fellow-editors (Charles Rivers Carroll and Edward Carroll) discuss Scott and Cooper. Both novelists, for all their genius, were cursed with too much facility, and had done too much hasty work at the demand of publishers and readers. Cooper in the *Heidenmauer* (1832) had erred in choosing a foreign subject; he had succeeded better in his American novels because "Long and familiar contemplation of his country and its associations, admirably prepared him for their illustrations." See John C. Guilds, Jr., "William Gilmore Simms and the *Cosmopolitan,*" in *Georgia Historical Quarterly,* XLI, 31-41.

93. *Southern Literary Gazette,* I (Sept., 1828), 8.

94. *The Cosmopolitan,*" I, 14-15.

95. *Letters,* I, 144.

96. *The Damsel of Darien,* 9.

97. *Views and Reviews,* II, 177. Simms prefaces the following quotation by noting

that Paulding "enjoys considerable American reputation as a humorist," but that he had "never esteemed him greatly in this character." *Southern Patriot*, May 4, 1847. See also *Southern and Western*, II (Sept., 1845), 216.

98. *Letters*, I, 147.

99. *Letters*, I, 67. Simms's objection that Bird made his characters talk alike has been noted earlier.

100. *Southern Patriot*, March 10, 1846.

101. *Letters*, III, 122.

102. *Letters*, III, 183-84.

103. *SQR*, XXI (April, 1852), 530, and XXII (July, 1852), 203-220.

104. *The Wigwam and the Cabin*, 39. In Ch. I of "The Two Camps," Simms explains that his character and Horse-Shoe "were drawn from not dissimilar sources."

105. *Southern Patriot*, July 20, 1846.

106. *Letters*, II, 174-75.

107. *Letters*, II, 42-43.

108. *Idem*.

109. *Southern and Western*, II (Dec., 1845), 426.

110. *Southern Patriot*, March 2, 1846.

111. *Letters*, II, 99.

112. *SQR*, XX, 265-66 (July, 1851); *SQR*, XXII (Oct., 1852), 543.

113. Charleston *Mercury*, June 7, 1860. In *The Marble Faun*, the major defect is that Hawthorne had "a too great desire to make not only a story, but a picturesque survey of Italy," but it will richly repay those readers, especially, whose views are "somewhat metaphysical."

114. Perry Miller, *The Raven and the Whale* (1956), 107, 147. See also John Stafford, *The Literary Criticism of "Young America"* (1952). Although Simms was aware of the personal criticism rampant in his day, he did not approve of it; he wrote to James Lawson that "criticism now-a-days does not so much depend upon the book as upon the author. It is the man, not the volume, that is most commonly under the knife" (*Letters*, I, 100).

115. *Letters*, I, 440.

116. *Letters*, V, 55.

117. *Southern Patriot*, April 9 and 25, 1846. Miller, *op. cit.*, 158, considers, I think erroneously, these reviews as "the faithful Simms, obeying orders" given by Duyckinck. Miller, evidently unaware of how long Simms had advocated nationalism in literature, exaggerates Simms's subservience to the "Young America" group.

118. *SQR*, XVII (July, 1850), 514-20.

119. *SQR*, XVII (April, 1850), 259-60.

120. *SQR*, XVI (Oct., 1849), 260.

121. *SQR*, XXI (Jan., 1852), 262.

122. *SQR*, XXII (Oct., 1852), 532.

123. *SQR*, XXII (July, 1852), 261.

124. *SQR*, XVI (Oct., 1849), 245-46.

125. *Southern and Western*, I (June, 1845), 434-35; *Letters*, V, 388. In the "Literary Docket," Charleston *Mercury*, Aug. 20, 1859, he praised the purity of her "taste and style, the simplicity and grace of the writer, the quiet domestic interest . . . the just moral developed; and the general good sense, spirit and propriety" of the novelist.

126. "Our Literary Docket," Charleston *Mercury*, July 12, 1859; Charleston *Courier*, June 4, 1867. In the earlier review, Simms mentions De Forest's two travel books.

127. *Letters*, II, 29. The following quotations appear, in order, on II, 96, 105, 117. In *The Magnolia*, NS II (June, 1843), 391-400, Simms praised *The Career of*

Puffer Hopkins as an attempt "to produce a book which should be characteristic and national in its features."

128. *Views and Reviews*, II, 147, 151.

129. *Letters*, IV, 168-69, 181, 191n.

130. *Letters*, IV, 181. Simms believed this to be an important function of the critic: "He is bound to point out faults—if his discrimination is adequate to such a duty; and, if not, he had better go through a course of Pope's Essay on his own art" ("American Criticism and Critics," *Southern Literary Journal*, II (July, 1836), 396).

131. Charleston *Mercury*, Jan. 20, 1860. After the war Simms wrote various notices of new works by Cooke. In the Charleston *Courier*, May 22, 1867, he praised *Surry of Eagle's Nest* for its rapid movement, vigorous action, effective scenes, and graphic incident, but qualifies this by noting that the "narrative, which is wonderfully full, free, and flowing," runs away with Cooke, and makes him too little heedful of his characterization. But Cooke was forced by necessity to write far too rapidly—"a pitiable fate for the author—the poet—the artist."

132. Charleston *Courier*, Nov. 4, 1868.

133. Charleston *Courier*, Feb. 4, 1868. In a letter to Lawson the year before (*Letters*, V, 88) written on the back of a "Prospectus of *Southern Society*," Simms called attention to its "formidable list of writers." Among these were Simms, Cooke, Timrod, Hayne, and Lanier.

134. *Martin Faber*, I, 154. See H. H. Clark, "Changing Attitudes in Early American Literary Criticism," in Floyd Stovall (ed.), *The Development of American Literary Criticism* (1955), 52.

135. See R. H. Fogle, "Organic Form in American Criticism: 1840-1870," in Stovall, *op. cit.*, 65, 82-83. As Fogle notes, this organic concept has recently been perceptively described in Arthur Lovejoy's *Great Chain of Being* (1936).

136. *Views and Reviews*, I, 214-15.

137. *Ibid.*, I, 25.

138. *Letters*, III, 275.

139. *Letters*, IV, 422.

140. *Letters*, 275, 262.

141. *Letters*, I, 223. This is really the second part of an article on Southern Literature, although in the form of a letter to the editor; it was published in *The Magnolia*, III (Feb., 1841) 69-74. Here Simms objects to imitative poetry, and states that no American poet deserves "the glorious epithet of 'Builder' " (p. 216) —a favorite expression with him. In *Views and Reviews*, II, 147-48, he compares a poem to a building, and the poet's "faculty as a *builder* [is] the highest evidence, perhaps, of poetical endowment."

142. *Letters*, IV, 454.

143. *Letters*, IV, 616. This was written to the poet Charles Warren Stoddard, Oct. 24, 1866, giving an evaluation of Stoddard's poetry. In "A Few Words about Poetry," in the Columbia *Phoenix*, April 21, 1865, Simms had written that "Poetry is essentially *winged* thought." In a review appraising Macaulay's "thoughtful, instructive, and eminently valuable historical and philosophical essays" (Charleston *Mercury*, Feb. 20, 1856), Simms recorded his own belief that "philosophy only does mole-fashion, what poetry does eagle-fashion." But he added that the truth "is attainable, by the honest worker, in either region."

144. Trent, 7; *Letters*, III, 261. Earlier he had limited his claim: "I regard poetry as my forte, particularly in the narrative and dramatic forms" (*Letters*, II, 257).

145. See Hayne's letter to Taylor in *The Correspondence of Bayard Taylor and Paul Hamilton Hayne*, ed. by Charles Duffy (1945), 94-95; and D. M. Mc-Keithan, *A Collection of Hayne Letters*, 428. However, in a review of Simms's poems in *Russell's Magazine*, II, 152-60, Hayne compared Simms's poetry with that

of the Elizabethan dramatists in its "directness of diction, its abrupt audacity and defiance of conventional trammels, its compressed vigor."

146. *Letters*, I, 221-22. There are five mss. of "Poetry and the Practical" in the Charles Carroll Simms Collection. An 80-page ms., dated Jan. 4, 1851, was delivered as a lecture in Augusta, Georgia. The second ms. adds little. Simms then revised and enlarged, until he had three mss. of 46 pages, 32 pages, and 50 pages. These were delivered as three lectures in Charleston, May-June, 1854. Page references in the text without Roman numerals refer to the single lecture; with Roman numerals, to the three lectures. In III, 41, Simms marked through Virgil, and substituted Horace.

147. *Letters*, III, 225; first published in *The Magnolia*, III 69-74.

148. Letters, IV, 432. In the Dedication to *Areytos, or Songs of the South* (1846), Simms had described his lyrics as improvisations inspired by "the spontaneous emotion, the sudden flight of fancy, or the voluntaries of sentiment and passion. We must take such performances as so many short bird-flights."

149. In the review in *Russell's*, II, 159, Hayne notes that Simms had an "apparently invincible repugnance to the distasteful duty of correction."

150. Trent, 145-50. Here Trent is considering *Grouped Thoughts and Scattered Fancies* (1845): "There are eighty-four of these quatorzains—for with a few exceptions they cannot be called sonnets." Trent's criticism is somewhat invalidated by his pedantic definition of a sonnet, and more by his statement that he is interested in using the poems to illustrate the defects of Southern poetry. A reader less interested in proving a point may well think that some of the poems are interesting and stimulating.

151. *Southern Patriot*, July 31, 1860.

152. Charleston *Courier*, April 5, 1867. This is a review of *The Book of the Sonnet* (1867), edited by Leigh Hunt and S. Adams Lee. The commentary on American sonnets is by Paul Hamilton Hayne and George Henry Boker. Simms enjoyed speculation about the indebtedness of Spenser to Sidney, and of Elizabethan sonnet-writers to Wyatt and Surrey, and eventually to Petrarch and Dante.

153. *Letters*, V, 356.

154. *Letters*, III, 169. Perhaps Simms overstates his point, since the letter is to Thomas Holley Chivers. However, in the ms. of "Poetry and the Practical," 70, he asserts: "Mere verse-making constitutes but a small part of the poetic faculty."

155. *Letters*, I, 155. Possibly Simms's qualification should be noted: "At least I have sought to make it such, and as such I require that it should be judged." In his review of Wordsworth (SQR, NS II [Sept., 1850], 4-7), Simms discusses possible definitions of poetry, and decides there are no hard-and-fast rules for determining where prose ends and poetry begins, and vice versa. He frequently praised a prose-writer for having poetical qualities: for example, De Quincey is described as a "remarkable essayist, endowed equally with the Poetical and the Metaphysical faculties" (Charleston *Mercury*, Feb. 6, 1855).

156. *Letters*, III, 170

157. *Letters*, V, 409-10.

158. *Letters*, II, 257.

159. *Letters*, IV, 443. In *Views and Reviews*, I, 37, he calls Wordsworth "probably the greatest contemplative poet that has ever lived."

160. Simms, *Poems Descriptive, Dramatic, Legendary, and Contemplative*, 154-57. Simms omits Dryden from his "Heads of the Poets," but considering how often he links "Shakspeare, Milton, and Dryden," there seems good reason for putting Milton second and Dryden third in his ranking of the English poets.

161. *Ibid.*, 159.

162. *Views and Reviews*, I, 37-40.

163. Simms's longest and best treatment of Wordsworth is in his "Poetical Works of Wordsworth," *SQR*, NS II (Sept., 1850), 1-23. Part of the essay is devoted to Henry Taylor. The above quotations are from this essay, and from *SQR*, NS II (Nov., 1850), 540. But Simms constantly uses Wordsworth as a touchstone by which to judge contemplative poets. In the *Columbia Phoenix*, June 15, 1865, Simms in an article, "Wordsworth on Taste and Culture," especially praised the English poet for being inspired by nature unadorned, and not prettified. In *Letters*, II, 137, he praised Wordsworth and Bryant for "associating the moral with the physical."

164. "Wordsworth on Literature," in the Columbia *Phoenix*, June 21, 1865.

165. *SQR*, NS II, (Sept., 1850) 22-23.

166. *Ibid.*, 11: *SQR* NS X (Oct., 1854), 535; *SQR* XVI (Oct., 1849), 260. In *Letters*, I, 282, he wrote Lawson: "I am not so sure that you do not underrate Cowper." Simms notes occasionally the evil influence that French poetry had on English, during and after the Restoration; in *Views and Reviews*, I, 90, he deprecates "the substitution, in England, of French for English poetry—the clinquant of a false, for the hearty ring of the genuine metal."

167. *Ibid.*, 22.

168. *Idem*. In the Charleston *Courier*, April 29, 1868, under the title "Robert Southey's Work," Simms welcomed a reprinting of his work.

169. *Letters*, I, 12. Simms refers to Sir Philip Sidney, and adds that he does not see "any reason for his enthusiasm" for the old ballads. But Byron had some kinship with the balladwriters: his "egotism and passion—his vain pride—his intense kindlings—his stubborn resolution not to do right because his enemies censure his wrong doing—declare the genuine English character" (*Views and Reviews*, I, 39).

170. Simms, *Poems*, II, 158.

171. As late as 1868, Simms was comparing certain of his poems with Byron's as "not descriptive but dramatic, passionate, not contemplative. . . . It is quite as coherent and as much a tale as the Giaour" (*Letters*, V, 151-52).

172. In a review, "Montgomery's Messiah," *Magnolia*, IV (Jan., 1842), 6.

173. *The Wigwam and the Cabin*, 71.

174. *Magnolia*, IV, 6.

175. *Views and Reviews*, I, 82-83.

176. Simms, *Poems*, II, 158.

177. *Views and Reviews*, I, 96.

178. *Poems*, II, 157-58.

179. *The Forayers*, 235. Dennison certainly had "his own artless manner"— a phrase that Simms perhaps injudiciously applies to Burns.

180. *Views and Reviews*, I, 40.

181. In *Letters*, V, 88, he amusingly paraphrases Keats's *Endymion*: "it is a *thing of Promise*, which on a Bank Note, is a thing of Beauty, and so, as Shelley sings, a joy forever."

182. *Letters*, V, 267. He also asked for a copy of Coleridge's work.

183. Simms, *Poems*, II, 159.

184. *Southern Literary Gazette*, I (Sept., 1828), 42. The review (41-47) objects to Hunt's making himself the most important character in the book, and to his reducing Byron to "a level low indeed." Mr. Duncan Eaves ("An Early American Admirer of Keats," *PMLA*, LXVII [Sept., 1952], 895-98) thinks the tone "unmistakably Simms's." I agree, but the entire article cannot be by Simms, for the reviewer notes that Lord Byron was fearless, "as we heard a very intimate friend of his say in London" (p. 43). James W. Simmons, his fellow-editor, may have written all the article, or the two editors may have written it together. Certainly Simms approved of the ideas on Keats and Shelley.

185. In "The Love of Study," *Southern Literary Gazette*, NS I (May 15, 1829),

19, Simms quotes a sonnet "said to have been written by John Keats," but it has not been identified as by Keats. Simms also misquoted slightly two lines from "The Eve of St. Agnes" in "The Progress of Civilization," *American Monthly Magazine,* III (August, 1834), 365.

186. *SQR,* NS II (Sept., 1850) , 21; *SQR,* NS II (Nov., 1850), 535.

187. *Letters,* V, 616.

188. *Letters,* II, 416. Although not mentioned in this letter, Simms included Philip James Bailey and Henry Taylor in his "Heads of the Poets," *Poems,* II, 161.

189. Simms, *Poems,* II, 159.

190. *SQR,* NS II (Sept., 1850), 256-57.

191. *Letters,* IV, 529.

192. *Letters,* V, 150.

193. Charleston *Courier,* Jan. 16, 1867. Apparently Simms did not see *The Queen Mother, Rosamond—Two Plays* (1860) until after he had read some later works. Probably his edition did not indicate that it was a reprint, for he assumed this was a new work. In the Charleston *Courier,* June 19, 1866, he writes that "Atalanta and Chastelard have been justly exceedingly praised and admired, and the present poem has many of the merits and all the defects of its predecessors . . . there is no sense of latent power in these poems."

194. *SQR,* NS II (Sept., 1850), 233-47. In the *Southern Patriot,* Oct. 8, 1845, he called *Festus* "a book for your student of metrical metaphysics," and notes it was modelled after *Faust.*

195. "Later Poems of Henry Taylor," *SQR,* XV (July, 1849) 484-526. See also *SQR,* NS II (Sept., 1850), 21, where he links Tennyson and Taylor as the "greatest poets now living in England," but the structure of their verse "depends upon the noble theory of Wordsworth's best practice." Also, they have received their philosophical ideas and mental discipline from Wordsworth.

196. Simms, *Poems,* II, 160. But Simms noted unfavorably that Campbell "nibbled" some "fine lines" from Philip Freneau.

197. *Southern and Western,* I (May, 1845), 358-59; Charleston *Mercury,* Feb. 16, 1860.

198. Charleston *Mercury,* May 24, 1860.

199. "Our Book Table," Charleston *Courier,* Feb. 24, 1866.

200. *The Partisan,* 390. In *Woodcraft,* 239, he notes incidentally that Thomas Gray's "The Bard" is "much undervalued . . . a production very far superior, in all poetic respects, to the over-lauded elegy of the same writer."

201. *The Scout,* 295. This foppish surgeon, Hillhouse, quotes pedantically and without much understanding from Milton, Pope, Shakespeare and Ovid—pp. 298, 300, 325, 363.

202. *Eutaw,* 335. Simms objects especially to their use of "antiquated divinities" and artificial speech.

203. An amusing example (*Katherine Walton,* 62): a bibulous British officer says to justify his consumption of Madeira and Jamaica: " 'Drink deep,' was the counsel of the little poet of Twickenham."

204. *Letters,* V, 174-77.

205. *Letters,* I, 367, and V, 105.

206. *SQR,* NS II (Sept., 1850), 15.

207. *Letters,* I, 256, 265. Although couched in the form of a letter to the editor, this was really an article and was published in *The Magnolia,* III (Aug., 1841), 376-80.

208. "Copyright Law," *SLM,* X (Jan., 1844), 13.

209. *SQR,* NS IV (Oct., 1851), 538.

210. *Southern Literary Gazette,* I (Dec., 1828), 237-53. Simms also presents a qualified defense of Byron's moral and religious views, 250-51, 253.

211. "Montgomery's Messiah," *Magnolia,* IV (Jan., 1842), 1-14. A note to this article states that "this article was in great part written in 1832, when the Messiah was published." The earlier article appeared in the *Knickerbocker,* IV (Feb., 1834), 120-34, under the cumbrous but accurate title, "John Milton vs. Robert Montgomery. Or a Modest Comparison of Paradise Lost and Regained, of the One, with the Messiah, Now Published in the Sacred Annual, of the Other." All the quotations are from *The Magnolia.*

212. Homer also was one of these. Some poets, like Cowper and Gray, had "genius with little blood." Byron and Burns died young, with their passions unconquered. Simms opens the article cited above by quoting from Andrew Marvell, "that rough and sturdy citizen, and scarcely less rough and sturdy poet."

213. *SQR,* XVII (Oct., 1852), 544. See also *SQR,* XV (April, 1849), 260-61, and XVI (Oct., 1849), 240, where in a review of Lowell's *Fable for Critics* he spoke of Emerson as "really half-witted." Simms was personally and critically exasperated by Lowell's judgments. However, he was on friendly terms with Margaret Fuller; in the *Southern Patriot,* July 9, 1846, he described her as "a woman of thought, who *feels* her subject, and is one of our most human and genial philosophers." Reviewing Thoreau's *Walden* after sectional as well a philosophical lines had tightened (Charleston *Mercury,* Feb. 8, 1855), Simms called it a "queer, well-written book" that revealed Thoreau as "carrying out the antique Puritan philosophy to its proper results, in all social matters." But Thoreau's "intellect we should greatly wrong, did we not describe it as one well calculated to inspire the respect and compel the watchful consideration of yours. His book is full of a speculative interest."

214. *Southern and Western,* II (Nov., 1845), 342-60, esp. 348-49. Simms reviewed *The Conduct of Life* in the Charleston *Mercury,* Jan. 29, 1861, and re-stated his views: "Perhaps the chief merit of Carlyle and Emerson really consists in this. They re-*commend* to our ears a useful commonplace, which had fallen into vulgarity. They enforce an old moral by a new costume. They, briefly, allegorize the sermon and epigrammatize the truth. . . . [Emerson] is rather excursive than deep; and is suggestive rather than profound. You will read him with pleasure and profit, at times; and there is this advantage in his obscurities, that respecting him as a man of fine talents, he provokes you to study."

215. *Letters,* I, 157-58.

216. *Southern Literary Gazette,* I (Nov. 1828), 157-58, 192.

217. *Letters,* V, 208.

218. "W. C. Bryant," *Magnolia,* IV (April, 1842), 193-201, esp. 199-200. Simms practically drags in a compliment to Bryant in a novel (*Eutaw,* 150): after quoting "The groves were God's first temples," he adds that Nelly Floyd "had no knowledge of this beautiful chant of one of our best native poets."

219. Charleston *Mercury,* Dec. 13, 1859.

220. *Letters,* V, 150.

221. *Southern and Western,* II (July, 1845), 67-8.

222. Charleston *City Gazette,* June 30, 1830. This was in a review of James W. Simmons's *The Age of Rhyme.* Simms felt that Simmons had underrated Bryant and Halleck. Ten years later, however, he wrote Lawson (*Letters,* I, 172): "I fully agree with you that he is not to be spoken of in the same breath with Bryant.'

223. *Letters,* I, 172. He also thought that Halleck, "a natural aristocrat," disdained the popular judgment and partly for that reason wrote too little. Sometimes he wrote above the popular taste: "in his satire, the weapon he uses is the small sword, not the bludgeon. It is a polished blade, and, however mortal the thrust, did not mangle the victim." (*Letters,* V, 149-50).

224. *Letters,* I, 172.

225. *Southern and Western,* II (Nov., 1845), 347-49.

226. *Letters,* II, 68.

227. *Letters,* V, 263-64, and a review of Longfellow's *New-England Tragedies* in the Charleston *Courier,* Nov. 19, 1869: "These things are at once dull and feeble, lacking equally in power, pathos and poetry. The wonder is that Mr. Longfellow, who is confessedly an artist—much more decidedly artist than poet—should have exhibited the bad taste of choosing such themes, brutal, if not bald, for the latest exercise of his muse. But the greater wonder is that Mr. Longfellow should so blunder as to attempt the Drama at all."

228. *Letters,* II, 74; II, 90; and I, 71, respectively.

229. *Letters,* I, 233.

230. Charleston *Mercury,* Nov. 22, 1855.

231. *SQR,* NS II (Sept., 1850), 255-56, Charleston *Mercury,* Feb. 8, 1855.

232. *Southern and Western,* II (Nov., 1845), 342-60.

233. Charleston *Courier,* Dec. 30, 1848, and *SQR,* XVI (Oct., 1849), 239-42. See also *Letters,* II, 567.

234. *Letters,* II, 467-69, and *Southern and Western,* II (Nov., 1845), 348-49.

235. *Letters,* III, 414.

236. Charleston *Mercury,* Feb. 24, 1860. Simms notes that *The Autocrat* "never reached us."

237. *Letters,* III, 96-97.

238. *SQR,* NS III (April, 1851), 563-64.

239. *SQR,* NS, VII (Jan., 1853), 265.

240. Charleston *Courier,* April 5, 1867. See Jay B. Hubbell, "Five Letters from George Henry Boker to William Gilmore Simms," *Pennsylvania Magazine of History and Biography,* LXIII (Jan., 1939), 66-71.

241. The quotation is from one of the "Lorris" Letters, Charleston *Mercury,* Dec. 22, 1854. See also SQR, NS VII (Jan., 1853), 265, and especially "Recent American Poets," *SQR,* XVI (Oct., 1849), 224-32. See also a letter to Taylor in *Letters,* III, 333-34.

242. *SQR,* NS VIII (July, 1853), 284.

243. *Letters,* II, 43, 90, and III, 170.

244. *Southern Patriot,* March 2, 1846.

245. *Southern Patriot,* Nov. 10, 1845. This article mainly defends Poe's lecture in Boston, but it also characterizes him as "an admirable critic . . . methodical, lucid, forcible;—well-read, thoughtful, and capable, at all times, of rising from the mere consideration of the individual subject, to the principles, in literature and art, by which it should be governed." Poe had criticized Longfellow and other Boston favorites; moreover, Poe's poetry was "too original, too fanciful, too speculative" to be grasped by the ordinary audience.

246. *Letters,* III, 169-70.

247. *Southern and Western,* II (Oct., 1845) , 278-81. See also *Southern Patriot,* Aug. 7, 1845.

248. *Letters,* III, 168-70; *SQR,* NS VIII (July, 1853), 273. In *SQR,* NS VII (Jan., 1853), 265-66, he remarks that Chivers's *Eonchs of Ruby* "blush their own praise," but that the book must be "kept in lavender for future use."

249. *The Complete Works of Thomas Holley Chivers,* I, 139. This volume of correspondence was edited by Emma Lester Chase and Lois Ferry Parks.

250. *SLM,* IX (Dec., 1843), 715-20; *SQR,* V (Jan., 1844), 103-18. In letters to Duyckinck, Simms complained frequently of Mathews' perversity.

251. Letter to Tuckerman, in *Letters,* III, 70-71. Simms valued Tuckerman much more highly as a writer of prose, and treated this in an extensive review-article, "Tuckerman's Essays and Essayists," *SQR,* NS I (July, 1850), 370-406.

252. *SQR,* NS I (April, 1850), 261.

253. *Letters,* III, 346-47. However, in a letter signed "Lorris," Charleston *Mer-*

cury, May 30, 1856, Simms takes the editor to task for not reviewing at length Meek's *The Red Eagle:* "I do not like to see our native authors, even in their crude beginnings, passed over neglectfully in our domestic courts of criticism. . . . Mr. Meek has a fine imagination, a lively fancy, an excursive thought, and a grace and force of expression which with proper pains-taking must assure him of the highest excellence in style."

254. *Letters,* II, 307-08, and III, 38. In "John Esten Cooke of Virginia" (Charleston *Mercury,* Oct. 21, 1859), Simms wrote that the two brothers shared "in large degree, the poetical faculty," and regretted that John's "claims as a poet have been obscured . . . by his superior successes in prose."

255. This was an idea that Simms frequently stated. Probably the best essay embodying this idea is in *Russell's Magazine,* III (April, 1858), 36-37, in a review of Howard Caldwell's *Poems.* Caldwell had written perceptive essays for *Russell's* on French writers ("Beranger," I [April, 1857], 37-45; "Victor Hugo," I [June, 1857], 259-77), but Caldwell argued in them that poetry attained its maturity in the lyric, in which "the full glories of subjectivity appear" (I, 37), and that the lyric follows "the *caprices of music,* rather than the rules of art" (39) . This view did not coincide with Simms's ideas. Moreover Caldwell's poetry is imitative, lacking in music, and sometimes downright prose, although it also reveals "the glow of youth, the warmth of a genial nature, the sympathies of a true humanity. . . . We say to Mr. Caldwell . . . You are only now *preparing* yourself to write poetry. But what you have written, assures us that you have poetry in you." Caldwell never forgave Simms for this review.

256. See Jay B. Hubbell, *The Last Years of Henry Timrod,* 155-56, 167; *Letters,* II, 563-64; III, 352, 369. His most practical tribute was in editing an anthology of the writings of his fellow-townsmen, *The Charleston Book* (1845). But in the Preface he felt it necessary to stress that many pieces, being the work of amateur writers, have "that air of didactic gravity, that absence of variety, and of the study of artistical attributes" that professional writing should have. To compensate, the reader will find "a liveliness of fancy, a fluency of expression, and a general readiness of resource."

257. "Recent American Poets," *SQR,* XVI (Oct., 1849), 224-32, esp. 228. See also *Letters,* II, 563-64, where Simms writes: "every poetaster of Charleston looks upon me as an enemy. Yet scarcely a Southron has ever received a kind word in the South, unless from my pen; and even [J. M.] Legaré is indebted to me for a genial notice."

258. "The Writings of Washington Allston," *SQR,* IV (Oct., 1843), 363-414. On his poetry, see 381 ff. In praising Allston as a painter, Simms notes: "The great genius thinks rather of the work itself, than of its rewards" (390). Contrasting Allston with amateurs generally, Simms remarks that "Nothing, that we know, has ever come from amateur authorship, but *dilettantism,* affectation, pert pretense, and the most miserable conceit" (396). In *A Supplement to the Plays of William Shakespeare,* 5, Simms declares flatly that the young author or artist learns most from studying imperfect early works, thus acquiring "a proper idea of the toils, the obstacles, and the trials" that even the genius must undergo. He adds: "It is mere *dilettantism* alone, which shrinks from such a development—preferring only the knowledge of the perfect results of labor, without being troubled with its processes."

259. Quoted in Trent, 297.

260. *Letters,* V, 426.

261. *Letters,* V, 97.

262. Simms's tribute, "The Late Henry Timrod," was published in *Southern Society,* I (Oct. 12, 1867), 18-19; it is reprinted in Jay B. Hubbell's *The Last Years of Henry Timrod,* 153-65.

263. Hubbell, 154-56, 158. In *Letters*, IV, 592, Simms commented on Timrod's lack of flexibility, and added: "He is one of the best of the Southern Poets, refined and highly polished, with fine meditative tone, and a pure and graceful fancy."

264. *Letters*, V, 290. In this letter Simms advised Hayne that "you should, as you could, make your reputation out of the story of Sappho. . . . The point, if you will remember, is the conflict between Sappho's passions and her intellect" (289). Apparently Hayne did not take the advice.

265. To Hayne in *Letters*, IV, 430-32. Simms was in part defending himself against Hayne's criticism of his own lyrics as fugitive poems. They were instead, Simms claimed, *"Happy inspirations."*

266. *Southern Patriot*, July 31, August 1, 2.

267. *Letters*, IV, 540.

268. Preface, *War Poetry of the South*, VI.

269. *Letters*, III, 70.

270. Simms was by no means alone in making this distinction, and in this country Hawthorne's comments have been even more influential. But Simms's observations were independently made, and still have value.

271. *Letters*, I, 156-57. Here, Simms was perturbed because Lawson proposed to write an article "finding fault with Bryant." Lawson's "rashness of judgment . . . tempts you to be too soon satisfied with the light you have upon a subject, and leads you to a decision before you have sufficiently examined it under all lights." In the Epilogue to *Metamora*, line 36, Lawson had written that "The critic's merit is to find a fault" (*Letters*, V, 436).

272. *Egeria*, 19; second sentence quoted in Hubbell, *The South in American Literature*, 594. Simms's prescriptions may have been wise, but I find his advice to other writers the least attractive part of his reviews.

275. *Letters*, II, 230. Simms later tried to interest various publishers in another collection of his critical articles, but without success.

7. COOKE

1. *Southern Literary Messenger* (hereafter referred to as *SLM*), I, 324 and 388. Cooke's handwriting was not easy to read, with the result that "A Song of the Seasons" was printed as by Zarry Zyle, instead of Larry Lyle (232, 388, 402). When the critic objected to Cooke's use of "bugle-bee," the author first noted that Keats had used it in the "Eve of St. Agnes"; he then re-wrote the quatrain using the suggested word "bumble-bee," so that "he had come at *bumble* call." As Cooke ironically notes, this is "a vast improvement." He justifies the use of "soughing blasts" by the authority of Wyatt and Shakespeare.

2. See John D. Allen, *Philip Pendleton Cooke* (1942), 23-28 (hereafter cited as Allen, *Cooke*). This and Allen's much longer, unpublished Vanderbilt dissertation are indispensable for any study of Cooke's life and works. I am also indebted to him for making available to me a complete typescript of Cooke's writings. Material not in the published biography will be cited as Allen, *Dissertation*. I have also made extensive use of David K. Jackson's valuable article, "Philip Pendleton Cooke," in *American Studies in Honor of William Kenneth Boyd* (1940), and a rather slight use of May Alcott Thompson's unpublished Columbia M.A. thesis (1923).

3. Allen, *Cooke*, 24-27. The only one of these youthful poems that had any merit, in his estimation, was "Rosalie Lee."

4. *SLM*, XXVII (June, 1858), 419-32; quotation on 420. This essay, and Rufus W. Griswold's in *The International Magazine*, IV (Oct., 1851), 300-03, seem to me the best contemporary accounts of Cooke. I have used the reprinted version of Griswold's article in *SLM*, XVII (Oct.-Nov., 1851), 669-73.

5. *SLM*, IX (Dec., 1843), 744; *Froissart Ballads*, 174-78 (in a revised version).

6. Preface, *Froissart Ballads;* Allen, 80n. For a good example of his use of literary allusions, see "Life in the Autumn Woods."

7. *SLM*, XII (April, 1846), 202. In a note here, and on the title page of *Froissart Ballads* (translated in the Preface), Cooke quotes the original:

> Ennui venuta certa fantasia
> Che non posso cacciarmi de la testa
> Di scriver un historia in poesia
> Affato ignota, o poco manifesta.

These, Cooke notes, are the opening lines to the Roman prelate Forteguerri's *Ricciardetto.*

8. See Allen, *Cooke*, 23-28 and 41-45. Cooke promised to send material for *Burton's Gentleman's Magazine*, but warned Poe that "I cannot promise anything like the systematic contribution which I was guilty of in White's case, for the 'madness of scribbling' which once itched and tickled at my fingers-end has been considerably cured by a profession and matrimony." When Beverly Tucker asked his advice about the dialogue in *Viola*, Cooke made a few suggestions, but added: "Such trivial changes are the mere varieties of wording with which literary men try and amuse themselves. The only secret that I know for making poetic measure sound rough without becoming unmusical, is to violate the right placing of an accent here and there, and to terminate the line with a word of two or more syllables where the accent is on the penultimate syllable, leaving the ultimate a metrical superfluity." Cooke sometimes deliberately shifted accents in order to produce discord (quoted in Allen, *Cooke*, 81-82).

9. Rufus W. Griswold, "Philip Pendleton Cooke," *International Monthly Magazine*, IV (Oct. 1, 1851), 300-03; *SLM*, XVII (Oct.-Nov. 1851), 669-73. See also *Passages from the Correspondence and Other Papers of Rufus W. Griswold*, (1898), 191-92.

11. Griswold, *Passages*, 191. When Kennedy requested copies of his poems for inclusion in Griswold's *Poets and Poetry of America*, Cooke replied: "I have no 'port folio.' My verses are scattered about on *scraps* of paper of all colours, shades, and degrees of antiquity" (quoted in Allen, 68).

12. *International Monthly Magazine*, IV (Oct. 1, 1851), 302. Several passages from Cooke's letters were reprinted in *Southern Poets* (1936), 349-51.

13. *SLM*, XII, 201n. Griswold especially objected to "that *vassalage* of opinion and style, which is produced by a constant study of the literature of that nation, whose language we speak." Cooke thought Griswold "should have loved" American poets "better than to say it" (200).

14. Allen, *Dissertation*, 309. Allen also doubts (207) that Cooke "consciously held to any formal theory of the function of the modern romance. . . . Of himself as an artist he seems to have been essentially unself-conscious: In his own eyes he was a talented Virginia gentleman who desired to achieve fame and modest fortune through the employment of his pen."

15. Letter to N. B. Tucker, Dec., 1835 (quoted in Allen, *Cooke*, 25).

16. *SLM*, I (April, 1835), 397-401.

17. *SLM*, I (June, 1835), 557-65; quotation on 557. Cooke twice refers to the *Edinburgh Review* article, 559n and 562n.

18. *Ibid.*, 558.

19. *Ibid.*, 558-59.

20. *Ibid.*, 560. Cooke notes (559) that Aeschylus has been criticized severely for his mistaken ideas of the use of allegory; one error is "his introduction of STRENGTH, as a character who assists Vulcan in binding Prometheus to his rock."

21. *Ibid.*, 562. Cooke had little use for Ben Jonson, regarding him as having followed "the Grecian model too closely"; had mild praise for some verses by

Elizabeth; and regarded Cowley as appealing mainly to lovers, who find "pleasant aliment in the metaphysical and metaphorical love verses of this unnatural poet."

22. Cooke quoted, as throwing "more light upon the true character of Milton's mind, so far as sublimity is concerned, than anything I have seen," Dr. Hugh Blair's comparison: "Homer's [sublimity] is generally accompanied with fire and impetuosity; Milton's possesses more of a calm and amazing grandeur. Homer warms and hurries us along; Milton fixes us in a state of astonishment and elevation. Homer's sublimity appears most in the description of action; Milton's in that of wonderful and stupendous objects." Cooke also adapts, from Coleridge's *Table Talk* about Schiller and Shakespeare: "Both are sublime, but Homer's is the *material* sublime."

23. *Ibid.,* 563-64.

24. *Ibid.,* 565.

25. *SLM,* II (Jan. 1836), 101-06; references on 101.

26. *Ibid.,* 101-02. At his worst, however, his "soporific verses are of more worth than all the narcotics ever squeezed from the pores of the poppy."

27. *Ibid.,* 102-03. The main fault with the satires is that frequently they are "too frigid and naked."

28. *Ibid.,* 103-05.

29. *Ibid.,* 105-06.

30. *SLM,* I, 557 and 564. Poets like Cowley had unfortunately "made Pindar their master and forgot Horace."

31. *Ibid.,* 560. In the magazine, *Lava* is given. Shelly and Shelley seem to have been interchangeable in the printer's mind. Cooke complained bitterly of the "many typographical errors" (Allen, 25).

32. Quoted in Allen, *Cooke,* 59-60.

33. Letter, June 6, 1851; in Boston Public Library. See also J. E. Cooke's article, *SLM* XXVI (June 1858), 419-32. Cooke was, of course, already familiar at least with Tennyson's magazine verse.

34. Allen, *Cooke,* 85-86. Allen considers his style nearer to that of Keats than to any other of his contemporaries.

35. Quoted by D. K. Jackson in *Essays in Honor of William Kenneth Boyd,* 312. White used this on the cover of the Sept. 1835 *Messenger.* The brackets are in the original.

36. Letters quoted in Allen, 42-43, and in many biographies and editions of Poe. Cooke objected to the archaic "saith Lord Verulam"; Poe changed it to read, "says Bacon, Lord Verulam."

37. Quoted in Allen, *Cooke,* 45-46.

38. Allen, *Cooke,* 45.

39. Allen, 72-73.

40. *SLM,* XIV (Jan. 1848), 34-38.

41. "Old Books and New Authors," *SLM,* XII (April 1846), 199-203; quotation on 200. Here Cooke called Poe a "poet and critic of high powers."

42. *Ibid.,* 199. On 201, Cooke calls "The Knight's Tale," treating of the rivalry of Palamon and Arcite for the hand of Emilie, "the noblest of the Canterbury Tales." Under the title he quotes: "Uprose the sun, and uprose Emily."—Chaucer.

43. *Ibid.,* 199.

44. *Idem.* "He may desire to be original, as Wordsworth did at one period of his life—but that illustrious example warns him against the sort of originality which takes to the mud of the way-side, because the way itself has been beaten smooth by others." Cooke readily admitted direct if unconscious imitation. In a note appended to "Lines," in *Graham's,* XXIX (Sept. 1846), 143, he wrote that his line, "Thy Soul stood beckoning in thine eye," is "nearly identical with a song written by the Earl of Carbery (1653). It sprung up in my mind as original, and I wrote it

as such. My verses are too flimsy in their texture to meddle with, or I would put another in its place."

45. *Ibid.*, 200.

46. *Ibid.*, 201. See n. 13. In the Preface to *Froissart Ballads,* Cooke notes: "The reader may be disposed to undervalue poems professing to be versifications of old stories, on the ground of a want of originality. I ask only, in anticipation of this, that he will recollect the fact that, from Chaucer to Dryden, such appropriations of old story were customary with the noblest poets of our English language." Cooke especially appeals to the authority of Chaucer and Keats.

47. *Ibid.*, 201. Cooke adds in a footnote: "this title of love and reverence, bestowed by one poet upon another,—Dante styles Virgil 'meo maestro,' Dryden calls Spenser 'my master'; and a page of the like instances might be written,— would be taken as grave evidence of servility, if an American poet used it."

48. *Ibid.*, 202-03. Cooke notes that Pike acknowledged his indebtedness to Coleridge. The common American edition, he adds, includes the work of Coleridge, Shelley, and Keats in the same volume. In any case, Pike's poems prove that "the spell of Keats was also on him."

49. "Dante," *SLM*, XII (Sept. 1846), 545-52. Italy was out of favor, and her literary works might be replaced by Mrs. Randolph's *Virginia Housewife.* This might have one advantage: "defiant of all odds, we unhesitatingly declare, that we prefer Mrs. Randolph to Mrs. Hemans—the 'Virginia Housewife' to the 'Vespers of Palermo.' "

50. *Ibid.*, 545-46. Cooke briefly compares a stanza in terza rima translated by Hayley to the blank verse translation by Cary. In three lines, "the despotism of rhyme enforces a false termination to the first, wholly interpolates the second, and crowding the text in the third, drops a part of it for want of room."

51. *Ibid.*, 546. Cooke's poem, "The Famine Tower," is on 551-52; it was re-titled "The Story of Ugolino" in *Froissart Ballads.* Cooke confessed that "We make our version from Cary; it is, therefore, a version twice-removed from Dante. Such things are often done, but we believe this of ours to be the first admission of the sort ever made." This footnote does not appear in *Froissart Ballads.*

52. *Ibid.*, 547-48.

53. *Ibid.*, 549-50. Once again Cooke draws on the *Edinburgh Review.* May A. Thompson in her thesis on Cooke, 31, writes that "In the Cooke homestead were stacks of the old editions of the *Edinburgh Review,* and here the boy spent many golden hours."

54. *Ibid.*, 550-51. Cooke emphasized the need of mystery; Sue's mistake was, in the later and relatively worthless sections, to make his character of Monsieur Rodin too definite, with the result that we "dismiss him as a dirty little wretch."

55. "Living Novelists," Ch. I, XIII (June, 1847), 367-73; Ch. II, XIII (Sept. 1847), 529-36; Ch. III, XIII (Dec. 1847), 745-52. The quotations are on 745.

56. *Ibid.*, 745. However, in "Leaves from my Scrap Book," *SLM*, I (April, 1836), 314-16, Cooke dissents sharply from T. S. Grimké's statement that "I think Homer, as a poet, inferior to Scott," and demonstrates the unreasonableness of this judgment by translating some of Scott's poetry into Greek and Latin. If Scott suffers by translation, "it is only fair to presume that Homer and Virgil suffer as much in our eyes." Modern readers "perceive the merits of our modern poets; we are blind to the merits of the ancients."

57. *SLM*, XIII (June 1847), 367.

58. *Ibid,* 369-70.

59. *Ibid.*, 372. Willis's own practice "squints so singularly in the direction of this odd system of training, that we take the counsel to be serious in spite of its oddity."

60. *Ibid.*, 372. Browne seems to be writing "in three languages; his English

goes lumbering under Greek and Latin, but it is apparent that art, or the love of parade and effect, is not the reason that it does so."

61. *Ibid.*, 372-73.

62. *Ibid.*, 529-30. The critic is on safe ground if he can compare the poet "of love and wine with Anacreon, the pastoral poet with Theocritus or Virgil." Allegory had become entrenched in medieval thought, but "Otway's crust shows the fate of the dramatist." Lovelace in his time had pleased practically everyone except "that stern critic Cromwell."

63. *Ibid.*, 531, 533, 535. Cooke never explains this critical aberration, but insists that "We must pardon much to Dumas for haste," and that (with James) "It is no more than simple justice to pardon meagreness and sameness of plot in the fiftieth book of an author."

64. *Ibid.*, 553. Dumas' terse conclusions "seem inherent to the subject. . . . This is rather an unusual merit." Dr. Allen has well described (*Dissertion*, 337-38) Cooke's "A Morning with Cagliostro," *SLM*, XVI (Dec. 1850), 743-52, as "a good-natured burlesque of those characteristics of Dumas that Cooke had noted in the second of his essays in contemporary novelists." In the same mood is his burlesque of a fable from Ovid's *Metamorphoses*: "Joseph Jenkin's Researches into Antiquity: Erisicthon," *SLM*, XIV (Dec. 1848), 721-26.

65. *Ibid.*, 535. James's ideas and style are precisely matched: "tame, fluent thought with a tame, fluent style."

66. *Ibid.*, 535-36. Cooke also praised James for his love of chivalry (a subject close to Cooke's heart), and as "one of the most upright, gentle, and honorable men in the world."

67. *SLM*, XIII (Dec. 1847), 745-46. He digresses to note that Pope and Bolingbroke had introduced from France a "piquant grace" into English prose. Johnson had "returned to the pomp of the old Latinity," but this was a matter of personal taste. Modern prose writers were in general superior to the older writers, whether in the Latin or the Gallic tradition. Of two highly-praised comtemporary stylists, Cooke notes: Macaulay is "a magnificent ship-of-the-line, cruising in the seas of history and art, creeds and constitutions, and defending the truth everywhere with terrific force: but the metaphor holds good in this, also, that his style is as monotonous as the thunder of cannon. The style of Lord Brougham is angular, and as rough as a rasp."

68. *Ibid.*, 747-50.

69. *Ibid.*, 750. Cooke dedicated *Froissart Ballads* to John Pendleton Kennedy, as literary head of the clan. Cooke also noted, on American fiction, that he "used to devour the 'Spirit of the Times.'" Albert Pike had credited Coleridge with arousing his poetic passions; Cooke in a paraphrase credited Porter with arousing his passion for sports (quoted in Griswold, *SLM*, XVII (Oct.-Nov., 1851), 669-73.

70. *Ibid.*, 750-51. Cooper's preference for *The Bravo* was "one of those freaks of parental love, common enough with authors and mothers." *The Last of the Mohicans* was "very meanly written," but in his best work, *The Deerslayer*, "the winter of sixty radiates a warmer poetry of thought than the summer of thirty."

71. Letter to Rufus W. Griswold, June 16, 1851; in Boston Public Library.

72. *SLM*, XV (Jan., 1849), 46-54; (Feb., 1849), 101-08; (March, 1849), 148-54; quotation on 151. Even the liberal John R. Thompson objected to some of Cooke's fictional liberties: after praising highly the general conclusion of *The Gregories of Hackwood* (*SLM*, XV, Sept. and Oct., 1848, 537-43, 612-22), he asked pointedly: "Was there not a dramatic impropriety, however, in the *denouement*? There was no human witness of the last act of the old man's drama. . . . How could we know, therefore, the details of the catastrophe?" (Letter to Cooke, Oct. 17, 1848; in Univ. of Virginia Library; quoted in Allen, *Dissertation*, 325).

73. *SLM*, XIII (June, 1847), 367.

8. CHIVERS

1. Titles will be listed individually in the following notes. Most of the manuscripts are in the Chivers Collection, Duke University Library (hereafter cited as Chivers Col., DUL). For permission to quote freely from them, I am indebted to Mr. Ben Powell, Librarian, and to the officials of the Duke University Library. For help in using them, I am especially indebted to Mr. Jay B. Hubbell, Jr. When no other citations are given, a numeral at the end of a paragraph indicates that all quotations therein are from the same ms. Indispensable for any study of Chivers are S. Foster Damon's *Thomas Holley Chivers: Friend of Poe* (1930); Richard Beale Davis's excellent edition of *Chivers' Life of Poe* (1952); Charles H. Watts' *Thomas Holley Chivers* (1956); and *The Correspondence of Thomas Holley Chivers*, edited by Emma Lester Chase and Lois Ferry Parks (1957).

2. "The Beauties of Poetry," Chivers Col., DUL. Chivers wrote an essay under this title, then apparently condensed it, using many of the same ideas, illustrations, and even wording. He adds: "Poetry is that sweet-singing Sibyl which this indulgent Mother [Nature] has throned upon the High Places of the earth to woo them back again to her affectionate bosom."

3. "The True Messiah of Liberty," Chivers Col., DUL. Even St. John, he noted, obtained only a partial vision. In "The True Shekinah of God," Chivers Col., DUL, he claimed that "God chose the Poets of old to be the true Revelators of his Divine Will."

4. "The True Prophet of God," Chivers Col., DUL. Chivers was pessimistic about the modern spiritual world, for he declared that the "truth is, this world, as it is now governed—being, as it is, entirely under the dominion of the Devil—is not a fit abiding place for any of the true Sons of God." (In *Chivers' Life of Poe*, Edited with an Introduction by Richard Beale Davis, 1952, p. 30).

5. "On the True Nature of Poetry," Chivers Col., DUL. He repeats the idea that the true poet is the "only sublime Worker."

6. "On the True Nature of Poetry (Preface)," Chivers Col., DUL. Probably in order that it could be published independently, the article listed in n. 5 was prepared from this longer work. Chivers planned an anthology or anthologies under various titles: "The Dial of Poesy; or, The Princes of Parnassus" has the typical sub-heading, "Comprehending many of the most Brilliant Gems of the Greatest Poets of Ancient and Modern Times." Chivers objected when Lord Macaulay described poetry as fiction, and like a magic lantern; poetry might be a dream, but dreams were prophecies, and intuitively true ("The True Poet and His Poetry," Chivers Col., DUL).

7. Preface, *Memoralia* (1853). Most of this preface, and that to *Nacoochee*, has been reprinted in *Southern Poets*. The wording in the text above is largely repeated in "Hebrew Poets," Chivers Col., DUL, and in many other articles.

8. "The Beauties of Poetry, II," Chivers Col., DUL. Almost the same words are used in the first essay. Other typical examples occur in "On the True Nature of Poetry (Preface)," where Adam is described as the perfect man capable of conversing with the Angels; and in "On the Revelation of the Divine Idea through Greek and Hebrew Poetry," (Chivers Col., DUL), where he is "the truly Divine Man." In the *Georgia Citizen*, Oct. 23, 1852, Chivers qualifies this by saying that in the God-inspired man among the older Hebrews "it was David's Harp which was then vibrating in his soul. . . . This was truly living out the divine life—for none but a divine man could have heard that which had long before died into silence in the souls of all the world."

9. Preface, *Nacoochee* (1837). These delineations by the sensitive poet may "seem to outshine realities, but do not, because they spring from the fountains of things that exist." But since men are fallible, few people realize this; and only

the intuitive poet or artist is "capable of giving birth to other beings brighter than himself."

10. Letter to Poe, Aug. 27, 1840, in *The Correspondence of Thomas Holley Chivers* (V. I of *The Complete Works of Thomas Holley Chivers*), edited by Emma Lester Chase and Lois Ferry Parks, 1957, p. 9. Impeccably edited, this volume is essential in any study of Chivers. Hereafter cited as *Correspondence*.

11. Preface, *Memoralia* (1853). Chivers frequently praises the beauties of the physical earth; in the Preface to *Nacoochee* he asserts that there "is nothing in the world that is not equivalent in brightness to the poetical manifestations of it." At the same time, nothing in the natural world (mountains, streams, etc.) is equal to the creations of man.

12. *Search After Truth* (1848), 35-37. In his extremely valuable book, *Thomas Holley Chivers: His Literary Career and His Poetry* (1956), Charles H. Watts II quotes this phrase and notes (p. 253, n. 117) that "to couch an eye" means to remove a cataract. The phrase was a favorite one with Chivers.

13. *Search After Truth*, 35. In a letter to Poe, Aug. 6, 1844 (*Correspondence*, 29), Chivers glorifies the body: "it is through the perfected body of man that his soul is made perfectly manifest. A perfect body is the only mediator of the soul. It is the body which connects the soul with the external world. . . . True wisdom is the perfect revelation of the right relations subsisting between the soul of Man and the external world. This revelation is the immortality of Man speaking out of the temple of his mediatorial body." In the *Georgia Citizen*, April 19, 1851, he praises the Greeks for their handsomeness, and laments the number of ugly people in the modern world.

14. Preface, *Atlanta* (1853). Here, "Ministering Angels wait upon the soul of every true Poet to lead him into the way of all Beauty." In defending Transcendentalism, Chivers asked Poe, "what is Revelation, but Transcendentalism?"; and later asserted that "all *true* Poetry is certainly transcendental" (*Correspondence*, 9, 23; see also 32-35).

15. *Chivers' Life of Poe*, 32. This idea recurs often; for example, in "The True Shekinah of God" (Chivers Col., DUL), he writes that "it is only the *real person* who is the *real genius*, or *Artist*."

16. *Correspondence*, 53. Earlier he had written to Poe that "the embers of enthusiasm are still glowing with a quenchless heat in the centre of my heart. Music and poetry are my chief delights. Poetry, I consider the perfection of literature. Without it, the lips of the soul are dumb. It is the beautiful expression of that which is most true. It is the melodious expression of the unsatisfied desires of the heart panting after perfection" (*Correspondence*, 14).

17. "Lyrical Poetry" (end), Chivers Col., DUL. Chivers frequently stresses the necessity of writing "at white heat."

18. "The Dial of Early Days," Chivers Col., DUL. This two-page ms. has the sub-title, "Preface to the Early Poems," and is dated Boston, Nov. 10, 1852. Watts (59-60) discusses a projected *Woodland Melodies; or, The Dial of Early Days*, with a Preface dated April 10, 1850. For a long and interesting letter on his early poetry, see *Correspondence*, 187-202.

19. Preface, *Memoralia*. That the idea and the form should, ideally, come into the poet's mind simultaneously is a doctrine frequently stated in Chivers' articles.

20. *Chivers' Life of Poe*, 79. This idea will be discussed later, especially in treating Chivers' criticism of Poe. In "The True Poet and His Poetry," Chivers Col., DUL, he notes that well-educated people appreciate "that Poetry which is the result of an equal blending of Nature and Art—although Nature, after all, is the only *true* Art."

21. Preface, *Memoralia*. Chivers uses the same idea and wording in "On the Art of Poetry," Chivers Col., DUL. A true poem has a literal and a spiritual, an

outward and an inward beauty. It must be a perfect fusion of "Art and Passion." Only a perfect man, Christ, could write a perfect poem.

22. Preface, *Memoralia*. This distinction between Gothic and Greek poetry is of cardinal importance in any consideration of Chivers' criticism.

23. "On the Revelation of the Divine Idea through the Greek and Hebrew Poetry," Chivers Col., DUL. In "Hebrew Poetry" (Chivers Col., DUL), he claims that "Lyrical Poetry, in its most Gothic state, was the primeval dialect of the Edenic or Perfect Man."

24. "On the Art of Poetry," Chivers Col., DUL. Here he adds to other comparisons that art is to poetry as wings to birds, body to soul, or soul to spirit: "the *Existere* of its divine *Esse.*"

25. *Chivers' Life of Poe*, 93. See n. 20.

26. *Chivers' Life of Poe*, 93-9; 47; 73; 94, respectively.

27. *Correspondence*, 14, 23. In his *Poe*, 94, Chivers insists that this must be "an ideality of soul . . . which must be Gothic."

28. *Correspondence*, 14. However, he wrote several poems to or about musicians, and in his newspaper articles frequently discussed their performances.

29. "Music the Soul of Poetry," Chivers Col., DUL. Poetry is "the Adam, the *male* principle of creation." As the perfect union of man and woman consummates perfect harmony in this world, so it is by "union of Poetry and Music that a Revelation of the Divine Idea can be vouchsafed to this world." In *Correspondence*, 186-87, Chivers claimed that his articles on the opera had been published. They have not been located.

30. "The True Prophet of God," Chivers Col., DUL. In "The Mastix" (Chivers Col., DUL), he writes that it "is the melody of a Poem which gives it a glory. This melody is entirely dependent on the rhythm. If that be deficient, the Poem is not a perfect work of Art."

31. Preface, *Virginalia*. In "Lyrical Poetry" (Chivers Col., DUL), he uses practically the same language, adding that the refrain "is very little understood either in England or America. . . . It is to Lyrical Poetry precisely what the Chorus was to the Greek tragedy but infintely more necessary inasmuch as it is indispensable to the perfection of it." He started a separate article entitled "On the Refrain" (Chivers Col., DUL), but apparently never completed it; only one page has survived.

32. "Of Rhythm and Metre," Chivers Col., DUL. Alliteration is good, but when carried too far, as in "Endymion," leads to hypnotism. Chivers includes an extract from Bayard Taylor partly because it was praised by "that great critic Edgar A. Poe." But the rhythm was borrowed from Tennyson's "Dream of Fair Women": "How this could have escaped Poe, is beyond my conjecture."

33. For an excellent example, see his letter to Poe, *Correspondence*, 58-60.

34. "Tennyson," Chivers Col., DUL. Chivers left an incomplete four-page ms., from which this quotation is taken, and a five-page one, which is mainly just a clearer copy.

35. *Correspondence*, 131, 138.

36. *Correspondence*, 63.

37. *Correspondence*, 23. In "Lyrical Poetry" (Chivers Col., DUL), he insists that "the Critic must be the Artist to understand Art."

38. *Correspondence*, 63. Even Poe left something to be desired: "When he read Poetry, his voice rolled over the rhythm of the verse like silver notes over golden sands—rather monotonously and flute-like. . . . He made use of very little Art in his recitations— never uttering any declamatory tones, or using the lowest Theatrical emphasis, but the most modest, chaste and delicate delivery. From this it must be evident to everyone that his Readings were not very effective; and such is the very fact. His reading of Lyrical Poetry was certainly very melodious and beauti-

ful, but he lacked that well-attuned power of modulation in accent, emphasis and cadence, necessary to make either an Epic or Dramatic writing effective" (*Chivers' Life of Poe,* 63).

39. "The True Poet and His Poetry," Chivers Col., DUL.

40. In a four-page fragment labelled Preface (Chivers Col., DUL). It is dated April 3, 1842, and signed E.B.S. It seems to be a preface to a novel: the author claims to have written a "mythical Satire," making use not only of "the *romance* of *reality,* but the *reality* of romance."

41. "On the Art of Poetry," Chivers Col., DUL, and "Of Rhythm and Metre," Chivers Col., DUL. In a preface to *Alba Regalis* (see n. 48), he praised the Elizabethan dramatists for having developed a "suitable langauge . . . the purely dramatic Style—that is, the tragico-poetic rhythms of a naturally impassioned dialogue."

42. "On the Art of Poetry."

43. Preface, *Nacoochee.*

44. "The Beauties of Poetry," Chivers Col., DUL. He also emphasizes its subjective value: "True poetry is the beautiful expression of that which is most true. . . . It is the diamond key by which we unlock the inner sanctuary of the soul."

45. *Correspondence,* 189-90.

46. *Correspondence,* 49 and n. 30, 51.

47. Watts, 5, 95. Since Watts has done what seems to me a definitive study of literary influences on Chivers, I have deliberately scanted this aspect.

48. This four-page fragment in the Chivers Col., DUL, has the misleading title, "The Duchess of Malfi." Chivers never gets around to discussing Webster's play. In a preface prepared for his unpublished play *Alba Regalis, or The Red Rose of Scotland,* Chivers noted: "When I wrote this tragedy, it was not because I knew the difference between one Dramatic Style and Another, but because I did not know. . . . There are two kinds of Plays, the Poetic as well as the purely Dramatic tragedy. . . . I have attempted to prove in my play of *Alba Regalis* that a purely Poetic Tragedy would be the most Dramatic of all Plays" (Chivers Col., DUL; see also *Correspondence,* 95).

49. "Shakespeare," and "Definitions of Poetry by Various Authors," Chivers Col., DUL. In the latter he asks, "What is the Chinese wall compared with Hamlet or Antony and Cleopatra?"

50. Watts, 98-99, 113.

51. "Lyrical Poetry," Chivers Col., DUL.

52. "The Beauties of Poetry," Chivers Col., DUL.

53. *Ibid.*

54. *Correspondence,* 20, 23.

55. "Lyrical Poetry," Chivers Col., DUL. See Watts, 125-32. In "The Mighty Dead," Shelley is praised as poet of love and liberty, "The ISRAFEL among the Sons of Song." Chivers also characterizes him (*Georgia Citizen,* Oct. 18, 1851) as "eminently a great reformer."

56. "Shelley," *Southern Literary Messenger,* Feb. 1844, X: 104-06. It is subtitled "Extract from a Lecture on 'The Genius of Shelley.' "

57. *Chivers' Life of Poe,* 46. In "Philosophic Marginalia," Chivers praises "Adonais": "Who but Shelley would have personified Death as not only the slayer of Keats, but the remorseful writer of his immortally-crystalline Epitaph?"

58. "Lyrical Poetry," Chivers Col., DUL. See Watts, 117-25.

59. *Chivers' Life of Poe,* 47. See Watts, 132-37, and John O. Eidson, *Tennyson in America* (1943).

60. *Correspondence,* 53-54, 59. In the article "Tennyson," however, he argues that "In Memoriam" is not only inferior to Shelley's and Milton's elegies, but it does not really resemble them.

61. "Lyrical Poetry," Chivers Col., DUL.
62. "Tennyson," Chivers Col., DUL.
63. "Tennyson." In his *Poe* (94-95), Chivers wrote that the "Elizabethan Bards wrote Gothic Poems; Tennyson, Greek AEidolons. . . . The Elizabethan Bards wrote out of the heart, Tennyson out of the brain." Here and in *Correspondence*, 106, he insists that "Tennyson is entirely devoid of passion—the primum mobile of the true Poet."
64. *Georgia Citizen*, Aug. 2, 1850. See Watts, 103-05.
65. "Lyrical Poetry," Chivers Col., DUL.
66. *Correspondence*, 54. For discussion of Horne by Poe and Chivers, see *Correspondence*, 23 and 65, and *Chivers' Life of Poe*, 40.
67. "Lyrical Poetry," Chivers Col., DUL.
68. Manuscript fragment on Poets, Chivers Col., DUL. For Moore's early influence, see Watts, 99-102.
69. *Correspondence*, 106-07. In defending his originality, Chivers added: "I never read anything of Wordsworth that pleased me."
70. "Wordsworth," a one-page item, Chivers Col., DUL. Even his best work, the Lucy poems, lacked feeling.
71. *Correspondence*, 79.
72. "Definitions of Poetry by Various Authors," Chivers Col., DUL. To Chivers, poetry was "the objectivity of the subjectivity . . . the invisible becoming visible— the impersonal becoming personal."
73. "Examination of Coleridge's Definition of Poetry, Tragedy and Comedy," Chivers Col., DUL. The ms. never gets to tragedy or comedy. At the end of "Definitions" he objected to Coleridge's definitions, but again the ms. breaks off before he discusses the matter. Perhaps the closest Chivers gets to clarifying his disagreement is in an incomplete Introduction to an unnamed drama: "The world began with Comedy. The author of this protoplay was God. The actors Adam and Eve. The theme love. The scene, the Garden of Paradise. The time of the action, the beginning of the world. . . . But what is a Comedy? Marriage. What is a marriage? The exchanging of one self for another—the self of wisdom for the self of love. . . . Comedy cannot, therefore, be what Coleridge calls 'unlimited jest. . . .'
"Then what is tragedy? Death—the sublimest, most pathetic, most lamentable that ever occurred on the earth was that of Christ on the Cross. . . . This should, also, be the type of all Tragedies." Chivers adds that Greek tragedy had for its theme a mythology in which the disordered, finite will of man was subordinate to the perfect, infinite will of a Supreme Power; Shakespearean tragedies had for their themes the historical occurrences of "the New Dispensation of Religion in which the True God of Heaven is the Arbiter of Man's actions in time."
74. "On the Refrain," Chivers Col., DUL.
75. "The Lyrical Poets of Scotland," Chivers Col., DUL. Chivers thinks that Lowell's "Rosaline" owes much to Mayne's work.
76. "Lyrical Poetry" and "The Beauties of Poetry," Chivers Col., DUL.
77. "Lyrical Poetry," Chivers Col., DUL. He had used practically the same wording about Wordsworth, and in "Wordsworth" he indicates that Montgomery had more passion but also more didacticism.
78. *Chivers' Life of Poe*, 40; *Georgia Citizen*, Oct. 11, 1851. In the *Georgia Citizen*, July 5, 1851, he declared that "Festus is no Poem in the true acceptation of the term. . . . It possesses all the faults of Keats' Endymion, with but very few of its beauties. Mr. Bailey is no artist. . . . No Poem can last, as a whole, which does not appeal, in its artistic perfection, to the well-attuned perception of the *truly critical* Reader. . . . A Poem is no place for the teaching of Hegelian Metaphysics—the peculiar province of Poetry being the creation of beauty."
79. "Lyrical Poetry," Chivers Col., DUL.

80. "The Mighty Dead," Watts, 95-98.

81. "Thomas Chatterton," Chivers Col., DUL.

82. *Georgia Citizen*, Aug. 15, 1851; "Definitions of Poetry by Various Authors," Chivers Col., DUL.

83. "Lyrical Poetry," Chivers Col., DUL. Here, too, Chivers insists that it is the rhythm of a poem "which constitutes the originality."

84. "Lyrical Poetry." Chivers started several articles on Milton (Chivers Col., DUL); this passage re-appears in a one-page fragment.

85. "The Beauties of Poetry," Chivers Col., DUL.

86. "Definitions of Poetry by Various Authors," Chivers Col., DUL.

87. "Milton's Paradise Lost Compared with Homer's Iliads," Chivers Col., DUL. Chivers uses the plural because he considered the Greek epic a series of lyrics.

88. Preface, *Atlanta:* "no poem of any considerable length, from the very nature of the revelations subsisting between the power of the soul to receive, and the impressions to be made, can be pleasing."

89. "Milton's Paradise Lost Compared with Homer's Iliads." The sole superiority of *Paradise Lost* is in the new theology of Jesus. When Simms reviewed *The Lost Pleiad* (1845) unfavorably, writing that "man ought not to complain," Chivers started a rejoinder (Chivers Col.) justifying lamentations, and citing as supporting witnesses Jeremiah, Coleridge, Shelley, and especially Milton in "Lycidas" and in "the opening" of Book III of *Paradise Lost*.

90. *Eonahs of Ruby*, 167.

91. Four manuscript pages, mainly quotations with brief commentary, from *Paradise Lost*. In "Definitions of Poetry" he quotes with approval Milton's phrase, "simple, sensuous, and passionate," and notes its superiority to Poe's idea of passionless poetry.

92. "Shakespeare," Chivers Col., DUL. Chivers crossed out a sub-title, "Extract from a Lecture." He quotes at length from *Venus and Adonis* and *The Rape of Lucrece* to prove that Shakespeare, when untrammeled by dramatic exigencies, had attained artistic perfection in poetry.

93. Thus he discusses the origin of *orphan* in *Merry Wives of Windsor*, and of *lob* in *Midsummer Night's Dream*, and the meaning of the drinking scene in *Othello*, in manuscripts entitled "Dramatic Criticism," Chivers Col., DUL. He thought Collier and Knight frequently wrong in their punctuation, as well as in their emendations.

94. "Definitions of Poetry by Various Authors," Chivers Col., DUL.

95. "Lyrical Poetry," Chivers Col., DUL; in the *Georgia Citizen*, June 14, 1851, he wrote that "I have just received, from London, a book which I would not exchange for its weight in gold. It is an old play, in Five Acts, written by John Lily [*sic*]."

96. See *Correspondence*, 122-23.

97. "Vittoria Corombrona," Chivers Col., DUL. His unfinished article on the *Duchess of Malfi* breaks off before there is any discussion of Webster's play. For his interest in buying modern editions of Elizabethan dramatists, see *Correspondence*, 272-76.

98. "Gothic Songs of England," Chivers Col., DUL.

99. The Prospectus of *The Stylus* (reprinted in *Georgia Citizen*, Nov. 9, 1850) claimed that "It will be wholly American—entirely original in form and matter." Discussing George Gilfillan's biography of Emerson (*Georgia Citizen*, July 5, 1851), Chivers wishes to know what he means "by saying that 'in spite of the penumbra of prejudice against American verse, more fugitive floating Poetry of real merit exists in its literature than in almost any other.' . . . Does he not *know* that America has produced the best *Lyrical Poetry* of any land under the sun?" See also Watts, 183 ff.

100. *Correspondence*, 8, 23.

101. *Correspondence*, 9, 23.

102. "Manuscript Fragment on Poets," Chivers Col., DUL. In the *Georgia Citizen*, Aug. 21, 1850, he calls Emerson a "Literary Ganymede—or in other words, an Ambrosial Eclecticist."

103. *Chivers' Life of Poe*, 48-49; *Georgia Citizen*, Feb. 23, 1851.

104. "Longfellow in Limbo; or, A Most Faithful Review of His 'Hiawatha,'" Chivers Col., DUL. Much of this material was published in the *Georgia Citizen*, Jan. 19 and Feb. 16, 1856. He and John Gierlow discussed in letters Longfellow's plagiarism; see *Correspondence*, 247 ff.

105. "Manuscript Fragment on Poets," Chivers Col., DUL.

106. *Chivers' Life of Poe*, 45-46.

107. A photostat fragment entitled "J. R. Lowell," Chivers Col., DUL. Here he also calls Rufus Griswold the "Lord Mogul of American Letters," who has written a Preface to *Paradise Lost*: "Shades of the immortal Milton! Look down with pity —not indignation."

108. *Georgia Citizen*, April 5, 1850. See also his letter to Duganne, *Correspondence*, 106-08.

109. *Georgia Citizen*, March 21, and Aug. 2, 1850.

110. "Manuscript Fragment on Poets," Chivers Col., DUL. Poe's poems were "above the Popular taste—else they *would* have sold—as readily as any of those of Willis or Longfellow" (*Chivers' Life of Poe*, 26).

111. "Preface," Chivers Col., DUL.

112. *Correspondence*, 139. Briefly noting Caroline Lee Hentz in the *Georgia Citizen*, July 5, 1850, he writes that her recent drama is "worth all the Tales and Nouvelettes that she ever wrote. A *true* Dramatic Poem is the highest manifestation of the perfect genius."

113. *Georgia Citizen*, June 5, 1852.

114. *Chivers' Life of Poe*, 25-26, 98. Chivers crossed through a paragraph: "there is not a man in the world who knew Poe who will not say that he was infinitely a better man than Griswold ever was in his best moments."

115. *Ibid.*, 28-29.

116. *Ibid.*, 29, 33, 59-62. See also his letters to Poe, in *Correspondence*.

117. *Ibid.*, 43. See also 73 and 77. Chivers makes the same point in many essays, notably at the end of "Definitions of Poetry by Various Authors."

118. *Ibid.*, 33.

119. *Ibid.*, 80, 85-87, 96.

120. *Ibid.*, 97. See also *Correspondence*, 14.

121. *Chivers' Life of Poe*, 97.

122. *Ibid.*, 132.

123. *Ibid.*, 73, 76-78.

124. *Ibid.*, 78-80.

125. *Ibid.*, 38; repeated in a crossed-out passage, 65 n. In *Correspondence*, 14, he wrote Poe that he had always thought "highly of your talents as a poet, and the best critic in this Country."

126. *Correspondence*, 23. See also 14 and 48-49.

127. *Chivers' Life of Poe*, 89.

128. *Correspondence*, 23.

129. *Chivers' Life of Poe*, 83. In "Definitions of Poetry by Various Authors" he notes: "Poe said that Poetry must *not* be sensuous, or passionate, but *spiritual*. This is what he said to me—stating, at the same time, that all that kind of Poetry which was passionate was just precisely '*no Poetry at all.*'" Both in his *Poe*, 92, and in the *Georgia Citizen*, Oct. 18, 1851, Chivers quotes Poe's "true passion is

prosaic, homely," and complains, "This he said in speaking of Mrs. Welby's poetry —than whom a more passionate woman never existed."

130. *Correspondence*, 23 and 25, n. 9.

131. *Ibid.*, 48.

132. *Georgia Citizen*, July 12, 1850, and Oct. 11, 1851.

133. *Correspondence*, 106-08. See Watts, 149-60. Chivers even objected (*Georgia Citizen*, June 26, 1852) to imitation by a medium: "In the first place, Poe never wrote any such Poetry as this—therefore, could not have dictated it to Mrs. Lydia H. Tenney. She was therefore, never an amanuensis of his—nor does she possess the least aptitude in her mind to be so. In the second place, Poe would never dictate, from a SUPERIOR SPHERE, to a mind in *this*, or *inferior* one that of which he was not the original—particularly in an ungrammatical language."

134. *Correspondence*, 136-38.

135. "The Valley of Diamonds," *Georgia Citizen*, July 12, 1850, and "Letters from the North," *Georgia Citizen*, Oct. 11, 1851.

136. One of the most vicious appeared in the *New York Quarterly*, April, 1853, II: 161-63. See Watts, 73 ff.

137. *Waverley Magazine*, VI (April 9, 1853), 233. The reviewer thinks that "the originality of his style and views may very well arrest attention."

138. *Waverley Magazine*, VII (July 30, 1853), 73. One of the most valuable treatments of this subject is S. Foster Damon's chapter, "The Problem of Plagiarism," in his *Thomas Holley Chivers*, 198-219.

139. *Waverley Magazine*, VII (Aug. 13, 1853), 105, 108.

140. "Honey from Hybla," *Waverley Magazine*, VII (Aug. 20, 1853), 120. See Watts, 81-83.

141. "Poe's Plagiarism," *Waverley Magazine*, VII (Oct. 1, 1853), 216.

142. "The Mastix," Chivers Col., DUL. There seemed to him "no kind of Rhythm to be compared" with the trochaic for the elegy, because of its "peculiar adaptation to the impression of pathetic tenderness."

143. Thus he wrote Simms (*Correspondence*, 137-40, 1852) of his book "entitled *Hortus Deliciarum; or, the Garden of Delights*, in which I have given an analysis of Poetry from its Gothic up to its Greek manifestations. You will therein see a '*New Thing*' under the Sun.' " He also considered as possible titles, "Fruit from the Tree of Life" and "The Valley of Diamonds." Under the last title he published articles in the *Georgia Citizen*, June 14-Sept. 20, 1850. On a projected anthology, see n. 6.

144. A rough draft of an undated announcement in the Chivers Col., DUL, gives in summary form so many of Chivers' critical ideas that it seems worth quoting at length: "Dr. T. H. Chivers very respectfully announces . . . that he will deliver a course of lectures on the divine Art of Poetry, which is the jewelled crown of all Arts. . . . As he has devoted his whole life to the worship of the Beautiful, he would most earnestly entreat those who have never tasted of the Ambrosia of Heaven to come to his Symposium. . . . Syllabus: 1. Introduction to the General Subject, in which will be discussed the True Nature of Poetry (as being the Revelation of the Divine Idea). 2. A dissertation upon Poetry from its Gothic up to its Greek manifestations. 3. On the Ancient Hebrew and Greek Poetry with specimens of the style and peculiarity of oriental Imagery. 4. On the Rhythm, Metre and Refrain of Poetry. 5. On the Art of Poetry in general, inclu[ding] the use of a Poetical Language. 6. On Beauty. 7. On Lyrical Poetry with recitations from the greatest of the English and American Poets. 8. On the Poetry of Elizabeth Barrett Browning with recitations. . . ."

145. *Correspondence*, 139. Chivers adds: "let me tell you that this is the *glory of all Poetry*."

9. GRAYSON

1. Grayson's autobiography has not been published. The manuscript and a typescript edited by Robert Duncan Bass (1933) are in the South Caroliniana Library, University of South Carolina, Columbia. Practically all of Grayson's remarks on literature are in Ch. XI. In the following notes, the first page number is to Grayson's manuscript; the second, to Bass's typescript. I have used some material from my earlier article, "Legaré and Grayson: Types of Classical Influences on Ante-Bellum Critics," in *Segments of Southern Thought.*

2. *Russell's Magazine,* I (July, 1857), 327-37. I have reprinted "What Is Poetry?" as an appendix in *The Essays of Henry Timrod* (Athens, Georgia, 1942), 135-54, with notes on 172-76. I have listed page references to the article, and to the reprint cited as *Essays.*

3. *Autobiography,* 122-23, 247-48. Grayson here is referring only to poetry. His arguments against secession, notably in the *Letters of Curtius,* indicate clearly that he was strongly influenced by Jonathan Swift and that he knew Swift's work thoroughly. In his *Memoir of James L. Petigru* (Charleston, 1866, 42-44), Grayson recalled that at South Carolina College they had spent a night "over the wild wit of Rabelais"; daylight found them "engaged in the coarse but irresistible merriment of the modern master of broad humor and boisterous wit." They also read aloud to each other from the writings of Horace, Bacon, Dryden, and Pope.

4. *The Hireling and Slave,* Charleston, 1854; re-published in 1856, with additional poems, as *The Hireling and the Slave, Chicora, and Other Poems.* Grayson adds twenty-one pages of prose notes to buttress his argument, and on the title page has brief supporting quotations by M. G. ("Monk") Lewis and Thomas Carlyle. Grayson seems to most readers more effective in his attack than in his defence.

5. Preface, XV-XVI (1856 ed., XIV-XV). In 1854 he attacked Harriet Beecher Stowe, who "with prostituted pen assails/ One-half her country, in malignant tales;/ Careless, like Trollope, whether truth she tells,/ And anxious only that the libel sells" (44; see also Notes, 94-95). In 1856 he added four lines and a prose footnote attacking *A Key to "Uncle Tom's Cabin"* as a compilation of slanders: "To the false tale she adds its falser Keys" (41).

6. *Essays,* 142; *Russell's,* I, 330. Grayson seems never to have doubted that Horace had presented the definitive theory of poetry.

7. *Autobiography,* 122-23, 247-48.

8. *Essays,* 136; *Russell's,* I, 327. In the *Autobiography* (135; 275), the poet is simply "a very pains taking individual and works as hard at his trade as any other intellectual laborer. . . . He toils after thoughts, words, and images. Sometimes they come readily. Sometimes they refuse to come at all. His tools are pen and ink. His inspiration is the same as that of every other mental workman, the excitement of thought."

9. *Essays,* 137; *Russell's,* I, 328. Grayson did not believe that poets had such powers. They have the diversities and peculiarities of temperament common to men not because they are poets but because they are men: "It would be as rational, perhaps more so, to ascribe Byron's licentiousness to his deformed foot than to his genius for poetry" (*Autobiography,* 139, 283).

10. *Essays,* 137-38; *Russell's,* I, 328. The greatest of English poets—Chaucer, Spenser, Shakespeare, and Milton—were men of high moral character; but poetic genius did not excuse evil: "The best songs are the crackling of thorns under a pot compared with the interests of truth and virtue" (*Autobiography,* 140, 285-86).

11. He tells with approval of Coleridge's schoolmaster, James Bowyer, who made fun of young poets for using "lyre" when all they meant was pen and ink (*Essays,* 136; *Russell's,* I, 327).

12. *Essays* 138-39; *Russell's*, I, 328-29.

13. *Essays*, 139; *Russell's*, I, 329. Hannay's *Satire and Satirists* was published in 1854.

14. *Essays*, 140; *Russell's*, I, 329-30. Grayson also quotes approvingly Wordsworth's defence of using "the naked language" to describe "some of the most interesting passions of men," even if the language is at times "indelicate or gross or vulgar."

15. *Essays*, 141; *Russell's*, I, 330.

16. *Essays*, 141-43; *Russell's*, I, 330-31. Grayson spells it "Marinere": possibly a misprint, but probably intended to emphasize its kinship to archaic ballads.

17. *Essays*, 143; *Russell's*, I, 331-32.

18. *Essays*, 143-44; *Russell's*, I, 331-32.

19. *Essays*, 144-46; *Russell's*, I, 322-33. Grayson agreed with Coleridge's judgment that there was too much "matter of factness" about Wordsworth's poetry, but it was an effect, not a cause. In his *Autobiography* (unnumbered leaf between 124 and 125; 251-52), Grayson drily remarks about Timrod's response to the charge that Wordsworth was mechanical in his enthusiasm: "I said so once and was nearly annihilated by an indignant admirer who overwhelmed me with quotations to prove how much I was in error. The quotations did not change my opinions."

20. *Essays*, 147-48; *Russell's* I, 333.

21. *Essays*, 149; *Russell's*, I, 333-34. In attempting to illustrate his theory, Grayson turns a brief passage from Milton's "Tractate on Education" into five lines of blank verse. The demonstration is not exactly convincing.

22. *Essays*, 150; *Russell's* I, 335.

23. *Essays*, 151; *Russell's*, I, 335-37.

24. *Essays*, 153-54; *Russell's*, I, 336.

25. *Russell's*, III, 516: "Poetry, Objective," and "Poetry, Subjective."

26. "The Poet's Reward," in *The Hireling and the Slave, Chicora, and Other Poems*, 147. Grayson uses as a headnote a passage from Coleridge beginning: "Poetry has been to me its own exceeding great reward." Not only does poetry console us for false friendship and faithless love; it consoled Milton for his blindness, Dante for his exile, Homer for his wandering, and Cowper for his partial loss of reason.

27. Paul Hamilton Hayne has recorded (*Southern Bivouac*, IV, NSI, 335, Nov. 1885) that in his last brief meeting in 1862 with Grayson, his friend was reading *Les Miserables* and pronounced it "the most powerful fiction since the time of W. Scott." Grayson "dwelt upon the spirit and originality" of the novel, and called Hugo a "prodigious genius," whose "most glaring faults are the offspring of power. He is a Titan, the more conspicuous among a generation of Pigmies." Hayne also notes that Grayson was mainly interested in politics and in history, and that most of his contributions to *Russell's* were on political matters.

10. TIMROD

1. Timrod's critical essays have been reprinted in full in *The Essays of Henry Timrod*, edited by E. W. Parks (Athens, Ga., 1942), together with all his identifiable editorials on literature (hereafter cited as *Essays*). Full biographical information in given in that book. Many of his extant letters and editorials are in Jay B. Hubbell's indispensable study, *The Last Years of Henry Timrod*, 1941 (hereafter cited as Hubbell, *Timrod*). I am indebted to R. L. Meriwether and E. L. Inabinett for permission to use the unpublished Timrod material and letters in the South Caroliniana Library of the University of South Carolina. William Fidler has printed

Timrod's letters to Rachel Lyons in the *Southern Literary Messenger,* II (Oct., Nov., Dec., 1940) 527-35, 605-11, 645-51; and in *Alabama Review,* II (April, 1949), 139-49.

2. Paul Hamilton Hayne (ed.), *The Poems of Henry Timrod* (1872) 30-31. "A Vision of Poesy" is on pp. 137-61. It also appears in *Poems of Henry Timrod* (Memorial Edition, with memoir by J. P. K. Bryan, 1899 and 1901), 74-100. Page references are to this edition, hereafter cited as Timrod, *Poems.*

3. Timrod, *Poems,* 75. Timrod noted that the "ground of the poetic character is a more than ordinary sensibility" (*Essays,* 73).

4. *Ibid.,* 85. The following quotations in this paragraph are from pages 85-90.

5. *Ibid.,* 90-92. Quotation on 91.

6. *Ibid.,* 92-100. Quotations 98-99.

7. To cite one old and one very recent example: G. A. Wauchope, *Henry Timrod: Man and Poet* (Bulletin of the University of South Carolina, 1915), 22, and G. A. Cardwell, Jr., *The Uncollected Poems of Henry Timrod* (Athens, Georgia, 1942), 4.

8. *The Poetical Works of Percy Bysshe Shelley* (edited by Mrs. Shelley; Boston, 1881), I. Above quotations, 162-63.

9. Timrod, *Poems,* 75-76, 81-85.

10. Shelley, *op. cit.,* 164-66. Following quotation, 163.

11. Timrod, *Poems,* 93.

12. *Ibid.,* 85, 88.

13. Shelley, *op. cit.,* 157-58.

14. Timrod, *Poems,* 99.

15. Several critics have thought they detected a stronger influence than I can find. Peirce Bruns (in the *Conservative Review,* I: 263-77, May, 1859, p. 268) makes by far the strongest statement that I have seen; he thinks there is little resemblance between Wordsworth's handling of nature, and Timrod's: "Timrod, in this regard, at least, is far nearer to Shelley." Walter Hines Page (in the *South-Atlantic,* I: 359-67, March, 1878, p. 365) says that two or three stanzas of "A Summer Shower" remind him by their exquisite movement and beautiful fancy of Shelley's "Cloud." Jay B. Hubbell (*The Last Years of Henry Timrod,* Durham, 1941, p. 127) suggests that Timrod's "Song" (first line: "The Zephyr that toys with thy curls") is "reminiscent of Shelley's 'Love's Philosophy.' "

16. In "What Is Poetry?" and "A Theory of Poetry," in *Essays,* 70, 114.

17. Shelley, "A Defence of Poetry."

18. In varying forms, this distinction appears in three of Timrod's essays: "The Character and Scope of the Sonnet," "What is Poetry?", and "A Theory of Poetry." For a good, brief discussion of his essays, see G. P. Voigt, "Timrod's Essays in Literary Criticism," in *American Literature,* VI: 163-67, May, 1934.

19. Hayne, *op. cit.,* 19.

20. Timrod, "What is Poetry?"

21. Timrod, "A Vision of Poesy," *Poems,* 75.

22. *Ibid.,* 85-88.

23. "The Character and Scope of the Sonnet," *Essays,* 65. This essay was first published in *Russell's,* I, (May 1857), 156-59; reprinted in *Essays,* 61-68. Timrod uses practically the same phrasing in "A Theory of Poetry," *Essays,* 119:

I look upon every poem as strictly a work of art, and on the Poet, in the act of putting poetry into verse, simply as an artist. If the Poet have his hour of inspiration (though I am so sick of the cant of which this word has been the fruitful source, that I dislike to use it) it is not during the work of composition. A distinction must be made between the moment when the great thought strikes for the first time along the brain, and flushes the cheek with the sudden revelation of beauty, or grandeur,—and the hour of patient and elaborate execution. The soul of the Poet, though constrained to utter itself at some time or other, does not burst into song as readily as a maiden of sixteen bursts into musical laughter. Many poets have written of grief, but no poet with the first agony at his heart, ever sat down to strain that grief through iambics. Many poets have given expression of the first raptures of successful love, but no poet, in the delirium of the joy, has ever babbled it in anapests. Could this have been possible, the poet would be the most wonderful of improvisers, and perhaps a poem would be no better than what improvisations always are.

It would be easy to prove the truth of these remarks by the confessions of the Poets themselves. Poe has described to the world the manner in which he slowly built up the poem of the Raven. A greater poet than Poe speaks of himself as "not used to make a present joy the matter of his song," and of his poems, which the "Muse accepts, *deliberately* pleased," as *"thoughtfully* fitted to the Orphean lyre." The labour through which Tennyson has attained that perfection of style which is characteristic of his poems, must have been almost infinite. And Matthew Arnold—a poet not widely known in this country, but one who in the estimation of the English critical public—sits not very far below Tennyson—separates as I have separated the hour of insight, from the hour of labour.

Of his own poem "Katie," Timrod wrote to Rachel Lyons, *SLM*, II (Nov. 1940), 609, that "I am more than usually distrustful as to the merit of the composition. It was so purely an inspiration; it was written with such facility; and with such small recourse to art in the execution, that I am much afraid that your verdict will be that 'I have done a thing which ought not to have been done.' It has had, however, the approbation of the critical few to whom I have yet submitted it."

24. Hayne, *op. cit.*, 26. Hayne gives no hint as to whether these depreciators were personally known to Timrod. In the essay, a scornful reference is made to Samuel Rogers' attack on the sonnet: "That complacent poet has remarked that 'he had never attempted to write a sonnet, as he could see no reason why a man, who had anything to say, should be tied down to fourteen lines.' He adds, somewhat condescendingly, that it 'did very well for Wordsworth, as its strict limits prevented him from lapsing into that diffuseness to which he was prone.' That a poet who was wont to confine himself to four couplets a day, as much we suspect from actual sterility in word and thought, as with any design of polishing his verse, should speak in terms of such cool disparagement of the style of Wordsworth, is amusing enough. But with the banker's strictures upon the author of Laodamia, we have nothing to do. What shall we say in reply to that objection which turns upon the impossibility of compressing the thoughts of Mr. Rogers within the compass of fourteen lines. The answer lies in a nutshell. It is plain that Mr. Rogers had never reflected upon the nature of the sonnet." Too many readers, also, understood very little about poetry, and cared less. If he read poetry aloud to a group, Timrod soon discovered that too often the "subtle melody has fallen on deaf ears. The deep thought, the lofty imagination have not been comprehended at all. 'Very good, I dare say, but—I am no critic,' or, 'quite pretty, but after all, give me a song of Moore's.' The enthusiastic reader shuts the book with an internal malediction" (*Essays*, 61-62).

25. Grayson's essay appeared in *Russell's*, I (July 1857), 327-37; Timrod's in *Russell's*, II (Oct. 1857), 52-58. I have reprinted both articles in *The Essays of Henry Timrod*. See also the article on Grayson in this book. At least two unwary biographers have quoted from Grayson, and attributed the quotation to Timrod, with the result that Timrod's critical ideas were completely falsified.

26. Joseph LeConte, "On the Nature and Uses of Art," in the *Southern Presbyterian Review*, XV (Jan., 1863), 519-20.

27. Timrod quotes at length from Grayson, *Essays*, 70-72, before beginning his reply. Timrod's comments on words are on 74-76. He asserted that verse can never be prose, though much of it may not be poetry: "while we acknowledge the work of Lucretius to be a poem, we may yet declare that much of it is not poetry." The prose of Jeremy Taylor and of Milton is often "sensuous, picturesque, and passionate," and therefore poetic, so that "without denying the passage from Milton's Tractate on Education [quoted by Grayson] to be prose, we may yet assert that it contains the genuine elements of poetry" (76-78). Equally, Timrod denies that "because it is impossible to call Ivanhoe a poem, it must follow that it does not contain a single element of poetry." Here, too, Timrod is making a careful distinction between the objectified form, the poem, and the subjective essence, poetry.

28. "A Theory of Poetry" was delivered as a lecture at Columbia, South Carolina, in 1863-64. The manuscript is in the Charleston Library Society. Apparently the essay was first published in three parts in *The Independent*, LIII (March 28, April 4 and 11, 1901), 712-16, 760-64, 830-33, with an introductory note by Henry Austin. It was reprinted in the *Atlantic Monthly*, XCVI (Sept. 1905), 313-26. Neither text is completely reliable. It was again printed from Timrod's manuscript in *Essays*, 103-32.

29. *Essays*, 107-11. Timrod quotes with approval Charles Lamb's dictum that the reader should have "docile thoughts, and purged ears." He also wrote that "It has been correctly remarked of the extracts which go by the name of the beauties of Shakespeare, that those passages lose more by being torn from the context than the dramas themselves would lose by being deprived of those passages altogether. This is true also, though doubtless not to so great an extent, of Paradise Lost, and it could not be true if each book, or part of a book, could affect us as strongly when considered as portions of a series of poems, as when regarded as fractions of a harmonious whole" (109). Timrod also believed that interested readers could concentrate for a much longer period than Poe did: "I am disposed to think that the young lady who pores till midnight over a metrical novel of Scott's, and wakes up the next morning with her bright eyes dimmed and a little swollen, or the young poet who follows for the first time the steps of Dante and his guide down to the spiral abysses of his imaginary hell, could not easily be induced to assent to the truth of these assertions. The declaration made with such cool metaphysical dogmatism that 'all excitement[s] are through a psychal necessity, transient' needs considerable qualification" (*Essays*, 105).

30. *Essays*, 113. Timrod also notes specifically that "I have said nothing from which it could be inferred that I regard size as a criterion of excellence. It is one thing to say that a poem of twelve books may be good, and another thing to say that a poem is good because it contains twelve books. I am not going to deny, however, that a poem may be extended to so great a length as to preclude the possibility of its operating upon our feelings with unity of effect, as witness the Fairy Queen. Yet, it should be observed in justice to Spenser that *that* production is in fact, what Poe maintains the epic of Milton to be, a succession of poems having no real connection with each other. Perhaps the same may be said of the Iliad of Homer. I do not refer to the Columbiad because if that ponderous production could be crushed into a space no bigger than that occupied by an epigram, not a drop of genuine poetry could be forced from it. If I should be asked to fix the limit beyond which a poem should not be extended, I can only answer that that must be left to the taste and judgment of the Poet, based upon a careful and appreciative study of the few great masters. The ordeal of criticism will settle afterwards how far unity has been preserved or violated. In general it may be remarked that the plot of a poem should be so compact,

as not to involve scenes and subjects of too great diversity. As a consequence of this principle, I have always regarded the Divine Comedy of Dante in its progress though Hell, Purgatory and Heaven as three distinct poems" (111).

31. *Essays*, 114. Timrod again protests against the confusion "of the subjective essence and the objective form." Poetry may be revealed in music, painting, sculpture, or architecture, but here he is concerned only with "the development of Poetry in words" (113, 119). He also notes that Poe's theory leads to the conclusion that "Tennyson is the noblest of poets. . . Poe is next to the noblest. At the same time I must do Poe the justice to acquit him of the petty vanity of wishing to lead his readers to such a conclusion" (115). Timrod admired both Tennyson and Poe, but he would not admit their superiority to Milton and Wordsworth.

32. *Essays*, 117-18. Poe, he felt, had erred in "confounding Truth with Science and Matter of fact" (123).

33. *Essays*, 120-21. Wordsworth in particular, through "his majestic calm," could bring calmness to those who "study (not read) him in his own poetical and philosophical spirit. I am quite sure that nobody could devote a month or many months to that grand old bard, without being made wiser and better" (Letter to Rachel Lyons, *SLM*, II [Dec. 1940], 651).

34. Letter to his sister Emily, March 25, 1861, in Timrod-Goodwin Collection, South Caroliniana Library. W. P. Trent (*William Gilmore Simms*, 233-34) thinks Timrod's inability to conceal his dislike of poor poetry may have led to a temporary estrangement with Simms: "Timrod was critical by nature and Simms was vulnerable in many places. Timrod knew that he could write real poetry, while Simms could not, and it probably vexed him to hear the elder man airing his often crude views upon poetical subjects in his positive Johnsonian manner." But Trent also quotes (297) from a letter in which Timrod wrote to Simms that "Somehow or other, you always magnetize me on to a little strength." And in the *Daily South Carolinian*, May 3, 1864, Timrod wrote: "We had the pleasure of welcoming to our office, yesterday, WILLIAM GILMORE SIMMS, Esq., poet, critic, novelist, historian, and one of the oldest living editors of the South. No man has done half so much as this wondrously prolific writer to create a Southern literature, whether by the achievements of his own broad genius or by the generous encouragement which he has lavished upon young aspirants." Also, Timrod was not unduly sensitive about criticism of his own work; he wrote to Rachel Lyons, *SLM*, II (Nov. 1940), 610, that "I can endure any amount of criticism with perfect equanimity. If I think the criticism correct, I am not too proud to profit by it; if it seem to me unjust, it would not affect me though it came from the lips of an angel."

35. Columbia *Daily South Carolinian*, Jan. 19, 1864.

36. These letters to Hayne are listed in the order of the quotations: July 10, 1864, in Hubbell, *op. cit.*, 32: "I do not know whether you have published any verses lately, but if so, you may possibly be surprised that they are not copied in the Carolinian. The reason is that I never see a literary paper. Fontaine immediately seizes on them for his wife who keeps them on file. If you should ever wish anything to appear in the Carolinian,—I mean of course after you have sold it to some other paper not too mean to buy it—you must send it to me." March 30, 1866; quoted in Hubbell, *op. cit.*, 59. On March 7, 1866, Timrod used the same phrase to Hayne, but without relating it to poetry (Hubbell, *op. cit.*, 51): "I like usually to plunge *in medias res.*" Hayne's prize-poem was "The Confederates in the Field"; Timrod's, "Address Delivered at the Opening of the New Theatre at Richmond" (1863).

37. See "A Vision of Poesy" and "A Theory of Poetry"; also, the discussion

and notes below; and "A Rhapsody of a Southern Winter Night," in *Poems*, 109-13.

38. The poem is titled, perhaps significantly, "A Little Spot of Dingy Earth"; in Cardwell, *Uncollected Poems*, 67-71. The quotations are from 70-71.

39. "Youth and Manhood," in *Poems*, 24-26.

40. "Why Silent," in *Poems*, 45.

41. Sonnet V, "Some truths there be are better left unsaid"; in *Poems*, 173. The same thought appears also in "A Rhapsody of a Southern Winter Night," III:

> While in the fears that chasten mortal joy,
> Is one that shuts the lips, lest speech too free,
> With the cold touch of hard reality,
> Should turn its priceless jewels into dust.

He was also convinced that a poet could not fully understand what he intuitively knew or felt. See Sonnet XIV, "Are these wild thoughts, thus fettered in my rhymes," and the poem "Dreams," in *Poems*, 182 and 101-02.

42. "Retirement," in *Poems*, 136. See also "Sonnet—In the Deep Shadow," in *Uncollected Poems*, 53; "Vox et Praeterea Nihil," in *Poems*, 31; Sonnet VI, "They dub thee idler, smiling sneeringly," in *Poems*, 172. Timrod also made effective literary use of both the sleep-dream and the day-dream; see my article, "Timrod's Concept of Dreams," *South Atlantic Quarterly*, XLVIII (Oct. 1949), 584-88.

43. See, for typical examples, "To Anna," in *Uncollected Poems*, 92; "A Vision of Poesy," section II; Sonnet X, in *Poems*, 178; "Why Silent," in *Poems*, 45; also, two letters from Emily Timrod Goodwin to Hayne (Nov. 23, 1867, in Timrod-Goodwin Collection, South Caroliniana Library): "With regard to our brother's age I must be candid with you. The year of his birth was written down by my father as the 8th of December 1829 [actually, W. H. Timrod recorded Henry's birth in his day-book as occurring Dec. 8, 1828]; but Hal always said 1830. He thought he had accomplished so little that he made himself a year younger than he really was." On Oct. 22, 1867, in a letter to Hayne describing her brother's death, Emily wrote (quoted in Hayne, *op. cit.*, 61-62; Ms. in Timrod-Goodwin Collection): "After the Doctor went, he said to me, 'And is this to be the end of all—so soon! and I have achieved so little! I thought to have done so much. I had just before my first attack fallen into a strain of such pure and delicate fancies. I think this winter I would have done more than I have ever done; I should have written more purely, and with greater delicacy."

44. See the opening paragraphs of "The Character and Scope of the Sonnet."

45. "A Vision of Poesy," in *Poems*, 87-88.

46. See "A Theory of Poetry"; also note 108.

47. "A Vision of Poesy," in *Poems*, 88 and 97-99.

48. The best example of this is the conclusion of "The Cotton Boll," in *Poems*, 11.

49. For an excellent discussion of this subject, see J. B. Hubbell, "Literary Nationalism in the Old South," in *American Studies in Honor of William Kenneth Boyd* (Durham, 1940), 175-220.

50. With his essay, "Literature in the South," *Russell's*, V (Aug. 1859), 385-95; reprinted in *Essays*, 83-102.

51. Timrod notes that "not once, but a hundred times" he has heard Simms, "the first of Southern authors alluded to with contempt by individuals who had never read anything beyond the title-pages of his books" (85). He divides critics into three classes: the bigots, who "know Pope and Horace by heart, but who have never read a word of Wordsworth or Tennyson"; the slaves of nationalism and authority, who are willing to accept another critic's judgment that Drake's "Culprit Fay" is the greatest of American poems, and are indignant if "Tennyson

be mentioned in the same breath with Longfellow"; the autocratic, who pass judgment without knowledge: "it is good to be independent; but it is not good to be too independent.... Nor is that independence, but license, which is not founded upon a wide and deep knowledge of critical science, and upon a careful and respectful collation of our own conclusions, with the impartial philosophical conclusions of others." In the South, the problem was further complicated by the demand for "Southernism in literature" (86-87). There is an abundance of literary material in the South, but no individual writer should feel obligated to confine himself to them (90-91). Timrod also regrets that poetry and novels are generally considered "a very light and superficial sort of writing. . . . Of two writers, one of whom should edit a treatise on the conic sections, and the other should give to the world a novel equal in tragic power and interest to the Bride of Lammermoor, the former would be considered the greater man by nine persons out of ten" (91-92). Timrod justifies poetry (although it should need no vindication) because "beneath all the splendour of its diction and imagery, there is in its highest manifestations at least a substratum of profound and valuable thought"; fiction, because more "of human nature can be learned from the novel of Tom Jones than from a History of the whole Roman Empire—written, at least, as histories are commonly written.... We do not hesitate to say, that of two persons, one of whom has only read Hume's chapter on Richard I, and the other only the Ivanhoe of Scott, the latter will be by far the better acquainted with the real history of the period" (94-96). But appreciation is "a plant of slow growth." Of Southern writers, only Poe "has received his due measure of fame. The immense resources and versatile powers of Simms are to this day grudgingly acknowledged, or contemptuously denied. . . . While our centre-tables are littered with the feeble moralizings of Tupper, done up in very bright morocco . . . there is, perhaps, scarcely a bookseller in the United States on whose face we should not encounter the grin of ignorance, if we chanced to inquire for the Froissart Ballads of Philip Pendleton Cooke" (96-97). Timrod entered a plea for a just but strict criticism, with "No quarter to the dunce" as its motto, and for a rigorous but appreciative study of English literature (97-99).

52. On January 13, 1864, the Columbia *Daily South Carolinian* announced in its columns the valedictory of R. W. Gibbes, M.D., and its new ownership by F. G. De Fontaine & Co. De Fontaine was to be editor, and as "associate editor we have secured the services of HENRY TIMROD, ESQ." He was responsible for the editorials; he helped also with other sections of the paper. In a letter to Hayne, Timrod disclaims the authorship of most of the book notices. All the editorials that contain literary criticism are printed in *Essays*, in the notes to "Literature in the South" and "A Theory of Poetry." J. B. Hubbell, *op. cit.*, 133-45, reprints five of them. The first of his editorials, entitled "Southern Literature," appeared Jan. 14, 1864.

53. "Southern Nationality," Jan. 16, 1864, and "Nationality in Literature," Jan. 19, 1864. The quotation in this paragraph is from "Nationality in Literature."

54. "National Songs," Jan. 24, 1864. In a letter to Rachel Lyons, Sept. 6, 1861, *SLM*, II (Nov. 1940), 609, he wrote: "I tried, not long ago, to write a national song; but my work failed to satisfy me and I destroyed it.

"There seems to be some especial difficulty in writing a song of this nature. There is really not a single good one in the language; for 'Rule Britannia' and 'The Star-Spangled Banner' are both worthless as poetry. Even Tennyson has failed in his attempts in this line; witness, for instance, the doggerel of his 'Riflemen, riflemen, riflemen, form!' And but the other day all the Yankee poets (and it cannot be denied that there are some noble ones among them) were trying, with the incentive of a prize of five hundred dollars before them, to manufacture a national hymn; yet they all signally failed."

55. "War and Literature," Feb. 28, 1864, and an editorial without a title, Sept. 15, 1864.

56. Quoted in Hubbell, *op. cit.*, 43.

57. The *Daily South Carolinian* stopped with the burning of Columbia on Feb. 17, 1865. Its printer, Julian A. Selby (*Memorabilia and Anecdotal Reminiscences of Columbia, S. C.*, Columbia, 1905, 101) writes that as Sherman's army approached he and Timrod "issued a 'thumb-sheet' two or three times a day," with shells dropping near the building. Timrod wrote some editorials, 1865-66, for the *Phoenix* (started in Columbia March 21, 1865, but moved before December to Charleston). Trent, *op. cit.*, 292, says that Timrod did not "contribute a line for weeks together." Timrod (letter to Hayne, March 30, 1866; in Hubbell, *op. cit.*, 60) writes that Fontaine "started the Carolinian" again in Charleston: "I have hacked for him for four months, and have not yet received one month's pay. The truth is, Fontaine *can't* pay."

58. J. P. K. Bryan, in Introduction, *Poems*, xxxiii.

59. Hayne, *op. cit.*, 18-19.

60. *Ibid.*, 21.

61. "A Theory of Poetry," *Essays*, 124-35; and "Literature in the South," *Essays*, 99.

62. In a thoughtful discussion of Timrod's life and work, Peirce Bruns (in *Conservative Review*, I: 268, May, 1899) disagreed flatly with this; but he apparently was not familiar with Timrod's prose: "It has been said that he was most deeply influenced by Wordsworth. But this is manifestly erroneous. The mistake, we suppose, has arisen from Paul Hayne's statement that Timrod's favorite poem was Wordsworth's "Intimations of Immortality from Recollections of Early Childhood,' a poem which is certainly the most un-Wordsworthian of all the Lake Poet's works. Surely there can be no resemblance between the 'cloudy pantheism' of Wordsworth and the clear-cut, definite forms under which Timrod envisaged the flowers of nature. Timrod, in this regard, at least is far nearer to Shelley." Trent, *op. cit.*, 235, states without qualification of Timrod: "That he was dominated by Tennyson . . . is perfectly true." There are obvious borrowings in thought from Wordsworth's "Ode on Intimations of Immortality" in Timrod's "Dramatic Fragment," *Poems*, 105-06.

63. Letter to Rachel Lyons, in "Unpublished Letters of Henry Timrod," edited by William Fidler, *SLM*, II (Nov. 1940), 610-11.

64. "A Vision of Poesy," in *Poems*, 86-89 and 99.

65. *Poems*, 169.

66. "A Dedication," in *Poems*, 37.

67. "A Vision of Poesy," in *Poems*, 78. In the poem "Dramatic Fragment," 105-06, he says that "We are born . . . in miniature completeness"; we do not change, but only grow and develop; and childhood is "a sort of golden daylight."

68. "A Theory of Poetry." Later quotations in this paragraph are from the same article (*Essays*, 117, 120-21).

69. Fidler, *op. cit.*, II: 651. Emily Timrod Goodwin, in writing of her brother's love of nature, did not mention the influence of Wordsworth, but emphasized the influence of their mother (Letter, Emily to Hayne, Sept. 25, 1872, in Timrod-Goodwin Collection, South Caroliniana Library; quoted in Hayne, p. 41): "It was from *her*, more than from his gifted father, that my brother derived that intense, passionate love of Nature which so distinguished him. Its sights and sounds always afforded her extreme delight. Shall I ever forget the almost childish rapture she testified, when, after a residence in the pent-up city all her life, she removed with me to the country? A walk in the woods to her was food and drink, and the sight of a green field was joy inexpressible.

"From my earliest childhood, I can remember her love for flowers and trees and for the stars; how she would call our attention to the glintings of the sunshine through the leaves; to the afternoon's lights and shadows, as they slept quietly, side by side; and even to a streak of moonlight on the floor."

70. "The Summer Bower," in *Poems,* 106-08.

71. W. G. Simms, "The Late Henry Timrod," in *Southern Society,* I: 18-19, Oct. 12, 1867; also in Hubbell, *op. cit.,* 153-65.

72. Hayne, *op. cit.,* 24.

73. "Lines to R. L.," in *Poems,* 131. An allusion which takes for granted a knowledge of Tennyson is given in "Lines," *Poems,* 191:

> I saw, or dreamed I saw, her sitting lone,
> Her neck bent like a swan's, her brown eyes thrown
> On some sweet poem—his, I think, who sings
> Œnone, or the hapless Maud:

R. L. was Rachel Lyons. The poem was first published in *Russell's,* VI (Feb. 1860), 459. For an excellent account of Tennyson's influence on Timrod and other Southern poets, see John O. Eidson's *Tennyson in America* (Athens, Ga., 1943) .

74. Typed copy of letter to Emily, from Charleston, Feb. 10, 1862, in Timrod-Goodwin Collection, South Caroliniana Library. The original is missing.

75. While she owned the book, Mrs. Lloyd wrote to W. A. Courtenay (March 15, 1898; letter in *Memories of the Timrod Revival 1898-1901,* Charleston Library Society): "I have a little worn copy of Tennyson which he always carried with him. It never left him. He had it from the time when he was almost a boy. It is marked by him, and some of the pages turned down by him." It may be noted that Mrs. Lloyd was frequently given to over-statement.

The one pencilled note deals with the line from Section II of "The Princess": "The Rhodope that built the pyramid." Timrod noted: "Herodotus says that this pyramid wrongly ascribed by some to Rhodope was built by Mycerinus." This testifies more to a knowledge of the Greek historian ("Euterpe," Ch. CXXXIV) than to his known appreciation of Tennyson. Timrod has also marked a few lines in "Œnone," in "The Palace of Art," in "A Dream of Fair Women," in "In Memoriam," and in "Maud."

76. For another example, see *Poems,* 136-37. Timrod's eight-volume set of Milton (London: Pickering, 1851) is now in the Timrod Museum at Florence, S.C. It reveals no notes or markings; presumably Timrod owned a copy of Milton earlier. On a fly-leaf, in Timrod's writing but without a date, is the notation, "from his esteemed, departed friend, Mrs. Emma P. Blake." The material in the Timrod Museum has only association or sentimental value.

77. Letter to Hayne, March 7, 1866; in Hubbell, *op. cit.,* 54. In an undated letter to Emily from Copse Hill (probably May or August, 1867; Timrod-Goodwin Collection, South Caroliniana Library) he described Jean Ingelow as a "worthy successor of Mrs. Browning's"; and on Aug. 24, 1864, he closed an editorial on the imperfections of contemporaneous judgments with her "titanic lines," beginning "Every age,/ Through being beheld too close, is ill-discerned / By those who have not lived past it." Ludwig Lewisohn (*Books We Have Made,* 53; scrapbook in Charleston Library Society, from Charleston *News and Courier,* Sundays July 5-Sept. 20, 1903) suggests that "A 'Dramatic Fragment' is an attempt in the jerky, but picturesque, blank verse of Elizabeth Barrett Browning."

78. See page 5 of introduction, and "A Vision of Poesy," in *Poems,* 90. The semi-personal, semi-literary comparison is well illustrated by L. Frank Tooker's comment (in the *Century,* LV, n.s. 33: 932-34, April, 1898): "The reader is constantly reminded of the cumulative sadness that was the lot of Keats, as he is reminded of the latter's excessive sensibility of temperament. Indeed, in spirit the two poets were essentially kin, though in poetic insight and expression—in the

true province of the poet—Timrod, of course, dwelt on a lower plane. He also dwelt in a different atmosphere, for while the influence of Keats may be traced in his work, the feeling, the local coloring, the habit of thought, are his own."

79. Ms. in Charleston Library Society. These poems have all been published in Cardwell, *The Uncollected Poems of Henry Timrod* (1942).

80. Hayne, who disliked Byron, expressly notes (p. 67) "the absence from his works of all morbid arraignments of the Eternal justice or mercy; all blasphemous hardihood and whining complaint—in a word, all *Byronism* of sentiment."

81. "Song—When I bade thee adieu," published in *Russell's Magazine*, I: 489, Sept. 1857; in *Uncollected Poems*, 108; the opening section of "The Character and Scope of the Sonnet" reveals his doubt of Moore's validity as a poet. The manuscript poem is in *Autographic Relics*, and may have been written several years earlier. I agree with Cardwell (*op. cit.*, 3-4) that "in spirit and subject matter, Timrod's early verse seems much like the poetry of Moore."

82. "In Bowers of Ease," in *Autographic Relics*, and in *Uncollected Poems*, 78; see also 119, n. 68. Timrod consistently spells the poet's name Thompson; a few editions show this spelling, and Timrod may have owned one of them.

Worth noting among these very early poems is Timrod's parody of Charles Wolfe's "The Burial of Sir John Moore after Corunna." The first two lines show its schoolboy, mock-occasional character: "Not a grin was seen, not a giggle heard / As the tutor breath'd his last." The poem is described as "his first known effort," but is dated 1844. It is printed in *Uncollected Poems*, 23.

83. See "A Theory of Poetry," *Essays*, 124.

84. "Field Flowers," in *Uncollected Poems*, 100.

85. Editorial without title, *Daily South Carolinian*, Aug. 3, 1864. The only other author named is Shakespeare; Timrod contrasts England's narrowness of policy with his universal sympathies. The newspaper's spelling: etherial.

86. Hayne, *op. cit.*, 31; see also "A Theory of Poetry," *Essays*, 112.

87. See "The Character and Scope of the Sonnet," *Essays*, 62.

88. "Names of Months Phonetically Expressive," in Hayne, *op. cit.*, 50-51. Hayne gives no source, but says that it was written "after the surrender at Appomatox." Somewhat similar remarks appears in the *Daily South Carolinian*, Oct. 2 and 4, 1864, but there Timrod says: "The reader must, himself, make what he can of November. We don't like the month, and shall, therefore, say nothing about it."

89. "Address Delivered at the Opening of the New Theatre at Richmond," in *Poems*, 69-73. See also "Field Flowers," in *Uncollected Poems*, 99-102; and the later, revised version, "Two Field Flowers," in Hubbell, *op. cit.*, 128-30.

90. "A Dedication," in *Poems*, 38.

91. Letter from Emily Timrod Goodwin to Hayne, quoted in Hayne, *op. cit.*, 9, and in Hubbell, *op. cit.*, 170. The romantic story may not, however, have impressed Henry as much as it did Emily.

92. June 4, 1867; quoted in Hubbell, *op. cit.*, 83.

93. Letter, Emily Timrod Goodwin to Hayne, Oct. 22, 1867 (in Timrod-Goodwin Collection, South Caroliniana Library). Timrod thought that he might "make an effort, like Mrs. Dombey," and regain his health.

94. Letter from Emily Timrod Goodwin to Edith Goodwin, Oct. 29, 1867, in Timrod-Goodwin Collection, South Caroliniana Library. A letter from Emily Goodwin to Hayne (Oct. 22, 1867; see note 93) describes the same incident in a slightly different form.

95. Letter to Hayne, March 7, 1866, Hubbell, *op. cit.*, 54. Hubbell identifies the Simms attribution as in *Beauchampe* (New York, 1856), p. 118. Timrod mentions this erroneous identification again in a letter to Hayne, March 26, 1867 (Hubbell, *op. cit.*, 76). Hayne, *op. cit.*, 56, also talks of Timrod's quoting Ford or Fletcher.

96. Sonnet XI, in *Poems*, 179.

97. *Poems*, 144-46. Hayne, *op. cit.*, 37, gives it as "A Call to Arms." Two of the mild conceits from the poem, and typical of the kind that Timrod wrote, are:

> And feed your country's sacred dust
> With floods of crimson rain!
>
> . . . . .
>
> Does any falter? let him turn
> To some brave maiden's eyes,
> And catch the holy fires that burn
> In those sublunar skies.

I suspect that Hayne was referring to the second example, or possibly to the personification of the Southern woman as the lily, and the man as the palm-tree.

98. Letter to Rachel Lyons, Feb. 3, 1862, in *Southern Literary Messenger*, II: 646, Dec., 1940. See also note 114.

99. "Madeline" was first published in *The Southern Literary Messenger*, XVIII: 212, April, 1852; in *Poems*, 32-36. "La Belle Juive," in the *Charleston Daily Courier*, Jan. 23, 1862; in *Poems*, 57-59; Timrod enclosed a manuscript copy to Rachel Lyons in his letter to her, Jan. 20, 1862.

100. See *Essays*, n. 13, 167. Also deleted was a prefatory sentence: "It is indeed to a sort of discontent with the unrealities and imperfections of earth, and in the perception of a higher existence than the life which we actually lead, that the world owes the inspiration of some of the noblest poems in its possession." Timrod also accepted the innate goodness of the very young child; Wordsworth's "Ode on Intimations of Immortality" he considered, "if we except perhaps Milton's 'Hymn of the Nativity,' to be the noblest ode in the language." In it, Wordsworth "has flung a new and sacred lustre over the life of Infancy" (*Essays*, 127). Timrod also objected to critics who tried to apply a "quibbling common sense" to a supernatural story, and called upon the authority of Coleridge to distinguish between a "poet's philosophical notion of common sense" and a literal definition. With William J. Grayson in mind, he noted sarcastically: "There must be a vast difference between the taste of a man who regards the Ancient Mariner as the noblest of all ballads, and the taste of another who has read through that poem with no other sensation than what is vulgarly termed a turning of the stomach" (*Essays*, 78). Timrod does not make it clear that he is the one who regards it as the "noblest of all ballads," although this seems to me to be implied.

101. His three-volume set of Bacon (*Novum Organum, Advancement of Learning,* and *Essays*) is in the Timrod Museum at Florence, S. C. It is not marked or annotated.

102. Both *Russell's* and the *Messenger* used many brief quotations from English authors and magazines. Timrod himself, or a colleague, inserted many short pieces into the columns of the *Daily South Carolinian* in 1864: items from or about Carlyle, Thackeray, Dickens, Wilkie Collins, Lamb, Sidney Smith, Herbert, Cotton, Lamartine, Artemus Ward, Josh Billings, Whittier, T. B. Aldrich, and so on. The editorial shears apparently worked on English, Northern, and Southern papers without much discrimination; probably, on whatever came to hand. In writing to the South Carolina author Clara Dargan, asking her for contributions to a proposed paper, Timrod said that her story, "Philip, My Son," "in my opinion, would compare favourably with the best of Blackwood's" (quoted in Hubbell, *op. cit.*, 90). On May 5, 1864, he editorialized hotly about an "extract from an article" by Oliver Wendell Holmes in the *Atlantic Monthly*. Holmes is called an "objurgatory doctor," though perhaps an honest abolitionist; but in response to Holmes' question as to what stand Tennyson and Dickens have taken on slavery, Timrod answers that Dickens "has probably penetrated the true character of the political PECKSNIFFS of the North," and that Tennyson's "pure and lofty name" has been taken in vain by "the small Boston versifier."

103. Letter from Henry to Emily, July 29, 1853, in Timrod-Goodwin Collection, South Caroliniana Library.

104. Letters to Hayne, March 7, 1866, and March 26, 1867; quoted in Hubbell, *op. cit.*, 54 and 76.

105. Letter to Rachel Lyons, Dec. 10, 1861 (in University of Alabama Library).

106. Letter to Hayne, July 10, 1864; quoted in Hubbell, *op. cit.*, 32.

107. By July 11, 1867, Timrod was familiar enough with Swinburne's work to write Hayne (Hubbell, *op. cit.*, 88): "Your criticism of Swinburne also pleases me much; but I must express my regret that you have left his obscurity untouched."

108. Letter to Hayne, April 13, 1867 (in Timrod-Goodwin Collection, South Caroliniana Library). The serial was *Joscelyn.*

In a letter to Rachel Lyons, July 7, 1861; in *Southern Literary Messenger,* II (Nov., 1940), 605-06, Timrod criticized "the 'Beulah' of your friend Miss Evans" as a "very clever work," but without any especial excellence or "any marked originality in the style and characters of the story." He objects particularly that "Beulah's transition from scepticism to Faith is left almost wholly unaccounted for."

For Miss Evans' theory concerning poets, Timrod had only contempt: "I think it would not be difficult to show that Poetry is *not* merely a noble *insanity*; and that the errors and eccentricities of poets have not been *in consequence* of, but *in spite* of the influence of the poetical temperament. In fact, the poet, in his completest development, involves the metaphysician, and is a more sound, wholesome, and perfect human being, than the gravest of those utterers of half-truths who set up as philosophers."

109. Quoted in Hayne, *op. cit.*, 54.

110. *Ibid.*, 54-58. After Timrod's death, Emily wrote to Hayne (May 17, 1870; in Timrod-Goodwin Collection) that Henry had once read to her some lines from Whittier, "which he had copied while at your house." Henry Austin (in *The Bookman,* 9:343, June, 1899) thought that some of Timrod's lines reminded one of Whittier. H. T. Thompson, *Henry Timrod,* 117, says that after Timrod's "The Past" appeared in the *Southern Literary Messenger* (May, 1850), Whittier praised the poem in a letter to Hayne. Hayne, *op. cit.*, 21, relates the story without mentioning Whittier's name, and speaks of the "encouraging effect" of the letter on Timrod.

111. In Timrod-Goodwin Collection, South Caroliniana Library.

112. Hayne, *op. cit.*, 18: J. P. K. Bryan, in *Poems,* xxxiii. A former student of Timrod's who is supposed to have inspired his "Præceptor Amat," Miss Felicia Robinson, says that Timrod "spent as much of his time as his duties would allow in reading and studying, and was rarely without some book in his hand. . . . He was a very learned man, being devoted to the Classics, and able to read fluently French, German, Latin and Greek" (quoted in Wauchope, *Henry Timrod,* 12-13). Simms (in *Southern Society,* I: 18, Oct. 12, 1867) wrote: "He was a good Latin scholar, something of a Grecian, and possessed a fair general acquaintance with some of the Continental languages." Henry Austin, *op. cit.*, 342, thinks one line of "A Dedication" is "well-nigh as luscious with liquids as its prototype in Vergil's First Eclogue." H. T. Thompson, *Henry Timrod,* 15, tells of acquiring "a copy of Cooper's Vergil now unfortunately lost, which Timrod had used at school, and which the writer afterwards used. The pages of this old book were embellished with caricatures in pencil, and accompanied with doggerel verses in Timrod's handwriting which embodied pungent and sarcastic criticism of his classmates."

113. Letters, March 15, 1898, and March 30, 1900, in *Memories of the Timrod Revival 1898-1901* (bound Ms. volume in Charleston Library Society).

114. Professor Cardwell seems definitely convinced of this. In the Introduction to *Uncollected Poems of Henry Timrod,* 4-5, he notes: "Some possible classic

parallels there are. The quatrain *'There is I know not what about thee,'* is of course similar to Martial, I. xxxii (cf. also Catullus, LXXXV): but it is clearly playing upon Brown's famous impromptu translation rather than upon Martial's original. One may compare both *'Sweet let not our slanderers'* and *'Let V——y prattle'* with Catullus, V, but the similarities are quite general. For an example of a faint reminiscence of the *Anacreontea,* compare Ode 8 (numbering of the Loeb edition) with the verses *'For high honours.'* For another faint echo of a classic poem, compare *'Six months's such a wonderful time'* with Horace, I. v. Here, as in the instance of Martial, I. xxxii, mentioned above, an English intermediary or poem on a similar theme (cf. Suckling's 'Out upon it!') is probably to be assumed." Peirce Bruns, *op. cit.,* 270, says that "from all Timrod's lighter verse there breathes gently . . . the faint, sweet perfume of Catullus' 'Dainty Volume,' " and compares Timrod's "A Dedication" with Catullus, LXXV.

115. Timrod's pocket-size copy, now in the Charleston Library Society, included the works of three Latin poets: *Catulli, Tibulli, et Propertii, Opera* (London, 1822). I give an example of each type of annotation: IV: utrumque . . . pedem, underscored, with note "The lower corners of the sails and the ropes by which they were made fast were called *pedes";* limpidum lacum, underscored, with note, "Lake Benacus." X: caput unctius referret, "a metaphor for becoming rich." XXXII: meridiatum, "to pass the noon, to take one's siesta." LI: "Ad Lesbiam," "The first three stanzas of this poem are translated from Sappho's celebrated ode preserved by Longinus." LXI: Julia Manlio . . . bona cum bona / Nubit alite virgo, "Julia will her Manlius wed, / Good with good, a blessed bed. Leigh Hunt." LXIII: ll. 6-8, "Note the abrupt transition to the feminine gender"; l. 75, "Condemned as a spurious line by the best commentators." LXXXIX: omnia plena puellis / Cognatis, "crowds of female cousins—idiomatic as omnia miseriarum plenissima (Cicero)."

The Tibullus has no marks or notes; the Propertius a few underlinings, two or three notes on words, and one change in punctuation: I, XX, 32, "Ah! dolor ibat," to "Ah dolor! ibat."

116. *Cornelii Nepotis Vitae* (The Regent's Classics. Pocket Edition. London, 1819); bound in the same volume, *Pomponii Melae, De Situ Orbis, Libri Tres* (London, 1819); *P. Papinii Statii Opera* (London, 1822) .

117. March 7, 1866; quoted in Hubbell, *op. cit.,* 53-54.

118. Letter to Hayne, March 26, 1867; quoted in Hubbell, *op. cit.,* 76.

119. In the same poem, Timrod speaks of a "much-valued edition of Homer," and of "the Greek's multitudinous line." Walter Hines Page, in the *South-Atlantic,* I (March, 1878), 367, writes that "A Mother's Wail" is Timrod's most nearly perfect poem, and to the reader of Simonides seems almost Greek-like.

120. On W. H. Timrod's war service, see G. A. Cardwell, Jr., "William Henry Timrod, the Charleston Volunteers, and the Defense of St. Augustine," in *North Carolina Historical Review,* XVIII (Jan., 1941), 27-37. The "Song of Mignon" is printed in *Uncollected Poems,* 103-04; Simms seems to have been writing of an original poem by Timrod.

121. Letter to Emily, July 4, 1851 (in Timrod-Goodwin Collection, South Caroliniana Library). In the letter to Hayne, March 7, 1866, he speaks of Davidson's critical *niaiseries,* which deserve only "a round dozen *'grands coups de pieds dans le derrière.'* "

122. Now in the Timrod Museum at Florence, S. C.

123. See Hayne, *op. cit.,* 8-17, and Hubbell, *op. cit.,* 165-78; Timrod's Daybook, in the Charleston Library Society, has been preserved only for the four years 1825-1829, and 1836. James McCarter, who employed Timrod for over ten years, wrote to Hayne in 1867: "His wonderful powers of conversation, his genial manner, his pleasant and amiable temper, his exquisite humour, and pungent wit, soon gathered

round him a knot of clever young men, who relished his company, and enjoyed his jokes," so that his workshop was called Timrod's Club (Hubbell, *op. cit.*, 173-74). Hayne quotes several of his later poems, including "To Harry."

124. A tiny volume of 78 pages. The first poem, "Quebec," is subtitled "In Imitation of Campbell's Hohenlinden"; "A Dream" is a weak, conventionalized poet's vision of a "beauteous maid" who vanishes when the poet wakes; "To Pyrrha" has above the title, "Horace, Book I, Ode V, Imitated"; various poems celebrate the charms of such pastoral ladies as Julia, Celia, Thyrsa; on p. 61 the poet calls himself Strephon; several poems are remotely in the Cavalier tradition, with the air sometimes listed under the title (p. 57, "Song." / "Air—The Glasses Sparkle on the Board"); a few are sonnets; "Sullivan's Island" is a didactic poem in heroic couplets. The most interesting, "Noon. An Eclogue" has three negro characters, Sampy, Cudjoe, and Quashebo; and some negro dialect which the author explains in footnotes. The poem is a deliberate mixture of dialect and high-flown language; two women who are talked about are Clarissa and Jemimah. Many of the blank pages of the Daybook contain later poems.

125. Hubbell, *op. cit.*, 166: "In an undated letter Emily Timrod Goodwin wrote to Hayne: 'I heard him regret deeply that he had ever allowed them to appear in print, so meanly did he think of them.' "

126. W. G. Simms, in *Southern Society*, I: 18-19, Oct. 12, 1867; quoted in Hubbell, *op. cit.*, 155.

127. For a vivid account of this group, see P. H. Hayne, "Ante-Bellum Charleston," in *The Southern Bivouac*, I (Nov. 1885), 327-36.

128. Unfortunately, no record of this criticism exists, except in the writings of Hayne and Bruns on Timrod. Yates Snowden ("A Reminiscence of Henry Timrod," Charleston *News and Courier*, Dec. 20, 1903) tells of one gathering of five young men: Timrod, Bruns, John della Torre, William A. Martin, and the unnamed narrator. Bruns claimed that della Torre had discovered the Latin original of a recent poem of Timrod's; della Torre read as the original his own translation into 13th century Latin. Timrod, non-plussed, protested innocence until the other men laughed at him and admitted the hoax. Years later, Rachel Lyons Heustis remembered especially Timrod's "entire absence of jealousy or unkind criticism of contemporary poets," and his willingness to listen to criticism of his own verse (letter to W. A. Courtenay, March 20, 1899, in *Memories of the Timrod Revival 1898-1901*).

11. HAYNE

1. *Poems of Paul Hamilton Hayne* (1882), 164-65; Hayne, "Memoir of Henry Timrod," in *The Poems of Henry Timrod* (1873), 17.

2. See Kate H. Becker, *Paul Hamilton Hayne: Life and Letters* (1951), 5-6, 10-11. The reviews in "Our Book Table," in the *Southern Literary Gazette* are in general disappointing; they are, properly, notices rather than reviews, and are unsigned. In a signed Valedictory Editorial on Dec. 18, 1852, W. C. Richards stated that Hayne had been the editor for the past six months. In a letter to E. L. Didier. (Nov. 29, 1881; Hayne Collection, Duke Univ. Library) Hayne gives the date as May 21, 1852; he bought out Richards in Dec. 1852, but the magazine ceased publication in 1853. There is a considerable amount of literary gossip, and in the magazine and the bi-weekly Supplement there are printed or re-printed many poems by Timrod (frequently under the pseudonym Aglaus), Hayne, and Simms, as well as serials of Simms's *Golden Christmas* and *The Sword and the Distaff*. In an editorial (July 10, 1852) Hayne praised Simms (as Father Abbott) for having taught Charlestonians "to look abroad at \home." But Hayne's distrust of his critical powers in this period is clearly stated on Dec. 4, 1852: in a notice

of Macaulay's *Lays,* Moore's *Irish Melodies,* and other books, he wrote that of "the literary merit of these books it would be mere impertinence to speak in this notice."

3. *Russell's Magazine,* I (May 1857), 182. Hayne edited *Russell's* from its beginning in April 1857, to its death in March 1860. He selected for quotation or wrote most of the "Editor's Table"; wrote nearly all of the book reviews; and contributed poems, stories, and articles.

4. Daniel Morley McKeithan, *A Collection of Hayne Letters* (1944), 88. This book is indispensable for any study of Hayne's criticism. Letter of May 17, 1860. Hereafter cited as McKeithan.

5. *Russell's,* III (June, 1858), 284. Hayne also objects to Southern periodicals overpraising Southern writers, calling it an "amiable dishonesty, for dishonesty it really amounts to." However, he confesses he too may have sinned. In the body of the review, though not in the headnote, he writes *Taylor* instead of Turner several times.

6. This unsigned, three-part editorial appeared in the *Southern Literary Gazette,* Oct. 2, 9, 16, 1852. It has all the distinguishing marks of Hayne's style. The article to which Hayne objected had appeared in the *North British Review;* on Oct. 23, Hayne notes that if the author was an American, as he had heard, the article was even worse than if by a Briton. But the English themselves tended to disregard all but the greatest of their own early writers; Chaucer, Spenser, Shakespeare, and perhaps Beaumont and Fletcher continued to be valued, but the others were unfairly neglected. Earlier, on July 3, 1852, the *Gazette* had carried an unsigned editorial praising an article in a British periodical entitled "Contemporary Literature of America." The article was only a summary, with names of authors "of many of whom we know nothing"; but at least a British reviewer had noticed American writers without sneering at them. The editorial may well be by Hayne, but has few of his characteristic felicities and peculiarities of style.

7. *Russell's* IV (Jan. 1859), 348-53, especially 352-53. Hayne's list of unfairly neglected Southern poets is large and uncritical. This neglect was not merely sectional: in the *Southern Literary Gazette,* Dec. 4, 1852, he had written that Barlow, Trumbull, and other early American poets "have sunk into as deep an oblivion as if they had never penned a line." This was unjust, and some publisher should re-issue their complete works.

8. McKeithan, 85; letter to John Esten Cooke, Nov. 4, 1859. Simms reviewed Caldwell's *Poems* in *Russell's,* III (April, 1858), 36-47. In the *Southern Quarterly Review,* NSVI (Oct., 1852), 533-34, Simms reviewed unfavorably a pamphlet containing Overall's poem, "The Funeral of Mirabeau." So had Hayne or a contributor in the *Southern Literary Gazette,* Aug. 28, 1852; the poem was not worth publishing "separately and alone."

9. Jay B. Hubbell, *The Last Years of Henry Timrod,* 28. Davidson was "a fool of the *worst* kind, inasmuch as he possesses just sufficient talent to impose on superficial scholars." But Hayne as editor of *Russell's* in April, 1859 (V: 83) welcomed the news that Caldwell and Davidson were planning to start a literary weekly in Columbia, S. C.: "Both these gentlemen are well and honorably known to the people of our state, and of the South, as poets and essayists." Caldwell had contributed "admirable papers on Victor Hugo, Béranger and other French celebrities, while Mr. Davidson is generally known as the author of the appreciative essay on Edgar Poe, which appeared in our *second volume*" (161-73). In late 1869, Hayne was infuriated by *Davidson's Living Writers of the South* (see McKeithan, 227-28).

10. *Russell's,* IV (Feb., 1859), 479-80 and IV (Jan., 1859), 376. Hayne was objecting to the morbidity and unwholesomeness in the poetry of James Gates Percival. In Charles W. Hubner's *Representative Southern Poets,* 77-78, he is quoted

as believing even Byron "might have been a far nobler character if his consort had been a different woman." She was "densely, impenetrably stupid," capable of believing the lies she poured into the ears of Mrs. Stowe.

11. McKeithan, 127; *The Correspondence of Bayard Taylor and Paul Hamilton Hayne,* edited by Charles Duffy (1945), 24. Hereafter cited as Duffy. Hayne is quoting from an article in the Wilmington, North Carolina *Morning Star,* March 11, 1876. When Hayne was literary editor of *Southern Opinion* (Richmond, Virginia), he published an equally violent article on Whitman in the Sept. 7, 1867, issue: Whitman had started a new school of verse writers, if not poets, in the United States; his works "unite the incoherent extravaganza of Nat Lee with a pruriency of sentiment and reflection which, amazing as we may deem it, actually throws the feculence of Swinburne into the shade." Hayne objected to Whitman's over-use of punctuation marks and to his endless cataloguing; perhaps most of all, stylistically, to his "peculiar" versification: "It consists in the arrangement of the baldest prose into couplets and paragraphs of uneven length, which no system of prosody the world has ever known could be made to interpret."

12. See, for example, *Russell's,* II (Dec., 1857), 274-76 and IV (Jan., 1859), 376-78, for a vigorous defence of Longfellow, Irving, and Bryant against British attacks. For private admission of defects in Simms's work, see Duffy, 94-95 (to Bayard Taylor), and his letter, Aug. 4, 1870, in Richard Beale Davis's "Paul Hamilton Hayne to Dr. Francis Peyre Porcher," *Studies in Philology,* XLIV (July, 1947), 535-36.

13. McKeithan, 41. Hayne uses nearly the same wording in a letter to Moses Coit Tyler, April 9, 1873 (McKeithan, 314). In writing his biography of Timrod for the *Poems,* "The *Past,* with all its bitterness, its sorrows, its despair,—*too vividly* pressed upon me—to admit of any attention being paid to the special graces of *style.*"

14. *Russell's,* VI (Nov., 1859), 175-76. Hayne thought Timrod at his best in blank verse. His amatory poems had "given rise to an idea that his genius is rather fanciful, sensuous, and passionate, than truly imaginative. 'The Vision of Poesy' will effectually dispel this error."

15. Charleston *Mercury,* March 18, 1862; quoted in Hubbell, *Timrod,* 20. See also Hayne's Memoir, in *Poems of Henry Timrod,* 66-67. Hayne praised the "simplicity, clearness, purity, and straightforward force of his imagination."

16. Hubbell, 99-100. Hayne wrote several poetic tributes to Timrod; in his *Complete Poems* are "Under the Pines: To the Memory of Henry Timrod," and "By the Grave of Henry Timrod." An uncollected sonnet is printed in Hubbell, *The Last Years of Henry Timrod,* 19. For *Southern Opinion,* Oct. 19, 1867, he wrote a memorial notice; in that magazine he printed or re-printed many poems by Timrod and Simms.

17. *Russell's,* VI (March, 1860), 568: The other five are Milton, Tennyson, Keats, Matthew Arnold, and Richard Henry Stoddard. Clearly Hayne was mentally excluding the dramatic blank verse from consideration.

18. Duffy, 94-95. See n. 12. In *Southern Bivouac,* NSI (Oct., 1885), 268, Hayne called Simms "a virile and upright spirit, constitutionally incapable of fraud or meanness, and chastened, at last, into pathetic gentleness; a man greater than his works. . . ." See also McKeithan, 420.

19. W. P. Trent, *William Gilmore Simms,* 230-32; *Russell's,* II (Nov., 1857), 152-60; *Southern Bivouac,* I (Oct., 1885), 257-68; quotation on 262. Simms's fecundity, added Hayne, "reminds one of Lope de Vega." In 1878 he wrote that, "tho I once tried *hard* to think *otherwise—,* Simms can scarcely be called a *Poet!* He has written some *sweet individual* pieces, and *passages of force* & *suggestiveness* may be culled, here & there, from his longer compositions; but somehow, he lacked the

higher inspiration . . . his *true Genius* was *essayical, controversial,* (as his *superb political* treatises show), and also conspicuous in the more characteristic of his novels & romances."

20. *Russell's,* II (Nov., 1857), 152-60. Hayne thinks (154) that only Simms's blank verse has "received careful and studious elaboration." Hayne also feels (160) that Simms never received deserved encouragement in Charleston. He also regretted (letter to Simms, McKeithan, 220) that Simms had been forced to expurgate a ballad before publishing it.

21. *Russell's,* II (Dec., 1857), 240-59; see especially 241 and 259. Hayne justifies any leniency (259) because "reviewers have followed the malicious policy of so confounding the chaff with the wheat, as very nearly to conceal the latter from the public view; and, secondly, that his autorial blemishes are generally of the kind that expose themselves. They are to be found, not so much in the thought as in the mode of expression—not so much in the spirit and design of his works, which are invariably of a high order, as in rudeness of form and structure, and frequently injudicious carelessness of detail." Whether "such artistic imperfections will out-balance the solid and forcible results of imagination, genius and invention, is a question, the reply to which we leave, with a modest but unhesitating confidence, to Posterity."

22. *Russell's,* II (Nov., 1857), 178. Hayne ostensibly quotes the review to prove to a correspondent that in *Norman Maurice* an American had written an "original play which deals with contemporary events and characters."

23. *Russell's,* III (July, 1858), 370. When professional authorship is unprofitable, as in Charleston, the gifted amateurs must be depended on "for the development of a higher and purer taste, and for the establishment of a respectable organ."

24. *Russell's,* I (July, 1857), 327-37; reprinted in my *Essays of Henry Timrod* (1942), 135-54. See also the article by Grayson in this book. Timrod's essay with the same title appeared in *Russell's,* II (Oct., 1857), 52-58.

25. *Russell's,* III (Sept., 1858), 571. Hayne also prints a long extract from the poem. But his finest tribute to Grayson is in his discussion of John Russell and Russell's club-like bookstore, and the starting of *Russell's Magazine.* Russell introduced Hayne to Grayson in 1857; Grayson wrote the lead article for the first issue, "The Edinburgh Reviewer Reviewed." This was a defense of the South, in response to an article that Hayne thought had been written by an American "Puritan Renegade." Here, Hayne treats mainly Grayson's political and historical writings, *Southern Bivouac,* I (Nov., 1885), 331-35. In this article Hayne discusses the literary and intellectual life of Charleston, praising the Roman Catholic Bishop Lynch, the Rev. James W. Miles, Dr. S. Henry Dickson, his son-in-law J. Dickson Bruns, Basil Gildersleeve, and various others. Most of them contributed to *Russell's* (327-36). Hayne's letter to Kingsbury, Jan. 25, 1859, is in the Southern Historical Collection, University of North Carolina Library, and published in Francis B. Desmond's "Editor Hayne to Editor Kingsbury: Three Significant Unpublished Letters," *North Carolina Historical Review,* XXXI (Jan. 1955), 97-98. Kingsbury's article on Grayson in *The Leisure Hour* is "one of the few comprehensive critiques."

26. *Russell's,* III (April, 1858), 90-92 and III (June, 1858), 274-75. Bryan was drawing a good picture "of the *second and third class Poet,* and *not* of the great masters of song."

27. *Russell's,* V (July, 1859), 370-72. In this memorial notice, Hayne quotes in full Legaré's long poem, "Thanatokallos."

28. *Southern Review,* VII (Jan., 1870), 123-58; quotation on 147. He devotes only two pages to Legaré as a writer, although he admired him as a "*magnificent genius, and profound scholar*" (McKeithan, 319). Hayne published a shorter,

slightly revised version in the *Southern Bivouac*, NSI (Sept., 1885), 193-98; the longer version was reprinted in his *Lives of Robert Young Hayne and Hugh Swinton Legaré* (1878).

29. Quoted in Kate H. Becker, *Paul Hamilton Hayne*, 114. For *Southern Opinion*, April 11, 1868, he reviewed *Tiger-Lilies* as "(with many glaring faults) the most original and thoughtful tale we have read for a long time," and was delighted that a "young author has recently arisen at the South, for whom we venture to predict a brilliant future." Hayne also reprinted Lanier's poem "Barnacles." To Bayard Taylor, he confessed disappointment with the "centennial Cantata" (Duffy, 81). Hayne's poetic tribute, "The Pole of Death," was published in *Harper's New Monthly Magazine*, LXV (June, 1882), 98, and in *Complete Poems*, 322. See also *The Letters of Sidney Lanier* (1945) in the Centennial Edition, under the general editorship of Charles R. Anderson.

30. Introductory Notice to *The Poems of Frank O. Ticknor, M.D.*, 1879. Hayne frequently included Ticknor in his lists of Southern poets whose work deserved to be in anthologies. In his "Confederate War Songs," *Southern Bivouac*, NSI (June, 1885), 35-43, Hayne lists Ticknor, James Ryder Randall, and Henry Timrod as the outstanding war poets, although "a conspicuous philosophical element, and also a 'reserve of power' not compatible with the lyric pure and simple," prevented Timrod from achieving fiery ardor. Ticknor's wording was sometimes careless, but he had "fire of conception" and "simple forthrightness of execution." Randall had vigor and sonorousness, while Timrod revealed the "superiority of moral and spiritual to material forces." Hayne has brief laudatory remarks, also, on John R. Thompson, Abram J. Ryan, A. J. Requier, Henry Lyndon Flash (quoting his best poem, "Zollicoffer"), John Esten Cooke (also quoting his best poem, "The Band in the Pines"), and S. Treackle Wallis. He did not include Margaret Junkin Preston, to him the most gifted of Southern female poets, with a mind "comprehensive, brilliant, and creative." Neither does he include Simms.

31. *Russell's*, II (Feb., 1858), 476-77. But Meek's poetry was not equal to his prose (in the same review, Hayne discussed Meek's *Romantic Passages in South Western History* and *Songs and Poems of the South*). Likewise, when C. C. Jones attempted to do something about the neglected grave of Richard Henry Wilde, Hayne wrote him on Sept. 29, 1885, that "one sad simple strain ["Lament of the Captive"] which goes straight to the heart of Humanity, will long preserve his name. . . . *Technically* the song has serious faults." Hayne objects to the judgment that "in the blending of *sound* and sense," the next to the last line is "unrivalled in English verse." This, Hayne wrote sharply, struck him "as absurd." Tennyson and Swinburne had done better (the latter especially in "The Garden of Proserpine), and with less of commonplaceness and with far more originality (Letter in Duke Univ. Library).

32. *Russell's*, V (Sept., 1859), 568-70. Most of the review consists of quotations. He admitted that Thompson's poetical powers were not lofty, although they were "very considerable." For some typical Hayne letters to Thompson, see McKeithan, 50-51 and 123-34; on Whitman, 127.

33. *Russell's*, III (April, 1858), 80-82. Hayne reprints the Preface and the first six stanzas. Hayne indicates no familiarity with Chivers' earlier work.

34. *Russell's*, VI (Dec., 1859), 279; Becker, 58. Reviewing *Arthur Gordon Pym, and Other Stories*, in *Russell's*, I (April, 1857), 48-54, Hayne noted a union of powers usually considered "as antagonistic. His imagination was truly noble and comprehensive." But some "preternatural gloom of morbid association pervaded his intellect. . . . But in his wildest flights, his most erratic investigations, we discover a coherency of logic, an absolute mathematical propriety, a keen activity of the analytical judgment." Hayne's final sentence: "We conclude, as we began,

by expressing our conviction of the extraordinary genius manifested in these productions, and the firm belief that their author's claims to immortality are at least equal to the claims of any other American writer whatsoever."

35. *Russell's*, IV (Jan., 1859), 370-72. Hayne used this material again in *Southern Opinion*, March 28, 1868. The early work of this "weird genius" was "unelaborated" when compared with the revised poems.

36. See Becker, 59-61, for poem and letter; McKeithan, 343-45. In a brief notice in *Russell's*, V (Aug., 1859), 476, Hayne comments upon "the entire absence of anything like moral sense in Poe's character." He also thinks that, "Great as Poe's genius undoubtedly was," he has been too much imitated. For Hayne's defence at a dinner in Boston of Poe's genius, see Hubbell, *The South in American Literature*, 546.

37. Letter of May 4, 1858; Desmond, "Editor Hayne to Editor Kingsbury," *NCHR*, XXXI (Jan., 1955), 92-101. In a review of Hayne's poetry in the *Leisure Hour* (Oxford, N. C.), March 4, 1858, Kingsbury called his sonnets "among the best in the language." Kingsbury published at least one of Hayne's poems, and republished many poems and stories. Hayne reciprocated by writing in *Russell's*, III (July, 1858), 382, that the *Leisure Hour* was edited with "taste, ability, and judicious care."

38. McKeithan, 100-01. On p. 35, in a letter to R. H. Stoddard, Aug. 28, 1859, Hayne wrote that the "position of a literary man at the *South* is anomalous, & by no means agreeable." He complains of small sales of his books, and of receiving no pay for editing *Russell's*. For similar letters to Horatio Woodman and R. H. Dana, Jr., in 1860, see Hubbell, *The South in American Literature*, 746. In 1873 Hayne wrote to M. C. Tyler that H. S. Legaré, Simms, P. P. Cooke, and Timrod all had suffered materially from early literary fame, for Southern communities looked down upon the writer "with a *species of scorn*, as a half crazed enthusiast, having no firm, wholesome root in the soil of social existence" (McKeithan, 319-20).

39. Duffy, 71-72. In a letter to John T. Trowbridge (ed. R. A. Coleman, in *American Literature*, X (Jan., 1939, 483-86; Feb. 29, 1869), Hayne makes the same complaint, and adds: "in *my* most unfortunate section, Literature has never had room, or air to breathe." In several letters to Margaret Junkin Preston in 1872-73, he makes much the same complaints. The originals are in the Hayne Collection, Duke University Library, but Hubbell, 752 and 754, gives representative samplings.

40. McKeithan, 4; for representative letters to Whipple, see McKeithan, 62-67. The letter to Mrs. Preston is in the Hayne Collection, Duke University Library.

41. McKeithan, 70-71.

42. McKeithan, 53-54. In a letter to Simms, April 30, 1870 (McKeithan, 233-34), Hayne described Bryant's translation of the *Iliad* as "very literal, marvellously correct, but lacking fire."

43. McKeithan, 339-40; letter to Moses Coit Tyler, June 1, 1874. Becker, 110, gives a slightly different phrasing. For some representative letters to Lowell, see McKeithan, 99-107. That of Dec. 28, 1859 (99-100), shows Hayne's ready willingness to accept criticism and attempt to profit by it. In Aug., 1875, Hayne wrote to Lowell: "Your works, (*prose* and *poetry*) have been invaluable to me, and many a lyric & sonnet of yours I know by *heart*" (McKeithan, 105).

44. McKeithan, 146-48. Several of his poetic tributes, especially to Longfellow and Whittier, are in his *Poems*.

45. *Russell's*, I (May, 1857), 188 and IV (Nov., 1858), 187-89. Although the "pure thoughts, the sweet, clear, natural expression" charmed him and "served to commend the 'Courtship' to all hearts," he was doubtful about the use of hexameters: "The laws of English versification depend not on quantity but on accent, and we

greatly doubt the success of any attempt to depart from them." Hayne preferred blank verse, but was "too much pleased with his poetry to quarrel with the dress," for Longfellow's poetry is "pure, healthy, and health-giving." Hayne objected to a British reviewer's over praising Thomas Buchanan Read at the expense of Longfellow: "overpraise is worse than the most virulent depreciation."

46. McKeithan, 143. See also 147, where Hayne sees no reason why a poet "should not be a Christian, and a gentleman!" Hayne was worried about religious doubt (partly because he shared in it, in spite of his attempts not to do so; see "A Little While I fain would linger yet"); in *Southern Opinion*, Aug. 10, 1867, he generalized: "The spirit of our age is essentially iconoclastic. We are breakers of images and destroyers of sacred things." In spite of his friendship and admiration for Longfellow, he attempted to keep his published comments dispassionate. Reviewing Longfellow's translation of Dante's *Divine Comedy*, he first noted that Dante was the sole Italian author in whom everyone claimed an equal right, but that Longfellow had attempted too much: "Instead of the marvelous harmony of Dante's versification, we have too often foisted upon us the dreariest and heaviest *prose*. . . . Fidelity is dearly purchased at *such* price." Longfellow's translation was honest and he could praise some features of it, but Cary's was better (*Southern Opinion*, Oct. 26, 1867). See also his letter to Longfellow, McKeithan, 143-78. After Longfellow's death, he wrote to Hubner, McKeithan, 74: "The world loved that man, as few of our kind have ever been loved before. . . . Despite a fame which had spread over three-fourths of our globe; despite wealth, position, the flattery of unnumbered multitudes, often growing into adulation, he kept both the whiteness and the humility of his spirit, recognizing, like Tennyson, the comparative nothingness of mortal renown . . . he was equally considerate to the humblest and loftiest of mankind."

47. McKeithan, 119. Although Whittier and Hayne remained close friends, and Hayne praised him in poems and letters, Hayne nonetheless constantly made a distinction between the politician and the poet: for instance, in *Southern Opinion*, Nov. 23, 1867, he regretted that Whittier prided himself so on his New England birth; he is "a fine, noble genius, perverted by the wretched sectionalism of the Puritan; unconsciously narrowing those sympathies which, undisturbed and uninfluenced, might have been truly cosmopolitan. . . . As an *artist*, we sincerely admire him." At his best, Whittier belongs to "the school of Wordsworth"; his language is "invariably pure and limpid"; his love of men and nature pure. But abolitionism had led him to "the harshest notes of Prejudice, and—as Carlyle would express it—a 'sour unwisdom.' " In spite of this, the "*core* of the man's heart and genius is sweet and sound." Hubbell, 756, quotes from a letter to Mrs. Preston (Duke Univ. Library; April 15, 1873): "the grand old man!! A fanatic, all his life, and yet so profoundly sincere; hating what he deemed crime, but ever tender towards the supposed Criminal."

48. Letter to Charles W. Hubner; excerpt in Hubner's *Representative Southern Poets* (1906), 73. He also noted that "In literary immortality . . . I have no faith. A few clarion names and golden threads of song may truly survive for a long time, but their term of existence must also arrive."

49. *Poems*, 340. The poem was written to Emerson "on his 77th Birthday." Hayne speaks of Emerson as seeking "with travail of brain" to penetrate "the veiled mystery of immaculate Truth," and possibly receiving "the white splendor of God's grace from heaven?". The remark on "Threnody" is in *Russell's*, IV (March, 1859), 564; Hayne quotes at length from the poem. In the *Southern Literary Gazette*, Dec. 18, 1852, Hayne noted with some bafflement that he had read "the eloquent mystic with a pleasure similar to that with which we gaze upon a sky of mingled cloud and starlight." But he did not always feel kindly toward

Emerson: in *Southern Opinion*, July 20, 1867, he praised the young Scottish poet Robert Buchanan for his "vivid picturesque power, and clear minuteness of detail," similar to Crabbe's but lifted above it by "an ethereal delicacy of imagination"; on April 4, 1868, he noted that Buchanan, whom "we once praised so highly in this department, has been, in plain language, making an ass of himself, by his injudicious, violent, absurd advocacy of the claims of Walt Whitman and Ralph Waldo Emerson."

50. *Russell's*, IV (March, 1859), 561-62. Reviewing *The Autocrat of the Breakfast Table* (IV, 384), Hayne wondered "whether a series of essays, containing so much of deep truth and subtle philosophy . . . were ever before so generally popular. . . . this work is a benefaction to the whole country." See also Victor H. Hardendorff, "Paul Hamilton Hayne and the North" (Duke Univ. Thesis, 1942), 55-61.

51. *Southern Literary Gazette*, July 3, 1852; *Russell's*, III (July, 1858), 384. As usual, Hayne gives extracts. In a letter to E. C. Stedman (McKeithan, 251; Feb. 10, 1878), Hayne noted that he had met Aldrich "in a very brief, casual way" in Boston, and "of course, I greatly admire his delicate and beautiful genius." Much later, he wrote to Hubner, McKeithan, 78, that for "Aldrich's art, indeed, I have the profoundest admiration," but he lacked "the grander elements of emotion and passion. Seldom, if ever, do his lyrics take hold of the deeper strings of one's heart. Here Lowell towers above him; so does Longfellow; so again do Whittier, Stoddard, and not a few others; yet Aldrich's self-knowledge, his unerring consciousness of his own limitations, seems in itself genius."

52. McKeithan, 115. Even nature's beauty is enhanced by the "companionship of *such* a woman, & poet as Mrs. Thaxter."

53. *Russell's*, I (April, 1857), 84. It may be worth noting that although later he considered Bret Harte rather vulgar, Hayne called *The Lost Galleon* a "very clever volume of verses," and quoted an extract (*Southern Opinion*, April 4, 1867). But he felt that Harte had only "a thin vein of genius" (Hubner, 78).

54. In a poetic tribute (*Poems*, 269), Hayne wrote that "art and nature wisely blend in thee!" In a letter to E. C. Stedman, Feb. 10, 1878 (McKeithan, 251), Hayne describes Fawcett as "the *most regular* of my Northern correspondents. . . . I have learned *not* merely to *admire* the *Poet*, but heartily to *love* the *man*." Hayne especially admired "Fidelitas." See also Hardendorff, 99, 106-07.

55. Especially, letter to Stoddard, Oct. 3, 1856 (McKeithan, 17); however, see the letters to Stoddard, 3-46. In *Southern Opinion*, Oct. 19, 1867, he remembered Stoddard's collection of poems when he was twenty-four as the "maturest collection of verses we ever remember to have read, by an author so young. A fastidious, dainty, elaborate *finish* characterizes his style." He had studied the English poets, "especially Herbert and Herrick." In the *Southern Literary Gazette* (1852-53), Hayne reprinted several of Stoddard's poems.

56. *Russell's*, I (April, 1857), 91, for general praise of Stoddard as poet, and the statement that his "The Fisher and Charon" is "probably the most subtle and harmonious production in blank verse ever published in this country"; and VI (March, 1860), 568. This editorial is mainly in praise of Timrod, but notes Timrod's indebtedness in some poems to Tennyson.

57. *Russell's*, I (April, 1857), 90-91; *Poems*, 268. See also Jay B. Hubbell, "George Henry Boker, Paul Hamilton Hayne, and Charles Warren Stoddard, Some Unpublished Letters," *American Literature*, V (May, 1933), 146-65; Duffy, 9, 13. In a letter to R. H. Stoddard (Feb. 10, 1857; McKeithan, 27) Hayne was indignant at *Putnam's* for patronizing Boker and Stoddard, while praising highly Julia Ward Howe's *Passion Flowers*. Hayne promised to write "a careful, impartial, & *analytical* critique upon *Boker & yourself*." This appeared in *Russell's*, as above. In one letter he not only inquired about Boker and Louis Godey, but also men-

tioned that "I have had a charming correspondence with *Mrs. Rebecca Harding Davis*, the author, you know, of that *powerful* novel, 'Dallas Galbraith.' "

58. The quotation is from a letter to Stoddard (Aug. 24, 1855; McKeithan, 11-12). For their literary relationship, see Charles Duffy's excellently edited *Correspondence of Bayard Taylor and Paul Hamilton Hayne*, 1945. Hayne's memorial notice and evaluation appeared in the *Andover Review*, II (Dec., 1884), 548-60.

59. McKeithan, 236-37. For Hayne's letters to Stedman, see McKeithan, 236-302. Stedman included seven of Hayne's poems in his *An American Anthology 1787-1900;* what would undoubtedly have pleased Hayne even more if he had been alive to see the book, Stedman included six poems by Paul's son, William Hamilton Hayne.

60. *Poems*, 263. Late in life, he wrote Hubner (McKeithan, 79) that he had completely given up hope of visiting England, "and the pang is bitter. . . . Fate seems to have determined that I shall die, as I have lived for a quarter of a century, among the solitudes of the Pine Barrens."

61. McKeithan, 12.

62. *Russell's*, IV (March, 1859), 560. Hayne had used exactly the same phrase in his Preface to *Sonnets and Other Poems* (1857). This was Simms's opinion also. In his *Memoir* (27) of Henry Timrod, Hayne quotes with approval Timrod's laudatory remarks on Wordsworth and Matthew Arnold.

63. McKeithan, 403 (Letter to Moses Coit Tyler, Jan. 31, 1886; Hayne calls *Tiresias and Other Poems* a "wonderful book for a man who will soon be an Octogenarian"); *Russell's*, VI (Dec., 1859), 278-79: Hayne argues that Tennyson, like Milton earlier, is ahead of his age and therefore not appreciated, whereas Pope and Congreve, "legitimate children of their respective times," were "flattered and overwhelmed with praises." In 1859 he especially envied James T. Field's "companionship with *Tennyson* . . . he enjoyed the inestimable privilege of hearing *Tennyson* read 'Queen Guinevere' " (McKeithan, 63-64).

64. *Russell's*, III (June, 1858), 271-74; see also IV (Oct., 1858), 84-85. Hayne incidentally praises Ben Jonson and Marlowe. On Wordsworth's poems he writes: "Were we to lose the 'Excursion,' and every other work dramatic and lyrical, which emanated from the genius of Wordsworth, his *Sonnets* (and especially those to Liberty) would form an imperishable monument to his fame."

65. *Russell's*, I (May, 1857), 181, 467, 469; III (July, 1858), 346, 351. A Northern reviewer had charged Tennyson and Robert Browning with obscurity; he had preferred "a *true* charge against Browning," but why bring "a *false* one" against Tennyson. Hayne vigorously defends Tennyson's clarity of thought and expression, even in "In Memoriam" (181-82).

66. Duffy, 39; *Russell's*, II (Feb., 1858), 479; McKeithan, 356-57 (letter to Moses Coit Tyler, Sept. 30, 1876). Hayne frequently makes allusive references to Scott's characters; for one example see McKeithan, 217.

67. *Southern Field and Fireside*, I (March 17, 1860), 338; II (June 30, 1860), 43. In the second paper listed, the conversation proceeds to Owen Meredith's *Lucile*, the success of which had been "wonderful if not complete." Whittington then quotes from Herrick and indicates to his wife the older poet's reputation.

68. *Russell's*, V (Sept., 1859), 565-68; quotation on 568; see also VI (Feb., 1860), 472. *Poems*, 26: this is one of Hayne's best sonnets.

69. Duffy, 14; *Russell's*, VI (Oct., 1859), 82-87; quotation on 85. In this memorial notice, Hayne regrets that Hunt is not better known in the United States. For the following quotation, *Russell's*, V (June, 1859), 275; here Hunt is described as probably "the oldest writer of distinction—not excepting De Quincey, now living, and *still engaged in literary labour,* in Great Britain." Reviewing *The Complete Poetical Works of Leigh Hunt*, in *Russell's*, II (Nov., 1857), 186-87, Hayne praises his "dainty, fanciful and delicate Muse."

70. *Russell's*, IV (Feb., 1859), 433-43; quotations on 439, 438; see also I (May, 1857), 185. Hayne's purpose was to give "a sketch of the man, and of the author, especially the poet."

71. Letter, Feb. 3, 1859, *North Carolina Historical Review*, XXXI (Jan., 1955), 99-101; *Scott's Magazine*, Atlanta, I (Feb., 1866), 154-61; *South-Atlantic*, Baltimore, V (March, 1880), 208-17; VI (July, 1880), 2-11.

72. *Russell's*, VI (March, 1860), 569; V (Sept., 1859), 542-49; quotations on 542 and 549; Hayne quotes liberally. He thought "Guinevere" better than the other three; it is "as *near* perfection, as such a performance can be" (547).

73. *Russell's*, I (May, 1857), 182. See n. 65, and McKeithan, 250, where he quotes from Browning's "Parting at Dawn," in order to disagree with him on a poet's "need of a world of men." See n. 75.

74. *Poems*, 269. But Hayne soon lost some of his enthusiasm for Swinburne. When he reviewed *Laus Veneris* (*Southern Opinion*, June 22, 1867), he began by noting that, some twenty-five years before, Philip James Bailey's *Festus* had, with its audacity of design and skill of execution, roused a critical furore; but Bailey's later work had all proved disappointing. Tennyson had profited in the long run from maturing slowly. Swinburne, like Bailey, had taken critical and reading circles by storm, but his recent work was inferior. Hayne objected to his "lewd comparisons"; also, there was "no form of secret, abhorrent crime, which Swinburne does not celebrate." Swinburne's imagination seemed to him "intense, but narrow." Yet he also felt (*Southern Opinion*, Sept. 7, 1867) that Swinburne had started a new school of poetry in England. On Jan. 6, 1874 (McKeithan, 145-46), he wrote to Longfellow that because he was neither a Christian nor a gentleman, "Swinburne's sonorous stanzas are likely to become '*vox, et praeterea nihil*' (always excepting his '*Atalanta in Calydon*')." But in 1878 he enjoyed "the great honor & pleasure of a correspondence with Swinburne" (McKeithan, 257). Hayne also enjoyed a brief correspondence with Dante Gabriel Rossetti (McKeithan, 286).

75. *Russell's*, I (April, 1857), 93. See McKeithan, 250, for an apt quotation on the divided nature of the poet, one driving him to the world, one to solitude. Here, Hayne claimed to prefer solitude to society.

76. *Poems*, 270. In *Southern Opinion*, Sept. 21, 1867, he wrote: "As a lyrist, Miss Ingelow is exquisite."

77. *Russell's*, I (June, 1857), 274-75: a review of *Aurora Leigh*; if autobiographical, it makes Mrs. Browning unlike the tender, delicate, slightly pedantic poetess he had pictured, and instead a strong-minded genius. The work is a disappointment to her admirers: "As a novel, Aurora Leigh is common-place. . . . As a poem, it is entitled to far higher praise." Hayne returned to this in *Russell's*, III (April, 1858), 82-83: Mrs. Borwning's *Sonnets from the Portuguese* "give her own personal experiences so simply and profoundly that they have the same justification as Shakespeare's sonnets . . . [but] when I read 'Aurora Leigh' I knew she could never be 'the greatest of female writers.'" For Marston he felt a warm personal regard and carried on an extensive correspondence with him; he wrote Stedman of "My beloved friend, *Marston*, whose private letters are *marvels* of interest, & brilliant epistolatory force" (McKeithan, 297).

78. *Russell's*, II (Dec., 1857), 278. Hayne wondered why "that wonderful poem" *Orion* had not been re-issued by an American publisher. Bailey wrote somewhat similar poetry; see *Russell's*, IV (Jan., 1859), 379-82: Hayne thought his *The Age* undervalued, as his *Festus* had been overvalued. It had only "fragments of rhythmical beauty," but as a satire *The Age* was effective.

79. Letter to Bayard Taylor, Feb. 23, 1871, in Duffy, 43-45. The letter includes a sonnet to William Morris which is not in Hayne's *Poems*; it was published without italics in Lanier's *Music and Poetry*, 198. Hayne objected to William Dean Howells' sneering at Morris's poetry (Duffy, 60, 63). In *Southern*

Opinion, Oct. 26, 1867, he called Morris the young English poet "whose genius, we have no hesitation in affirming, is superior to any other poet who has appeared in that country since the death of Keats." Hayne was reviewing *The Life and Death of Jason.*

80. *Poems,* 178. See McKeithan, 379-80 and Duffy, 40-43. For an extended treatment of this poem and Hayne's attitude, see my article, "Hayne's Adaptation of Chaucer's Franklin's Tale," in *Essays in Honor of Walter Clyde Curry* (1954), 103-15. In a notice of a superb new edition of *The Canterbury Tales,* Hayne wrote that Chaucer is unfairly neglected; he was "England's earliest, and in some respects, noblest singer" (*Southern Opinion,* May 9, 1868).

81. *Complete Poems,* 257, 138, 156, respectively. For his own dislike of materialism and his desire to escape from the "sordid zeal with which our age is rife," see his "My Study," 30. The sonnet begins: "This is my world!"

82. *Russell's,* III (July, 1858), 321-33; quotations on 321, 322, 324, 328. In a long headnote, Hayne announced that he proposed to begin "after some preliminary remarks . . . with Christopher Marlowe and end with James Shirley." Hayne's purpose was to glean from his predecessors in the field "such facts, observations, and deductions as may be of interest to the ordinary reader." He confessed that readers who turned to the plays "will be amazed at the amount of folly, coarseness, and buffoonery which deface some of the most characteristic of their work. But these are patent, and on the surface, and instead of being inextricably interwoven with the texture of the nobler thoughts and feelings, (as is the case with several modern poems of repute) they stand apart in the nakedness of their deformity." But no reader's morals are likely to be contaminated, for vice is presented as hideous; the old dramatists may, in fact, be pronounced "*moral teachers* of a high order." Also, "it cannot be denied that their most successful scenes, their grandest delineations of character, and noblest flights of eloquence and poetry, are quite as remarkable for purity of thought and elevation of sentiment as for force of diction and imagination" (321). At the end, Hayne notes that he is mainly indebted "to the most trustworthy of authorities, the Rev. Alexander Dyce"; he also relied heavily on William Hazlitt.

83. *Russell's,* V (May, 1859), 179. Hayne is mainly dealing with Cervantes, who possessed "a genius only less than Shakespeare's."

84. *Russell's,* III (Aug., 1858), 480; Letter to John R. Thompson, new editor of the Augusta *Southern Field and Fireside,* May 22, 1860 (McKeithan, 123-25).

85. Timrod, "The Character and Scope of the Sonnet," *Russell's,* I (May, 1857), 156-59; reprinted in *The Essays of Henry Timrod;* Hayne, Preface to *Sonnets and Other Poems* (1857); Simms, *Russell's,* III (Sept., 1858), 536, as headnote to a sequence, "The Child Sleeping in its Mother's Arms" (for the first three sonnets, see III, 222). Simms notes that he is addressing only "that class of readers who have learned to recognize poetry as a proper medium for philosophy." Simms reviewed *The Book of the Sonnet* in the Charleston *Courier,* April 5, 1867, and disagreed sharply with Hunt and Hayne on the need for regularity in the English sonnet.

86. All the quotations are from Hayne's Preface to *Sonnets and Other Poems* (1857). Hayne agreed with Simms that the English sonnet was not really suitable for love poems: it "addresses to the Scholar. It is too delicate a piece of workmanship, too fine in its adjustment, and harmonies to please the ear, or the fancy of the casual reader." Haynes concludes the prose Preface by quoting Wordsworth's "Scorn not the Sonnet." Several of his sonnets in the book discuss poetry: in the Dedicatory Sonnet to his mother, he called the sonnet a "small elaborate lyre"; in "Great Poets and Small" (3), he makes a plea for minor poetry: the thrush and the linnet sing "a happy note," even though they are not equal to the thrush or the skylark; in two sonnets on the Poet (5-6), Hayne admits the

general tendency to think of him as idle, yet the poet may attain immortality when "Stock depreciates, even Banks decay." One sonnet (15) was "suggested by the description of Fairfax Rochester, in chapter XXXVIII of 'Jane Eyre.' " There are also poetic tributes to Goethe (18) and Shelley (37).

87. Quoted in Hubbell, "George Henry Boker, Paul Hamilton Hayne, and Charles Warren Stoddard," *American Literature*, V (May, 1933), 146-65. For Boker's approval of the design but dissatisfaction with the execution of the work, see Sculley Bradley, *George Henry Boker*, 242, and Duffy, 12. In *Southern Opinion*, Sept. 21, 1867, Hayne noticed the work, but confined himself mainly to a discussion of Hunt's comparison of English and Italian sonnets, briefly crediting the American section to S. Adam Lee. Hayne also took occasion to praise the sonnets of Simms and Timrod. He admired Hunt's essay as "an exhaustive, vigorous, & learned treatise on a subject, little understood or appreciated, even among professional literary men" (Duffy, 13).

88. *The Book of the Sonnet*, edited by Lee Hunt and S. Adams Lee, 1867, pp. 96-127. I have followed Hayne's discussions sequentially.

89. *Russell's*, III (July, 1858), 382. I have quoted from several of Hayne's letters to its editor, T. B. Kingsbury.

90. McKeithan, 146 (previously noted in connection with Swinburne). In Duffy, 50, he notes that the "groundlings" hate "philosophy, thought, metaphysical deductions."

91. *Russell's*, II (Feb., 1858), 464-65. Thought, Hayne declared, "is essentially invincible and immortal."

92. *Complete Poems*, 296. Hayne wrote many poems on poetry; see, for example, 26, 28, 30, 32.

93. Respectively, McKeithan, 237 and 18.

94. Duffy, 9-10. As late as 1881, Hayne wrote to W. R. Alger that when "a man has derived *great instruction;* no less than *pleasure,* from the works of another, I think that he should (if practicable), acknowledge such a debt to his Benefactor" (McKeithan, 75; see also 248-49, where he expresses to Stedman a desire for a "noble *esprit de corps,* which urges one to recognize a brother or sister in *Art,* everywhere, & at all seasons").

95. *Russell's*, I (May, 1857), 182. This would apply to plays and long narrative poems as well as to novels, in Hayne's view.

96. Duffy, 62. This letter to Taylor was written in 1875.

97. Duffy, 62. In *Southern Opinion*, Aug. 17, 1867, Hayne declared that even *Tom Jones* and *Roderick Random* were "but coarse caricatures" when compared with *Jane Eyre* and *The Mill on the Floss.*

98. Quoted in Becker, 6. He wrote Tyler in 1882 (McKeithan, 399) that "When a boy, I actually *wore out* my '*Robinson Crusoe*' by eternal handling, and believed as firmly in the veritable existence of 'Robin' & his 'man Friday' as I did in my *own.*" In 1870 he wrote to Simms that he was preparing a book for Hurd and Houghton, "a *simplified Froissart* for children" (McKeithan, 232-33). Parts of this (possibly all that Hayne wrote) were published in the *Riverside Magazine for Young People*, and reprinted in *Burke's Magazine for Boys and Girls*, beginning March 1871. The projected book was never published.

99. Duffy, 39, 60; see also 63. Hayne repeats this last phrase almost exactly in the *Southern Bivouac*, IV or NSI (Oct., 1885), 264.

100. *Russell's*, II (March, 1858), 568, and IV (Jan., 1859), 384. For all his liking for historical romances, Hayne had only mild praise for G. P. R. James, although he published two of James's poems in the *Southern Literary Gazette*, Aug. 21, 1852; in the same issue, he indicated that he was no great admirer of W. H. Ainsworth.

101. *Russell's,* V (Sept., 1859) , 571; Letter to Margaret Junkin Preston, Jan. 16, 1872 (Duke Univ. Library).

102. McKeithan, 376-77; 184; 445 respectively. In "The Whittington Club," Hayne has Bishop discuss Dickens' *Tale of Two Cities,* which is generally and rightfully admired for its pathos and psychological insights (*Southern Field and Fireside,* I [March 31, 1860], 354).

103. *Russell's,* I (April, 1857), 83. *Putnam's Monthly* had sneered at the South through an editorial revamping of the *Pickwick Papers*: "Mr. Dickens is one thing, but Mr. Putnam, playing Dickens, is another affair, and not tolerable to Gods or Men." In *Southern Opinion,* April 4, 1868, Hayne protests against Dickens's not visiting the South; he should see the region before judging it, for Dickens, a moralist, "has conveyed to us the loftiest, purest, sweetest lessons of charity."

104. *Southern Field and Fireside* I (March 24, 1860), 346. These papers took the form of dialogues on literature between a James Whittington and a Henry Bishop; the series started March 17, 1860. Whittington read his essay upon Thackeray's *Virginians.* Bishop felt that Thackeray's "very nose radiates benevolence." The opinions, however, are Hayne's. Years later, in praising Mary R. Mitford as woman and author, especially of *The Village,* Hayne added: "Miss Mitford's critical instinct were generally correct, as witness her invariable and hearty appreciation of Walter Scott, and other first-class writers; and yet, it is true, that she blundered awfully sometimes—what could be more amazingly shallow, and a trifle impertinent, than her depreciation of Thackeray, especially of his Chef d'oeuvre, Esmond" (Hubner, 76-77). In the *Southern Literary Gazette,* Dec. 18, 1852, he had briefly praised *Henry Esmond,* calling it "complicated and interesting"; earlier, on Aug. 15, 1852, he had praised Thackeray's *Book of Snobs* because it "abounds with the rarest humor, and the most sparkling aphorisms of experience and philosophy." But he also objected (Dec. 4, 1852) that in his lectures Thackeray had dealt too minutely with the darker side of Dean Swift's character. On July 3, 1852, the *Gazette* reprinted an article on the life of Thackeray.

105. *Russell's,* II (Nov., 1857), 181-82; V (July, 1859), 375; in a favorable review of a book by Bulwer Lytton's son: *Poems,* by Owen Meridith; *Russell's,* III (Aug., 1858), 468-71.

107. Respectively, *Russell's,* I (June, 1857), 279; I (April, 1857) , 95; I (May, 1857), 169-74; quotation on 169.

108. *Russell's,* I (Aug., 1857), 471, 477. Reviewing *The Professor,* Hayne judged it too analytical, too lacking in plot and movement, and less mature than *Jane Eyre,* although it could "stand upon its intrinsic merits." In *Russell's,* I (July, 1857), 378-80, he wrote a favorable review of E. C. Gaskell's *Life of Charlotte Brontë*: the biography displayed a "rare union of conscientiousness and of sympathy," dealing honestly with "a Tragedy of sombre hue" in the story of a strange remarkable family, and in the life of a great novelist. In *Southern Opinion,* May 30, 1868, Hayne wondered, with new and superb editions of Dickens, Thackeray, and Bulwer available: Why isn't there one of Charlotte Brontë's work? He has been asked for a biographical sketch, and gives an appreciative one, with some notice of her sisters. These also are praised in the review of Gaskell's biography.

109. *Russell's,* I (Aug., 1857), 479. Of the Appendix to *The Romany Rye,* Hayne notes: "The prejudices of the writer are here ridiculously apparent." Hayne especially objects to Borrow's calling Scott "the descendant of 'cow-stealing' marauders."

110. *Russell's,* I (Aug., 1857), 473. Hayne had liked "the dashing author of 'Charles O'Malley,' 'Harry Lorrequer,' and works of a kindred stamp."

111. *Russell's,* IV (March, 1859) 564-65. Hayne notes unfavorably that this is

"a republication of an English work of fiction, the hero of which is an American."

112. *Russell's,* V (Aug., 1859), 475. In *Southern Opinion,* Aug. 17, 1867, Hayne called Trollope "a pre-Raphaelite in literary art," and ambitious to present truthfully the English middleclass to which he belongs. The charge that there is nothing heroic in Trollope's work is "not merely unfair, but absurd," for Trollope takes "for his specialty the actual men and women of the age, as they think and act within the bounds determined by the strict laws of conventionalism." In the book being reviewed, *The Last Chronicle of Barset,* the "best qualities of the author's style and genius have been conspicuously displayed."

113. *Russell's,* II (Nov., 1857), 187-88; McKeithan, 45. *White Lies,* the book being reviewed, was "a story of uncommon merit." The month before, he had noticed the first two of four parts, expressed disappointment, but deferred judgment (II, 94-95). Hayne was glad that he had not been "guilty of a very common piece of critical dishonesty, namely, of settling the position of a work of art, with scarcely any knowledge of its contents."

114. Duffy, 62. This seems to me an excellent example of Hayne's eclectic taste, when compared with his praise of historical romances.

115. Hayne reviewed *The Literary Life of James K. Paulding,* compiled by his son, in *Southern Opinion,* July 27, 1867. He praised Paulding as a Democrat and an effective pamphleteer. As writers, "Irving possessed the most grace, correctness, and elegance of expression, but Paulding the stronger genius. . . . But Paulding was careless of his literary fame, was not, in fact, a professional *litterateur* at all." In the *Southern Literary Gazette,* Oct. 16, 1852, he briefly noticed a reprint of Catherine M. Sedgwick's *A New England Tale* (1822) as "a natural and pleasing moral story."

116. *Russell's,* I (Aug., 1857), 471-72; McKeithan, 351. He also objected to the London *Athenaeum's* calling Hawthorne's stories "pleasant works of fiction, nothing more." In the *Southern Literary Gazette,* July 31, 1852, he called *The Blithedale Romance* one "of the best of our author's works, with his fascinating peculiarities of style, full of that clear, nervous, but delicate diction, for which Hawthorne is remarkable." On Sept. 18, 1852, he regretted that Hawthorne had written a campaign biography of Franklin Pierce.

117. Letters to John G. James, Jan. 31, 1878, and April 3, 1878, in McKeithan, 420, 428. On 420, Hayne writes: "Full of faults, he was nevertheless '*a man, every inch of him.*'"

118. Letter of Aug. 4, 1870, in Richard Beale Davis's "Paul Hamilton Hayne to Dr. Francis Peyre Porcher," *Studies in Philology,* XLIV (July, 1947), 533-36. Hayne is to some degree defending his article, "William Gilmore Simms," in *Appleton's Journal,* IV (July 30, 1870), 136-40. In the article as in the letter (and later in his article in *Southern Bivouac,* NSI [Oct., 1885], 257-68), Hayne emphasized that "the man was far greater than his works." In the article Hayne notes that in this memorial notice he has refrained from a critical appraisal.

119. *Russell's,* I (June, 1857), 251-55. Hayne noted Simms's personal knowledge of the frontier, which provided "the simplest and rudest materials. . . . The story dispenses with all adventitious aid, and depends for its interest wholly upon the masterful development of characters rich in their very homeliness, their outspoken vigor of thought, and the demonstrative energy of their action and passion." In *Russell's,* VI (Dec., 1859), 276-77, he quoted a long passage from the *North American Review* praising *The Cassique of Kaiwah* and earlier novels.

120. *Russell's,* V (June, 1859), 287. Hayne promised to "devote some space to the examination of this book" in the next issue, but failed to do so.

121. *Russell's,* VI (Dec., 1859), 288. However, the comment is at the end of a long and favorable review of John Esten Cooke's *Henry St. John, Gentleman.* As early as July 17, 1852, in the *Southern Literary Gazette,* Hayne noted with pleas-

ure in an English magazine a favorable comparison of Cooper with Scott, although two weeks later in the same magazine he praised a reprint of Scott's "inimitable works."

122. Hayne requested a serial from Cooke in 1855, two years before the magazine appeared (McKeithan, 67); for one of Hayne's offers, see McKeithan, 84; quotation on 85. In the review (VI, 286) he praised Philip Pendleton Cooke's ballads for their "ringing rhythm."

123. McKeithan, 91; March 16, 1877. Hayne promised to notice *Canolles,* but I have not located the review. In *Southern Opinion,* June 27, 1868, he reviewed *Fairfax:* Cooke "carries us back to his favorite epoch and his favorite historical localities"—Virginia in pre-revolutionary days—in a "tale of rapid movement and tragic *dénouement.*" Although "cleverly drawn," the characters are types with which we have long been familiar." Hayne reprints Cooke's "My Acre," calling it "the best poem we have seen from his pen for years."

124. *Russell's,* VI (Aug., 1859), 474-75. In the same issue there is an article on *Sea-Cliff* (429-36; probably not by Hayne). It begins: "We are glad to welcome Mr. De Forest once more. He is one of those genial natures that are always welcome to his friends and to the world as often as they choose to repeat their visits." *Sea-Cliff* is praised as being "really American in scenery, incidents and character." De Forest "cannot fail to succeed as a writer of fiction," and he is especially "happy in his delineation of female character" (435-36).

125. *Southern Opinion,* Sept. 7, 1867; *Southern Bivouac,* NSI (Nov., 1885), 330. In the same paragraph he remembered also Stoddard's "Herod Agrippa and the Owl," which in his opinion deserved "to rank with the best of his blank-verse poems."

126. Respectively, *Russell's,* I (July, 1857), 377; II (Nov., 1857), 191-92; McKeithan, 384 (a letter to Moses Coit Tyler, Dec. 31, 1878). The fact that the author was from Atlanta did not keep her from being "equally ignorant & vulgar"; mistaken praise of such work was in part responsible for Southern "literary *backwardness.*" Hayne thought that Fanny Fern's conceits "would certainly delight Thackeray."

127. "Literature at the South: The Fungus School," *Southern Magazine,* XIV (June, 1874), 651-55.

128. McKeithan, 399; letter to Moses Coit Tyler, Dec. 11, 1882. He added that if he could procure a small edition of Burton's *Anatomy of Melancholy,* "I would carry it always in my pocket!"

129. Duffy, 39-40; Jan. 9, 1871. Later Hayne wrote that he supposed the book too philosophical to be popular (50). He also tried to secure a copy of *The Story of Kennett* (61).

130. "Ante-Bellum Charleston: II," *Southern Bivouac,* NSI (Oct., 1885), 257-68; quotation on 264. In this article on Simms, Hayne presents an imaginary conversation between Howells and James in which they contemptuously dismiss the romances of Scott, Cooper, and Simms, and the work of Poe.

131. Duffy, 63-64. Hayne adds, typically: "The Lord forgive me, if I have allowed a poor personal pique to mislead my opinions." See also, for a letter to Howells, J. DeLancey Ferguson, "A New Letter of Paul Hamilton Hayne," *American Literature,* V (Jan., 1934), 368-70. Hayne was personally distressed when Howells, reviewing his *Legends and Lyrics* in the *Atlantic Monthly,* April, 1872, "accused me of having (in 'The Wife of Brittany' & 'Daphles') imitated Morris!! While the *facts* of the case are *that the W.O.B.* was composed between the years 1863-4, *before Morris was ever known in America;* & 'Daphles' I was correcting the proof of, *when I first saw Morris' 'Jason.'* " Hayne was correct, but the charge of plagiarism, as he considered it, rankled (McKeithan, 277).

132. Hayne published a three-part article on Gayarré in the *Southern Bivouac,*

NSII (June, July, Aug., 1886) , 28-37, 108-13, 172-76. For an excellent article with generous quotations from their letters, see Charles R. Anderson, "Charles Gayarré and Paul Hayne: The Last Literary Cavaliers," in *American Studies in Honor of William Kenneth Boyd,* 221-81. On J. C. Harris to Hubner (McKeithan, 79), Hayne wrote that he was "heartily glad to hear of his success. He richly deserves it."

133. *Southern Bivouac,* I (Sept., 1885), 193-202; quotation on 196. He complained that "It has grown into a habit among too many of the periodical writers of our day to elevate 'the new South' at the expense of the 'Old' in all matters pertaining to literary and intellectual enlightenment. . . . Let me say to them, in the words of the bluff old English lexicographer, 'Free your minds, gentlemen, from cant.' "

INDEX